Global Legal Insights
Bribery & Corruption

Third Edition
Contributing Editors: Jonathan Pickworth & Jo Dimmock
Published by Global Legal Group

GLOBAL LEGAL INSIGHTS - BRIBERY & CORRUPTION

THIRD EDITION

Contributing Editors
Jonathan Pickworth & Jo Dimmock, White & Case LLP

Production Editor
Sam Friend

Senior Editor
Suzie Levy

Group Consulting Editor
Alan Falach

Group Publisher
Richard Firth

We are extremely grateful for all contributions to this edition.
Special thanks are reserved for Jonathan Pickworth and Jo Dimmock for all of their assistance.

Published by Global Legal Group Ltd.
59 Tanner Street, London SE1 3PL, United Kingdom
Tel: +44 207 367 0720 / URL: www.glgroup.co.uk

ISBN 978-1-910083-69-7
ISSN 2052-5435

Printed and bound by CPI Group (UK) Ltd, Croydon, CR0 4YY
November 2015

CONTENTS

Preface   Jonathan Pickworth & Jo Dimmock, *White & Case LLP*

PREFACE

We are very pleased to present the third edition of Global Legal Insights – Bribery & Corruption. This book sets out the views of expert legal practitioners on the enforcement environment for bribery and corruption in 29 countries around the world. The authors have identified developments in enforcement since the last edition, mapped the latest trends and anticipated changes that may be coming down the track. The book also benefits from a number of new contributions that were not in the previous edition, notably new chapters in relation to Cyprus, Ghana, Hong Kong, Portugal, Serbia, Sri Lanka and the UAE.

Worldwide, 176 countries have signed up to the UN Convention against corruption and companies everywhere are committing to the fight. But doing business around the world is not getting any easier. Investigation and enforcement of bribery allegations show no sign of abating.

No industry is immune. From oil and gas, defence and pharmaceuticals to financial services and now even sport, corruption is very much in the global spotlight.

In the United Kingdom the first Deferred Prosecution Agreement is expected soon, and more onerous sentencing has come into force. In Brazil, investigations are as prolific as anywhere in the world right now. However, the US remains the most feared of all the world's enforcers, even though others are snapping at its heels.

We are very grateful to each of the authors for the contributions they have made to this book. We hope that it provides a helpful insight into what will remain a hot topic for enforcement and compliance.

Jonathan Pickworth & Jo Dimmock
White & Case LLP

Albania

Adi Brovina & Dritan Jahaj
Haxhia & Hajdari Attorneys at Law

Brief overview of the law and enforcement regime

The legal regime (whether civil or criminal) relating to anti-bribery and anticorruption in Albania is constituted by:

(1) The Criminal Code of the Republic of Albania approved by Law no.7895, dated 27 January 1995, as amended (the "Criminal Code"). The first and second section of the Criminal Code (criminal acts against the activity of the state committed by public officials) amended by Law no. 9272, dated 16 September 2004, clearly defines criminal offences relating to anti-bribery and corruption.

(2) The Criminal Procedure of the Republic of Albania approved by Law no. 7905, dated 21 March 1995 as amended (the "Criminal Procedure Code"), governs the investigation procedures of bribery and corruption.

(3) Law no. 9754, dated 14 June 2007 "On the criminal liability of legal entities", which provides for the criminal liability of legal entities where the offence has been committed on behalf of the legal entity or for the benefit of the legal entity through its bodies or representatives.

(4) Law no. 9643, dated 20 November 2006 "On public procurement", which also contains anticorruption provisions.

(5) Law no. 9367, dated 07 April 2005, "On the prevention of the conflict of interests in the exercising of public functions" as amended (the "Conflict of Interest Law"). The rules defined by this law are obligatory for implementation by, *inter alia*, every state institution, central or local, and every organ or subject created by and/or under the above subjects, including state or local undertakings, commercial companies with a controlling participation of state or local capital, non-profit organisations and other legal entities controlled by the above subjects.

(6) Law no. 9508, dated 10 April 2006 "Public collaboration in the fight against corruption".

(7) Law no. 9049, dated 10 April 2003 "On the declaration and audit of assets, financial obligations of elected persons and certain public officials" (hereinafter the "Declaration of Assets Law").

(8) The upgrading of the legislative framework for the fight against corruption in Albania was manifested in the ratification of two Council of Europe conventions: the Criminal Law Convention against Corruption (2001); and the Civil Law Convention against Corruption (2000).

(9) In 2006, Albania also became party to the United Nations Convention against Corruption (UNCAC), a consequence of which is the Implementation Review Mechanism, established in 2009 to enable all parties to review their implementation of UNCAC provisions through a peer review process.

The main bodies involved in investigating and enforcing such activity, and the sanctions imposed

The Criminal Code of the Republic of Albania provides for offences of corruption regarding: active corruption (bribery) of persons exercising public functions (Article 244 of CC); active corruption (bribery) of senior state or local elected officials (Article 245 of CC); and the exercise of influence on persons exercising public functions (Article 245/a of CC).

It also provides for: abuse of office (Article 248 of CC); abuse of contributions made by the State (Article 256 of CC); passive corruption (bribery) of persons exercising public functions (Article 259 of CC); and passive corruption (bribery) of high state officials or local elected officials (Article 260 of CC).

As well as: active corruption (bribery) of judges, prosecutors and other justice officials (Article 319 of CC); passive corruption (bribery) of judges, prosecutors and other justice officials (Article 319/c CC); and offering rewards and promises (Article 328 of CC).

The main bodies involved in the identification and prevention of bribery and corruption are the Prosecutor Office, the High Inspectorate of Declaration and Audit of Assets, and all structures created for such purpose within the public bodies.

The penalties provided by Albanian legislation for cases of bribery and corruption are the following:
- Active corruption of persons exercising public functions is punished with a prison term of six (6) months up to three (3) years.
- Active corruption of high state officials and of the local elected/representatives is punished with a prison term of one (1) year up to five (5) years.
- Passive corruption of persons exercising public functions is punished with a prison term of two (2) years up to eight (8) years.
- Passive corruption of high state officials and of the local elected/representatives is punished with a prison term of four (4) years up to twelve (12) years.

The usual sentences given to legal entities responsible for committing an offence are a fine and termination of the entity. Moreover, legal entities may be punished additionally with: a) the closure of one or more activities or structures of the legal person; b) the establishment of administrative control; c) prohibition to participate in procurement procedures of public funds; d) removal of access or use of licences, authorisations, concessions or subsidies; e) prohibition to publicly seek funds and financial resources; f) removal of the right to exercise one or more activities or operations; and g) the obligation to publish the court verdict.

Fines, in terms of Article 9 of law no. 9754, dated 14 June 2007 "On the criminal liability of legal entities", consist in the payment, in favour of the state, of an amount of money within the limits provided in the same law.

Depending on the type of offence, the applicable fines are as follows: a) for crimes under the Penal Code which provide for a penalty of at least 15 years of imprisonment or life imprisonment, the legal person shall be punished by a fine of 25m ALL (approximately €178,571) up to 50m ALL (approximately €357,142); b) for crimes that, under the Criminal Code, envisage a sentence of at least seven to 15 years' imprisonment, the legal person shall be punished by a fine of from 5m ALL (approximately €35,714) up to 25m ALL (approximately €178,571); and c) for crimes that, under the Criminal Code, envisage a sentence of less than seven years, the legal person shall be punished with a fine of 500,000 ALL (approximately €3,571) to 5m ALL (approximately €35,714). In the case of liability of legal persons for committing a criminal offence, the legal person shall be punished with a fine of 300,000 ALL (approximately €2,134) to 1 million ALL (approximately €7,114).

Overview of enforcement activity and policy during the past two years

According to the Code of Criminal Procedure, the prosecution and the judicial police are the investigation bodies.

In order to implement the constitutional amendments of 2012, and to limit the immunity of high officials which had not yet been implemented in practice, in 2014 the "Anti-corruption package" was approved. Amendments to the Criminal Procedure Code and amendments to the Anti-Mafia Law graded the corruption of high officials as a serious criminal offence.

Cases that have been prosecuted (or received other civil sanctions where applicable) and the sanctions:

According to the Tirana Judicial District Court for 2015, 22 cases were judged on the offence provided by "Active corruption of persons exercising public functions" provided by article 244 CC. In all the above-mentioned cases, the court found the defendant guilty, leading to a conviction, including: decision no. 2, dated 12 January 2015; decision no. 1054, dated 7 April 2015; and decision no. 979, dated 31 March 2015, etc.

Significant cases currently under investigation:

Significant cases currently under investigation include those involving three judges, a prosecutor and two attorneys accused of passive corruption.

Current trends of enforcement action:

In the framework of the National Strategy for Development and Integration, overall implementation of the new anti-corruption strategy is being prepared, aimed at strengthening the integrity of the judiciary, prosecution, etc., as well as judges, prosecutors and other justice officials.

The main task is to ensure the cooperation and interaction of these bodies with other state bodies to take measures against corruption, as well as cooperation and interaction with NGOs, civil society and the public.

In 2008, an anti-corruption strategy was adopted and action plans to implement the strategy have been drafted each year. The latest action plan includes measurable indicators, which should enable the monitoring of progress, as endorsed by the inter-ministerial working group responsible for preparation, drafting and follow-up of implementation of the anti-corruption strategy. The Department for Internal Administrative Control and Anti-Corruption (DIACA), which also performs internal controls on all administrative bodies, coordinates all relevant activities.

Among the policies put in place to prevent corruption, it is important to mention the law on the declaration and auditing of civil servants' assets and a law for the prevention of conflicts of interest while engaged in public work.

Law and policy relating to issues such as facilitation payments and hospitality

Facilitation payments are not allowed by the Albanian legislation. The facilitation payments defence should be carefully considered while doing business in Albania. Normally in Albania, various central and local government agencies and state and municipal entities officially establish computerised systems for the expedited performance of their services (i.e. issuance of licences, registering a company, etc.). Therefore, any payments other than such official fees may be viewed as corruption under Albanian law.

The Albanian law distinguishes between a simple gift and unjustified benefits. For the gift to be qualified as unjustified benefits, a person must give money or other valuables to an Official with the intent that the Official performs (or refrains from performing) certain actions in that person's favour or in favour of a third party. However, there are still no apparent *de facto* rules and procedures for gift-giving to Officials, though the cases defined in acts of the competent organs that permit the receipt of gifts or preferential treatment for reasons of State protocol are excluded.

Therefore, a company or an individual presenting a gift to an Official may bear a risk of such gift being treated as a corrupt payment or provision of unjustified benefits (i.e. commit corruption crimes punishable under the Criminal Code), depending on the value of the gift, the intent of the gift-giver, the circumstances and the time frame.

Article 23 of the Conflict of Interest Law defines that it is prohibited for an official to seek or to accept, directly or indirectly, gifts, favours, promises or preferential treatment – given because of his position – from an individual, natural person or private legal person.

An official to whom gifts, favours, promises or preferential treatment is offered according to the above should:

(a) refuse them and, if the offer was made without his knowledge or in advance, return it to the offeror or, if this is impossible, officially submit it to his superior or to the nearest superior institution;
(b) try to identify the person who offers them and his motives and interests;
(c) in any case, immediately inform his superior or the nearest superior institution about the gift, favour, promise or preferential treatment offered or given, the identity of the offeror when he can be identified, and the circumstances, as well as stating his point of view about the possible reasons for this event and its relation to his duties as an official;
(d) continue the exercise of duty normally, especially concerning that for which the gift, favour, promise or preferential treatment was offered, and continually keep his superior informed about every possible development; and
(e) if the offering or granting of the above-mentioned goods is related to the commission of a criminal offence, report it to the competent organs for criminal prosecution.

According to the Decision of Council of Ministers no. 714, dated 22.10.2004, the employee may be allowed to keep gifts, without being obliged to declare them if they exceed a value of 10,000 ALL (approximately €70) for gifts, while if the gifts are expensive, he must declare them within 30 days and submit them to his/her direct superior in the human resources unit of the institution.

The giving of gifts or hospitality to government officials and public servants is considered as active bribery and prohibited by Articles 244, 245 and 245/1, first paragraph, 319, 319/b and 328 of the Criminal Code.

The same consideration should also be made in relation to the giving of gifts and hospitality in the private sector, as far as it constitutes a corruptive practice. The relevant provision prohibiting such practice is Article 164 (a) of the Criminal Code.

Key issues relating to investigation, decision-making and enforcement procedures

Investigations and enforcement related to bribery offences mainly emanate from the police and the prosecutor's services, and potential victims' complaints in Albania. The court is the competent decision-making authority whose decisions are enforceable. According to case law, all defendants require <u>application for summary trial</u> (when the court evaluates that the case may be solved in the state where the acts occurred, and decides to perform the accelerated trial). When a sentencing decision is given, the court lowers the punishment of the imprisonment or fine by one-third (1/3).

Under Article 280 of the Albanian Criminal Procedure Code, the prosecutor and judicial police receive notice of criminal offences *ex officio* and through the notification of others. Also, Articles 281, 282 and 283 of the Albanian Criminal Procedure Code provide for criminal reports by public officials, criminal reports by medical personnel and criminal reports by citizens.

"Digital Station" is the application presented by the Ministry of Internal Affairs and the Foundation "Vodafone", which will serve the citizens and the State Police to ensure quality of service, law enforcement and the fight against corruption. Citizens may choose to remain anonymous or identified.

Further, the General Prosecution Office has recently created, on its official website, a new page where any citizen can directly report corruption cases including the names of the persons involved in such cases. Furthermore, within the General Prosecutor's Office is the Directorate of Investigation and Control of Economic Crime and Corruption. The director of such is responsible for more effective cooperation of both the Task Force Directorate and entities in its composition with other departments of the Prosecutor General and with the Task Force Directorate prosecutor's offices at lower levels, for better achievement of the prosecution operation and its tasks.

Recently, the committee of laws approved the "Anti-corruption package" proposed by the Ministry of Justice. This provided that exceptionally high-level officials, as stated in Article 141 of the Constitution, which, due to its competence, are automatically investigated by the Prosecutor General and judged by the Supreme Court. All other senior state officials and elected local officials, who are not included in the scope of Law no. 152/2013 "On Civil Service", will also be investigated and, if found guilty, tried for corruption by the Prosecution of Serious Crimes and the Court of Serious Crimes.

Overview of cross-border issues

Albania has become increasingly aware that bribery and corruption are the main obstacles to political, economic and social development in Albania as well as to EU accession. The government has, with the ultimate objective of the modernisation of governance, proclaimed uncompromising war and zero tolerance against bribery and corruption. This movement has started through the ratification of international conventions on the war against corruption such as the United Nations Convention against Corruption, the Criminal Convention of the Council of Europe against Corruption, and the Civil Convention of the Council of Europe against Corruption, etc.

In its planned strategy against corruption for the period 2015-2020, the government has fixed as its main objectives (1) the improvement of international judicial and police cooperation with the establishment of joint investigation teams for international crime, (2) joint training with foreign counterparts, (3) the strengthening of cooperation with foreign counterparts by increasing the number of operations and exchanges of information, and (4) the improvement of international judicial and police cooperation in the war against economic and financial crime.

The war against corruption has already provided satisfactory results by an increase of police joint investigations, exchange of information and arrests.

Corporate liability for bribery and corruption offences

Criminal liability of legal entities was introduced by Law no. 9754, dated 14.06.2007 "For the criminal liability of legal entities". This law, even though it is not exclusive to bribery and corruption offences, plays a determinant role in the issue of criminal liability of legal entities.

Legal entities are responsible for criminal offences committed: (a) in its name or on its behalf, from organs and representatives of the legal entity; (b) in its name or on its behalf, from a person who is under the authority of a person who represents, governs, or manages the legal entity; and (c) in its name or on its behalf, resulting from the lack of control or supervision from the person who governs, represents or manages the legal entity. Both Albanian legal entities and foreign legal entities may be subject to criminal penalties.

The law further defines the "*organs or representatives of the legal entity*" as any physical person who is in charge of the representation, governance, management or supervision of the activity of the legal entity or its structures. This definition is relatively large and includes in the list of probable offenders any physical person who has a managing or supervisory role in the company. If such responsibility is exercised by a collective organ, the legal entity is no less responsible.

Convicted legal entities may be subject to primary and additional penalties. The primary penalties are financial fines or the termination of the legal entity. Additional penalties may be of a different nature; the most common penalty applied in the case of bribery and corruption offences is exclusion from participating in tenders or public procurement procedures, as well as the granting of concessions, licences or authorisations.

The termination of the legal entity is ordered in case (a) the legal entity has been established with the objective of committing the criminal offence, (b) the legal entity has conducted its activity in service of the criminal offence, (c) the criminal offence has caused serious consequences, and/or (d) the legal entity is a recidivist.

The criminal liability of legal entities is not frequently requested by the prosecution office. It is becoming, however, more common in cases of highly publicised events and offences resulting in serious consequences. From the other side, bribery and corruption offences are, as a general rule, prosecuted towards the physical persons actually responsible for the offence; convictions of legal entities are particularly rare.

Proposed reforms / The year ahead

Corruption and the fight against it continue to be one of the major challenges and priorities for Albania. In the context of reforms, few have been undertaken. Through the adoption of Law no. 119/2014 "for the right to information", there is an improved possibility for citizens and entities to control the activity of the state. Further, regarding transparency in the use of budgetary funds, in the legal changes in March 2014 the Council of Ministers adopted a decision to carry out electronic tendering procedures for concessions and public-private partnerships.

In May 2014, amendments to the Declaration of Assets Law and conflicts of interest were approved, increasing the number and frequency of controls on the High Inspectorate of Declaration and Audit of Assets and Conflict of Interest (IDAACI) and forcing disclosure of cash-in-hand over a certain value and seeking their deposit in the bank.

The changes in the Criminal Procedure Code during 2014 transferred jurisdiction for active and passive corruption of judges, prosecutors, judicial officials, senior officials of the state and local elected officials to the Serious Crimes Prosecution and the Serious Crimes Court. The amendments to the Anti-Mafia Law in 2014 also expanded powers for seizure and confiscation of illegal assets stemming from corruption in all criminal offences that fall in the sphere of competence of the Serious Crimes Court. Amendments to the State Police Law in September 2014 sanctioned the establishment of a National Investigation Bureau, tasked with investigating cases of corruption.

Following these amendments and the identified problems, challenges still remain in the investigation and prosecution of corruption.

Adi Brovina
Tel: +355 4 22 80 170 / Email: adibrovina@lawfirmh-h.com.al
Mr. Brovina was called to the Albanian National Bar in 2012. He graduated in law from Jean Moulin LYON III University, where he successfully completed Masters' degrees of the first and second level in advanced corporate law (2008), and of the first level in European law (2009). He is currently undertaking doctoral studies. He has completed a traineeship at the European Court of Human Rights. His practice focuses on commercial and contract law.
Mr. Brovina speaks Albanian, English, French and Italian.

Dritan Jahaj
Tel: +355 4 22 80 170 / Email: dritanjahaj@lawfirmh-h.com.al
Av. Jahaj joined Haxhia & Hajdari Attorneys at Law in 2013. He was admitted to the Albanian Bar Association in 2008. Av. Jahaj graduated in Law from the Faculty of Law, University of Tirana. Currently he is undertaking Master's studies in penal law at the Faculty of Law, University of Tirana. His practice focuses on: criminal law; litigation; penal law; employment law; tax and customs law; and administrative law, etc.
Av. Jahaj speaks Albanian, English and Italian.

Haxhia & Hajdari Attorneys at Law

Blvd. "Dëshmorët e Kombit", Twin Towers, Tower 2, 9th Floor, Tirana, Albania
Tel: +355 4 22 80 170 / Fax: +355 4 22 80 171 / URL: http://lawfirmh-h.com.al

Australia

Greg Williams & Tobin Meagher
Clayton Utz

The law and enforcement regime

<u>Legal regime</u>

Australia is a federation comprising six States and two self-governing Territories. The Australian Constitution specifies those areas in which the Commonwealth has power to legislate and leaves the residue to the States. Corruption and bribery are largely State matters.

Each of the States and Territories criminalise both public sector and private sector bribery.[1] However, many of these offences are technical in nature and therefore difficult to enforce.

The Australian federal government (the Commonwealth) has laws which prohibit bribery of federal public officials,[2] as well as laws which prohibit the bribery of foreign public officials.

<u>Foreign public sector bribery</u>

Australia ratified the Organisation for Economic Co-operation and Development (OECD) Convention on Combating Bribery of Foreign Public Officials in International Business Transactions (OECD Convention) in 1999. Australia is also a party to the United Nations Convention against Corruption (UNCAC) of 2003. Both treaties require State Parties to criminalise bribery of foreign public officials in the course of international business.

Australia has given effect to its treaty obligations in Division 70 of the *Criminal Code Act 1995* (Cth) (Criminal Code). Section 70.2(1) makes it an offence to provide, offer or promise to provide a benefit not legitimately due to another person, with the intention of influencing the exercise of a foreign public official's duties in order to obtain business or a business advantage.

"Foreign public official" is broadly defined to include:
- an employee or official of a foreign government body;
- a member of the executive, judiciary or magistracy of a foreign country;
- a member or officer of the legislature of a foreign country;
- a person who performs official duties under the law of a foreign country; and
- an employee or official of a public international organisation, such as the United Nations.

"Benefit" is also broadly defined to mean "any advantage" and is expressly not limited to property.

The offence created by section 70.2(1) captures bribes made to foreign public officials either directly or indirectly via an agent, relative or business partner. While a key element of the offence is that the defendant must have *intended* to influence the foreign public official, it is not necessary to show that such an intention was expressed.[3] Section 70.1(1A) makes it clear that liability under section 70.2(1) will arise whether or not the bribe achieved its desired purpose of obtaining or retaining business or a business advantage. In determining whether a benefit was legitimately due, a court must disregard whether the benefit in question was customary, necessary or required in the particular circumstances. The value of the benefit is also to be disregarded.

Section 70.2 has extra-territorial reach. Liability arises if the bribery occurred in Australia, and also where it occurred outside Australia, so long as the person who engaged in it was an Australian citizen or resident, or a body corporate incorporated in Australia.[4]

The maximum penalty for an individual who is convicted under section 70.2(1) is 10 years' imprisonment, a fine of AU$1.7m, or both. A corporation can be fined the greatest of: AU$17m; three times the value of any benefit obtained directly or indirectly that can be reasonably attributed to the bribe; or, where the value of the benefit cannot be determined, 10% of the corporation's annual turnover for the 12 months up to the end of the month in which the conduct constituting the offence occurred. Bribery may also give rise to money laundering charges under Division 400 of the Criminal Code.

In addition to criminal penalties, any benefits obtained by foreign bribery can be forfeited to the Australian government under the *Proceeds of Crime Act 2002* (Cth). That Act establishes a regime that allows proceeds of Commonwealth-indictable offences to be traced, restrained and confiscated by a court. It also confers power on a court to order that a person appear before it to demonstrate that unexplained wealth was acquired by lawful means.

Defences to foreign public sector bribery

The Criminal Code provides two defences to the offence of foreign bribery under section 70.2(1). The first defence is engaged where the conduct in question was lawful according to the written law of the place where the conduct occurred.[5]

The second defence is in respect of facilitation payments. If the value of the benefit in question was of a minor nature, provided in return for expediting or securing the performance of a minor 'routine government action', and a record of the details of the conduct was created as soon as practicable, a defendant will have a good defence against liability.[6]

For the purposes of the defence, routine government action is an action of a foreign public official that is commonly performed by that person, including things like granting permits or licences, processing government papers and providing access to utilities. Routine government action does not involve a decision whether to award new business, or to continue existing business with a person. Setting the terms of new or existing business is also excluded. While sections 26-52 and 26-53 of the *Income Tax Assessment Act 1997* (Cth) provide that domestic or foreign bribes cannot be deducted under the Act, facilitation payments are not considered bribes, so are tax-deductible as losses or outgoings.

A defendant bears the onus of proving a defence.

Domestic bribery offences

The Criminal Code also criminalises bribery of Commonwealth public officials. Section 141.1(1) provides that it is an offence for a person to dishonestly provide or offer a benefit to another person, or cause a benefit to be so provided or offered, if done with the intention of influencing an Australian Commonwealth public official in the exercise of his or her official duties. A Commonwealth public official will be guilty of a criminal offence under section 141.1(3) if he or she dishonestly requests, receives or agrees to receive a benefit with the intention either of having his or her duties influenced, or of fostering a belief that such influence will be wielded. The maximum penalties for individuals and corporations convicted of these offences are the same as those for offences under section 70.2 of the Criminal Code.

Section 141.1 has extra-territorial reach. A person will be liable whether or not the conduct constituting domestic public sector bribery occurred in Australia, and whether or not the result of the bribery was obtained in Australia so long as it involved an Australian Commonwealth public official.

There are also State and Territory provisions which prohibit bribery of public officials, although those provisions are often the same as those which prohibit private sector bribery.[7]

Domestic private sector bribery

The Criminal Code does not criminalise bribery in the private sector; the States and Territories are left to legislate in this area. Indirect Commonwealth regulation is provided to some extent by the prescription of directors' duties in the *Corporations Act 2001* (Cth) (Corporations Act) and by the market-sharing and price-fixing provisions in Part IV of the *Competition and Consumer Act 2010* (Cth).

At the State and Territory level generally, it is illegal to corruptly give or offer inducements or secret commissions to, or receive them from, employees or agents of corporations and individuals.[8] Conduct will be 'corrupt' only if engaged in with the intention of influencing the recipient to show favour.

An example of the State and Territory provisions are those in the *Crimes Act 1900* (NSW), the relevant statute for the State of New South Wales (NSW). In that statute:
- Section 249B(1) prohibits an agent from corruptly receiving or soliciting (or corruptly agreeing to receive or solicit) any benefit from another person as an inducement, a reward, or on account of doing or not doing something, or showing or not showing favour to any person in relation to the affairs or business of the agent's principal. It also prohibits the receipt of any expectation which would tend to influence the agent to show or not show favour to any person in relation to the affairs or business of the agent's principal. Section 249B(2) imposes mirror offences on persons who give or offer an agent any such benefit.
- Section 249D(1) prohibits a person from corruptly giving a benefit to another person for giving secret advice to a third party where the person giving the benefit intends the advice to influence the third party to enter into a contract with the person giving the benefit, or appointing the person who gives the benefit to any office. Section 249D(2) makes it an offence to corruptly receive such a benefit.
- Section 249E makes it an offence for a person who offers or gives a benefit to a person entrusted with property (or any person entrusted with property who receives or solicits a benefit for anyone) without the consent of each person beneficially entitled to the property or the Supreme Court of NSW as an inducement or reward for the appointment of any person to be a person entrusted with the property.
- Section 249J provides that it is not a defence that the receiving, soliciting, giving or offering of any benefit is customary in any trade, business, profession or calling.
- The definition of "agent" is a wide one and includes employees: section 249A.

The legislation in the States and Territories varies as to the penalties that may be imposed for private sector bribery. Generally, individuals are liable for between three and 21 years' imprisonment.[9] Under the NSW Crimes Act, an individual can be imprisoned for up to seven years, and may also be ordered to repay all or part of the value of any benefit received or given by that person. He or she may also be disqualified from holding civic office for up to seven years. Where bribery is perpetrated by a corporation, some jurisdictions provide for fines instead of imprisonment.

Whistleblower protection

There is no general legislative protection for whistleblowers who report bribery. However, there are some specific legislative protections. For instance, Part 9.4AAA of the Corporations

Act protects an officer or employee of a company from victimisation if he or she discloses information in good faith to the Australian Securities & Investments Commission (ASIC) or an auditor, director or senior manager of the company where the discloser has reasonable grounds to suspect that the information shows the company, or an officer or employee of it, has contravened the Corporations legislation (meaning the Corporations Act, the ASIC Act and certain rules of court). Similar protection is provided by provisions of the *Banking Act 1959* (Cth), the *Insurance Act 1973* (Cth), the *Life Insurance Act 1995* (Cth) and the *Superannuation Industry (Supervision) Act 1993* (Cth). In some instances, bribery will constitute an offence under certain of these Acts, in which case the whistleblower may be entitled to rely on the relevant protections offered.

Public officials are protected under the *Public Interest Disclosure Act 2013* (Cth) (PID Act). The PID Act seeks to encourage public officials to report suspected wrongdoing in the Australian public sector, while protecting those who make public interest disclosures from reprisals.

The June 2014 Report of the Senate Economics Reference Committee on the Performance of ASIC made a number of recommendations in respect of whistleblower protection, including an expansion of the provisions in the Corporations Act, a review of the adequacy of Australia's current framework of protecting corporate whistleblowers, and a recommendation that the government explore options for reward-based incentives for corporate whistleblowers.[10]

A report published on the Transparency International Australia website concluded that Australia had significant room for improvement, particularly in relation to the private sector.[11]

Investigation and enforcement agencies

Australia has adopted a multi-agency approach to combatting corruption. Australia's main criminal law enforcement agencies in bribery cases are the Australian Federal Police (AFP) and the Office of the Commonwealth Director of Public Prosecutions (DPP). State-based investigations are generally conducted by the fraud squad of the particular State police department, with prosecutions being undertaken by State Directors of Public Prosecution.

The AFP is active in detecting and investigating corruption as part of its statutory obligations to investigate serious crimes against federal laws and against Commonwealth property, revenue and expenditure.

While allegations of corruption will generally be referred to the AFP, other agencies that may become involved in investigation processes include: the Australian Commission for Law Enforcement Integrity; the Australian Crime Commission; the Inspector-General of Intelligence and Security; and the Office of the Commonwealth Ombudsman. The DPP is largely responsible for prosecuting offenders under the anti-bribery provisions of the Criminal Code.

Corruption involving or affecting the public sector (including State government agencies, local government authorities, members of Parliament and the judiciary) is also dealt with at State level through independent bodies such as the NSW Independent Commission Against Corruption (ICAC).[12] While it cannot charge individuals or corporations with offences, the ICAC has wide-ranging power to investigate "corrupt conduct" involving NSW public officials or public bodies/authorities. Reports following an investigation can be given to parliament, the police or released publicly. The scope of ICAC's powers in respect of conduct by private individuals was the subject of a High Court judgment (*ICAC v Cunneen* (2015) 89 ALJR 475). The Court determined that ICAC did not have power to investigate conduct of private individuals which could affect the efficacy, but not probity, of public officials. The NSW government has since passed legislation retrospectively validating investigations undertaken by ICAC before the High Court's judgment.

However, in August 2015, an Independent Panel appointed by the Premier of NSW to review ICAC's powers recommended against legislation to reverse the High Court's decision, but instead proposed expanding the definition of corrupt conduct in ICAC's governing legislation to include certain types of conduct by private individuals which might undermine confidence in public administration. The types of conduct include certain types of fraud on the public revenue and fraud in relation to applications for public licences, permits or clearances. There were two high-profile ICAC investigations in 2013 relating to alleged corruption in the issue of mining licences. The Independent Panel also recommended limiting ICAC's power to make findings of corrupt conduct to cases involving serious corruption. The NSW government has indicated that it will accept the Panel's recommendations.

Overview of enforcement activity and policy during the past two years

Cases prosecuted

The first case prosecuted under Australia's anti-bribery laws centred upon Securency International Pty Limited (Securency), a subsidiary of the Reserve Bank of Australia. It arose from allegations by a company insider that Securency had paid nearly AU$50m to international sales agents to bribe central banking officials in Malaysia, Indonesia and Vietnam in order to secure banknote supply contracts. Investigations were jointly conducted by the AFP, the United Kingdom's Serious Fraud Office and Malaysia's Anti-Corruption Commission, leading to raids and searches in all three countries.

Following the AFP's investigation, dubbed 'Operation Rune', the AFP charged Securency, Note Printing Australia Limited ('NPA') and several of the companies' former senior managers with offences of bribing foreign officials under section 70.2(1) of the Criminal Code. Committal hearings commenced on 27 July 2011 and marked the first ever bribery prosecution under the anti-bribery provisions of the Criminal Code. Some details of the case against Securency were the subject of a suppression order, but that order was lifted in June 2015 (*Commonwealth DPP v Brady* [2015] VSC 246). The Court's reasons disclose that the proceedings involve offences in connection with banknote printing contracts for Malaysia, Indonesia, Vietnam and Nepal between 1999 and 2004. There have been 112 court sitting days spent on committal hearings. It is expected that there will be separate trials for each country, each of which will run for multiple months.

The suppression order made in June 2014 prevented disclosure of the names of certain foreign politicians in Malaysia, Indonesia and Vietnam who had been named in connection with the alleged criminal conduct, but were not alleged in the proceedings to have been a party to any of the alleged bribes. It was lifted following the publication of a copy of the suppression order (including the names of the individuals concerned) on Wikileaks and the subsequent widespread publication of their names by press outside Australia.

One former Securency officer, the former Securency CFO, David John Ellery, pleaded guilty to a charge of false accounting in July 2012. Mr. Ellery admitted that he had created a false document enabling the payment of AU$79,502 to a Malaysian intermediary. One month later, he received a six-month suspended sentence. Mr. Ellery had previously raised his concerns internally with respect to accounting anomalies within Securency.

The second charges under Australian anti-bribery laws were laid by the AFP in February 2015 against two directors of an Australian construction company, Lifese. The directors are charged with conspiracy to bribe a foreign public official in connection with building contracts in Iraq. A third man has also been charged. These proceedings are at an early stage.

In March 2015, two men (one formerly employed by an Australian bank and the other by the Australian Bureau of Statistics (ABS)) were sentenced to 7¼ and 3¼ years of imprisonment respectively after pleading guilty to charges of insider trading, abuse of public office, money laundering and identity theft. The offences related to an agreement between the men that ABS employee would provide to the other sensitive and unpublished ABS data, obtained in his capacity as a Commonwealth public official, and that the other would use that information to trade in margin foreign exchange derivatives. Those trades resulting in gross profits of over AU$8 million, being the largest insider trading profit to come before an Australian court.

In March and April 2015, NSW police charged two former executives of Commonwealth Bank of Australia with receiving bribes in return for the grant of IT contracts to a US company, ServiceMesh. The charges resulted from the Bank reporting anomalies it had uncovered to the police. These charges are brought under domestic anti-bribery laws. This matter is also the subject of a NSW Crime Commission investigation.

Current investigations

In April 2015, the OECD's Follow Up Report to its Phase 3 Report on Australia (discussed further below) recorded that the AFP had 17 foreign bribery investigations underway (an increase on seven as at October 2012). The AFP does not generally publish details of its ongoing investigations, but some which have been referred to in the press include:
- An investigation into alleged corrupt practices of Australian multinational mining company, BHP Billiton. in its promotional activities that preceded the 2008 Beijing Olympic Games. BHP Billiton has reached an agreement with the SEC in relation to this conduct (see below), but the AFP investigation continues.
- An investigation of a prominent Australian company, which self-reported to the AFP after an internal audit uncovered possible foreign bribery. It is reported that the company alerted the AFP to a possible breach involving payments made by a Singapore-based subsidiary to facilitate a wharf construction project in Iraq. Further unrelated allegations reportedly levelled at the company relate to a senior employee having channelled steel worth AU$500,000 to a third-party project in Indonesia.

In March 2014, the Australian government established a Royal Commission into Trade Union Governance and Corruption. This inquiry is in relation to governance arrangements and alleged financial irregularities as well as bribes, secret commissions and other unlawful payments made in the context of these entities. The Royal Commission and is now due to report at the end of 2015. The Commission's activities have been highly controversial and in August 2015 the Commissioner heard (and ultimately rejected) an application to disqualify himself on the basis of apprehended bias.

ICAC has a number of ongoing investigations. There are some particularly high-profile ICAC investigations which are worthy of mention. Operations Credo and Spicer, both commenced in 2014, concern dealings between a company known as Australian Water Holdings and various members of the NSW Parliament. They involve allegations of misuse of public office by some members of the NSW Parliament, as well as corruption in relation to the giving and receiving of political donations by members of the NSW Parliament. These investigations are ongoing, although they were temporarily halted as a result of the High Court's decision in *Cunneen* (see above). However, although they have not been completed and no findings have been made by ICAC, they have already resulted in the resignation of the Premier and several Ministers of the New South Wales Government.

In 2013, two other investigations into the grant of mining exploration licences (Operations Jasper and Acacia) resulted in corrupt conduct findings against a number of former members of the NSW Parliament and senior mining executives.

Current trends of enforcement action

It is evident from the scarcity of prosecutions to date that Australia is still in the early stages of enforcing anti-bribery laws in relation to foreign public officials. However, significant progress has been made in the level of enforcement action over the last three years. The catalyst for that progress appears to have been the Phase 3 Report on Implementing the OECD Anti-Bribery Convention in Australia, issued by the OECD Working Group on Bribery in late 2012 (OECD Phase 3 Report). The OECD Phase 3 Report noted that a substantial proportion of Australia's international economic activity is exposed to foreign bribery risks, particularly in the mining and resources sector and the agriculture sector. While fuels and mining products accounted for almost 60% of Australia's exports in 2011, agricultural produce constituted over 12% of total exports. In 2011, China was Australia's biggest export destination and India was ranked fifth. Australia's geographic location also sees it play a significant economic role in neighbouring Polynesian and South Pacific countries, many of which pose serious corruption risks.

The OECD Phase 3 report criticised Australian enforcement efforts and was particularly scathing about the failure of the AFP to resource, prioritise and pursue foreign bribery investigations. It also criticised the AFP for a lack of sufficient co-ordination and co-operation with both its international contacts and other Australian regulatory and enforcement agencies. More generally the report said that Australia should improve its measures to ensure that public officials reported suspicions of foreign bribery and to protect whistleblowers and expressed concern about the lack of transparent policies and guidelines for the debarment of persons convicted of foreign bribery.

The AFP and the Australian government responded to the OECD Phase 3 Report with a number of initiatives. These include:

• at the time of the Phase 3 Report the AFP had already in April 2012 established a Foreign Bribery Panel of Experts which now has responsibility for ensuring that allegations of foreign bribery are investigated thoroughly;

• the AFP has entered into a Memorandum of Understanding (MOU) in respect of collaborative working arrangements and the sharing of information with each of ASIC and the Australian Prudential Regulation Authority. In an October 2013 speech, ASIC Chairman Greg Medcraft made it clear that while the AFP was responsible for investigating foreign bribery and corruption, and taking criminal action through the courts, ASIC would look at allegations concerning directors' duties in appropriate cases;

• in February 2013, the AFP established dedicated Fraud and Anti-Corruption teams in five capital cities; and

• the establishment in July 2014 of the Fraud and Anti-Corruption Centre (FAC), a centre hosted by the AFP, but also involving officials from a range of government departments, regulators (including ASIC and the Australian Taxation Office), and investigation and enforcement agencies. The FAC's role appears to be to improve co-ordination amongst agencies, to develop standards and procedures for fraud and anti-corruption investigation and to provide training to investigators.

These developments were all noted in the OECD Working Group's Follow-Up to the Phase 3 Report & Recommendations (OECD Follow-Up Report), published in April 2015. This report noted that since the OECD Phase 3 Report 15, new allegations of foreign bribery had surfaced and the number of matters under investigation by the AFP had increased from seven to 17. While noting that good progress had been made in implementing the recommendations of the Phase 3 Report, the Follow-Up Report identified the following areas for further work:

- increased enforcement of foreign bribery, corporate liability and false accounting provisions;
- the extension of whistleblower protection in the private sector;
- the introduction of transparent debarment processes for government procurement agencies; and
- further action on the OECD's recommendations for legislative change in a number of areas.

The OECD Follow-Up Report confirms that the effectiveness of Australia's enforcement agencies has increased significantly since 2012. Not surprisingly this has resulted in a greater number of foreign bribery allegations. The progress of the Securency prosecutions suggests that it will be a number of years before the increased enforcement translates into high-profile convictions. However, companies doing business in Australia should not be lulled into a false sense of security because much is happening behind the scenes.

Law and policy relating to facilitation payments and hospitality

Facilitation payments

A facilitation payment is a small bribe or 'grease' payment made to a public official to secure or expedite the performance of a routine procedure to which the payer is legally entitled. Typical examples of routine procedures involve processing visas and other government papers, and granting permits or licences for conducting business in a country.

In the Commentaries on the OECD Convention, facilitation payments are distinguished from bribery on the basis that a small facilitation payment does not constitute an attempt to obtain or retain business or other improper advantage. However, a different approach is taken in the UNCAC, in which no distinction is made between bribery and facilitation payments.

The former approach has been adopted in Australia, where the Criminal Code excludes criminal liability for facilitation payments. However, the OECD recognises that the operation of the defence can be problematic. While the practice of Australian companies making facilitation payments appears to be prevalent, there is general confusion about the scope of the defence, and a lack of understanding about what constitutes a facilitation payment. Individuals and corporates alike need to be aware that they will only be able to rely upon the defence if the payment is of a minor nature, made for the sole or dominant purpose of securing a routine government action of a minor nature, and the details of the payment are properly recorded as soon as is reasonably practicable.

Although the OECD Convention does not require countries to criminalise the use of facilitation payments, there has been a gradual shift in mood, and such payments are no longer widely considered acceptable. In 2009, the OECD recommended that, in view of the corrosive effect of small facilitation payments, States Parties to the OECD Convention should:

- periodically review their policies on and approach to small facilitation payments in order to combat this practice; and
- encourage companies to prohibit or discourage the use of small facilitation payments, because such payments are usually illegal in the foreign countries in which they are made.

In November 2011, the Australian government published a public consultation paper in relation to the facilitation payments, seeking responses from interested stakeholders on a proposal to repeal the facilitation payments defence. The proposal has been viewed favourably by the OECD, although whilst the Government has said it remains under active consideration, it does not appear to be a high-priority agenda item.

The OECD Phase 3 Report noted that there were inconsistencies between the record keeping requirements for facilitation payments in the *Criminal Code* and those in Australia tax legislation dealing with the claiming of deductions which should be reconciled. As the OECD Follow-Up Report noted, nothing has yet been done in this regard.

Hospitality

Australian legislation does not expressly explain the circumstances under which providing gifts and hospitality may amount to bribery. As the law currently stands, the giving of such benefits will only be unlawful if done with the intention of influencing a public official. There is little in the way of guidance on this area from Australian regulators. The principal guidance for Commonwealth public officials is under the *Public Service Act 1999* (Cth), which has a series of relevant standards set out in the Australian Public Service Code of Conduct, and the Australian Public Service Values, under the umbrella of the Australian Public Service Commission Guide to its Integrated Leadership System. The Department of Foreign Affairs and Trade has its own Code of Conduct for Overseas Service. State and Territory Governments also have their own public services with their own codes of conduct, which may be supplemented by agency-specific codes.

In certain business transactions, providing a level of hospitality to prospective clients may be required. Vigilance is recommended in this area to ensure compliance with anti-bribery laws, particularly when engaging with public officials. Some issues to consider in determining whether hospitality is appropriate are: whether the company providing it has a clear policy on gifts and hospitality and whether that policy is being complied with; whether the expenditure is reasonable and is accurately recorded; and whether the hospitality might reasonably be suspected of influencing the recipient's decision-making processes.

The BHP Billiton case is a timely reminder of the particular risks associated with the provision of hospitality to public officials. On 20 May 2015, BHP Billiton agreed to pay to the SEC a US$25 million penalty to settle SEC charges that it violated the FCPA by failing to devise and maintain sufficient internal controls over its global hospitality programme connected to the company's sponsorship of the 2008 Summer Olympic Games in Beijing. BHP Billiton is subject to a continuing AFP investigation in relation to this conduct.

Key issues relating to investigation, decision-making and enforcement procedures

Self-reporting

In Australia, self-reporting of foreign bribery to the AFP is encouraged but is not mandated by any legislative or formal framework. At the time the OECD Phase 3 Report was published, at least three companies had self-reported evidence of bribery committed by persons related to them. In each case, the AFP proceeded with ongoing investigations.

The AFP has indicated that it expects to see more self-reporting by companies; however, this has not been matched by legislative amendments or clear prosecution guidelines. While there are few, if any, formal incentives from a criminal law perspective, a potential benefit to self-reporting is that the AFP may be more inclined to work with the corporation in question, and keep it better informed during the investigation process. There may also be leniency at the prosecution stage, although a number of other factors would also be considered in accordance with the Prosecution Policy of the Commonwealth.

Plea bargaining

A plea bargain can take two forms, the first being an agreement between the prosecution and the defence that the defendant agree to plead guilty to a particular charge in return for more serious charges being dropped. This type of plea bargain is allowed in Australia and, in certain circumstances, the DPP may be able to provide a defendant with testimonial or prosecutorial immunity. In addition to agreeing to drop certain charges in return for a guilty plea, the DPP may agree to proceed with a charge summarily rather than on indictment, or agree not to oppose a defence.

The Prosecution Policy of the Commonwealth provides guidance on negotiations between the prosecution and the defence about charges to be prosecuted. Charge negotiations are specifically encouraged and can occur at any stage of a prosecution, and at the DPP's initiation. This practice will meet the requirements of justice as long as the charges to be continued bear a reasonable relationship to the nature of the defendant's criminal conduct, provide an adequate basis for the imposition of an appropriate sentence, and are supported by evidence.

The second form involves a defendant pleading guilty to a charge in return for a lesser sentence being imposed by a court. This form of plea bargaining has been virtually precluded by the High Court in *Barbaro v the Queen* (2014) 253 CLR 58, which holds that prosecutors are not required and should not be permitted to proffer even a sentencing regime to a judge.

The OECD Phase 3 Report recommended that a clear framework be provided to address uncertainties around self-reporting and plea bargaining. Issues requiring clarification include how a person or company might be expected to cooperate, the credit to be given for cooperating with the AFP, measures for monitoring compliance with a plea agreement, and the prosecution of natural persons related to companies. This recommendation has been addressed by the AFP and DPP developing a presentation for industry about the benefits of co-operation.

Civil *versus* criminal prosecution

Foreign and domestic public sector bribery offences are prosecuted in Australia under provisions of the Criminal Code. At the State and Territory level, private sector bribery is also prosecuted criminally. There are only some circumstances in which acts of bribery may also give rise to civil claims. Civil penalty proceedings under the *Corporations Act 2001* (Cth) (which are brought by ASIC) for breaching directors' duties are an example.

Examples of cases in which ASIC has pursued directors or officers for breach of section 180 of the Corporations Act (for failing to exercise due care, skill and diligence) include *ASIC v Ingleby* [2013] VSCA 49 and *ASIC v Lindberg* [2012] VSC 332, which both arose out of the so-called 'Oil for Food' programme. These cases highlight the need for directors and officers to ensure that proper systems are in place to combat bribery and corruption within their organisations, and the importance of not ignoring 'red flags'.

Overview of cross-border issues

Parallel investigations

As the drive to enforce the anti-bribery regime gathers momentum and the regime itself becomes more sophisticated, Australian agencies are increasingly using parallel investigations and collaborating with overseas agencies.

An International Foreign Bribery Taskforce (IFBT) was established in May 2013 as a platform for specialist investigators from Australia, the United States, Canada and the United

Kingdom to work together to combat foreign bribery. The IFBT facilitates collaboration and cooperation between experts from the AFP, the Federal Bureau of Investigation, the Royal Canadian Mounted Police and the City of London Police Overseas Anti-Corruption Unit. The IFBT aims to enhance the response of these like-minded countries to foreign bribery by encouraging experts to share knowledge, skills and methodologies.

Australia is also an active member of the G20 Anti-Corruption Working Group, which aims to enhance the prevention of corruption-related activities. The G20 met in Australia in November 2014 and the Leaders' Communique at the end of that meeting included an endorsement of the G20 2015-2016 Corruption Action Plan.

Another multilateral anti-corruption forum to which Australia contributes is the Asia-Pacific Economic Cooperation (APEC) Anti-Corruption and Transparency Experts Taskforce. Australia was a key participant in developing the APEC Code of Conduct for Business and has since worked with Chile, Thailand and Vietnam to implement it. For the purpose of disturbing the financing of corrupt activities, Australia also collaborated with other APEC members to promote the use of anti-money laundering systems, and hosted several international conferences on this topic.

Overseas impacts

Australia's geographic location and footprint in certain high-risk economic activities expose it to impacts from overseas laws concerning bribery and corruption, as set out above. In addition to the mining and resources and agriculture sectors, another area of risk is the construction sector, particularly in Asian markets (and in particular China) where Australian companies are increasingly turning given investment opportunities.

Overseas impacts are also felt in Australia, due to the increasingly international nature of business. An example is provided by the differences in anti-bribery laws in Australia and the United Kingdom. While in Australia facilitation payments are allowed and there is no strict liability bribery offence for corporations, the opposite is true in the United Kingdom. Australian-based companies doing business in the United Kingdom must be aware of the need to comply with the strict anti-bribery regime in place there, and may be required to implement company-wide procedures and policies to ensure compliance.

Corporate liability may arise under foreign laws even where there is no obvious jurisdictional nexus. It is increasingly common for international business partners to demand that their Australian counterparts comply with foreign laws. International business contracts may require that Australian companies warrant their compliance with foreign anti-corruption laws or provide annual certificates of compliance with them.

Corporate liability for bribery and corruption offences

Section 70.2(1) of the Criminal Code creates the offence of providing, offering or promising to provide a benefit not legitimately due to another person, with the intention of influencing the exercise of a foreign public official's duties to obtain business or a business advantage. This offence captures the conduct of individuals and corporations alike; however, to establish the criminal liability of a corporation, the Criminal Code requires that both a physical and mental (or 'fault') element be satisfied.

The physical element of the offence under section 70.2(1) is attributed to a corporation if the conduct was committed by an employee, agent or officer of the body corporate acting within the actual or apparent scope of that person's employment or authority.[13] The fault element, being the requirement of intention under section 70.2(1), is satisfied if the corporation "expressly, tacitly or impliedly authorised or permitted the commission of the offence".[14] Authorisation or permission can be established in several ways, including by proving that:

- the corporation's board of directors or a 'high managerial agent' (a senior officer) carried out the conduct, or authorised or permitted the commission of the offence;
- the corporation had a corporate culture that directed, encouraged, tolerated or led to non-compliance with the legislative provisions; or
- the corporation failed to create and maintain a corporate culture requiring compliance with the relevant anti-bribery laws.

The scope of corporate liability provisions in the Criminal Code is broad. In particular, the provisions relating to corporate culture direct attention to the adequacy of a corporation's anti-bribery compliance programme.

Proposed reforms / The year ahead

There have been a number of stalled attempts in recent years to either amend Australia's foreign bribery legislation or to reform the national governance framework. In particular, in September 2011 the Commonwealth Government announced a commitment to developing a National Anti-Corruption Plan. Despite a public consultation process which concluded in 2012, a National Plan is yet to be released.

The stalled proposal to repeal the facilitation payments defence is described above.

On 24 June 2015, the Australian Senate asked its Economic References Committee to conduct an Inquiry into the measures governing the activities of Australians with respect to foreign bribery, with specific reference to the effectiveness of, and any possible improvements to, Australia's implementation of its obligations under the OECD Convention and UNCAC. As part of that Inquiry the Committee is asked to address the effectiveness of, and any possible improvements to, existing Commonwealth legislation governing foreign bribery. The Terms of Reference expressly cover ancillary matters such as the resourcing of enforcement agencies, self-reporting and whistleblower protection.[15] Submission to the Committee closed on 24 August 2015. The Committee is due to report by 1 July 2016. It is likely that the Committee will hold public hearings in early 2016.

The Committee's report is likely to establish the framework for the next stage in the development of Australia's anti-bribery and corruption regime. It is too early to tell what the Committee's recommendations might be, but the terms of reference are broad enough to allow for the possibility of wholesale reform of both legislation and enforcement.

Endnotes

1. *Crimes Act 1900* (NSW), s 249B; *Crimes Act 1958* (Vic), s 176; *Criminal Law Consolidation Act 1935* (SA), s 150; *Criminal Code Act 1899* (Qld), ss 442B-442BA; *The Criminal Code* (WA), ss 529-530; *Criminal Code Act 1924* (Tas), s 266; *Criminal Code 2002* (ACT), ss 356-357; *Criminal Code Act* 1983 (NT), s 236.
2. Part 7.6 of the *Criminal Code Act 1995* (Cth).
3. Proving offences under the Criminal Code requires proof of a physical element of the offence and a fault element of the offence. In the case of the fault element, intention to influence may be proved by showing that the person in question "means to bring [the result] about or is aware that it will occur in the ordinary course of events".
4. *Criminal Code*, s 70.5.
5. *Criminal Code*, s 70.3.
6. *Criminal Code*, s 70.4.
7. Various State and Territory legislation criminalises public sector bribery: *Crimes Act 1900* (NSW), s 249B; *Crimes Act 1958* (Vic), s 176; *Criminal Law Consolidation Act*

1935 (SA), s 150; *Criminal Code Act 1899* (Qld), ss 442B-442BA; *The Criminal Code* (WA), ss 529-530; *Criminal Code Act 1924* (Tas), s 266; *Criminal Code 2002* (ACT), ss 356-357; *Criminal Code Act 1983* (NT), s 236.

8. *Crimes Act 1900* (NSW), Part 4A; *Crimes Act 1958* (Vic), s 320; *Criminal Code 1899* (Qld), section 60 and 98C; *Criminal Law Consolidation Act 1935* (SA), ss 149 and 150; *Criminal Code Act* 1942 (Tas), s 72; *Criminal Code Compilation Act* 1913 (WA), s 61; *Criminal Code 2002* (ACT), s 356; *Criminal Code Act 1983* (NT), ss 59 and 88.

9. Maximum periods of imprisonment provided for by the various State and Territory legislation are: seven years under the *Crimes Act 1900* (NSW), s 249B; 10 years under the *Crimes Act 1958* (Vic), s 176; seven years under the *Criminal Law Consolidation Act 1935* (SA), s 150; seven years under the *Criminal Code Act 1899* (Qld), s 442I; seven years under *The Criminal Code* (WA), s 538; 21 years under the *Criminal Code Act 1924* (Tas), s 389(3); 10 years under the *Criminal Code 2002* (ACT), s 356; and three years under the *Criminal Code Act 1983* (NT), s 236.

10. Senate Economics References Committee, 'Performance of the Australian Securities and Investments Commission', June 2014 (http://www.aph.gov.au/Parliamentary_Business/Committees/Senate/Economics/ASIC/Final_Report/~/media/Committees/Senate/committee/economics_ctte/ASIC/Final_Report/report.pdf).

11. Wolfe, S *et al "Whistleblower Protection Laws in G20 Countries - Priorities for Action"*, September 2014. http://transparency.org.au/wp-content/uploads/2014/09/FINAL__-Whistleblower-Protection-Laws-in-G20-Countries-Priorities-for__-Action.pdf.

12. Other bodies include: the Independent Broad-based Anti-Corruption Commission in Victoria, the Crime and Corruption Commission in Queensland, and the Corruption and Crime Commission in Western Australia.

13. *Criminal Code Act 1995* (Cth), s 12.2.

14. *Criminal Code Act 1995* (Cth), s 12.3.

15. http://www.aph.gov.au/Parliamentary_Business/Committees/Senate/Economics/Foreign_Bribery/Terms_of_Reference.

Acknowledgment

The authors would like to acknowledge the assistance of Richard Abraham, Yehudah New, Magali Manon and Grace Ness in preparing this chapter and the work of King & Wood Mallesons who prepared the first edition of this chapter.

Greg Williams
Tel: +61 293 534 798 / Email: gwilliams@claytonutz.com
Greg Williams is a member of Clayton Utz's litigation group. Greg's experience ranges from acting in large-scale class actions and commercial litigation to advising on white-collar crime and regulatory issues.

Greg has recognised expertise in the field of bribery, fraud and corruption matters, and has written and presented widely on the impact of the international anti-bribery legislation in Australia. He has assisted clients with internal investigations relating to suspected breaches of both domestic and foreign laws and codes and advised in relation to their exposure to internal codes and compliance measures. He has written extensively about emerging trends in anti-bribery law, including the effect of the UK Bribery Act on Australian companies.

Greg has nearly 15 years of experience in the conduct of complex litigation, in particular product liability and class actions. He is listed in the *International Who's Who of Product Liability Defence* and *Life Sciences*, as well as in the 2016 Edition of *Australia's Best Lawyers* for his expertise in Product Liability and Class Actions Litigation.

Tobin Meagher
Tel: +61 293 534 842 / Email: tmeagher@claytonutz.com
Tobin Meagher is a partner within the Commercial Litigation Practice at Clayton Utz. He specialises in complex commercial litigation and disputes, with particular expertise in fraud/white-collar crime, contractual disputes, restrictive trade practices litigation and regulatory investigations.

Tobin has been involved in a number of significant commercial litigation matters for a variety of clients across a wide range of industries, including financial services, retail, telecommunications and energy and resources. He has also advised and represented a number of clients on the subject of regulatory investigation and enforcement proceedings.

Tobin has extensive experience in a variety of fraud matters, including matters involving the payment of secret commissions, bribery, conspiracy to defraud and fidelity insurance claims. He has advised clients on risks and responsibilities arising from international anti-bribery legislation, assisted clients the subject of regulatory investigation, and written and presented on emerging trends in anti-bribery law, including the effects of the UK Bribery Act and Foreign Corrupt Practices Act on Australian companies.

Tobin's asset recovery experience is recognised in the *International Who's Who of Asset Recovery Lawyers 2015* and he is also listed in the 2016 Edition of *Australia's Best Lawyers* for his expertise in Litigation.

Clayton Utz

Level 15, 1 Bligh Street, Sydney, NSW 2000, Australia
Tel: +61 293 534 798 or +61 293 534 842 / Fax: +61 282 206 700 / URL: http://www.claytonutz.com

Austria

Norbert Wess, Bernhard Kispert & Dietmar Bachmann
wkk law attorneys at law

Brief overview of the law and enforcement regime

The legal framework of corruption laws in Austria is well-developed and there is also a functioning institutional and legal system. Sometimes major corruption cases in Austria are investigated by a parliamentary committee and followed by criminal proceedings.

First, it must be pointed out that there is no specific written definition of "corruption" in Austrian law, but it is traditionally understood that the abuse of public duties to obtain a benefit is unlawful and moreover a criminal offence. In 2012 the Austrian legislator introduced for the first time the term "corruption" in the 22ⁿᵈ Section of the Austrian Criminal Code (*Österreichisches Strafgesetzbuch, StGB*).

The main legal provisions governing and dealing with bribery and corruption are laid down in the Austrian Criminal Code. They are characterised by the fact that a clear distinction is made between offences involving <u>public officials</u> and bribery in <u>commercial practice</u>. Furthermore, regarding public officials, Austrian criminal law distinguishes between offering and receiving/accepting bribes.

Section 22 of the Austrian Criminal Code comprises "criminal offences relating to public officials, corruption and other related criminal offences". These crimes (and others) are also relevant with regard to corporate liability, as the Act on Corporate Criminal Liability (*Verbandsverantwortlichkeitsgesetz*, VBVG) was introduced and provided for criminal liability of corporations in 2006.

In the context of bribery and corruption, the prosecution of active and passive bribery in the public and private sector (in particular holders of public offices such as politicians, judges, police officers, custom officials, etc.) represents the central part of Austrian criminal law.

The most severe form of corruption is the deliberate misuse of authority. To obtain an (unfair) advantage is, in that context, not a matter of fact, but usually a direct motive of delinquency. That also applies *inter alia* also to the abuse of office (§ 302 StGB) and breach of trust (§ 153 StGB).

Clause 153a of the Austrian Criminal Code (StGB) states that a person who possesses authority to represent a third party is not allowed to accept an advantage in the performance of his duties. In the context of all bribery and corruption-related provisions, an advantage covers cash and non-cash gifts, consultancy, agreements, etc. The Austrian Supreme Court of Justice (*Oberster Gerichtshof*) has repeatedly stated that a benefit can also consist of a non-pecuniary advantage.

As to corruption in the strict sense of criminal law, with respect to criminal offences involving public officials, Austrian Criminal Law differentiates between accepting and offering bribes. Moreover, the Austrian legislator notes that a public official (*Amtsträger*) means a person who works for a local, regional, national or international authority, state or international organisation and also every person who works for any public law entity.

Clauses 304, 305 and 306 of the Austrian Criminal contain the offence of receiving bribes, whereas clauses 307, 307a and 307b of the Austrian Criminal Code relate to offering and giving bribes.

Receiving/accepting a bribe	Offering a bribe
Clause 304 of the Austrian Criminal Code: A public official or arbitrator who **accepts a bribe** for the performance of an **official act in contradiction to official duties**.	Clause 307 (1) of the Austrian Criminal Code: A person who **offers a bribe** to a public official or an arbitrator for the performance of an **official act in contradiction to official duties**.
Clause 305 of the Austrian Criminal Code: A public official or arbitrator who accepts **benefits** for the performance or **omission** of an **official duty**.	Clause 307a Austrian Criminal Code: A person who **offers benefits** to a public official or an arbitrator for the performance of an **official act**.
Clause 306 of the Austrian Criminal Code: A public official or arbitrator who **accepts improper benefits** for an **impact**.	Clause 307b Austrian Criminal Code: A person who **offers improper benefits** to a public official or an arbitrator for an **impact**.
Clause 308 StGB: **prohibited intervention**	

Furthermore, these four categories are similar regarding one main element: the performance or omission of an <u>official act</u>. Pursuant to Austrian Criminal Law the consequences of the aforementioned criminal offences entail fines or imprisonment up to ten years, for example if the criminal offence exceeds the maximum value prescribed by law.

The second main category of Austrian bribery and corruption law provisions is the offering and receiving/accepting of <u>bribes in commercial practice</u>. As already mentioned, a central area of this category of bribe and corruption is included e.g. in the clauses 153, 153a, 168b and 309 of the Austrian Criminal Code.

Receiving/accepting an advantage and offering a bribe to an employee or authorised representative of a company	
Clause 309 (1) of the Austrian Criminal Code	**Clause 309 (2)** of the Austrian Criminal Code
An employee or authorised representative of a company **requesting, agreeing to receive or accepting an advantage** for his performance or omission of a **legal act** in contradiction to duty.	A person who **offers** (or **promises** or **gives**) an advantage to an employee or authorised representative of a company for his performance or omission of a **legal act** in contradiction to duty.

In general the legal consequences of bribery and corruption for a natural person are imprisonment and monetary fines. But the Austrian Criminal Code also states different value limits which have to be distinguished:

- the exception of any undue advantage specified in clause 305 (4) of the Austrian Criminal Code states that receiving an advantage is not a punishable act if it is permitted by law or the advantage has been given within the scope of an event, if there is a legitimate interest to attend this event. Receiving an advantage for the purpose of a public benefit is not punishable either, or if the advantage (or valuable product) has a law value and is in accordance with local custom;
- this also applies to the threshold limit of €3,000.00 specified in clauses 304 (2) 1st alternative, 305 (3) 1st alternative, 306 (2) 1st alternative, 307 (2) 1st alternative of the Austrian Criminal Code; and
- the threshold limit of €50,000.00 stated in clauses 304 (2) 2nd alternative, 305 (3) 2nd alternative, 306 (2) 2nd alternative, and 307 (2) 2nd alternative of the Austrian Criminal Code.

Criminal offence (Austrian Criminal Code)	Underlying offence (imprisonment/fine)	Threshold limit 1 over €3,000.00 (imprisonment/fine)	Threshold limit 2 over €50,000.00 (imprisonment/fine)
clause 153	≤ 6 months or ≤ 360 daily rates	≤ 3 years	1 to 10 years
clause 153 a	≤ 1 year		
clause 302	6 months to 5 years		1 to 10 years
clauses 304, 307	≤ 3 years	6 months to 5 years	1 to 10 years
clauses 305, 307a	≤ 2 years	≤ 3 years	6 months to 5 years
clauses 306, 307b			
clause 308			
clause 309			

A particular focus shall be put on the jurisdiction and competence of the court. In cases where the charge is brought to the court by the prosecutor after 1st January 2015, the jury must consist of two professional judges and two lay judges regarding (amongst others) several business crimes (e.g. clause 153 "breach of trust") in connection with a damage or a value-determining amount of more than €1m, bribery (clause 304 to 309) regarding bribes above €100,000.00 and financial crimes regarding amounts above €1m. Cases of severe abuse of authority (clause 302 (2) 2nd phrase) are additionally subject to appear before this specific jury if a damage or a value-determining amount of more than €100,000.00 occurs.

Overview of enforcement activity and policy during the past two years

Many significant cases have occurred during the last two years in Austria. Several prominent new cases of government and business corruption involving many public officials at the provincial and regional level, senior public officials and the central government have been investigated. All of these cases were made public and the findings of *Eurobarometer 2012*, for example, show that two-thirds of respondents have questioned the ethical standards of the Austrian political elite.

Consequently, criminal investigations in Austria have been paying more attention to cases of bribery and corruption in the last few years. Furthermore, almost all major enterprises and companies have set up compliance structures to investigate and avoid cases of bribery and corruption.

In the year 2013, the Austrian Public Prosecutor's Office against Corruption had to deal with 1,351 new cases related to bribery and corruption concerning 3,771 persons. Last year the number of new cases related to bribery and corruption minimally increased up to 1,359 cases. Thirty-one of the cases in 2013 were major cases reported by the press:

- On 25th October 2011 the Austrian National Bank (OeNB) reported to the Austrian Public Prosecutor's Office that there was some concerns that the subsidiary *Österreichische Banknoten- und Sicherheitsdruck GmbH* (OeSB) was involved in a bribery affair. After detailed examination by the public prosecutor the indictment stated that during the relevant period of time, i.e. from 2004 to 2011, bribes had been paid to Azerbaijani and Syrian public officials in order to obtain public contracts in the amount of more than €50m. The Court of the First Instance has already issued a judgment in which seven of nine accused were sentenced in this bribery affair. The convicted persons immediately filed an appeal against this sentencing. Finally, only two accused were acquitted, for a lack of evidence.

- In 2012, the German Public Prosecutor and the Austrian Public Prosecutor initiated investigations regarding the purchase of 18 'Euro-fighter' aircrafts. The reason for carrying out criminal investigations was that it was likely that bribes in the amount of millions of euros had been paid to Austrian officials in the performance of the transactions, even to members of the then Austrian government. The preliminary investigations are still ongoing and are not closed at this moment. Charges against the suspects are still not brought before court by the Austrian Public Prosecutor.
- A few months earlier on 2nd July 2012, the Austrian Public Prosecutor accused three members of the Board of Management of Telekom Austria AG, two authorised signatories of the Telekom Austria AG and one member of the Board of Management of the Euro Invest Bank AG of having manipulated the stock price of Telekom Austria AG. Telekom Austria AG succeeded in obtaining a remarkable court decision of the Court of First Instance: several defendants received prison sentences and the Telekom Austria AG as the 'damaged party' was awarded damages of a certain amount of €9.9m. In this context the judgment is subject to an appeal of which the Appeal Court's decision is still outstanding.
- Also quite notable and generating great media interest is the criminal proceedings against former football players and other individuals who have manipulated soccer matches of the Austrian Federal Soccer League (*Österreichische Fußball-Bundesliga*, ÖFBL). On 14th April 2014, the Austrian Public Prosecutor accused five former soccer players of the Austrian Federal Soccer League and five other individuals of acting as backers for the manipulation of bets ("betting fraud") by manipulating numerous soccer matches during the period between 2004 and 2013. The Court of First Instance has already passed judgments by which two notable former football players and other individuals were sentenced to prison for several years on the grounds of betting fraud. An appeal against the judgment of the First Instance was filed and at the time of writing the proceedings on appeal are still pending.

Law and policy relating to issues such as facilitation payments and hospitality

The Austrian Criminal Law regarding bribery and corruption states that a facilitation payment is a punishable act in the same manner as any other advantage. Worth mentioning as advantages here in particular are material and non-material advantages, like for example payments, valuable articles, any kind of services and any kind of social or professional benefits.

In the specific case of facilitation payments the Austrian legal opinion considers small sums to be equally criminal as bigger amounts of money or promised benefits, so that any payment to an official to induce or reward his performance of official duties, or in the performance of official activities, would violate the Austrian Criminal Code. Nevertheless the Austrian legislator specifies a few noteworthy exceptions, such as:

- In case of clause 153a of the Austrian Criminal Code where a monetary advantage of less than €100.00 is accepted, it is not liable to prosecution.
- In case of clauses 305 (1), 306 (1), 307a (1) and 307b (1), the clause 305 (4) of the Austrian Criminal Code specifies that an ("*undue*") advantage is not liable to prosecution if it is permitted by law or has been given within the scope of an event if there is a legitimate interest to attend this event. Receiving an advantage for the purpose of a public benefit is not punishable either, or if the advantage (product) has a law value and is in accordance with local custom.

Regarding hospitality, the Austrian legal opinion is that as long as it represents a valuable advantage, its criminal liability has to be assessed on the basis of criteria arising from the exceptions mentioned above.

Key issues relating to investigation, decision-making and enforcement procedures

Criminal offences regarding bribery and corruption in the private and public sector are both prosecuted by the Austrian Public Prosecutor, who is the competent authority for investigation in accordance with the Austrian Code of Criminal Procedure (*Strafprozessordnung*, StPO). But in recent years there has been a growing lack of public prosecutors who are specialised in offences relating to businesses. Therefore in 2011, the Austrian Legislator decided to create the *Zentrale Wirtschafts- und Korruptionsstaatsanwaltschaft* (WKStA) in Vienna which is the special Austrian Public Prosecutor's Office for the Enforcement of Business Crimes and Corruption. Presently, the WKStA has 23 public prosecutors, who are not only capable of reading and interpreting balance sheets but also have better understanding and in-depth knowledge of the rules of the economy.

Another important key issue occurred regarding the appointment of experts and the use of expert evidence in criminal proceedings. Until 1st January 2015, only the public prosecutor could appoint an expert during the preliminary proceedings. In the trial the same expert, who has already worked for the prosecutor during the preliminary investigations, was regularly appointed by the court. This expert represents the only expert of the trial. In addition, the accused have no right to appoint an expert of their own to whom the same rights are granted as the court's/the prosecutor's expert. These circumstances lead to an infringement of Article 6 of the European Convention for the Protection of Human Rights and Fundamental Freedoms – a provision which has constitutional status in Austria – and lays down that a defendant is guaranteed the right to a fair trial; this also includes the principle of equality of arms.

Ultimately, however, and this marks a major step forward from the point of view of the defendants, the Austrian Constitutional Court has asserted that this provision in clause 126 of the Austrian Code of Criminal Procedure was unconstitutional in the decision of 10th March 2015, G 180/2014 *et al*. The criminal cases that led to the Decision of the Constitutional Court are still pending at the Austrian Supreme Court (*Oberster Gerichtshof*). Now the Supreme Court is obliged to decide on the basis of the judgment of the Constitutional Court whether in each individual case the constitutional rights of the defendants have been infringed or not.

In the meantime – although before the judgment of the Austrian Constitutional Court – the system of the expert evidence has been changed by the Austrian legislator. Now the defendants/the defending counsels have the right to demand that the expert has to be court-appointed even in preliminary investigations. As a result, an infringement of the equality of arms principle should be avoided.

Overview of cross-border issues

Bribery and corruption is of course not only a major national problem involving Austrian national institutions and moreover the Austrian private sector. Therefore, Austria has concluded several multilateral agreements related to anti-corruption, including:
*   the United Nations Convention against Corruption;
*   the OECD Convention on Combating Bribery of Foreign Public Officials in International Business Transactions (Anti-Bribery Convention);
*   the Council of Europe Criminal Law Convention on Corruption (not ratified); and
*   Second Protocol of the Convention on the protection of the European Communities' financial interests.

In the past few years there has been great pressure from the national media as well as from the Council of Europe. In 2010, Austria was ranked 15th among 178 countries on the Corruption Perception Index of Transparency International, whereas in 2014 Austria was ranked 23rd in 2014 among 175 countries and territories.

The legal provision that crimes of corruption and bribery will be prosecuted in Austria regardless of the place where the crime was committed, if the offender is Austrian, is also of particular relevance (for companies as well as individuals). Additionally, these crimes are also prosecuted in Austria if the offence was committed in favour of an Austrian public official.

If an Austrian citizen as an employee or decision-maker of a company bribes a foreign public official, he/she will be punished pursuant to Austrian criminal laws. This applies regardless of the fact whether the crime was committed in Austria or abroad and whether it was an Austrian or foreign company.

Moreover, decision-makers or employees of foreign companies can be held criminally liable in Austria if they – even abroad or from abroad – bribe an Austrian public official.

This type of special regulation goes far beyond the original principle of territoriality. In reality, this means that bribery committed worldwide by Austrian citizens, or of Austrian public officials, can be prosecuted. This is also a reason why Austrian criminal justice authorities (have to) cooperate closely with foreign authorities.

Corporate liability for bribery and corruption offences

Following the principle of *"societas delinquere non potest"*, Austrian criminal law did not provide for corporate liability for bribery and corruption until the end of 2005. However, on 1st January 2006 the Austrian legislator introduced the Austrian Act on Corporate Criminal Liability (*Verbandsverantwortlichkeitsgesetz*) with the effect that legal entities are also liable if an employee or a decision-maker violates the Austrian Criminal Code in order to achieve a business advantage for the entity.

Regarding bribery and corruption there is corporate liability for active and passive criminal offences, which means offering and receiving a bribe justifies the liability of the entity concerned. Basically an entity is liable for any criminal offence of its decision-maker or employee if the criminal offence was performed for the benefit of the organisation or in breach of the organisation's duties. Only if the entity provides necessary and reasonable care to prevent criminal offences, in particular by implementing technical, organisational or personal precautions, may the liability be excluded.

Clause 2 (1) of the Austrian Act on Corporate Criminal Liability states that a decision-maker is a person with the power to act on behalf of the organisation under its bylaws, or any other individual representing the organisation.

The penalties for violating anti-corruption laws by companies include fines up to a maximum of €1.8m. The amount of the fine is based on 40 to 180 daily rates and based on the entity's profitability, taking into account its overall financial capacity. When determining the number of daily rates, the Austrian Court has to consider the severity of the crime, the extent to which the organisation benefitted, and the efficiency of precautionary measures taken to reduce criminal offences by its decision-makers or employees.

Proposed reforms / The year ahead

Recently, a far-reaching reform has been implemented by the Austrian legislator. In January 2013, a number of material changes were made (*Korruptionsstrafrechtsänderungs gesetz 2013*) with respect to the Corruption Law of 2012, amending the Austrian Criminal Code. Since 1st January 2015 the amendment of the Austrian Code of Criminal Procedure has become effective. The main innovation is that the term suspect (*Verdächtiger*) has been introduced. As long a person is (during preliminary investigation) not charged with a specific criminal offence, they are a suspect. When a person is charged with a crime (but an indictment has not yet been filed), and the person is explicitly incriminated to a specific criminal offence on the ground of definite facts, that person is designated *Beschuldigter*.

Recently the Austrian National Council determined the amendment of the Austrian Criminal Code as well (*Strafrechtsänderungsgesetz 2015*) entering into force in the beginning of 2016. The major changes concerning bribery and corruption are:

- Clause 153 of the Austrian Criminal Code (breach of trust) – the most important criminal offence regarding bribery and corruption – will be amended. In detail the term property loss gets replaced by a more restricted definition of loss. The purpose behind this amendment was to reduce the scope of application after huge criticism connected with the wide scope of application on this specific clause which arose during the last couple of years. The newly included paragraph (2) clarifies the abuse of law in the context "breach of trust". Simultaneously, threshold limit 1 is modified from €3,000.00 to €5,000.00 and threshold limit 2 is modified from €50,000.00 to €300,000.00.

- Clause 32 (1a) of the Austrian Code of Criminal Procedure is amended. From now on only the following crimes are subject to a jury consisting of two professional judges and two lay judges: clause 302 (abuse of authority); clause 304 (passive bribery); and clause 307 (active bribery). Criminal acts liable to clause 305 (acceptance of benefits), clause 306 (receiving benefits for influencing), clause 308 (forbidden intervention) and clause 309 (acceptance of gifts and bribery of employees and commissioners) are no longer subject to this specific jury.

- As already mentioned, clause 126 of the Austrian Code of Criminal Procedure has been a hot topic in recent years. Clause 126 (4) will be altered so that the accused can (principally) object to an expert because of his involvement in the preliminary investigations. But apart from this favourable adjustment of the clause 126 (4) the accused is still obliged to claim the expert's partiality for each individual case.

Nevertheless there are still areas in need of reform, such as the field of sports, betting and gambling. According to Austrian media reports the manipulation of bets ("betting fraud") is even more attractive than dealing drugs. But these criminal offences in the field of sports are punishable only under the specific criminal offence of fraud, clause 146 of the Austrian Criminal Code. According to this case, clause 146 of the Austrian Criminal Code states that there has to be a certain damage caused by fraud.

For the time being there is hardly any legal protection against bribery and corruption in sports. So there is probably a need to define a specific offence against manipulating bets. In this respect there are a lot of discussions among leading Austrian legal experts to introduce a specific criminal offence of "betting fraud".

But note that there is – of course – in clause 147 (1a) of the Austrian Criminal Code a provision regarding doping frauds in cases of severe damage.

Norbert Wess
Tel: +43 1 532 1300 / Email: n.wess@wkklaw.at

Norbert Wess is a partner of the firm and leader of the white-collar crime law team. He graduated from the University of Vienna as *Doctor iuris* (*Dr iur*) and also holds two postgraduate degrees in European Law (LL.M.) and Business Law (MBL). Within a short time he established himself in most of Austria's high-profile cases concerning white-collar crime and has earned a reputation nationally and internationally as one of the top defence lawyers in Austria.

Norbert Wess has a broad range of experience and is an active member of national and international criminal law associations. Furthermore he advises companies in matters of compliance and in-house investigations and he is publishing relevant literature regarding criminal law and also holding lectures and presentations in issues relating to white-collar crime, compliance and related topics.

Norbert Wess explains wkk law attorneys at law's core principles: "We are team players. We are promoting teamwork in order to exchange different point of views, form a solid structure and act as one person."

Bernhard Kispert
Tel: +43 1 532 1300 / Email: b.kispert@wkklaw.at

Bernhard Kispert is a partner at wkk law attorneys at law. He graduated from the University of Vienna and passed his Austrian Bar exam with distinction in 2005. During his activity as a lawyer he gained a lot of experience in civil and criminal proceedings, especially regarding sophisticated corruption and white-collar crime cases. In addition to his activities concerning Austrian Criminal Law, Bernhard Kispert has ongoing business relationships with several insurance companies charging him with the enforcement of extensive claims for damages.

Dietmar Bachmann
Tel: +43 1 532 1300 / Email: d.bachmann@wkklaw.at

Dietmar Bachmann graduated from the University of Vienna in 2009 and has been an associate at wkk law attorneys at law since 2012. He recently passed his Austrian Bar exam and closely collaborates with Norbert Wess. His practice covers a wide range of criminal disputes and during recent years he has gained a lot of experience in white-collar crime cases.

wkk law attorneys at law

1010 Vienna, Himmelpfortgasse, 20/2, Austria
Tel: +43 1 532 1300 / Fax: +43 1 532 1300 90 / URL: http://www.wkklaw.at

Brazil

Alberto Zacharias Toron, Edson Junji Torihara & Luisa Moraes Abreu Ferreira
Toron Torihara & Szafir Advogados

Brief overview of the law and enforcement regime

From the 1990s on, an anti-corruption regulatory framework was set forth to establish criminal and civil liability for acts of corruption and bribery as well as penalties for those convicted. Many statutes have been enacted, federal agencies were created and existing institutions reinforced to deal with corruption and bribery. However, "*although the transition to democracy in 1985 raised expectations of increased transparency and accountability, each of the five postauthoritarian presidential administrations has been sullied by accusations of corruption*".[1] In Brazil, there has always been a widespread perception that civil servants and businessmen caught in corruption were never punished or that the penalties were not harsh enough.

The last two years represented a shift in this perception with the Brazil Clean Companies Act and its federal regulation and with the criminal prosecution of the "*Mensalão*" and "*Operação Lava Jato*" cases.

Before moving on to what has changed (section two), it is important to explain – albeit briefly – the law and enforcement regime of anti-corruption law in Brazil.

Criminal liability

The active bribery of a Brazilian public official is a criminal offence under Article 333 of the Brazilian Criminal Code and it punishes the private party who offers the bribe. Article 317 of the Criminal Code makes it an offence for a Brazilian public official to accept a bribe. A statute enacted in 2003 increased the penalty for those crimes from between one and eight years of imprisonment to between two and 12 years of imprisonment, and there is a one-third increase in the penalty if the bribe is effective (i.e. if the public official acts because of the undue advantage that has been offered). There are specific offences related to corruption of foreign officials in international commercial transactions, added to the Criminal Code in 2002. In those cases, the penalty is still one to eight years of imprisonment, with a one-third increase if the bribe is effective (Article 337-B). Influence peddling is also a criminal offence under the Brazilian Criminal Code, and the penalty range is two to five years of imprisonment (Articles 332 and 337-C). There are also specific criminal statutes relating to bribery in public bidding (Statute n. 8666/93) and bribery of tax officials (Statute n. 8137/90) that constitute very similar offences but have slight differences in penalties.

In all of those cases, if the defendant is sentenced to four years of imprisonment or less, the penalty may be substituted for alternative sentences such as a fine and community service.

In case of a conviction, the defendant also has to return the stolen assets. The judge also has the discretion to force Public Officials to leave office, in case of a conviction.

In Brazil, corporate criminal liability is only allowed in environmental crimes, so a corporate entity may only be prosecuted for corruption in the civil regime.

There is no strict liability in Brazilian criminal law. Managers, officers and directors are only liable if they have personally engaged in criminal activities.

Another important aspect of criminal liability relating to bribery in Brazil is Statute n. 12683/12, which was passed in 2012 and included bribery as a predicate offence for money laundering.

Civil liability

Values stolen from Public Office, in Brazil, may also be recovered through a "public civil class action". Public civil class actions were created in 1985 (Statute n. 7.347), and authorise Public Prosecutors, some public bodies and civil associations to begin investigations focused on accountability and recovery of damages in cases related to the protection of collective rights, such as the environment, consumers' rights and economic rights.

If there is probable cause, the prosecution may secure an injunction preventing further payments in public bids or contracts under suspicion and may also freeze assets of those who are being investigated.

Investigating and prosecuting authorities

The **Public Prosecutor's Office** is the primary prosecuting agency for conducting criminal and civil lawsuits regarding corruption and bribery.

Prosecution is usually based on evidence gathered by investigations conducted by the **Federal and State polices**, but in cases of bribery and corruption there are other investigating authorities that may produce reports that will be used as evidence for legal (criminal or civil) action taken by the Public Prosecutor's Office, such as the Brazilian auditing institutions (e.g. "TCU"), the Brazilian Comptroller General Office, the Council for Financial Activities Control and the Administrative Council for Economic Defense.

Government auditing institutions play a central role in overseeing public spending. The most relevant federal auditing agency in Brazil is the **Federal Accounting Tribunal** ("**TCU**").

The **Brazilian Comptroller General Office** ("**CGU**") is a Federal Government agency in charge of assisting the President of the Republic in matters related to defending public assets and enhancing accountability through internal control activities, public audits and corrective and disciplinary measures.

The **Council for Financial Activities Control** ("**COAF**") was established for the purpose of regulating and applying administrative sanctions, receiving pertinent information as well as examining and identifying suspicious occurrences of illicit activities related to money laundering.

The **Administrative Council for Economic Defense** ("**CADE**") is an agency created to guide, inspect, prevent and investigate abuse of economic power.

In cases of transnational corruption, the **Department of Assets Recovery and International Co-operation** ("**DRCI**") within the Ministry of Justice plays a central role. DRCI is the responsible central authority in Brazil for mutual legal assistance both in criminal and civil matters and therefore is responsible for recovery of assets derived from illegal activity.

Enforcement activity and policy

A notorious corruption scandal in Brazil is a case of a bid for a public contract to build the Court's new headquarters for its tribunals of first instance in São Paulo, in 1992. The case study ("TRT Case"), published in 2013,[2] is a very interesting way to illustrate enforcement activity and policy in bribery and corruption in Brazil in the last 25 years.

In 2013, 20 years after the public bid, the Brazilian justice system was still prosecuting persons and companies involved and, according to the research, *"the case has led to parallel proceedings pending in more than ten judicial bodies in Brazil and Switzerland consisting of more than one hundred appeals and thousands of pages of legal minutiae. Despite all the fanfare, the chief parties involved in the case remain free from imprisonment and are appealing their convictions. The only exception among them is Nicolau dos Santos Neto (popularly known as "Nicolau"), who remains under house arrest"*. The public civil actions which initially froze the assets of those involved *"were not resolved by trial courts until October 2011—more than a decade after they were brought—and are now awaiting review and appeals"*. The recovery of the damages resulting from the scandal *"hinges on obtaining final, binding decisions against the defendants"* but *"the Brazilian State's biggest victory thus far has been the almost seven hundred thousand dollars that it recovered"* due to the sale of Nicolau's apartment in Miami and a half-billion-dollar agreement signed between the State and one of the companies involved.

In spite of many languishing proceedings, *"the TRT case has been regarded, by a variety of commentators, as a milestone for the justice system in dealing with political corruption"* and although *"it is impossible to establish a precise correlation between the myriad institutional transformations of the last two decades and the case studied here"*, it can be said that *"the justice system is a different one from the one that existed before the TRT case"* and many institutional changes were catalysed by the TRT Case.

A more recent and notorious corruption scandal is *"Mensalão"*, in which congressmen were accused of a vote-buying scheme through clandestine payments made by the Workers' Party (PT) – with money from fake advertising contracts signed by state-owned companies – to congressional allies in return for support for its legislative agenda. The President's chief of staff, José Dirceu, was accused and forced to step down.

The scandal broke down in 2005 and by the end of 2012, 25 of the 40 defendants were convicted and started to serve their sentences. Because most of the accused were congressmen with the right to be tried by the Supreme Court, the ground for appeals were minimal and the verdicts became definitive very quickly. Although there was not a radical institutional change regarding investigation of corruption scandal, *Mensalão "is viewed by analysts and legal experts as a landmark case in which, for the first time, high-ranking politicians were found guilty in a criminal trial and sentenced to prison terms for corruption charges"*.[3]

Overview of enforcement activity and policy during the past two years

Corporate liability for bribery and corruption offences: Brazil Clean Companies Act of 2013 (Statute n. 12.846/13)

The most relevant change in anti-corruption law in Brazil is its Clean Companies Act, effective in the beginning of 2014 and the presidential decree regulating the Act in the Federal Government (decree n. 8420/2015).

The Act applies to civil and administrative (not criminal) liability of business organisations, foundations, or associations and foreign companies with an office, branch or subsidiary in Brazil that commit acts of corruption (article 1). The Act covers the following activities:
• Promising, offering, or giving an undue advantage, directly or indirectly, to a public official, or a third person related to the official.

- Financing, sponsoring, or subsidising any offences set out in the law.
- Using another person or entity as an intermediary in order to conceal the company's real interests or the identity of the beneficiaries of bribery.
- Acts of fraud in public bidding.
- Obstructing investigations, audits, and the work of public agencies, entities, or officials.

The law applies to offences against Brazilian or foreign public bodies, irrespective of whether the offence is committed in Brazil or abroad, which means that the Act has extra-territorial application.

An important innovation of the act is the provision of strict liability. Corporate entities will be held liable regardless of their intention. The Act imposes strict liability on companies operating in Brazil for domestic and foreign bribery and provides no exception for facilitation payments. Prosecutors will simply need to prove that any of the illegal acts took place, without having to prove negligence.

Companies are not afforded a legal defence for implementing "adequate procedures" to prevent corrupt acts. Compliance programmes will be evaluated for sentencing purposes only.

The presidential decree that regulated the Clean Companies Act in the Federal Government (decree n. 8240/15) provides a list of elements that should be taken into consideration in evaluation of compliance programmes:

- commitment of high management and board members to the programme;
- policies and procedures applicable to everyone at the company and third parties;
- periodic training;
- periodic risk assessment;
- accurate and complete books and records;
- internal controls to assure the reliability of financial statements;
- specific procedures related to public procurement and interaction with government officials;
- independence, structure and authority of the compliance function;
- channels to report irregularities openly and broadly disseminated among employees and third parties, and mechanisms to protect good-faith whistleblowers;
- disciplinary measures applied in case of wrongdoing;
- procedures to immediately stop irregularities detected and to take measures to remediate damages caused;
- due diligence on third parties and in corporate and M&A transactions;
- continuous monitoring of the programme; and
- transparency in political contributions.

The decree recognises that an effective compliance programme must be risk-based, tailored according to factors such as: a company's size, structure, and industry; jurisdictions where it conducts business; reliance on third parties; and the degree of interaction with government entities, among other considerations.

Administrative penalties and judicial remedies can be applied in isolation or cumulatively, depending on the gravity of the offence.

Administrative liability

Administrative procedures are conducted by the "*highest authority of each body of Executive, Legislative and Judicial branch*". This provision in controversial because it depends on regulation by the Federal Government, States and Municipalities. The Federal Government issued a presidential decree regulating the act. For the bribery of foreign officials, the Brazilian

Comptroller General Office ("CGU") has exclusive authority to initiate administrative proceedings. For the bribery of domestic officials, the CGU retains authority to initiate such proceedings, but it is concurrent with the ministry whose officials were bribed. The City of São Paulo, for example, enacted a statute with the provision that its General Comptroller's Office is the only body that may launch and conduct administrative procedures in accordance with the Clean Companies Act. However, given Brazil's federative system, important questions remain concerning state and municipal authority to initiate administrative proceedings.

Administrative sanctions applied to corporate entities are: (i) a fine of between 0.1% and 20% of the corporate entity's gross annual turnover in the year prior to the commission of the offence. In the event that it is not possible to calculate the gross annual turnover, the law provides fixed administrative fines of up to R$60 million. In any case, fines should never be inferior to the illegal advantage obtained by the act; and (ii) the publication of the sentence in newspapers and news channels with great circulation, at the expense of the corporation.

Presidential decree n. 8420 provides detailed guidance for setting the maximum and minimum permissible fines as well as a method for calculating the fines actually to be imposed.

The payment of a fine does not exclude the company's obligation to fully repair the damage caused by the bribery.

Civil (judicial) liability

Administrative liability does not exclude civil liability of the legal entity (article 18). The Federal Government, States and Municipalities, through their Public Advocacy Offices or the Public Prosecutor's Office may file a judicial lawsuit in relation to the illegal acts set forth in the Clean Companies Act, in order to have the following penalties applied to legal entities (article 19):

- Loss of assets representing the illegal advantage obtained through the acts.
- Partial suspension of the legal entity's activities.
- Compulsory dissolution of the legal entity if it is proven that it was constituted to hide illegal interests or if it was frequently used to promote illegal acts.
- Prohibition from participating in public tenders, or receiving any form of public grants for up to five years.

The Public Prosecutor's Office or the Public Advocacy Office may request the freezing of assets, rights or values needed to secure the payment of the fine or to ensure full restitution for the damage caused.

Leniency agreements

The highest authority of each public entity may enter into a leniency agreement with legal entities that effectively collaborate with investigations, provided that: (i) the company is the first to come forward and demonstrate its interest in cooperating with the investigation; (ii) the company completely ceases its involvement in the investigated wrongdoing; (iii) the company admits its participation in the wrongdoing; and the collaboration results in: (iv) identification of those involved in the illegal act; and (v) rapidly obtaining information and documents that prove the wrongful acts under investigation (article 16).

The execution of the leniency agreement will exempt the legal entity from publicising the sentence in the media and will reduce the amount of the fine by 2/3.

The obligation to admit wrongdoing can present problems in cases where foreign authorities may also have jurisdiction, since other authorities may want to investigate the matter. Therefore, experts recommend that "*multinational companies considering self-disclosure should make sure they have a multi-country legal team formulating a strategy that takes into account potential legal actions in different countries*".[4]

Also, "*sanctions set forth in the Anti-Bribery Law include administrative sanctions (applied by the public administration directly) and judicial sanctions (applied by a judge). Companies that enter into leniency agreements with public authorities and satisfy their conditions will have their fines reduced by up to two thirds and exempted from the publication of the condemnatory decision. But certain judicial sanctions are not exempted. Companies could still be subject to loss of assets, partial suspension, and compulsory dissolution of the legal entity. While one would expect that partial suspension and compulsory dissolution would be used in more serious cases — perhaps those in which the legal entity was created for illegal purposes — to avoid being subject to loss of assets, companies should consider settling with all authorities with jurisdiction over the matter*".

Leniency agreements provisions in the act do not protect against criminal prosecution for individuals. However, it may be possible for authorities to expand the deal and include such protection, with the presence of the Public Prosecutor's Office.

As mentioned, construction companies investigated in "*Lava Jato*" have been one of the first to seek leniency agreements under Brazil Clean Companies Act. However, there has been heated debate between CGU, TCU and the Federal Public Prosecutors Office ("MPF"). The chief Federal Prosecutor has sent TCU a legal opinion defending that CGU may only sign leniency agreements with companies investigated in "*Lava Jato*" if MPF adheres to it. The former Chief of the Brazilian Comptroller General Office held that the Anti-Corruption Law granted to CGU the power to conduct agreements due to its credibility and reliability and that the law does not require any agreements to be authorised by TCU or MPF. As of October 2015, no leniency agreements have been formalised under the new law.

Companies can back out of a leniency agreement entered into with the Federal Government (decree n. 8420/15) at any time until its signing, in which case authorities have to return the evidence and cannot use it unless they come to it independently.

Significant cases currently under investigation and current trends of enforcement action: "*Operação Lava-Jato*" and collaboration agreements

A very recent corruption scandal still under investigation is "*operação Lava-Jato*" (referencing car-washing services) in which the federal police ended up unveiling an alleged fraud, corruption and money laundering scheme where construction companies supposedly made illegal payments to politicians and directors of Petrobras, a publicly traded energy and petroleum company controlled by the Brazilian Federal Government, in order to secure million- and billion-dollar contracts with the company. Bribes were allegedly split between Petrobras executives, parties that support the government and middlemen.

As the investigation enters its second year, the scandal has already led to the prosecution and imprisonment of important politicians, CEOs and the biggest construction companies of Brazil, as well as directors of "Petrobras", and has triggered a nascent movement seeking the impeachment of President Dilma Rousseff.

Using an investigation method called "*delação premiada*", in which those who are being investigated confess and implicate others in exchange for reduced penalties, investigators used the testimony of Alberto Youssef (a middleman) and Paulo Roberto Costa (a former direct of Petrobras) to arrest senior executives from big construction companies, Petrobras executives and politicians.

Even though collaboration has existed as a form of gathering evidence in Brazil for a while, formalised agreements have come into force after 2013 with the new Organized Crime Statute (n. 12.850/13). The statute defines organised crime, lists acceptable investigatory methods and regulates collaboration. In order for the penalties to be reduced, one or more of the following results must be achieved: identification of co-authors and their respective crimes; disclosure of the hierarchical structure and role division within the organisation; total or partial recovery of assets originated from the crimes; and the safe release of victims (article 4). Judge may grant a full judicial pardon, reduce the collaborator's sentence by up to two-thirds, or substitute prison with alterative sentences (e.g. community services and fine).

There is no question that collaboration has made all the difference in "*Lava Jato*". After senior executives from big construction companies, Petrobras executives and politicians were arrested, a great number of them started to collaborate, implicating others. Up to August, 2015, 28 collaboration agreements were signed with the Public Prosecutor's Office and affirmed by the judge.

According to the Public Prosecutor's Office: "*Were it not for the collaboration agreements between federal prosecutors and those under investigation, the Car Wash case would not have uncovered evidence of corruption beyond that involving Paulo Roberto Costa. We had evidence of bribes of less than R$100m [some US$31.5m at early April exchange rates]. Today we are investigating dozens of public officials as well as major companies, and there is evidence of crimes of corruption involving values far in excess of R$1bn [US$315m]. Just through the collaboration agreements, we have already recovered around R$500m [US$157m].*"[5]

Many lawyers, however, criticise those collaboration agreements due to a lack of detailed discipline. Another criticism "*is that collaboration, theoretically a voluntary process between equals, in fact entails a degree of compulsion by the stronger party*". In "*Lava Jato*", "*Federal police kept ... suspects in prolonged temporary custody, with the investigating judge ruling that some might flee the country; others might seek to tamper with witnesses or evidence*".[6]

Part of the reason why "*operação Lava Jato*" is considered by many to be a success is the work of Judge Sérgio Moro, who is overseeing the investigation. The judge is very quick in his decisions and treats the case with very high priority. He is considered by many as a national hero, even though many defence lawyers criticise him for violating procedural rights of the accused and for presiding over every investigation or criminal lawsuit originated from "*operação Lava Jato*", even in cases where the facts happened in other parts of the country. Recently, Brazil's Supreme Court ruled that cases unrelated to bribery in Petrobras (even if originated from *Lava Jato*) should not be tried in Curitiba by Sergio Moro.

As explained above, companies investigated by "*Lava Jato*" have also been one of the first to seek leniency agreements under Brazil Clean Companies Act.

Law and policy relating to issues such as facilitation payments and hospitality

The Clean Companies Act does not contain an exception for so-called "facilitation payments".

The Brazilian Criminal Code also prohibits facilitation payments: as mentioned above, it is a crime to offer undue advantage to a public official to perform an act or to delay or neglect a public duty, regardless of whether the act is within the public official's normal duties.

According to the Brazilian ethics code for civil servants, they cannot receive gifts, transportation, lodging, compensation or any kind of favour that has commercial value. Gifts distributed widely by entities as courtesy, propaganda or during special events may be accepted if they do not exceed the value of R$100.00 (one hundred reais) (decree n. 4081/02).

Overview of cross-border issues

Brazil signed the OECD Anti-Bribery Convention in 1997. The Convention led to a new law enacted in 2002 which included crimes of corruption and influence peddling of foreign public officials in the Brazilian Criminal Code (L. 10,467/02).

Also, in accordance with article 2 of the OECD Convention, the Brazilian Clean Companies Act set forth civil and administrative penalties for legal entities involved in bribery and corruption.

As mentioned above, the Department of Assets Recovery and International Co-operation ("DRCI") within the Ministry of Justice plays a central role in cases of transnational corruption. DRCI is the responsible central authority in Brazil for mutual legal assistance both in criminal and civil matters and through its Coordination General for Recovery of Assets, DRCI plays an important role in the recovery of assets of illicit origin.

In order to make asset recovery more effective, DRCI is responsible for performing the following activities:
*   Articulating and cooperating with the police, prosecutors and judges to recover, in Brazil and abroad, assets derived from illegal activity.
*   Elaborating studies to develop asset-recovery mechanisms.
*   Providing information and knowledge relating to money laundering.
*   Providing grants for management and early disposal of assets.

In cases of overseas bribery and corruption that affect Brazil, the investigation authority may request, via DRCI, legal assistance in order to gather evidence and recover assets.

In the "TRT Case" mentioned above, the *District Court of the Federal Tribunal in São Paulo* sent a letter rogatory to Geneva, explaining that a Brazilian citizen was under investigation for corruption and embezzlement of public money and requesting seizure and repatriation of all assets frozen in Switzerland. The Swiss judge granted the motion, but the *chambre d'accusation* that upheld the freeze held that a final decision from the Brazilian judiciary would be required for the assets to be forfeited and repatriated. In 2004 a new attempt to repatriate the frozen assets was made, this time by lawyers from Geneva retained by the Brazilian Federal Attorney General's Office. Five years later, the Swiss proceeding (P/5132/99) was concluded with a decision of forfeiture of the money frozen 10 years before. The decision was confirmed by the *Tribunal de Police de Geneve* in 2010 and became final in August 2012 with a decision of the *Federal Tribunal*.[7]

In 2013, US$4.8 million was repatriated, up to that point the largest amount recovered at once by the Brazilian government.

Collaboration agreements represented a shift in international asset recovery. By August 2015, a total of R$1.8 billion was recovered through collaboration agreements in "*Operação Lava Jato*", 50 times more than the R$35 million that had been recovered in the last 10 years through lawsuits. The speed with which the values were recovered and the huge difference in the amount recovered are due to the fact that, pursuant to collaboration agreements, the accused needs to give the prosecutors all information about bank accounts held in other countries, and subsequently give up those assets, in order to receive a mitigating sentence.

Proposed reforms / The year ahead

Proposed reforms to the Brazilian Criminal Code include criminalising the following conducts: **unjust enrichment**, if a public official owns or benefits from assets not compatible with their income; and **corruption in the private sector**, since, at the moment, in Brazil it is only a crime to practise corruption to the detriment of the government.

The wording of the proposed reform of the Criminal Code considers it a crime to purchase, sell, rent, receive, lease, loan or to enjoy goods or values inconsistent with the income received by the public official by reason of his office or by any other lawful means. According to the project, both the unjust enrichment and the crime that gave rise to this enrichment (if uncovered) will be punished.

The proposed criminalisation of corruption in the private sector is in accordance with the United Nations Convention against Corruption (incorporated in Brazil in 2006 through decree n. 5687), which states that countries are obligated to take anti-corruption measures in both the public and private sectors. The suggested text (article 167 of the projected new Criminal Code) is being criticised for establishing that only "the legal representative of the company or private institution" may be the author of the crime, even though bribes or other benefits may involve any employee or manager. Moreover, the text criminalises conduct which is characteristic of public servants and does not conform to private relationships.

It is impossible to say if these proposals will materialise, but there is no doubt that anti-corruption enforcement is being treated with high priority in Brazil. We can predict, for the coming years, new legislation to implement Brazil's Clean Company Act as well as strict new laws regarding bribery and corruption. We can also expect that companies operating in Brazil will take further steps to review their compliance programmes to ensure proper alignment with the requirements of the Act and its regulations.

* * *

Endnotes

1. POWER, Timothy and TAYLOR, Matthew, Accountability institutions and political corruption in Brazil, in Corruption and Democracy in Brazil, University of Notre Dame Press, 2011, p. 1.
2. This case study integrates the research on "transnational anti-corruption law in action" coordinated by Kevin Davis (NYU), Guillermo Jorge (San Andres) and Maira Machado (Direito GV) and is available at: http://www.law.nyu.edu/sites/default/files/upload_documents/Transnational%20anti-corruption%20law%20March%202014_NYU%20Colloquium%20(2).pdf.
3. www.wilsoncenter.org/event/the-meaning-and-implication-the-mensalao-brazils-largest-trial-political-corruption.
4. Carlos Henrique da Silva Ayres, Factors to consider before entering into leniency agreements in Brazil. (http://fcpamericas.com/english/brazil/factors-entering-leniency-agreements-brazil/#sthash.4abSueZw.dpuf.)
5. Brian Nicholson: Brazil's Operation Car Wash. (http://www.ibanet.org/Article/Detail.aspx?ArticleUid=7960b146-65c4-4fc2-bb6a-c6fbb434cd16.)
6. *Ibid.*
7. DAVIS, Kevin; JORGE, Guillermo; and MACHADO, Maira. Transnational anti-corruption law in action, p. 38. (http://www.law.nyu.edu/sites/default/files/upload_documents/Transnational%20anti-corruption%20law%20March%202014_NYU%20Colloquium%20(2).pdf.)

Alberto Zacharias Toron
Tel: +55 11 3822 6064 / Email: alberto@toronadvogados.com.br
Criminal lawyer and founding partner of Toron, Torihara & Szafir and a Criminal Law Professor at Fundação Armando Alvares Penteado (FAAP). He has LL.M. and PhD Degrees in Criminal Law at the University of São Paulo, and a Postgraduate Degree in Economic and European Criminal Law (University of Coimbra, Portugal) and in Criminal Law (University of Salamanca, Spain). He was a member of the Electoral Court of Appeals Justice, appointed by President Dilma Rousseff, for a two-year term of office (2014-2015). He is a Former Deputy General Secretary of the Brazilian Federal Bar Association 2007-2009, and a Former President of the National Committee for Lawyers Rights – Federal Bar Association 2007-2009. He is also a Former President of the Second Chamber of the Federal Bar Association, and a Former President of the State Committee for Drugs (CONEN/SP) 1995-1996. He is the author of the books: *"Crimes Hediondos – O mito da repressão penal"* (SP, Revista dos Tribunais, 1996); *"Inviolabilidade Penal dos Vereadores"* (SP, Saraiva, 2004) and *"Prerrogativas Profissionais do Advogado"* (Brasília, O.A.B., 2006).

Edson Junji Torihara
Tel: +55 11 3822 6064 / Email: edson@toronadvogados.com.br
Criminal lawyer and a founding partner of Toron, Torihara & Szafir, having obtained his Bachelor of Laws Degree (LL.B.) in Potifícia Universidade Católica (PUC). He also has a Postgraduate Degree in Business Criminal Law from Universidad Castilla La Mancha, Toledo, Spain, in 2007; and a Fundação Getúlio Vargas (GVlaw) 2004-2006 from the University of Coimbra, Portugal, in 2000. He is a founding partner of *Instituto Brasileiro de Ciências Criminais* (IBCCRIM) and *Instituto de Defesa do Direito de Defesa* (IDDD).

Luisa Moraes Abreu Ferreira
Tel: +55 11 3822 6064 / Email: luisa@toronadvogados.com.br
Criminal lawyer and partner of Toron, Torihara & Szafir, having obtained her Bachelor of Laws Degree (LL.B.) in Fundação Getulio Vargas (FGV) and Masters of Laws (LL.M.) at University of São Paulo. She has worked with criminal law and compliance since 2007. She advises and represents multinational clients on criminal liabilities and compliance issues. She represents companies and individuals in investigations and trials. She has participated and conducted collective research projects at FGV from 2011 to 2013 and in 2014 conducted LL.M. research in New York University School of Law (NYU Law). Selected publications include *"Case law regarding causal relationship between conduct and result to attribute criminal liability in Brazilian State Supreme Courts"*, Revista Direito GV 13 (2011), also published in English; *"The role of mandatory minimum sentences"*. Revista Ultima Ratio 3, Lumen Juris (2009); *"Corporate crimes: requirements for indictment respecting procedural safeguards"*; and *"Responsabilidade Penal na Atividade Econômico Empresarial"*, Quartier Latin (2009).

Toron Torihara & Szafir Advogados

Av Angelica, 688, cj 1111, CEP 01228-000, São Paulo, SP, Brazil
Tel: +55 11 3822 6064 / URL: http://www.toronadvogados.com.br

Canada

Riyaz Dattu
Osler, Hoskin & Harcourt LLP

Overview

Canada implemented its foreign anti-bribery legislation following its ratification of the *Convention on Combating Bribery of Foreign Public Officials in International Business Transactions* ("Convention") on December 17, 1998. The *Corruption of Foreign Public Officials Act* (CFPOA) came into force on February 14, 1999. Subsequent amendments have been made thereafter with the latest of these in June, 2013.

The principal criminal offence of bribery of foreign public officials is to be found in section 3 of the CFPOA. It reflects a consolidation of the principles of the bribery offence found in the Convention with the wording that already existed in the domestic corruption provisions of Canada's *Criminal Code*. All of the offences under the CFPOA are also included in the list of offences under section 183 of the *Criminal Code*. As a result, it is possible for Canadian law enforcement authorities, through the lawful use of a wiretap and other electronic surveillance, to gather evidence concerning the offence of bribery of foreign public officials cases.

Corruption of Foreign Public Officials Act

Subsection 3(1) is the principal bribery provision within the CFPOA, and provides as follows:

Every person commits an offence who, in order to obtain or retain an advantage in the course of business, directly or indirectly gives, offers or agrees to give or offer a loan, reward, advantage or benefit of any kind to a foreign public official or to any person for the benefit of a foreign public official:
(a) as consideration for an act or omission by the official in connection with the performance of the official's duties or functions; or
(b) to induce the official to use his or her position to influence any acts or decisions of the foreign state or public international organisation for which the official performs duties or functions.

This provision within the CFPOA, although based in part on the *Criminal Code*, is quite similar to the bribery provision within the *Foreign Corrupt Practices Act* of 1977 ("FCPA") in the United States. It makes illegal the giving of a benefit of any kind, in addition to those enumerated, to a foreign public official or for the benefit of such an official.

A foreign public official is defined in the CFPOA fairly broadly, as in the case of the FCPA, with minor differences:

"foreign public official" means:
(a) a person who holds a legislative, administrative or judicial position of a foreign state;

(b) a person who performs public duties or functions for a foreign state, including a person employed by a board, commission, corporation or other body or authority that is established to perform a duty or function on behalf of the foreign state, or is performing such a duty or function; and

(c) an official or agent of a public international organisation that is formed by two or more states or governments, or by two or more such public international organisations.

The issue of employees of state-owned or controlled corporations being considered foreign public officials has been considered in a recent Canadian enforcement case which is discussed below.

The June 2013 amendments expanded in a very significant way the scope of the CFPOA, and clarified a number of areas of ambiguity within the legislations. These amendments provided for the following:

- Introduced a books and records provision that imposes extensive and detailed requirements which prohibit certain bookkeeping practices and types of transactions (inadequately identifying, falsifying, hiding, destroying, recording of non-existent expenditures, or using false records), if related to bribery of foreign public officials. This provision of the CFPOA may be applied along with other provisions of Canadian law such as section 155 (financial disclosure) of the *Canada Business Corporations Act* and sections 361 (false pretence), 380 (fraud), and 397 (falsification of books and documents) of the *Criminal Code*.

- Significantly expanded the scope of Canadian prosecutorial jurisdiction to cover activities of Canadians (including officers and directors) and Canadian corporations, even if all the activities related to the alleged bribery take place or the falsification of books and records occurs outside Canada, thereby displacing the previous view that there had to be a "real and substantial link" between the offence and Canada. The basis for the offence will include conspiracy to commit, an attempt to commit, being an accessory after the fact or any counselling in relation to the offences of bribery or falsification of books and records.

- Increased the maximum term of imprisonment for individuals convicted under the CFPOA from five years to 14 years. The consequential result of this is that individuals found to have violated the CFPOA will not be eligible upon conviction for either conditional sentences or discharges. In addition, both individuals and corporations will continue to be subject to monetary fines at the discretion of a judge, who will not be restricted by a maximum prescribed amount.

- Clarified the definition of "business" by removing the words "for profit". The government's stated intent is to make this provision applicable to all businesses, regardless of whether they are seeking profits. It will therefore eliminate the potential defence that may have been available to non-profit organisations and unprofitable businesses that their activities were outside the ambit of the CFPOA.

- Provided exclusive authority to the Royal Canadian Mounted Police ("RCMP") to lay charges pursuant to the CFPOA against Canadian companies, Canadian citizens and permanent residents in Canada.

- Finally, the exception for "facilitation payments" – which in some very limited circumstances permits nominal payments made to expedite or secure the performance of an act of a routine nature by a foreign public official – will be eliminated on a date to be fixed by an order of the federal Cabinet.

The increased prison terms for Canadian nationals including officers and directors of Canadian corporations, the elimination of the territorial jurisdiction test, the increased exposure to CFPOA penalties by adding a books and records provision, and the elimination of exceptions and defences such as those for facilitation payments and businesses not earning profits, all point towards continuing vigorous enforcement by the Canadian government of the CFPOA.

Enforcement of the CFPOA

Niko Resources

On June 24, 2011, Niko Resources Ltd. ("Niko"), a TSX-listed international oil and natural gas exploration and production company, entered a plea of guilty to a single charge under the CFPOA. This was the first major enforcement action taken by Canada since the coming into effect of that legislation.

Niko pleaded guilty to the charge that between February 1, 2005 and June 30, 2005, it provided goods and services to a person for the benefit of a foreign public official to induce the official to use his position to influence acts or decisions of a foreign state, in order to obtain or retain an advantage in the course of business.

Through an Agreed Statement of Facts between Niko and the Crown, it was admitted that its Bangladesh subsidiary had provided a Toyota Land Cruiser SUV valued at $190,000 to the State Minister for Energy and Mineral Resources in order to influence him in dealings with that Niko.

Furthermore, the company also paid travel and accommodation expenses (valued at $5,000) for that official to travel to Calgary and New York and Chicago, to attend a conference and visit family.

Niko was required to pay $9.5 million in fines and was subject to a three-year corporate probationary term, during which it was required to implement and comply with an anti-corruption compliance programme.

Griffiths Energy

Griffiths Energy International Inc. ("GEI") entered a guilty plea on January 22, 2013 to a criminal charge under subsection 3(1) of the CFPOA, and agreed to a fine in the amount of $10.35 million. The criminal charge related to using the cover of sham consulting agreements to funnel or agree to funnel payments in the amount of US$2 million to two entities owned and controlled by Chad's ambassador to Canada and his spouse.

GEI acknowledged in its settlement agreement that the consulting agreements, even those pursuant to which no amounts were actually paid, violated the anti-bribery provision of the CFPOA, as they constituted agreements to provide, directly or indirectly, a benefit to a foreign public official so as to induce the official to use his position to influence decisions of a foreign state for which he performs duties and functions.

Karigar

Following the first trial under the CFPOA, Nazir Karigar, an agent for Ottawa-based technology company Cryptometrics Canada, was convicted for conspiring to bribe a foreign public official. On May 23, 2014, Mr. Karigar was sentenced to three years in jail at a federal penitentiary, notwithstanding his advanced age of 67 years and failing health. His sentencing occurred based on the law that existed prior to June 2013, as the events transpired prior to the date of the amendments when the maximum term increased from five years to 14 years.

The foreign bribery scheme related to attempts by Mr. Karigar to secure a contract for Cryptometrics Canada from Air India for the supply of biometric facial recognition security technology. Mr. Karigar provided Cryptometrics with a spreadsheet listing bribes to be paid to certain Air India officials. In June 2006, Cryptometrics' U.S. parent corporation transferred US$200,000 to Mr. Karigar's account, which Mr. Karigar claimed would be used to ensure that only Cryptometrics' bids qualified under a public tender. Under a later agreement, a further US$250,000 would be transferred to obtain the Indian Minister of Civil Aviation's approval of the Cryptometrics' bid. Ultimately, the Air India contract was not awarded to Cryptometrics, and there was no evidence that Mr. Karigar paid any bribe or the whereabouts of the funds transferred to him. Notwithstanding the absence of this evidence, the trial judge convicted Mr. Karigar holding that section 3 of the CFPOA also prohibits any scheme that amounts to a conspiracy or agreement to bribe foreign public officials.

Further enforcement activity after the conviction and sentencing of Mr. Karigar has occurred in this case. Charges were laid on June 4, 2014 by the RCMP against two U.S. nationals, Robert Barra (former Cryptometrics CEO) and Dario Berini (former Cryptometrics COO), and UK national, Shailesh Govinda, who worked with Cryptometrics. These further charges relate to bribing a foreign public official contrary to the CFPOA and fraud contrary the Criminal Code.

SNC Lavalin

On February 19, 2015, the RCMP National Division laid charges against the SNC-Lavalin Group Inc., its division SNC-Lavalin Construction Inc. and its subsidiary SNC-Lavalin International Inc. (together SNC). Each entity was charged with one count of corruption under paragraph 3(1)(b) of the CFPOA and one count of fraud under paragraph 380(1)(a) of the Criminal Code.

These charges against SNC resulted from a three-year criminal investigation in which the RCMP reviewed the company's business dealings in Libya. The alleged criminal activities took place over 10 years between 2001 and 2011 and relate to CAD 47.7 million in alleged bribes to public officials, and a supposed CAD 130 million fraud in relation to the construction of the Great Man Made River Project in Libya. Three individuals had previously already been charged as part of the Libya-related investigation, including former SNC executive vice-president Riadh Ben Aissa, who was extradited to Canada in October following the entering of a plea agreement in Switzerland. Several other former SNC-Lavalin executives and employees have been charged in connection with an investigation into a bridge building project in Bangladesh, and the company's operations in Algeria have also been under investigation. On September 10, 2014, a prominent Montreal tax lawyer was also charged with extortion and obstruction of justice for his part in the alleged scheme, which is said to have defrauded SNC-Lavalin of several millions of dollars.

The RCMP has indicated that it has 35 active CFPOA investigations.

Extractive Sector Transparency Measures Act

The *Canadian Extractive Sector Transparency Measures Act* (the "ESTMA") was proclaimed into force on June 1, 2015. The ESTMA's stated purpose is "to implement Canada's international commitments to participate in the fight against corruption through the imposition of measures applicable to the extractive sector". The legislation requires Canadian businesses involved in resource extraction to file and make publicly available reports on certain types of payments made to both domestic and foreign governments.

The ESTMA requires certain entities with connection to Canada, that are engaged in commercial development of oil, gas or minerals in Canada or elsewhere, or that control such entities, to report payments made to any government, whether foreign or domestic, in excess of CAD 100,000 in a given year. These reports are to be made available to the public.

Reports must be filed annually within 150 days of the end of each financial year of any entity subject to the ESTMA. However, the ESTMA provides that reporting is not required for the year in which the ESTMA comes into force, or for any prior year. As an example, a company with its fiscal year ending on December 31, 2015 will be obligated to report payments made from and after January 1, 2016 with its first report to be filed by May 30, 2017.

In addition, the reporting of payments made to Aboriginal governments or entities will be deferred for a two-year period following the date that the ESTMA comes into force, so the obligation to report such payments does not apply until June 1, 2017.

Natural Resources Canada (NRCan) has recently issued the following draft implementation tools for the ESTMA, which it created in consultation with industry, civil society organisations, Aboriginal experts, and provinces:
- Guidance to help businesses in the exploration and extractive sectors understand the requirements of the ESTMA;
- Technical Reporting Specifications for the reporting process including instructions on how to complete the reporting template and how reports are to be published; and
- Reporting Template in both XLS and PDF formats.

NRCan solicited comments on the implementation tools until September 22, 2015, following which it is expected that it will publish the final versions no later than November, 2015.

The Guidance provides an overview of the requirements of the ESTMA with illustrative examples, including guidance on whether a Canadian extractive business is an "entity" that engages in the "commercial development of oil, gas or minerals", whether it meets the criteria of an entity that is required to report under the ESTMA and what payments it is required to report:

Entity: The Guidance confirms that the term "entity" is to be interpreted broadly to include not only those prescribed by the ESTMA (i.e. any corporation, trust, partnership or other unincorporated organisation) but also similar types of organisations such as unlimited liability corporations, limited partnerships and royalty trusts, but does not capture individuals or sole proprietorships.

Commercial Development: The Guidance clarifies that the exploration or extraction of oil, gas or minerals "refers to the key phases of commercial activity" during the life cycle of a project, from prospecting to remediation, but is not intended to include "ancillary or preparatory activities" such as construction of an extraction site. The Guidance also confirms that businesses that provide goods or services associated with or related to commercial development of oil, gas or minerals would not constitute "entities" under the ESTMA, given that the activities they perform are outside the scope of commercial development. Contractors that provide such goods and services are not subject to the ESTMA by virtue of their contractual arrangements with a reporting entity.

Reporting Entity: The Guidance clearly states that a business must be subject to Canadian law in order to be subject to the reporting obligations under the ESTMA. Accordingly, a parent company that is not subject to Canadian law would not be required to report even if it wholly owns a Canadian subsidiary that is required to report. The Guidance also better defines how to apply the size-related criteria in determining whether an entity is required to report payments under the ESTMA:
- the CAD 20 million in assets and CAD 40 million in revenue tests are to be based on amounts reported in an entity's consolidated financial statements in one of its two most recent financial years for its global assets and revenue (and not those of any parent

company), and converted into Canadian dollars either using the exchange rate as of the entity's financial year end or the entity's method of translating the currency conversion used in its financial statements; and

- the number of employees should be based on the average of all employees over the two most recent financial years and should include full-time, part-time and temporary employees but not independent contractors (applying the Canadian common law definition of an employee).

Payments: In determining whether a payment is required to be reported under the ESTMA, the Guidance and the Technical Reporting Specifications emphasise substance over form. The Guidance provides a brief overview of the seven categories of "payments" that must be reported under the ESTMA, and directs reporting entities to use their reasonable judgment in cases where it may be unclear whether a payment should be reported under one category or another. The Guidance also specifies that, in determining whether a series of payments constitute payments to the "same payee," reporting entities must group together departments, ministries, boards, bodies and other authorities that perform or are established to perform a power, duty or function on behalf of a particular level of government (e.g. national/regional/ municipal) but encourages reporting entities, where practical, to list each department or agency to whom a payment is made. For example, fee payments to the National Energy Board, Environment Canada and NRCan (which are all Canadian federal bodies) would constitute payments to the "same payee" under the ESTMA, but the report should note three separate payments made to the National Energy Board, Environment Canada and NRCan.

The Guidance also notes that the Government of Canada is monitoring risks of potential conflict between the ESTMA and the laws of a foreign jurisdiction that may hinder reporting (for example, if the terms of a concession or licence are confidential and not to be disclosed by the reporting entity) and engaging directly with jurisdictions where measures exist that may raise concerns regarding the application of the ESTMA. Reporting entities that encounter challenges in meeting the reporting requirements under the ESTMA may provide details of these circumstances to NRCan.

The Technical Reporting Specifications contain step-by-step instructions on how to complete the reporting template in XLS or PDF form and how the form is to be made available to the public and NRCan, and includes requirements for project-level reporting and online reporting.

Finally, with the issuance of the implementation tools for the ESTMA for public comment, NRCan issued a substitution determination, confirming that reports submitted to European Union and European Economic Area member states that have implemented the EU Directive at a national level may be submitted to the Minister of Natural Resources as a substitute for a report prepared under the ESTMA, provided that reporting entities include an attestation statement in their report and indicate which jurisdiction the substituted report was originally filed, and that they file within the timeframe prescribed by the other jurisdiction. Reporting entities must also notify NRCan within the deadline under the ESTMA if the filing deadline in the other jurisdiction extends beyond 150 days after the end of its financial year.

Riyaz Dattu
Tel: +1 416 862 6569 / Email: RDattu@osler.com
Riyaz advises multinational and domestic businesses on international trade policy and investment matters, international trade strategies and market-access concerns. On international trade regulations, Riyaz assists clients in designing and implementing compliance programmes on money laundering and anti-terrorist financing, export and import controls, economic sanctions and other national security issues, and in carrying out due diligence in mergers and acquisitions and other international business transactions. Riyaz also acts as counsel in international trade and investment disputes involving the application of trade laws and regulations and the enforcement of treaties. He has acted as counsel from the time of the very earliest WTO disputes concerning Canada, and the first two investment arbitrations under Canada's bilateral investment promotion and protection treaties. During his more than 25 years of practice, Riyaz has advised and represented leading businesses in a full range of industry sectors.

Osler, Hoskin & Harcourt LLP

100 King Street West, 1 First Canadian Place, Suite 6200, P.O. Box 50, Toronto ON M5X 1B8, Canada
Tel: +1 416 362 2111 / Fax: +1 416 862 6666 / URL: http://www.osler.com

Cayman Islands

Martin Livingston & Adam Huckle
Maples and Calder

Brief overview of the law and enforcement regime

The Cayman Islands' Anti-Corruption Law (2014 Revision) (the "**Law**") came into force on 1 January 2010 with the intent of giving effect to the OECD Convention on Combating Bribery of Foreign Public Officials in International Business Transactions, as well as the United Nations Convention Against Corruption. The Law replaced the provisions relating to anti-corruption and bribery which previously existed under the Penal Code, and provides generally for four categories of corruption offences: Bribery (both domestic and foreign); Fraud on the Government; Abuses of Public or Elected Office; and Secret Commissions. There are also ancillary offences for failure to report an offence.

The Law also creates the Anti-Corruption Commission (the "**Commission**"), which oversees the administration of the Law. The Commission comprises the Commissioner of Police, the Complaints Commissioner, the Auditor General, and two 'appointed members', selected by the Governor from retired members of either legal practice, law enforcement or the judiciary.

Bribery

The key bribery offences under the Law are:

(a) *Bribery of public officers and elected members of the Cayman Islands Legislative Assembly*

It is an offence for a (Cayman Islands) public officer[1] or member of the Legislative Assembly ("**LA**"), to, directly or indirectly, solicit, accept or obtain (or agree to accept or obtain) for themselves or another person, any loan, reward, advantage or benefit (an "**improper payment**") with the intent to interfere with the administration of justice; procure or facilitate an offence; or protect an offender from detection or punishment. It is also an offence for any person to give or offer an improper payment to a public officer, or member of the LA, with such intent.

The penalty for bribery of a Cayman Islands public officer, or member of the LA, under the Law, is imprisonment for a term of 14 years.

(b) *Bribery of foreign public officer*

It is also an offence if any person, in order to obtain or retain an advantage in the course of business, directly or indirectly, promises, gives or offers, or agrees to give or offer, an improper payment to a foreign public officer,[2] save where such improper payment is either:

(i) permitted or required under the laws of the applicable foreign country or organisation; or

(ii) was made to pay the reasonable expenses incurred in good faith by, or on behalf of, the foreign public officer that are directly related to:

- the promotion, demonstration or explanation of the person's products or services; or

- the execution or performance of a contract between the person and the foreign country for which the officer performs duties or functions.

The penalty for bribery of a foreign public officer, under the Law, is imprisonment for a term of up to 14 years.

Where money is paid to a foreign public officer, the Law provides that such payment is not considered an improper payment to obtain or retain an advantage in the course of business, if it meets the criteria for a facilitation payment (see section below, 'Law and policy relating to issues such as facilitation payments and hospitality' for further detail).

Fraud on the Government

It is an offence for any person who:

(a) directly or indirectly, gives, offers or agrees to give or offer an improper payment to a public officer or a member of the LA,[3] in connection with:

   (i)   Government business;

   (ii)   Government claims, regardless of whether the relevant public officer or member of the LA (or other such person) is in fact able to cooperate, render assistance, exercise influence or do or omit to do what is proposed; or

   (iii) the appointment of any person, including himself, to an office;

(b) has or pretends to have influence with the Government, a member of the LA or public officer, and accepts a benefit for himself in connection with:

   (i)   Government business;

   (ii)   Government claims; or

   (iii) the appointment of any person, including himself, to an office;

(c) when dealing with a public officer or a member of the LA, provides benefit to such person without the prior written consent of the chief officer of the relevant government entity; or

(d) having made a tender to obtain a contract with the Government, provides or receives benefit in consideration for the withdrawal of their or another's tender.

The penalty for the offence of committing a fraud on the Government is a term of imprisonment of up to 10 years.

Abuses of public or elected office

Any person who purports to or agrees to sell either:

(a) an appointment to or resignation from a public office;

(b) a consent to any such appointment or resignation; or

(c) receives or agrees to receive a reward or profit from the purported sale thereof, commits an offence liable on conviction to imprisonment for a term of up to five years.

Any person who, in order to obtain or retain a contract with the Government, or as an express or implied term of such a contract, directly or indirectly provides a benefit to any person:

(a) for the purpose of promoting the election of candidates to the LA; or

(b) with the intent to influence or affect the election of any candidate to the LA, commits an offence liable on conviction for a term of imprisonment of up to 10 years.

Any person who purports to, or agrees to, sell either:

(a) an appointment to or resignation from a public office;

(b) a consent to any such appointment or resignation; or

(c) receives or agrees to receive a reward or profit from the purported sale thereof,

commits an offence liable on conviction for a term of imprisonment of up to five years.

Further, any person who:
(a) receives, agrees to receive, gives or procures to be given, directly or indirectly, an improper payment as consideration for cooperation, assistance or exercise of influence to secure the appointment of any other person to a public office;
(b) solicits, recommends or negotiates in any manner with respect to an appointment to or resignation from a public office, in expectation of a direct or indirect improper payment; or
(c) keeps, without lawful authority, a premises for transacting or negotiating any business relating to:
  (i) the filling of vacancies in public offices; or
  (ii) the sale or purchase of public offices; or appointments to, or resignation from public offices,
commits an offence liable on conviction for a term of imprisonment of up to five years.

Secret commissions

There is also a more general offence provision relating to secret commissions that may not necessarily need to involve a public official (whether local or foreign). The section provides that any person who gives, offers or agrees to give or offer to an agent any improper payment in consideration of any act relating to:
(a) the affairs or business of the agent's principal;
(b) for showing favour or disfavour towards any person in relation to the affairs or business of the agent's principal; or
(c) with the intent to deceive an agent's principal, gives the agent a receipt, account or other writing in which the principal has an interest that:
  (i) contains any statement that is false, erroneous or defective in any material particular; and
  (ii) is intended to mislead the principal,
commits an offence liable upon conviction for a term of imprisonment of up to five years.

Further, any agent who demands, accepts or offers or agrees to accept any improper payment to achieve (a), (b) or (c) above, from any person, also commits an offence liable upon conviction for a term of imprisonment of up to five years.

Reporting offences

The Law also provides for a mandatory reporting obligation in that any person from whom an improper payment has been solicited or obtained, in contravention of any provision of the Law, is also required to make a report to the Commission, or a constable, at their earliest opportunity. Failure to do so, without reasonable excuse, is an offence liable upon conviction to a fine of up to CI$10,000 (approximately US$12,000) and/or imprisonment for up to two years.

There are further offence provisions applicable to persons who provide false, misleading or inconsistent reports. The Law also makes it an offence to victimise a person who makes a report or disclosure to the Commission, or constable, of the bribery of a public officer or member of the LA, with a penalty of imprisonment for two years. The Law defines "victimisation" as an act:
(a) which causes injury, damage or loss;
(b) of intimidation or harassment;
(c) of discrimination, disadvantage or adverse treatment in relation to employment; or
(d) amounting to threats of reprisals.

Inchoate offences and vicarious liability

In addition to the primary offence categories outlined above, the Law also provides for "inchoate offences", which apply to the:

- attempt, conspiracy, or incitement to commit corruption offences; and
- aiding, abetting, counselling or procuring the commission of corruption offences.

The inchoate offences are liable on conviction to a fine of up to CI$5,000 (approximately US$6,000) and/or imprisonment for a term of up to two years.

Overview of enforcement activity and policy during the past two years

The Commission is supported by both the Royal Cayman Islands Police Service ("**RCIPS**") (through a dedicated Anti-Corruption Unit) and the Auditor General of the Cayman Islands in the investigation and determination of bribery and related offences under the Law. The investigative and enforcement arms of the regime are also complemented by a statutory freedom of information framework with an independent Information Commissioner and a free press.

The Commission's capabilities were recently strengthened by the provision of analytical, research and administrative support from the Commonwealth Secretariat. The Commission has adopted a multi-faceted approach to tackling corruption, which includes investigations, prosecutions and educational campaigns to improve the public's awareness of the Law.

However, the Commission does not have investigative resources of its own and must largely rely on the RCIPS to investigate any claims brought to it, introducing a risk that corruption cases may be deprioritised. Additionally, the independence of the Commission has been questioned, as it includes seats for the Auditor General and the Police Commissioner. Certain observers have argued that the Commission may be more effective if its members did not already have other full-time employment and would not be confronted by a potential conflict of interest if a matter actually involved some of their staff.

As at 24 November 2014 (the last date for publicly available records), there have been 113 complaints received and registered by the Commission since its inception (six of which have been received within the most recent reporting period of 1 July 2014 to 30 June 2015, although the figures for the remainder of this period are not currently publicly available). Of those complaints, 10 were 'pending' (awaiting further or significant information); 74 had been concluded; 10 were transferred to other investigative units for action; and nine were under active investigation.

There have been notable corruption cases since the introduction of the Law, two of which have progressed to trial and resulted in convictions. The first, *R v Webster*,[4] concerned a civilian employee of the RCIPS who pled guilty to two charges of misconduct of public office contrary to common law (i.e. not a charge under the new provisions of the Law), stemming from improper use of confidential police and immigration databases. Noting that there had been no previous cases in the Cayman Islands which would provide guidance as to the appropriate sentence, the Grand Court of the Cayman Islands referred to similar cases in the United Kingdom as persuasive authority. In part due to a lack of malice, or an intention to obtain a pecuniary benefit, a suspended sentence was imposed for 12 months.

In the second case of *R v Ebanks*,[5] a jury found a former Police Constable (PC) of the RCIPS guilty of two counts of soliciting a bribe and two counts of breach of trust. A social inquiry report has been requested by the presiding Grand Court Judge, with sentencing pending.

In *R v Myles*,[6] the former deputy chairman and director of the National Housing and Development Trust Board, who was accused of deceiving applicants of the Cayman Islands

Government's housing assistance scheme into unnecessarily purchasing homeowners' insurance, was convicted on seven deception offences and sentenced to six months' imprisonment. Although no official statements were released, it was widely reported that despite having initially been charged with breach of trust and abuses of public or elected office offences under the Law, these were later dropped due to an unforeseen technicality in the Law with respect to private sector appointees to the boards of government companies and authorities.

Certainly, the most prominent corruption case involved charges against the former Premier of the Cayman Islands. The initial charges had included two counts of misconduct in public office, four counts of breach of trust by a member of the LA, and five counts of theft in connection with the importation of explosive substances without a legal permit, although none were made pursuant to the Law. The former Premier was cleared by a Cayman Islands jury of all 11 charges in October 2014.

Law and policy relating to issues such as facilitation payments and hospitality

Facilitation payments

The Law recognises the limited business circumstances and/or cultural practices relating to facilitation payments and provides a statutory exception. Where money is paid to a foreign public officer, the Law provides that such payment is not considered an improper payment to obtain or retain an advantage in the course of business if:
(a) the value of the payment is small;
(b) the payment is made to expedite or secure the performance by a foreign public officer of "an act of a routine nature" that is part of the foreign public officer's duties or functions, including:
  (i) the issuance of a permit, licence or other document to qualify a person to do business;
  (ii) the processing of official documents, such as visas and work permits;
  (iii) the provision of services normally offered to the public, such as mail pickup and delivery, telecommunication services and power and water supply; and
  (iv) the provision of services normally provided as required such as police protection, loading and unloading of cargo, the protection of perishable products or commodities from deterioration, or the scheduling of inspections related to contract performance or transit of goods; and
(c) as soon as practicable after the payment and act of a routine nature are performed by the foreign public officer, the person making such payment makes a record of such payment or act, and the person has retained that record at all relevant times. Such a report must include:
  (i) the value of the payment;
  (ii) particulars of the act of a routine nature that was sought to be expedited or secured by the payment;
  (iii) the date or dates on which the payment was made and on which the act of a routine nature occurred;
  (iv) the identity of the foreign public official; and
  (v) the signature or other means of verifying the identity of the person making the report.

Hospitality

The Public Service Management Law (2013 Revision) concerns the narrower definition of "public officer" as the holder of any office of emolument in the public service, and includes any person appointed to act in any such office. Public officers are subject to "General Orders" which are contained within subsidiary legislation. Earlier versions of the General Orders regulated the acceptance of gifts by public officers. The specific provisions dealing with the acceptance of gifts have now been removed from the General Orders.

Public officers must be careful about receiving valuable presents (unless they are from personal friends) whether in the shape of money, goods, passages, subsidies or services or any other personal benefits.

Gifts received from foreign governments may be accepted where to do otherwise would be viewed by the particular foreign government as offensive, and where the public servant receives approval from the Governor of the Cayman Islands. There is no official guideline as to what constitutes a "valuable present", but previous wording was sufficiently wide to cover any gift.

The Public Servants Code of Conduct is overseen by the Commission for Standards in Public Life and provides that a public servant must disclose, and take reasonable steps to avoid, any conflict of interest (real or apparent) with his duties as a public servant, and must not use his official position for personal or familial gain.

As part of its regulatory handbook, the Cayman Islands Monetary Authority ("**CIMA**") issues a code of conduct for the directors of the Board of CIMA and members of its management committee ("**MC**"), who are expected to carry out their responsibilities to the exclusion of any personal advantage. For example, Board directors and members of the MC should not accept favours, fees or gifts from regulated institutions or the institutions' staff, professional companies or the general public, including commissions, special discounts or other forms of compensation, in order to avoid the appearance of improper influence on the performance of their official duties. All gifts received without prior notification from the sender must be declared immediately to the Managing Director of CIMA or in his/her absence to the Deputy Managing Director, who will deal with the matter appropriately.

Board directors and members of the MC are required to exercise discretion in accepting hospitality from any relevant organisations and professional advisers. Routine business lunches are accepted unless they become frequent or lavish. Attendance at expensive or exclusive sporting or cultural events which might draw criticism must be declined unless circumstances have been discussed with the Managing Director of CIMA.

Members are expected to turn down any invitation when they and their partner are the only guests, or where the host's party is only six or eight, and where the price of the tickets and accompanying fare is likely to exceed CI$100 (approximately US$120) per head. Invitations are to be automatically refused where they could be construed to be unusual or to risk creating a sense of obligation to the host, or bias in their favour (e.g. because of the circumstances of the invitation, or cost or rarity value of the event).

Key issues relating to investigation, decision making and enforcement procedures

The Commission is given broad powers to prevent and detect corruption offences under the Law. For example, the Commission may, upon successful application to the Grand Court of the Cayman Islands, order any person to refrain from dealing with a person's bank account or other property for a period not exceeding 21 days, if there is reasonable cause to believe that it relates to the proceeds or the suspected proceeds of a corruption offence. Further, the Commission may, in writing, require any person to provide information (excluding information communicated to professional legal advisers) for the purpose of clarifying or amplifying information relating to corruption offences.

Although the Attorney General must consent to the instigation of proceedings in relation to a corruption offence, a person may be arrested, charged, remanded into custody or released on bail before such consent is received.

The Law also expressly provides that, in any trial or proceedings for a corruption offence, the court, in relation to the proceeds of such an offence, shall apply the provisions of the Proceeds of Crime Law (2014 Revision).

Cross-border issues including mutual legal assistance

Mutual legal assistance is also extensively provided for under the Law, which allows the Commission to disclose any information received in relation to corruption offences to CIMA, as well as other designated institutions or persons. The Commission may also disclose any information to any foreign anti-corruption authority relating to conduct which constitutes a corruption offence, or would constitute a corruption offence if it had occurred in the Cayman Islands.

The Law also make offences extraditable and an offence occurs if the conduct:
(a) was committed wholly or partly within the Cayman Islands;
(b) was committed wholly or partly on board a Cayman-registered ship or aircraft (wherever it is located); or
(c) was committed wholly outside the Cayman Islands and the alleged offender:

    (i)   is a person with Caymanian status;

    (ii)   is a resident of Cayman; or

    (iii)   is a body corporate incorporated by or under a Cayman law.

The territorial provisions of the Law are much more extensive than any predecessor legislation, as corruption offences are deemed to be offences for which extradition may be granted, pursuant to existing Cayman Islands extradition laws and treaties. Moreover, corruption offences involving cross-border transactions and/or entities in different jurisdictions can also give rise to complex conflicts of law questions.

Although not Cayman law, it is noted that certain provisions of the United Kingdom Bribery Act 2010, which came into force in July 2011, have extraterritorial effect in certain British Overseas Territories, including the Cayman Islands.

For example, the offences of active or passive bribery (in the public or private sector) apply to acts committed overseas (where the act or omission would have been an offence, if done or made in the UK), provided the offender has a close connection with the UK. A close connection includes a British citizen, a British overseas territories citizen (which may include many Cayman Islands citizens), an individual ordinarily resident in the UK, or a body incorporated in any part of the UK. Furthermore, an offence of failing to prevent bribery (by not having adequate procedures) applies to companies, wherever incorporated, which conduct part of their business in the UK.

Corporate liability

While the offences under the Law are primarily directed to individuals, where an offence is proved to have been committed by a body corporate with the consent, connivance of, or be attributable to any neglect on the part of any director, manager, secretary or similar officer, including any person purporting to act in such a capacity, both the body corporate and the individual person shall be liable.

Proposed reforms / The future

In its June 2012 Annual Report, the Commission noted, in relation to the implementation of Part I of the Cayman Islands Constitution Order 2009 – the Bill of Rights, Freedoms, and Responsibilities, which came into force on 6 November 2012 – that respect and support for human rights are closely interlinked with anti-corruption initiatives.

In addition to continuing to successfully work in conjunction with the RCIPS Anti-Corruption Unit and the Auditor General to detect and expose corruption, the Commission has taken, and will continue to take, an active role in public awareness campaigns with other institutions and associations with similar or complementary objectives. For example, in April 2013 the Commission joined forces with the Cayman Islands Elections Office to educate and inform the public about the importance of integrity to the elections process.[7]

While there are currently no proposed reforms of the Law, publicised criticism stemming from the Law's perceived inadequacies in the *R v Myles* decision suggests that a legislative review of the Law as it applies to private sector appointees will be forthcoming.

* * *

Endnotes

1. A "public officer" includes a person holding public office, judge, magistrate, arbitrator, umpire, assessor, jury member, Justice of the Peace, or member of statutory body, tribunal or commission of enquiry.
2. A "foreign public officer" includes: (i) an employee/officer of a foreign government body; (ii) a contract worker for a foreign government body; (iii) a person appointed under foreign law, custom or convention; (iv) a member of the executive, judiciary, magistracy or legislature; (v) an employee, officer, contractual worker for a public international organisation; and (vi) an authorised intermediary of foreign public officer.
3. Including members of their families or any other person to their benefit.
4. Indictment No. 0085/2011, 7 May 2013; *R v Webster* [2013] 2 CILR 72.
5. Indictment No. 105/2012, 27 June 2014; *R v E.K. Ebanks* [2013] 2 CILR 381.
6. (Unreported) Indictment No. 70/2012, 13 June 2014.
7. http://www.electionsoffice.ky/index.php/the-news/224-acc-and-elections-office-partner-to-promote-integrity.

Martin Livingston
Tel: +1 345 814 5380 / Email: martin.livingston@maplesandcalder.com
Martin Livingston leads Maples and Calder's Cayman Islands Regulatory Financial Services Practice. He specialises in all aspects of regulatory, licensing, risk management and anti-money laundering. Martin also advises on duties of confidentiality and information exchange. He is the former President of the Cayman Islands Compliance Association (2003 to 2014) and is a regular speaker and author on regulatory law matters.

Adam Huckle
Tel: +1 345 814 5318 / Email: adam.huckle@maplesandcalder.com
Adam Huckle is an associate in the Cayman Islands office of Maples and Calder. He has a broad range of experience in dispute resolution and regulatory work, representing retail and investment banks, institutional trustees and other financial institutions.

Maples and Calder

PO Box 309, Ugland House, Grand Cayman KY1-1104, Cayman Islands
Tel: +1 345 949 8066 / Fax: +1 345 949 8080 / URL: http://www.maplesandcalder.com

China

Catherine E. Palmer, Tina Wang & Chi Ho Kwan
Latham & Watkins

Introduction

China has had strong anti-corruption laws for many years. On 1 January 1980, the *Criminal Law of the People's Republic of China* (the "**PRC Criminal Law**"), containing the criminal offences of bribery and corruption, came into effect. The *PRC Criminal Law* was further amended in 1997, with enhanced provisions on bribery and corruption offences.

The laws have now become more vigorous, with sustained enforcement following the coming to power of President Xi Jinping in 2013. President Xi has made the curbing and elimination of corruption one of his main goals. This has kick-started the beginning of a new era, which has brought a new focus on and appreciation of the strength and breadth of the Chinese anti-corruption laws.

The actions taken by President Xi have been felt even at the highest echelons of power. According to the statistics provided in a report by the Procurator-general of the Supreme People's Procuratorate, Cao Jianming, to the National People's Congress in March 2015, there were 41,487 cases. More than 50,000 persons are under investigation for corruption or dereliction of duty, representing an increase of around 7.4%. Indicative of the seriousness of the anti-corruption campaign, 4,040 state functionaries above the county level, including 589 state functionaries at the bureau level and 28 state functionaries at the provincial level, were investigated in these cases. As another example, banquets for representatives of the National People's Congress have given way to self-serve and alcohol-free buffets. This focus is also evidenced by the issuance of the Administrative Measures on Conferences of Central and State Departments (the "**Measures**") and the Provisions on Administration of Domestic Official Reception by Party and Government Organs (the "**Provisions**") in September and December 2013 respectively. The Measures aim at cutting expenditure on official meetings by central government departments. The Provisions contain strict and more detailed requirements and standards on where a business meal may take place and what must be excluded from a business meal. These developments are part of President Xi's overall efforts to eliminate opportunities for corruption and extravagance in connection with official meetings and receptions.

It is also noteworthy that the Chinese government invited the State Parties under the United Nations Convention Against Corruption to inspect China's compliance with the treaty during the review period from 2010 to 2015. This is indicative of the seriousness of the Chinese government's efforts in its anti-corruption campaign.

In November 2014, the Chinese government announced that a new anti-corruption bureau is to be established. It is anticipated that this new bureau will act as an anti-graft bureau and will investigate officials suspected of corruption. The bureau will also be combined with three existing bodies – the Anti-Corruption and Anti-Bribery Bureau, the Prevention of Duty-Related Crimes Department and the Investigation of Dereliction of Duty and Power Abuse Department. It will be established at vice-ministerial level, higher than a regular bureau.[1]

Foreign entities operating in China face the potential of being investigated and charged in connection with this sustained anti-corruption campaign. In the summer of 2013, GlaxoSmithKline ("**GSK**"), a British pharmaceutical company listed on both the London and New York stock exchanges, became the focus of the biggest corruption scandal in China involving a foreign company. The GSK chain of events was set in motion by two chains of e-mails accusing GSK of bribing doctors in order to promote GSK's medical products.[2] In September 2014, GSK was found by the Changsha Intermediate People's Court in Hunan Province, China to have offered money or property to non-government personnel in order to obtain improper commercial gains, and was found guilty of bribing non-government personnel. As a result of the Court's verdict, GSK was ordered to pay a fine of RMB 3bn (£297 million) to the Chinese government.[3] Five former GSK senior executives were sentenced to suspended imprisonment of two to three years.[4]

Following the GSK bribery investigation, the State Administration of Industry and Commerce stated that local Administrations of Industry and Commerce should pay more attention to industries affecting the public interest (including the pharmaceutical industry), strengthen their supervision over the bidding activities carried out by industry players, and conduct thorough investigations against any commercial bribery arising from the bidding process.[5] Four other foreign drug manufacturers – AstraZeneca PLC, Bayer AG, Sanofi SA, and Eli Lilly – were subsequently visited by the Chinese authorities.[6] Recently, in May 2014, the authorities also visited Roche Holding AG's offices in Hangzhou.[7]

The primary pieces of anti-bribery and anti-corruption legislation in China are: (i) the *PRC Criminal Law*; and (ii) the *PRC Law Against Unfair Competition* (the "**PRC Competition Law**"). The *PRC Criminal Law* applies to both "official bribery" (where government officials and state functionaries are involved) and "commercial bribery" (where private enterprises and/or their staff are involved), whereas the *PRC Competition Law* prohibits "commercial bribery".

In addition to this primary legislation, various government departments' administrative rules (such as the *Interim Regulations on Prohibiting Commercial Bribery*) and judicial interpretations issued by the Supreme People's Court and Supreme People's Procuratorate (such as the *Opinion on Issues concerning the Application of Law in the Handling of Criminal Cases of Commercial Bribery*) also contain anti-corruption provisions.

The Communist Party of China and the State Council have also issued internal disciplinary rules governing corruption or bribery of Communist Party members and Chinese government officials.

The PRC Criminal Law

The *PRC Criminal Law* prohibits: (a) "official bribery", which applies to a "state functionary" or an "entity"; and (b) "commercial bribery", which applies to a "non-state functionary".

The term "state functionary" is broadly defined, and includes civil servants who hold office in state organs, persons who perform public duties in state-owned entities or semi-government bodies, persons who are assigned to non-state-owned entities by state organs or state-owned entities to perform public duties, and persons who otherwise perform public duties according to the law.[8] The term "entity" includes state organs, state-owned companies, enterprises, institutions, and people's organisations.[9]

The term "non-state functionary" means any person or entity that is not a "state functionary" or an "entity" as defined in the *PRC Criminal Law.* Generally speaking, the criminal sanctions for bribery offences involving state functionaries are more severe than those involving non-state functionaries.

Under the *PRC Criminal Law*, both the offering and receiving of bribes constitute serious criminal offences in China. The offences are usually categorised as "bribe-giving" or "bribe-accepting" offences. The statutory offences are:

(i)   offering of a bribe to a state functionary;[10]
(ii)   offering of a bribe to a non-state functionary;[11]
(iii) offering of a bribe to an entity;[12]
(iv)   offering of a bribe by an entity;[13]
(v)   introduction to a state functionary of an opportunity to receive a bribe;[14]
(vi)   acceptance of a bribe by a state functionary;[15]
(vii) acceptance of a bribe by a non-state functionary;[16] and
(viii) acceptance of a bribe by an entity.[17]

On 29 August 2015, the National People's Congress promulgated the Ninth Amendments to the PRC Criminal Law, with amendments focusing on empowering judicial organs to more effectively combat corruption. In particular, these amendments:

(i)   expand the scope of monetary penalties as punishment for bribery offences (see the table setting out the penalties for various offences under the heading *Penalties under the PRC Criminal Law* below);
(ii) introduce the offence of persons or entities offering bribes to close relatives of, or any person close to, state functionaries or former state functionaries; and
(iii) raise the bar for mitigating circumstances to apply for reduced sentencing.

The amendments will come into effect on 1 November 2015.

The "bribe-giving" offence

The PRC Criminal Law generally prohibits an individual or entity from giving "money or property" to a state functionary, a non-state functionary or any entity for the purpose of obtaining "improper benefits".

"Money or property" includes cash, in-kind objects as well as various "proprietary interests that can be measured by money", such as the provision of: home decoration; club membership; stored value cards; travel expenses; shares in, or dividends or profits from, a company without corresponding investments in the company; payment through gambling; and payment for services that have not been provided, etc.[18]

In "bribe-giving" cases, a violation occurs when a party makes a bribe with the intent to seek "improper benefits", which include: (a) seeking benefits from a state functionary, non-state functionary or entity which would be a breach of law, regulations, administrative rules, or policies for that state functionary, non-state functionary or entity to provide; or (b) requesting a state functionary, non-state functionary, or entity to breach the law, regulations, administrative rules or policies to provide assistance or facilitating conditions. For commercial activities related to bidding and government procurement, giving money or property to a relevant state functionary in violation of the principle of fairness to secure a competitive advantage is considered giving money or property for the purpose of obtaining an "improper benefit".[19] Further, where "money or property" has been offered with an intent to seek "improper benefits", but the offence of giving a bribe is not consummated because of factors independent of the said intent, such action may nevertheless constitute a criminal offence attempt under PRC law.[20]

However, a person who gives money or property to a state functionary due to pressure or solicitation from that state functionary but who receives no improper benefit shall not be regarded as having committed the crime of offering a bribe.

Under PRC law, bribery may be distinguished from a gift by reference to the following factors:[21]

(i)   the circumstances giving rise to the transaction, such as the relationship between the parties, the history of their relationship, and the degree of their interaction;

(ii) the value of the property involved in the transaction;

(iii) the reasons, timing and method of the transaction and whether the party giving money or property has made any specific request for favour; and

(iv) whether the party receiving money or property has taken advantage of his/her/its position to obtain any benefit for the party giving money or property.

In other words, a person who gives money or property to a state functionary, non-state functionary or entity without requesting any specific favour may not be regarded as offering a bribe.

Effective from 1 May 2011, China extended the scope of commercial bribery to include illicit payments to foreign officials. The *PRC Criminal Law* now also criminalises the "giving of money or property to any foreign official or officer of a public international organisation" for the purpose of seeking "improper commercial benefits".[22] The inclusion of foreign officials in the definition extends the reach of China's anti-corruption laws beyond the country's borders, although the distinction between "improper commercial benefits" and "improper benefits" means that the scope of punishable actions involving foreign officials is slightly narrower than those where personnel of Chinese entities, as defined in the *PRC Criminal Law,* are the recipients of bribes.

The "bribe-accepting" offence

State functionaries, non-state functionaries and entities are also prohibited from accepting money or property or making use of their position to provide improper benefits to a person seeking such improper benefits.

Any state functionary forcibly seeking or soliciting and accepting cash or property shall be regarded as having committed the crime of accepting a bribe whether or not he or she ultimately provides an improper benefit to the offering party. Further, any person (whether a state functionary or non-state functionary) who takes advantage of their position to accept and keep for themselves a "kickback" or "handling fee" under any circumstances shall also be regarded as having committed the crime of accepting a bribe.

Again, "improper benefits" is also a key to the "bribe-accepting" offence, and it must be shown that the party accepting the bribe has used its power or position to seek a benefit for the party giving the bribe.

Monetary thresholds for enforcement

The monetary thresholds for commencing an investigation into offences under the *PRC Criminal Law* are relatively low, ranging from RMB 5,000 to RMB 200,000. A summary of the monetary thresholds is set out as follows:[23]

Offence	Threshold
"Bribe-giving" cases	
Offering of bribe to a state functionary	RMB 10,000

Offence	Threshold
Offering of bribe to a non-state functionary	RMB 100,000 where the person offering the bribe is an individual RMB 200,000 where the person offering bribe is an entity
Offering of bribe to an entity	RMB 10,000 where the person offering the bribe is an individual RMB 200,000 where the person offering the bribe is an entity
Offering of bribe by an entity	RMB 200,000
Introduction to a state functionary of opportunity to receive bribe	RMB 20,000 where the introducer is an individual RMB 200,000 where the introducer is an entity
"Bribe-accepting" cases	
Acceptance of bribe by a state functionary	RMB 5,000
Acceptance of bribe by a non-state functionary	RMB 5,000
Acceptance of bribe by an entity	RMB 100,000

Jurisdiction of the PRC Courts

Foreigners or foreign entities are subject to the same legislation when doing business in China.[24] Chinese criminal laws apply to crimes that take place within the territory of China, whether committed by Chinese nationals or foreigners.

Accordingly, the PRC courts would have jurisdiction over:

(i) bribery and other crimes that are committed by PRC or foreign individuals or entities within China;

(ii) bribery and other crimes that are committed by PRC or foreign individuals or entities on board PRC ships or PRC aircraft;

(iii) bribery and other crimes that are committed outside China with the intention of obtaining improper benefits within China;

(iv) bribery by PRC individuals of foreign officials or officers of a public international organisation outside China;

(v) bribery and other crimes committed by PRC nationals outside China which are punishable under the PRC Criminal Law by a fixed term imprisonment of three years or longer; and

(vi) bribery and other crimes committed outside China by PRC state functionaries or military personnel.

Penalties under the PRC Criminal Law

Criminal penalties vary depending on whether the party offering or accepting a bribe is an individual or an entity and, if the party is an individual, whether he is a state functionary or non-state functionary. As explained above, the criminal sanctions for bribery offences involving state functionaries are generally more severe than those involving non-state functionaries.

Where the individual has received more than one bribe, the amount of each bribe will be aggregated for the purpose of determining the appropriate penalty. The table below sets out the factors taken into consideration and the corresponding penalties for the relevant offences under the legislation:

Offence	Relevant factors	Penalty
"Bribe-giving" cases		
Natural person offering bribe to a state functionary	Where there is neither aggravating factor nor serious damage to the interests of the State	Criminal detention, or up to five years' imprisonment, and monetary penalties
	Where there is either aggravating factor or serious damage to the interests of the State	Five to 10 years' imprisonment and monetary penalties
	Where the aggravating factor(s) are particularly serious	10 years' to life imprisonment, monetary penalties, or confiscation of property
	Where the offender volunteers information on the bribery before prosecution	A lighter punishment within the stipulated range may be imposed or penalty may be waived
Natural person offering bribe to the family, relative or people otherwise with close ties to the state functionary		Criminal detention, or up to three years' imprisonment, and monetary penalties
	Where there is serious factor, or serious damage to the interests of the State	Three to seven years' imprisonment, and monetary penalties
	Where the aggravating factor(s) are particularly serious, or there is especially serious damage to the interests of the State	Seven to 10 years' imprisonment, and monetary penalties
Natural person giving bribes to a non-state functionary or to a foreign functionary or to an official of an international public organisation		Criminal detention, or fixed-term imprisonment for up to 10 years with monetary penalties, or fixed-term imprisonment of at least 10 years' or life imprisonment plus monetary penalties or confiscation of property
Natural person offering bribe to an entity		Criminal detention or up to three years' imprisonment, plus monetary penalties
Entity offering bribe to a state functionary	In respect of such entity	Imposition of a fine
	In respect of the employees of such entity who are directly in charge of the matter in question and the employees who are directly responsible for the crime (collectively, "Responsible Personnel")	Criminal detention or up to five years' imprisonment, plus monetary penalties
Entity offering bribe to a non-state functionary	In respect of such entity	Imposition of a fine
	In respect of its Responsible Personnel	Up to 10 years' imprisonment and monetary penalties

Offence	Relevant factors	Penalty
Entity offering bribe to another entity	In respect of such entity	Imposition of a fine
	In respect of its Responsible Personnel	Criminal detention, or up to three years' imprisonment, and monetary penalties
Introducing an opportunity to a state functionary to receive bribe	Where there is aggravating factor	Criminal detention, or up to three years' imprisonment, and monetary penalties
	Where the offender volunteers information on the bribery before prosecution	A lesser penalty may be imposed, or penalty may be waived
"Bribe-accepting" cases		
State functionary accepting bribe	Bribe involving a relatively large monetary amount or where there are other aggravating factors	Criminal detention or up to three years' imprisonment and monetary penalties
	Bribe involving a very large monetary amount or where there are other aggravating factors	Imprisonment for between three and 10 years, monetary penalties or confiscation of property
	Bribe involving an extremely large monetary amount or where there are particularly serious aggravating factors	10 years' to life imprisonment, monetary penalties or confiscation of property
	Bribe involving an extremely large monetary amount and serious damage to the interests of the State	Life imprisonment or death penalty, confiscation of property
Non-state functionary accepting a bribe	If the amount involved is relatively large	Criminal detention, or a fixed-term imprisonment of up to five years depending on the amount involved
	If the amount involved is substantial	Fixed-term imprisonment of more than five years, and/or confiscation of property
Entity accepting a bribe	In respect of such entity	Imposition of a fine
	In respect of its Responsible Personnel	Criminal detention, or up to five years of fixed-term imprisonment

Meaning of "aggravating factors" and "causing serious damage to the interests of the State"

According to the *Interpretation on Issues concerning the Specific Application of Laws in Handling Criminal Cases of Paying Bribes*, which was jointly issued by the Supreme People's Court and the Supreme People's Procuratorate and took effect as of 1 January 2013, any of the following circumstances shall be deemed as an aggravating factor:[25]

(i) The amount of bribe paid is more than or equal to RMB 200,000, but less than RMB 1m.

(ii) The amount of bribe paid is more than or equal to RMB 100,000, but less than RMB 200,000, whereas the bribe is:

    (a) paid to three or more people;

    (b) funded by illegal means;

(c)   paid to state functionaries who are responsible for supervising and administering matters in relation to food, drugs, work safety or environmental protection, etc. that cause serious harm to people's livelihood and infringe the safety of public life and property; or

(d)   paid to state functionaries at judicial or administrative authorities, thereby affecting administrative enforcement and judicial justice.

(iii) Other serious circumstances.

Any offering of a bribe to seek improper interests, which causes a direct economic loss of RMB 1m or more, shall be deemed as "causing serious damage to the interests of the State".[26]

Meaning of "particularly serious aggravating factors"

Any of the following circumstances shall be deemed as a particularly serious aggravating factor:[27]

(i)   The amount of bribe paid is more than or equal to RMB 1m.

(ii) The amount of bribe paid is more than or equal to RMB 500,000, but less than RMB 1m, whereas the bribe is:

(a)   paid to three or more people;

(b)   funded by illegal means;

(c)   paid to state functionaries who are responsible for supervising and administering matters in relation to food, drugs, work safety or environmental protection, etc. that cause serious harm to people's livelihood and infringe the safety of public life and property; or

(d)   paid to state functionaries at judicial or administrative authorities, thereby affecting administrative enforcement and judicial justice.

(iii) The bribe has caused a direct economic loss of RMB 5m or more.

(iv) Other serious circumstances.

Mitigating factors

Pursuant to Article 8 of *the Interpretation on Issues concerning the Specific Application of Laws in Handling Criminal Cases of Paying Bribes issued by the Supreme People's Court and the Supreme People's Procuratorate*, a person who offers or pays a bribe who truthfully confesses to his or her crime(s) after being prosecuted may receive a mitigated sentence. Further, a person who offers or pays a bribe may be exempted from prosecution or receive a mitigated sentence if he/she discloses any non-bribery offences that are proven to have been committed by the bribe-taker.[28]

However, the mitigation or exemption may not necessarily apply in the following circumstances:

(i)   Offering bribes to three or more people.

(ii) An administrative or criminal punishment has already been imposed for offering bribes.

(iii) The bribe is offered for the purpose of committing a crime.

(iv) A serious consequence has been caused.

(v)   Other cases to which mitigation or exemption from criminal punishment does not apply.

Limitation

The limitation periods for the prosecution of a crime are:

(i)   five years if the maximum penalty for that crime is a term of imprisonment of less than five years;

(ii) 10 years if the maximum penalty for that crime is a term of imprisonment of between five and 10 years;

(iii) 15 years if the maximum penalty for that crime is a term of imprisonment of no less than 10 years; and

(iv) 20 years (and may be extended on approval by the Supreme People's Procuratorate) if the maximum penalty for that crime is life imprisonment or death.

The PRC Competition Law

The prohibition of commercial bribery

The *PRC Competition Law* is intended to regulate business activities which may cause unfair competition. It prohibits, *inter alia*, "commercial bribery", which is defined as follows:

(i)   the use by a business operator

(ii) of the means of giving money, property or other benefits

(iii) to another person

(iv) in order to sell or buy goods or to obtain business transactions or other economic benefits.

Whilst not expressly set out in the relevant legislation, this offence appears to require an element of dishonesty. However, the threshold for the dishonesty is not defined.

The broad scope of prohibition

"Business operators" is broadly defined as legal persons, or other economic organisations and individuals who deal with commercial businesses or profitable services.

Pursuant to the *Interim Provisions on Prohibition of Commercial Bribery issued by the State Administration for Industry and Commerce*, "property" means cash and tangible assets, and includes promotional fees, advertising fees, sponsorship, research and development fees, consultancy fees, commissions and expense reimbursements paid in order to see or buy goods.[29] The term "other benefits" can include things such as the provision of tours and travel within China or abroad.[30]

Kickbacks and rebates

In particular, Article 8 of the *PRC Competition Law* expressly provides that any "off-the-book" kickback which is secretly provided to any individual or entity shall be treated as an offer of a bribe; and any acceptance of such kickbacks by any individual or entity shall be treated as an acceptance of a bribe.

However, the *PRC Competition Law* does offer a degree of leeway for business operators, as they may give or accept discounts or commissions in the course of a transaction, provided that such arrangements are transparent and are clearly recorded in the books of accounts. The party receiving the commission must have the legal qualifications necessary to provide the related services, and must also record the amount in its accounts.

Enforcement and penalties under the PRC Competition Law

If an offence of commercial bribery under the PRC Competition Law is sufficiently serious, the respective monetary thresholds to commence an investigation under the *PRC Criminal Law* as set out in Section II above may apply. Whether an act of commercial bribery is considered sufficiently serious will be considered on a case-by-case basis.

Depending on the severity of the situation, acts of commercial bribery under the *PRC Competition Law* may attract fines of between RMB 10,000 to 200,000. All illegal gains will also be confiscated, and prosecution will also be sought if the offence reaches the level of criminal conduct.

Prevention and remediation

The problems discussed above are global, and companies operating in China or in the global environment should implement policies and procedures to help prevent violations and remediate them as soon as any potential issue surfaces. Such policies and procedures should include elements of prevention, investigation and remediation.

Prevention – effective compliance programme

An effective compliance programme, which incorporates a comprehensive anti-bribery policy reflecting a strong stance against corruption from the board of directors and senior management, can lead to early identification of corruption risks. Such a programme should focus on the company's policies with respect to gifts, entertainment and other hospitality, and on dealings with third-party representatives and business partners, who should undergo due diligence to ensure compliance, sign anti-corruption representations and be subject to anti-corruption training as appropriate.

An audit function that periodically reviews company practices for corruption risk, and a group that oversees the implementation and maintenance of the anti-corruption programme, are both critical to early detection and prevention. Confidential reporting channels – for example a private hotline, through which employees can feel safe to report issues, has also proven effective in detecting risks. Such reporting avenues need to be accompanied with assurances that no retaliation will result from reporting corruption. Appropriate training for all levels of the organisation, as well as positive incentives that promote compliance with company policy and the law, should be prescribed. It is optimal that the programme be updated periodically to ensure it keeps pace with continuing developments in the anti-bribery laws and regulations in China.

Investigation – quick and adequate response to corruption allegations

Corporations must be prepared to conduct internal investigations of corruption allegations, whether raised as a result of the compliance programme or raised by enforcement agencies, the media or whistleblowers.

It is important and prudent to carefully choose the body responsible for conducting any internal investigation. There may be instances where an independent investigation is required. Allegations involving senior management, or investigations requiring specialist skills, should ideally be conducted by independent, external counsel.

The designated investigative body should be properly resourced and the scope of the investigation should be proportionate with the scope of the allegations. Any investigation in China should be conducted in accordance with Chinese privacy, labour and other local laws. Attorney-client privilege should also be maintained to provide confidentiality and protect against retaliation.

Remediation – appropriate corrective measures

Should an internal investigation corroborate corruption allegations, corporations must implement appropriate and adequate remedial measures with appropriate oversight by the board of directors.

Corporations should examine and correct gaps identified in the existing corporate policies and compliance programmes. It is also advisable for corporations to assess whether the identified issues affect its internal controls over financial reporting, and take appropriate remedial steps accordingly.

Consideration should also be given to whether the identified issues should be disclosed to authorities, having regard to the improper conduct and practices identified, the company's legal obligations, and disclosure obligations under local and/or foreign securities laws.

Conclusion

Anti-corruption enforcement is increasingly global in scope. As summarised above, China has begun aggressively enforcing its own anti-corruption laws on a sustained basis. This has and will continue to mean vigorous multinational anti-corruption enforcement targeting domestic and foreign companies and individuals.

With adequate preparation and resources, companies can effectively avoid costly risks. Corporations with business in China should have appropriate preventative measures, well-functioning investigation procedures and, if necessary, remediation measures so as to mitigate any potential financial and reputational risks. Those measures will help, if not eliminate, the risks that employees run afoul of China's anti-corruption measures, as well as anti-corruption laws of other jurisdictions. These risks will not go away without the right corporate attitude, resources and attention, and vigilance is key to protecting companies and individuals in this increasing enforcement environment.

* * *

Endnotes

1. http://www.chinadaily.com.cn/china/2015-03/14/content_19808542.htm.
2. http://www.businessinsider.com/mark-reilly-gsk-sex-video-and-china-bribery-allegations-2014-6.
3. https://www.gsk.com/en-gb/media/press-releases/2014/gsk-china-investigation-outcome/.
4. http://english.caixin.com/2014-09-22/100731794.html.
5. "SAIC: Focused Investigation of Commercial Bribery arising from Drug Sales", *China Business News*, August 21, 2013.
6. http://english.people.com.cn/90778/8350806.html.
7. http://online.wsj.com/news/articles/SB10001424052702303749904579577111605515346.
8. Article 93 of the *PRC Criminal Law*.
9. Article 391 of the *PRC Criminal Law*.
10. Article 389 of the *PRC Criminal Law*.
11. Article 164 of the *PRC Criminal Law*.
12. Article 391 of the *PRC Criminal Law*.
13. Article 393 of the *PRC Criminal Law*.
14. Article 392 of the *PRC Criminal Law*.
15. Article 385 of the *PRC Criminal Law*.
16. Article 163 of the *PRC Criminal Law*.
17. Article 387 of the *PRC Criminal Law*.
18. Article 7 of the *Opinion on Issues concerning the Application of Law in the Handling of Criminal Cases of Commercial Bribery*.
19. Article 9 of the *Opinion on Issues concerning the Application of Law in the Handling of Criminal Cases of Commercial Bribery*. See also Article 12, *Interpretation on Issues concerning the Specific Application of Laws in Handling Criminal Cases of Paying Bribes issued by the Supreme People's Court and the Supreme People's Procuratorate*.
20. Article 23 of the *PRC Criminal Law*.
21. Article 10 of the *Opinion on Issues concerning the Application of Law in the Handling of Criminal Cases of Commercial Bribery*.
22. Article 164 of the *Eighth Amendment to the PRC Criminal Law*, effective from 1 May 2011.

23. Thresholds set out in a circular issued by the Supreme People's Procuratorate in 1999 and a circular jointly issued by the Supreme People's Procuratorate and the Public Security Bureau in 2010.
24. Article 6 of the *PRC Criminal Law*.
25. Article 2 of the *Interpretation on Issues concerning the Specific Application of Laws in Handling Criminal Cases of Paying Bribes issued by the Supreme People's Court and the Supreme People's Procuratorate.*
26. Article 3 of the *Interpretation on Issues concerning the Specific Application of Laws in Handling Criminal Cases of Paying Bribes issued by the Supreme People's Court and the Supreme People's Procuratorate.*
27. Article 4 of the *Interpretation on Issues concerning the Specific Application of Laws in Handling Criminal Cases of Paying Bribes issued by the Supreme People's Court and the Supreme People's Procuratorate.*
28. Article 9 of the *Interpretation on Issues concerning the Specific Application of Laws in Handling Criminal Cases of Paying Bribes issued by the Supreme People's Court and the Supreme People's Procuratorate.*
29. Article 2 of the *Interim Provisions on Prohibition of Commercial Bribery issued by the State Administration for Industry and Commerce.*
30. Article 2 of the *Interim Provisions on Prohibition of Commercial Bribery issued by the State Administration for Industry and Commerce.*

Catherine E. Palmer
Tel: +852 2912 2626 / Email: catherine.palmer@lw.com
Catherine E. Palmer is a partner in the Hong Kong office of Latham & Watkins.
Ms. Palmer relocated to Hong Kong to lead the firm's Asia White Collar Defense
and Government Investigations Practice and Antitrust and Competition Practice.
Ms. Palmer is a former US federal prosecutor and previously has held various
positions in the firm, including as Co-chair of the White Collar Defense and
Government Investigations Practice and as Vice Chair of the global Litigation
Department.
Ms. Palmer focuses her practice on the representation of multinational companies
involved in criminal or regulatory investigations throughout the world, with an
emphasis on global corruption/bribery investigations, global antitrust cartel
investigations and investigations related to US trade and economic sanction
issues. Ms. Palmer has interacted with regulators throughout the world on behalf
of clients, including regulators in the US, EU, UK and Asia. Ms. Palmer works
closely with Latham's US White Collar Defense and Government Investigations
team and the firm's US and EU Antitrust and Competition teams to leverage the
firm's global assets throughout Asia and other parts of the world.

Tina Wang
Tel: +852 2912 2791 / Email: tina.wang@lw.com
Tina Wang is an associate in the Hong Kong office of Latham & Watkins and
a member of the Litigation Department.
Ms. Wang's practice focuses on international arbitrations, compliance and
regulatory matters. She advises local and multinational corporations in
connection with a range of multi-jurisdictional and cross-border litigation
and arbitration matters. She has also assisted multinational companies in
corruption/bribery investigations, internal risk assessments and global
antitrust cartel investigations.

Chi Ho Kwan
Tel: +852 2912 2632 / Email: chiho.kwan@lw.com
Chi Ho Kwan is an associate in the Hong Kong office of Latham & Watkins and
a member of the Litigation Department. Mr. Kwan specialises in civil fraud,
commercial litigation and arbitration proceedings. He also has experience
in a variety of regulatory matters and has experience in corruption/bribery
investigations and global antitrust cartel investigations.

Latham & Watkins

18th Floor, One Exchange Square, 8 Connaught Place, Central, Hong Kong
Tel: +852 2912 2500 / Fax: +852 2912 2600 / URL: http://www.lw.com

Cyprus

Costas Stamatiou & Andreas Christofides
Andreas Neocleous & Co LLC

Brief overview of the law and enforcement regime

Cyprus was a British colony until 16 August 1960, when it became an independent sovereign republic. On 1 May 2004, Cyprus formally joined the European Union, and on 1 January 2008 it became the fourteenth member of the Eurozone and the euro became the official currency.

Although approximately one-third of the island has been under Turkish occupation since 1974, this has no impact on the day-to-day life of most people, and Cyprus enjoys political and social security and stability, economic prosperity and a high quality of life. The so-called "Turkish Republic of North Cyprus" is recognised only by Turkey; the application of the EU *acquis communautaire* has been suspended there, and all references in this chapter are to the legitimate government of the Republic of Cyprus and the legislation enacted by it.

The main body involved in investigating bribery and corruption allegations and complaints is the police, which cooperates with specialist financial intelligence units such as the Unit for Combating Money Laundering (MOKAS). The Office of the Attorney General examines the findings of the police and decides whether a case should be heard by a court. The Audit Office of the Republic may also refer incidents of bribery and corruption to the Attorney General for investigation.

Cyprus's first law against bribery and corruption was introduced in 1920, when the island was a British colony. That law, which is still in force, has been updated and supplemented by several others. Today, the legal framework against bribery and corruption principally comprises:

* The Prevention of Corruption Law, Cap 161.
* The Civil Servants Law, Law 1 of 1990.
* The Criminal Code, Cap 154.
* The Law Ratifying the Criminal Law Convention on Corruption, Law 23(III) of 2000.
* The Political Parties Law, Law 175(I) of 2012.
* The Law on the Illicit Enrichment of Public Officials and Officers, Law 51(I) of 2004.

All these laws have been amended since they were introduced.

The Prevention of Corruption Law

Introduced in 1920, this law continues to have effect. Article 3 makes it a criminal offence, punishable on conviction with imprisonment for up to seven years, a fine of up to €100,000 or both, for an agent (which term includes a public employee) or employee to obtain a gift, or for any person to give a gift to an agent or employee, or to falsify a receipt with intent to deceive the principal or employer. Article 4 of the Prevention of Corruption Law increases the maximum term of imprisonment to seven years if the corruption relates to a government contract and article 5 provides that if any public official is proved to have received a payment or gift from a person seeking to conclude a government contract, the payment will be deemed to have been corrupt unless it is proved otherwise.

The Civil Servants Law

The Civil Servants Law governs the conduct of civil servants in general and makes specific provision regarding bribery of public officials at articles 69 and 70. No public official is allowed to receive or offer any gifts, including money, other goods, free travel or other personal benefits apart from gifts from personal friends, gifts made upon retirement and gifts that it would be contrary to the public interest to decline. Breach of the rules renders the civil servant liable to disciplinary proceedings under the Law. If during the course of his or her work a civil servant discovers or reasonably believes that an act of bribery or corruption has been committed by another civil servant, he or she is under an obligation to inform the relevant authority in writing, giving full details about the incident.

The Criminal Code

The Criminal Code is a compilation of criminal law provisions. It provides for criminal sanctions for bribery of public officials in articles 100 to 105A and of witnesses in article 118. Article 100 provides that any person employed in the public service who is responsible for the performance of any duty by virtue of such employment commits a criminal offence if he or she corruptly requests, receives, obtains, agrees or attempts to receive or obtains any property or benefit of any kind for himself or herself or any other person on account of any past or future action (including refraining from acting) on his or her part in the discharge of his or her duties. Similarly, anyone giving or offering such an inducement is guilty of an offence. In either case the penalty is imprisonment for up to three years, a fine of up to €100,000, or both. In addition, the individual's assets are subject to confiscation in accordance with applicable legislation.

Article 101 provides that any person employed in the public service who takes or accepts from any person any reward over and above his or her normal pay in respect of any performance of his or her duty is liable to imprisonment for up to three years, a fine, or both.

Article 102 defines a lesser offence of receiving any property or personal benefit of any kind on the understanding, express or implied, that favourable treatment will be given in return, punishable by imprisonment for up to two years, a fine, or both.

Article 103 makes it an offence, punishable by imprisonment for up to a year, for a public servant responsible for managing an asset or activity to favour his or her personal interests (for example by awarding business to associates) and article 104 makes it an offence, punishable by imprisonment for up to three years, a fine or both, for a public servant to submit false returns or reimbursement claims. Article 105 provides that any public servant who abuses his or her authority to carry out an act that is prejudicial to another person is guilty of a misdemeanour or, if the abuse is done for gain, of a felony punishable by imprisonment for up to three years. Prosecutions under these last three articles require the approval of the Attorney General.

Article 105A of the Criminal Code, described in further detail below, criminalises inappropriate attempts to influence any authority, committee, collective body or any member of such authority, committee or collective body, or any public official in the course of their duties related to any procedure of taking, appointing, promoting, allocating, transferring or of exercising administrative control in a governmental service, whether for the perpetrator's own benefit or for the benefit of someone else.

Article 118 deals with bribery of witnesses in legal proceedings. It makes it an offence, punishable by imprisonment for up to three years, to attempt to influence the testimony of a witness in any way.

The Law Ratifying the Criminal Law Convention on Corruption

The Law Ratifying the Criminal Law Convention on Corruption as amended transposes the provisions of the Criminal Law Convention on Corruption 1999, aligning Cyprus law with best practice in the field of bribery of foreign public officials, bribery in the private sector, trading in influence, money laundering of proceeds from corruption offences, account offences, participatory acts and corporate liability.

The Law incorporates the provisions of the Convention and the offences specified in it into domestic legislation, namely:
- active bribery of domestic public officials;
- passive bribery of domestic public officials;
- bribery of members of domestic public assemblies;
- bribery of foreign public officials;
- bribery of members of foreign public assemblies;
- active bribery in the private sector;
- passive bribery in the private sector;
- bribery of officials of international organisations;
- bribery of members of international parliamentary assemblies;
- bribery of judges and officials of international courts; and
- trading in influence.

The maximum penalty for each of the offences is seven years' imprisonment.

The Law defines 'public official' by reference to other legislation. Article 4 of the Criminal Code defines a public official as any person holding any of the following offices or performing the duties thereof, whether as a deputy or otherwise:
(a) any civil or public office or post, the power of appointing or removing a person to or from which is given to the President of the Republic, the Council of Ministers or any public commission or board;
(b) any post to which a person is appointed or nominated by law or by election;
(c) any civil post, the power of appointing to which or removing from which is given to any person or persons holding a public office or post of any kind set out in (a) and (b) above; and
(d) any post of arbitrator or umpire in any proceeding or matter submitted to arbitration by order or with the sanction of a court in pursuance of the law.

Article 4 also provides that the term 'public official' includes:
- a member of a commission of inquiry appointed or in pursuance of the law;
- any person employed to execute a process of a court;
- all persons belonging to the military or police forces of the republic;
- persons employed in a government department;
- a person acting as a minister of religion of whatsoever denomination insofar as he performs functions in respect of the notification of intending marriage, birth, baptism, death or burial but not in any other respect;
- persons employed by a municipal authority; and
- the "mukhtar" (head of a village) and members of the council of any community.

There is no definition of a foreign public official in the Law or other legislation and no reported Cyprus case law on the matter. In such circumstances Cyprus courts give words their ordinary meaning. Accordingly, the court is likely to refer to the definition of 'public official' found in article 4 of the Criminal Code, and adjust it appropriately. Furthermore, guiding reference may potentially be had – without any obligation of following – to section 6(5) of the United Kingdom Bribery Act 2010 which defines 'foreign public official' as an individual who holds a legislative, administrative or judicial position of any kind, whether appointed or elected, of a country or territory outside the United Kingdom (in the present case Cyprus), exercises a public function for or on behalf of a country or territory outside the United Kingdom, or for any public agency or public enterprise of that country or territory, or is an official or agent of a public international organisation.

The Political Parties Law

This Law repealed and replaced the Political Parties Registration and Funding Law of 2011 and now constitutes the main legal framework currently in force regulating the funding of political parties and establishing rules governing the transparency of their financial administration. Article 2 of the law defines a political party as "a body or association of persons having continuous character, statutory structure and national organisation range and having political, ideological or planned common objectives, which participates in elections or other representative bodies provided by the legal order and works together to influence the political will of the populace for the purposes of realising its political programme. The organisation, structure and functioning thereof in relation to matters the government and the society are dealing with, should be compatible with the legal framework provided for by the Constitution and the laws of the Republic and generally its presence in the socio-political life of the country shall provide sufficient guarantee for the importance of its purpose and its objective as a political party".

Article 4 of the law provides for state funding of all registered parties. Furthermore, state funds in respect of presidential elections are also distributed to the parties.

The Political Parties Law 2012 regulates private-sector financing of political parties. Article 5, which has been recently amended, allows political parties or affiliated organisations to receive lawful private monetary or in-kind contributions, whether named or anonymous, and limits the amount a natural or legal person may contribute to a party to €50,000 per year. Private contributions from companies registered under the provisions of the Companies Law or from physical persons are permitted as long as the activities of the companies or persons concerned are not illegal. Article 5(3) prohibits parties or affiliated organisations from accepting private contributions of any kind from legal entities of public or private law over which the state exercises control or from companies which are not registered in Cyprus under the Companies Law. However, public bodies are allowed to sponsor events organised by parties, limiting the amount of such sponsorship to €20,000 per year for each body. The total amount of anonymous contributions received by a political party or an affiliated organisation must be published in the daily press.

Article 7 of the Law requires at least 80 per cent of the expenses of political parties to be disbursed through the banking system.

Article 6 provides that political parties' income and expenses are to be audited by the Auditor General, an independent body under the Constitution. The political parties are obliged to keep detailed information and proper account books and prepare separate and consolidated financial statements for each financial year in accordance with International Financial Reporting Standards. Article 5(2) provides that a breach of the monetary limits in respect of donations to political parties constitutes a criminal offence on the part of both donor and recipient, punishable by a fine. Article 8 prescribes administrative fines of up to €20,000 for infringements of any of the other provisions of the law.

The Law on the Illicit Enrichment of Public Officials and Officers

This law codifies the offence of illegal acquisition of property by ministers, members of parliament, mayors and other senior officials and officers of the state. It provides for assets acquired in breach of its provisions to be confiscated. It repeals the earlier law enacted in 1965 and has since been amended in 2008. No prosecutions under it have ever been reported. There is currently no legislation obliging politicians or high-level officials to disclose their assets. The relevant provisions of a law adopted for that purpose in 2004 were found by the Supreme Court to be incompatible with constitutional provisions on privacy.

Parliament's Committee on legal affairs is currently considering a proposed amendment of Article 15 of the Constitution to allow asset disclosure for reasons of transparency of public life and prevention of corruption. Such an amendment would clear the way for other proposed legislative changes to strengthen the framework regarding the disclosure of assets of the president, ministers and members of parliament as well as other public officials.

Overview of enforcement activity and policy during the past two years

Corruption is not widely perceived to be an obstacle to business in Cyprus. There is a strong legal framework to combat corruption and effective public procurement and e-governance systems. Cyprus ranks in the top 20 per cent in Transparency International's 2014 Corruption Perception Index. Nevertheless, many people blame the 2013 banking sector crisis on an unhealthily close relationship between politicians and bankers that has contributed to corruption in some areas.

In recent years prosecutions for bribery have been few, and have generally involved low-level corruption such as the soliciting of bribes by police officers and lower-level officials in government departments such as the Department of Lands and Surveys. Successive governments have disowned and claimed ignorance of such corruption. It is only recently that a small number of high-profile cases have come before the Cyprus courts.

As part of the 2013 bail-out agreement with the European Commission, the European Central Bank and the International Monetary Fund, Cyprus committed to strengthen its banking supervision and regulatory framework and enhance the transparency of financial information. The government also appointed a committee to enquire into the causes of the financial crisis. Composed of former high-ranking judges, the committee's terms of reference include investigation of claims that banks had written off loans to politically connected debtors, and that others had benefitted from insider information before the imposition of capital controls. The committee has not yet concluded its investigations, which is leading to impatience on the part of the public and allegations and counter-allegations of corruption between the Attorney General and his deputy.

The Dromolaxia case

This case revolved around the purchase of an office building by the pension fund of the state-owned telecommunications authority at a price of €20 million, several times the open market value. The prosecution was made possible after the key participant in the transaction switched sides and turned prosecution witness. He initially faced charges in a separate but related trial along with two intelligence service officers, but the charges against him were dropped after he agreed to testify against the other defendants. The charges included corruption of a public official, accepting bribes and legalising ill-gotten gains, forgery of documents, fraud, abuse of a public official's fiduciary duties and obtaining money under false pretences. The final verdict was issued in January 2015, finding five persons guilty of various offences of corruption and fraud, and handing down prison sentences ranging from three-and-a-half to nine years.

The Cyprus University of Technology case

The Cyprus University of Technology ("CUT") case is currently being heard by Limassol District Court. A former director of finance at CUT and the head of the university's property management service have been charged with offences including conspiracy to commit a felony, receiving bribes, forgery, circulating a forged document, obtaining money through false pretences and abuse of authority. The charges relate to allegedly corrupt arrangements for procurement of student accommodation committed between 2005 and 2009, concerning three buildings rented by CUT for almost €16 million.

The Paphos Sewerage Board case

The Paphos District Court is currently hearing a case involving allegedly corrupt dealings of the Paphos Sewerage Board (PSB). According to investigators' findings, bribes were paid by private contractors to PSB members in order to secure construction and waste-management contracts. The five defendants include two former mayors, one of whom is currently a Member of Parliament, and town councillors.

According to the prosecution, between 1999 and 2003, while serving as Paphos mayor, one of the defendants received a considerable sum from a German company in order to secure the award of substantial contracts.

According to the indictment, two former town councillors are alleged to have received €400,000 in bribes from private contractors associated with the Paphos sewerage system, and another former town councillor is accused of having been bribed with €110,000.

A former Paphos mayor and a former PSB director are each serving a six-year jail sentence after confessing to having abused their power and taken bribes from contractors vying for PSB contracts.

Law and policy relating to issues such as facilitation payments and hospitality

Article 4 of Law No. 23(III) of 2000 transposes article 12 of the Criminal Law Convention on Corruption, which deals with trading in influence. It makes it a criminal offence, when committed intentionally, to promise, give or offer any undue advantage, directly or indirectly, to anyone who asserts or confirms that he or she is able to exert an improper influence over the decision-making of a wide range of persons in consideration therefor, whether the undue advantage is for himself or herself or for anyone else, in consideration of that influence, whether or not the supposed influence leads to the intended result. The categories of decision-makers include domestic public officials, members of domestic public assemblies, foreign public officials, members of foreign public assemblies, officials of international organisations, members of international parliamentary assemblies and judges and officials of international courts,

Furthermore, article 105A of the Criminal Code provides that any person who by any means attempts to influence any authority, committee, collective body or any member of such authority, committee or collective body, or any public official in the course of their duties related to any procedure of taking, appointing, promoting, allocating, transferring or of exercising administrative control in a governmental service, whether for his own benefit or for the benefit of someone else, is guilty of a criminal offence punishable on conviction with imprisonment for up to 12 months, a fine of up to €1,700 or both. It also provides that failure by any member of an authority, committee or collective body or any public official to report an approach for the purpose of obtaining preferential treatment within three days of the event is a criminal offence punishable on conviction with imprisonment for up to 12 months, a fine of up to €3,400, or both.

Key issues relating to investigation, decision-making and enforcement procedures

The Cyprus judicial process is traditional and has undergone little, if any, innovation or modernisation in recent years. Cyprus law has no provisions regarding plea agreements, settlement agreements, prosecutorial discretion or similar means without trial. While civil law remedies against corruption are also available (for example a victim of corruption may initiate civil legal proceedings for restitution on grounds of unjust enrichment, that is the significant increase of the property assets of a public official, which cannot be reasonably justified in relation to the individual's lawful income) they have rarely been used.

There is no specific law protecting whistle-blowers; instead, provisions regarding whistle-blowers are spread around other legislation. Article 369 of the Criminal Code provides that "[e]very person who, knowing that a person designs to commit or is committing a felony, fails to use all reasonable means to prevent the commission or completion thereof, is guilty of a misdemeanour", creating a defence against any prosecution based on their whistle-blowing activities. Article 69A of the Civil Servants Law requires public officials who become aware of instances of corruption to report them to their supervisor in writing, with supporting evidence. It is arguable that the requirement for reports to be in writing creates a disincentive to whistle-blowing, since it may require the whistle-blower to reveal his or her identity. The Labour Law requires objective grounds for dismissal of officials while article 9 of the 2004 Law Ratifying the Civil law Convention on Corruption (Law 7(III) of 2004 provides that a person who imposes an unjustified punishment on a whistle-blower for reporting corruption commits an offence punishable by imprisonment of up to six months, a fine of up to €5,110, or both. A whistle-blower that has been unjustifiably punished or dismissed or unfavourably transferred has a right to damages under the law.

In the private sector, the Unfair Dismissal Law offers vague guidance on protecting company employees from unfair treatment.

Many senior officials, as well as the Unit of Administrative Reform, the official body responsible for modernising the civil service, have called for a new law to protect whistle-blowers who disclose abuse of power or other illegal behaviour in the public and private sector. They argue that legislation expressly dealing with whistle-blowers, matching the obligation to report actual or intended misdemeanours with protection for whistle-blowers by making it a criminal offence to prosecute or victimise them, would be beneficial and instrumental in creating a culture of transparency and accountability through the medium of active citizen reporting on crimes and corrupt practices. As yet, however, no action has been taken.

Overview of cross-border issues

Cyprus offers international co-operation in corruption cases through formal rogatory letters, through Interpol and other channels for the exchange of police information, and between financial intelligence units such as the Unit for Combating Money Laundering (MOKAS). The central authority for the execution of requests submitted according to the provisions of the European Convention on Mutual Legal Assistance in Criminal Matters, the Council of Europe Criminal Law Convention on Corruption and the European Convention on Laundering, Search, Seizure and Confiscation of the Proceeds from Crime is the Ministry of Justice and Public Order, which forwards these requests to the appropriate authority for their execution. Furthermore, all Cyprus's bilateral agreements on legal and judicial co-operation include provisions for assistance in criminal matters.

Although the Cyprus Constitution prohibits extradition of nationals by article 14, which provides that no citizen shall be banished or excluded from the Republic under any circumstances, a Cypriot national who commits such an offence abroad can be prosecuted in Cyprus under the provisions of article 5(I)(d) of the Criminal Code, which deals with extraterritorial jurisdiction, and the relevant provisions of the Law Ratifying the Criminal Law Convention on Corruption.

Corporate liability for bribery and corruption offences

Law No. 23(III) of 2000 makes no distinction between natural and legal persons, but there is no codified offence corresponding to the UK offence of failing to prevent bribery contained in the Bribery Act 2010.

Proposed reforms / The year ahead

The latest EU Commission anti-corruption report found that perceptions of corruption in Cyprus were generally similar to the average for Europe as a whole. It concluded that Cyprus has demonstrated commitment to prevent and address corruption by amending legislation and establishing a coordinating body to combat corruption. However, in the opinion of the EU Commission, the small number of cases investigated, prosecuted or adjudicated in Cyprus indicates the need to strengthen the enforcement system and implement transparency and integrity safeguards facilitating detection and collection of evidence. The Commission recommended additional efforts to ensure closer coordination of relevant bodies, effective disclosure of assets and conflicts of interest, and greater transparency in the financing of political parties as well as in public procurement, and highlighted the following issues for attention:

- Strengthening the disciplinary regime for public servants, streamlining procedures to ensure effective investigation of corruption within the police and ensuring an effective coordination of anti-corruption policies by giving the coordinating body the necessary powers.
- Introducing codes of conduct for elected and appointed officials for them to declare assets periodically and to disclose potential conflicts of interests, with independent supervision and effective penalties.
- Reducing the thresholds for donations to political parties, limiting state-owned companies' freedom to sponsor political events, regulating donations to election candidates and campaigns, obliging parties to publish their financial statements and accounts online (including the identity of donors), and establishing external supervision of election candidates' income and expenditure. Developing uniform and effective tools to prevent and detect corruption in public procurement at national and local level, including internal and external control mechanisms and risk management tools within contracting authorities.
- Introducing new legislation offering protection to whistle-blowers who disclose abuse of power or other illegal behaviour in the public and private sector.

Considerable progress has been achieved with legal and institutional reform since the 2013 banking crisis and we expect to see this momentum continue.

Costas Stamatiou
Tel: +357 25 110000 / Email: stamatiou@neocleous.com
Costas Stamatiou was born in Limassol, Cyprus. He graduated in law from the University of Wales, Cardiff in 2001 and obtained a Master's degree in Legal Aspects of Marine Affairs from there in 2002 and a Master's degree in European Legal Studies from Bristol University in 2003. He was admitted to the Cyprus Bar in 2004. In 2009 he was appointed as a member of the shipping committee of the Cyprus Bar Association and for the past few years has also acted as a visiting law lecturer in local universities.
Costas speaks Greek and English and his main areas of practice are corporate, commercial, finance, shipping and energy law and associated litigation.

Andreas Christofides
Tel: +357 25 110000 / Email: andreas.christofides@neocleous.com
Andreas Christofides was born in Limassol, Cyprus. He graduated in law from the University of Sheffield in 2012 and was awarded an LL.M. by King's College London in 2013. Andreas joined Andreas Neocleous LLC in 2013 as a trainee and on completion of his legal training and admission to the Cyprus Bar in 2014 he continued his career as an associate in the litigation department.
Andreas speaks Greek and English and has a working knowledge of French. His main areas of practice are corporate litigation and general litigation, commercial law, admiralty and shipping.

Andreas Neocleous & Co LLC

Neocleous House, 195 Makarios Avenue, P.O. Box 50613, CY-3608, Cyprus
Tel: +357 25 110000 / URL: http://www.neocleous.com

France

Emmanuel Marsigny
EMMANUEL MARSIGNY AVOCATS

Brief overview of the law and enforcement regime

Bribery and corruption, as part of the wider economic and financial criminality field, are under particular scrutiny since 2012 and the revelations of several high-profile cases, some involving top French public officials.

As a consequence, recent reforms have hardened penalties and increased investigative powers.

The results of such trend are, at the moment, not visible through the final issues of proceedings but in the number of proceedings opened on those grounds.

Criminal offences

Bribery and corruption are dealt with by several offences, all contained in the *Code penal*, which are mainly: corruption; influence peddling; illegal taking of interest; and favouritism in public procurement.

Corruption

Public official corruption – whether French, foreign or international – and private corruption are criminal offences for both the corrupter ("active corruption") and the corrupted ("passive corruption") who can be prosecuted independently from one another.

Penalties are higher for public official corruption than for private corruption and were recently significantly raised (anti-tax fraud and large economic and financial criminality act n°2013-1117 dated December 6th 2013).

Public official corruption is defined as:
- for anyone to propose, illicitly, directly or indirectly, any offer, promise, donation, gift or benefit to a public official (French, foreign or international) in order for he or she to carry out or abstain from carrying out an act pertaining to his or her office, duty, or mandate, or facilitated by his or her office, duty or mandate or to yield to a request of such kind by such public official ("active corruption", Articles 433-1 and 435-3 of the penal code); and
- for a public official (French, foreign or international), to request or accept any offer, promise, donation, gift or benefit in order to carry out or abstain from carrying out an act pertaining to his or her office, duty, or mandate, or facilitated by his or her office, duty or mandate ("passive corruption", Articles 432-11 and 435-1 of the penal code).

Neither the performing of an act by the public official nor the actual payment of the bribe are needed for the offence to be constituted. "Active" and "passive" attempts at corruption are included in the offence definition and are therefore punishable.

Hence, neither does it matter when the proposal or acceptance to pay or the request or acceptance of the payment occurs. The offence may be constituted whether they occur before or after the performing of the act or the abstention of the public official.

French public officials are defined as persons holding public authority or in charge of a public service mission (widely construed as in charge of performing acts aiming at the satisfaction of the public interest), or by a person holding a public electoral mandate.

Foreign and international public officials are defined as persons holding public office or in charge of a public service mission, or an electoral mandate in a foreign State, or within a public international organisation.

The main penalties for "active" and "passive" corruption, whether domestic or international, are 10 years' imprisonment and a fine of up to €1,000,000 (€5,000,000 for legal persons) or up to twice the profits drawn from the offence.

Supplementary penalties are, notably:
- for natural persons: loss of civic, civil and family rights; disqualification from holding public office or any professional or social activity related to the infringement; prohibition to exercise an industrial or commercial activity (including managing a commercial company); and confiscation of the profits received by the corrupted; and
- for legal persons: prohibition to operate an activity related to the infringement; judicial supervision; exclusion from public procurement tendering; and confiscation of the objects used to commit the offence, the profits drawn from the offence or any unexplained wealth.

Private corruption is defined identically but:
- the corrupted is defined as a person holding, within the scope of his professional or social activity, a management position or any employment for any person, whether natural or legal, or any other body; and
- he or she must be solicited or must propose to carry out or abstain from carrying out any act within his position or facilitated by his position, in violation of his legal, contractual and professional obligations.

The main penalties are five years' imprisonment and a fine of up to €500,000 (€2,500,000 for legal persons) or twice the profits drawn from the offence.

Similar supplementary penalties for public officials' corruption offences are applicable.

Specific similar corruption offences exist for corruption of French and foreign magistrates (Articles 434-9 et seq. and 435-9 of the penal code).

Complicity: the accomplice to an offender is a person who knowingly, by aiding and abetting, facilitates an offence's preparation or commission; he is punishable as a perpetrator (Articles 121-6 and 121-7 of the penal code).

These provisions apply to each offence hereafter described.

Receiving: a receiver, under French law, is a person who conceals, retains, transfers a thing or acts as an intermediary in its transfer, knowing that that thing was obtained by a felony or misdemeanour. It also apprehends the act of knowingly benefitting in any manner from the product of a felony or misdemeanour.

It is punished by five years' imprisonment and a fine of up to €375,000 (Article 321-1 of the penal code).

These provisions apply to each of the offences hereafter described.

Statute of limitation: corruption – as every major offence – is subject to a three-year statute of limitation (Article 8 of the code of criminal procedure). This may sound a particularly short period, but French case law permits to postpone the starting point of the statute of limitation to the date where the facts appeared and could be observed under conditions enabling the exercise of the public action where they were concealed.[1]

Influence peddling

Where corruption (attempted or committed) is the reward of an act or abstention of the corrupted, influence peddling (attempted or committed) is the reward of the <u>abuse of an influence</u> with a view to grant the obtainment of distinctions, employments, contracts or any other favourable decision from a public authority or the government (Article 432-11 of the penal code).

The influence peddled may be real or simply assumed.

Both "active" and "passive" influence peddling are punishable, which means that the person who requests the abuse of influence as well as the person who would abuse its influence are punishable.

Unlike the peddling of influence <u>over an official of public international organisation</u>, which is specifically punished too (Articles 435-2 and 435-4 of the penal code), the peddling of influence <u>over a public official of a foreign State is not punishable</u>.

Penalties are harsher if the person who peddles its influence is a public official (identical to corruption penalties) than if he or she is a not a public official or if the peddled influence is over an official from an international organisation (five years' imprisonment and a fine of up to €500,000 or €2,500,000 for a legal person).

Influence peddling is subject to a similar postponement of the statute of limitation to the one described for corruption when the criminal facts were concealed.[2]

Unlawful taking of interest

Unlawful taking of interest is twofold: it encompasses both interests held by French public officials when in charge of public duties and interests taken after the end of such.

At first, it is prohibited for French public officials, as previously defined, to take, receive or keep any interest in a business or business operation, either directly or not, when, at the time in question, it has had the duty of ensuring, in whole or in part, its supervision, management, liquidation or its payment.

This offence is punishable by a five-year prison term and a €500,000 fine (€2,500,000 for legal persons), which may amount to twice the profit drawn from the offence (Article 432-12 of the penal code).

It is also prohibited for French public officials or government members to take or receive an interest by the way of work, consulting or shares in one of the privately held companies which, within the framework of its duties, he used to supervise, entered into a contract with, formulated an opinion on such contract, or regarding which he proposed decisions to the competent authorities before the lapse of a three-year period following the end of these duties.

This offence also applies to third party companies when 30% of shares are held by one of the privately held companies mentioned in the previous paragraph, State-owned companies operating in a competitive sector and subject to private law regulation, as well as joint-venture companies when the State and its components hold more than 50% of the capital.

This second offence is punishable by a three-year prison term and a €200,000 fine (€1,000,000 for a legal person), which may amount to twice the profits drawn from the offence (Article 432-13 of the penal code).

These offences aim to prevent French public officials from being placed in a situation where their personal interest contravenes or is likely to contravene the interest of the public good, for which they are or were responsible.

The unlawful taking of interest stated in Article 432-12 of the penal code embraces any kind of interests, whether material, intellectual, direct or indirect.

The mere fact of being placed in a situation where the personal interest is likely to contravene the interest of the public good can lead to a conviction, even if no harm or enrichment[3] ensues from this offence, making this offence one of the most stringent in OECD countries regarding conflict of interests.

Defendants tried to challenge the constitutionality of Article 432-12 of the penal code, but the case was dismissed by the French Cour de cassation on March 19th, 2014.[4]

A legislative attempt to modify the definition of that incrimination also failed, in January 22nd, 2015, due to disagreement between the Senate and the National Assembly on a new wording of this incrimination.[5]

Unlawful taking of interest is subject to a similar postponement of the statute of limitation to the one described for corruption, when the criminal facts were concealed.[6]

Moreover, as the unlawful taking of interest may be a continuous offence (when the French Public Official keep an unlawful interest), the limitation period only starts the day the offence came to an end.

Favouritism in public procurement

Favouritism in procurement is punishable for a French public official, or a person acting as a representative, administrator or agent of the State and its components, or State-owned company or joint venture with such companies, to obtain or attempt to obtain for others an unjustified advantage by the violation of rules on public procurement.

This offence is punishable by a two-year prison term and a €200,000 fine (€1,000,000 for a legal person) or up to twice the profits drawn from the offence (Article 432-14 of the penal code).

Companies benefitting from such unjustified advantage may be convicted as a receiver of that major offence.

Favouritism in public procurement is subject to a similar postponement of the statute of limitation to the one described for corruption when the criminal facts were concealed.[7]

Investigation and enforcement bodies

As a general principle in French law, criminal proceedings may be started by public prosecution or by civil complaints from persons who are likely to be direct victims of the offence.

Civil complaints grounded on corruption offences, since the 2013 aforementioned anti-tax fraud and great economic and financial criminality act, may also be filed by authorised anti-corruption associations.

In both cases they may be carried out either by the public prosecutor – who is not considered a judicial authority for not being independent from the executive power according to the European Convention on Human Rights – or, more frequently, by an investigating magistrate.

Complex corruption and similar offences cases are handled by those authorities within the relevant territorial specialised interregional jurisdictions (with wider territorial competence and increased means of investigations) or within the specialised interregional jurisdiction of Paris, which, moreover, has exclusive jurisdiction over international corruption offences.

The "Financial prosecutor" ("*Procureur de la République Financier*") has been created by the aforementioned 2013 anti-tax fraud and great economic and financial criminality act to increase prosecution means on bribery and corruption cases, among others. It has nation-wide jurisdiction.

The Paris tribunal has a specific financial office that houses specialised investigating magistrates and prosecutors as well as the "Financial prosecutor".

Under the supervision of these bodies, investigations are carried out by <u>central judicial police teams</u> specialised in financial criminality, mainly the central office for the repression of great financial criminality (*"OCRGDF: Office central pour la repression de la grande délinquance financière"*) and the central office of fight against corruption and financial and tax offences (*"OCLCIFF: Office central de lutte contre la corruption et les infractions financières et fiscales"*), whose staff was recently doubled. Lower profile cases are handled by regional specialised teams.

It is not rare that TRACFIN, the anti-money laundering and terrorism financing unit, which is a financial intelligence unit, provides assistance to investigating bodies by supplying information on suspect financial transactions.

Financial courts, whose role is to control regularity and reliability of public entities accounts and the quality of public funds management, play a part in the signalling of suspicions to judicial authorities. New directives on such cooperation were circulated at the end of 2014 and could result in an increase in information exchanges through this channel.

Besides these ordinary tribunals, the "Justice court of the Republic" (*"Cour de justice de la République"*) has jurisdiction over members of the government for offences occurring when in office.

It is worth mentioning that the recent focus on public officials' probity has also led to the creation of the "High authority for public life transparency" (*"HATVP: Haute autorité pour la transparence de la vie publique"*), in charge of receiving wealth and interests declarations from nearly 9,000 public officials (from government members to local authorities' elected members), controlling those declarations and their evolution during the course of the mandates.

Failure to comply with the obligation to file such accurate declaration is an offence punished by three years' imprisonment and a fine of up to €45,000, and, for government members, five years' imprisonment and a fine of up to €75,000.

Overview of enforcement activity and policy during the past two years

General figures

Between 2003 and 2013, the number of persons convicted for probity offences has been overall stable, with an average of nearly 300 per year.

The average length of proceedings until a final decision is rendered is around five to six years.

The penalties imposed (based on the analysis of convictions for only one offence) are mainly suspended imprisonment and fines, with an average, as an example, of around eight months and an €8,000 fine for corruption offences.

Supplementary penalties, such as disqualifications and confiscations, are very rarely imposed.

Although the figures are based on statistics of convictions for a unique offence, whereas important cases often imply multiple offence convictions (such as money laundering and misuse of company assets in addition to bribery and corruption), it is obvious that severe sanctions are rarely imposed until now.

However, the results of the recently hardened policy against bribery and corruption cannot be appraised yet, due to the length of proceedings.

It can be noted that there has been a significant rise in the investigations targeting local public officials for probity offences over the period 2008-2015 compared to the period 2001-2008 (a 70% rise in the number of targeted persons).

The scarce number of convictions for international corruption offences in international commercial transactions is highlighted by several international organisations and non-governmental organisations (five since the implementation of the OECD Anti-bribery convention of 2000), but there is a significant increase since 2012 in the number of proceedings opened on those grounds: 33 had been initiated in 2012; and 58 were as of December 2014 (of which 38 are still ongoing);[8] only a handful currently have companies as targets.

Significant cases prosecuted recently

A French aerospace, defence and security group and two of its employees were prosecuted for, allegedly, bribing Nigerian officials in order to be granted a €170 million contract to produce identity cards. After the sentencing of the company to a €500,000 fine and the acquittal of the managers by first degree jurisdiction, the court of appeal acquitted all the defendants whereas the prosecutor had requested no conviction for the company, since its executives were not prosecuted, but six months of suspended imprisonment for the employees (January 2015).

Two managers of a French oil and gas service group were sentenced to fines of €5,000 and €10,000 (January 2013) for foreign public official corruption in a case where $130 million of commissions were deemed to have been transferred in relation to the awarding of a $6 billion gas complex construction in an African country to several tenders. Although the case did not show personal enrichment, the prosecutor had requested much higher fines of €100,000 for each.

Several international groups and individuals are currently prosecuted in the "Oil for food" case for, allegedly, having bribed Iraqi officials to get around the "Oil for food" programme embargo. In the two separate current proceedings, first degree jurisdictions have acquitted all the defendants (July 2013 and June 2015), some were discharged by virtue of the "*ne bis in idem*" principle because they had concluded a plea agreement in the United States. The prosecution appealed those decisions.

A French former advisor of a former French President – prosecuted for illegal taking of interest for having taken the head of the entity resulting from a major bank merger in France after having participated in the operation supervision in his capacity of President advisor – was acquitted by first degree tribunal (September 2015), whereas prosecution requested two years of suspended imprisonment, a €30,000 fine and prohibition to hold any public function. The prosecutor appealed the decision.

A French former minister, prosecuted for influence peddling for having interceded to have the "*legion d'honneur*" granted to a manager in exchange for the employment of his wife, was acquitted, as well as the manager, in accordance with the prosecutor's request who at the end of the hearing dropped the charges that had been held by the investigating magistrate.

An environment services company and individuals were sentenced (April 2014) in a case of public procurement favouritism and corruption in the award of a contract by a municipality with a potential turnover around €30 million. An appeal was lodged and is still to be judged. The first degree jurisdiction sentenced the company to a €200,000 fine and its manager to a one-year conditional suspended prison sentence and a €20,000 fine.

Recently, several cases of unlawful taking of interest in the frame of wind farm development led to convictions. Most of these concerned the participation of local authorities' elected members in decisions on the establishment of wind farms on lands over which they had interests.

Significant cases under investigation

An oil company and two intermediaries were charged and sent for judgment for alleged foreign public official corruption in a Middle Eastern State in the awarding of oil and gas contracts in the late 1990s and early 2000s.

Several African States' public officials are under investigations for alleged money laundering in France, through investments in real estate and other goods, of the proceeds of alleged probity offences, purportedly committed in their countries.

Former advisors of a former French President are under investigation for benefitting from alleged public procurement favouritism in the award of contract for the providing of surveys to the presidency.

Suspected foreign public official corruption and influence peddling in the context of a €2bn aeronautic defence contract with a central Asian country is under investigations which are currently targeting a French former member of parliament, an advisor to the President and a lawyer.

Law and policy relating to issues such as facilitation payments and hospitality

Facilitation payments are not allowed under French law and are likely to constitute the offence of corruption.

Unlike many countries however, France has no statutory rules regulating gifts and hospitality offered to public officials.

A 2011 report of the "Reflection commission for the prevention of conflicts of interests in public life" (*"Commission de réflexion pour la prevention des conflits d'intérêts dans la vie publique"*) recommends regulating gifts and hospitality including by forbidding the acceptance of gifts worth over €150 and by providing that over the limit gifts that cannot be refused (protocol contacts) be handed to the entity to which the official belongs. No such statutory regulations have been adopted yet.

However, several codes and charters of ethics were recently created. Notably, since 2012, ministers sign an ethics charter which provides for the handing over to the public property service of all gifts over €150 and for the abstention to accept any invitation for a private journey by foreign governments or any legal or natural person whose activity is related to their department.

It must also be noted that a bill project is in discussion in parliament on the ethics, rights and obligations of civil servants (*"Projet de loi relatif à la déontologie et aux obligations des fonctionnaires"*). As of now, it does not include specific provisions on facilitation payments and hospitality but provides for the possibility to set ethical rules by decree.

Key issues relating to investigation, decision-making and enforcement procedures

The legislator introduced on December 6th, 2013 a new process for self-reporting in corruption and influence peddling cases, similar to the system of repentance that applies for ordinary offences, such as drug trafficking.

When the author or the accomplice of the offence has allowed the ceasing of the offence or the identification of the authors or accomplices, by repenting and warning the authorities, the prison sentence incurred is reduced by half (Article 433-2-1 of the penal code).

The French penal code also contains a plea-bargaining process, which may theoretically apply to bribery and corruption cases since the abolition on December 13th, 2011 of the restrictions to its scope (it now applies to every major offence, whereas it was previously confined to offences punishable by a five-year sentence at the most, and it is since applicable even at the end of an investigation conducted under the control of the investigating judge), which applied until then. But, to date, its implementation has been unsuccessful in white-collar crimes, leading Mr. Jean-Michel Hayat, Paris High Court's President, to call, on January 19th, 2015, for a "cultural revolution" by generalising the recourse to this procedure in this kind of offences.

The first attempts failed, as in a recent case involving a major foreign bank for tax evasion and money laundering, where the bank is said to have refused the prosecuting authorities' proposal.

One of the major impediments affecting this procedure is that the French legal system only allows settlement in conjunction with a guilty plea, which may impact potential civil proceedings.

There is no deferred prosecution agreement in France, but, theoretically, criminal law provides for a judicial supervision of legal entities upon the activity in the exercise of which an offence was committed, after being convicted (Article 131-46 of the penal code). This possibility is very rarely used.

The French legal system does not provide a special status for whistle-blowers but incorporates disparate provisions, which prevents layoffs as retaliation (Article L1161-1 of the Labour Code regarding corruption and Article 25 of the transparency in public life act n°2013-907, on October 11th, 2013, regarding conflict of interests).

Overview of cross-border issues

Jurisdiction issues

As a general principle, French criminal legislation on bribery and corruption applies to the following situations and to the offences that form an "undividable whole":

- offences committed, even partially, in France;
- complicity in France of offences committed abroad over which France has no jurisdiction, when there has been final conviction in the foreign State;
- offences committed abroad by French citizens when the offence is also punished by the foreign State where they occurred;
- offences committed abroad when the victim was a French citizen at the time in question; and
- offences committed abroad by a foreigner when the handing over of the incriminated person has been refused by France to a foreign State because the foreign penalty is contrary to French principles, or the foreign proceedings does not grant the fundamental rights and defence rights.

A special rule provides for the jurisdiction of French courts over certain cases of foreign public officials' corruption when corruption offences occurred abroad but the defendant is found in France.

By prosecuting offences located in France of money laundering or reception of proceeds coming from corruption offences committed abroad, French tribunals have a way to investigate cases for which they would not have jurisdiction over the corruption offence itself, on which they consequently investigate too in order to establish its existence.

As a current issue, over which recent decision were rendered, it is worth noting that tribunals recently judged that "*ne bis in idem*" principle applies when a defendant has concluded a plea agreement abroad. Prosecution cannot be held in such case.

International cooperation

During investigations, international judicial cooperation tends to be always more frequently used and to be quicker, especially inside the European Union where, in particular, the European arrest warrant makes it very simple and quicker to obtain the handing over of defendants.

In particular, it must be noted that when French investigating bodies are requested by foreign authorities to cooperate in cases of corruption abroad, they may and actually do open their own investigative proceedings on the grounds of money laundering when assets supposedly related to targeted persons are found in France. Such assets are seized with a very reduced margin to challenge the seizure.

It is interesting to point out the applicability in France of a "blocking statute", forbidding the disclosure, by any French natural person, any natural person established in France or any executive of a legal person established in France, of documents and information of an economic, commercial, industrial, financial or technical nature, to foreign authorities where such disclosure would impact French sovereignty, security, essential economic interests or public order.

Such blocking statute is an issue in foreign procedures such as non-prosecution or differed prosecution agreement and has recently been dealt with for major French groups facing such procedures by setting up a transmission channel through a "French governmental authority" in charge of checking that only useful information, to the exception of prohibited information, was transmitted.

Foreign legislation impact

Foreign legislation, like the Bribery Act in the United Kingdom and the Foreign Corrupt Practices Act in the United States, may have an impact on French international groups to which those pay particular attention.

Corporate liability for bribery and corruption offences

Pursuant to Article 121-2 of the penal code, corporate entities are criminally liable for the offences committed on their behalf by their organs or representatives. Recent case law tends to rule that precise identification of individuals who committed the offence is not a prerequisite to their conviction, when there is no doubt that the offence was committed by one of their organs, representatives or delegates on their behalf.

The applicable sentence to legal persons is five times the maximum amount of the fine, which apply to natural persons by the law sanctioning the offence (Article 131-38 of the penal code).

The French system does not currently provide for legally binding rules for business to adopt internal measures to prevent corruption, as it is known in the United States or in the United Kingdom.

On March 2015, the French Central Service of Corruption Prevention (the CSCP) provided guidelines towards French companies that operate abroad,[9] which apply on a voluntary basis, and set out the following key principles:
- top-level commitment: senior management has to be committed to prevent bribery and ensures it is implemented at every level of the organisation and with third parties;
- risk assessment: the risk assessment needs to be documented and updated on a regular basis, supported by a sufficient allocation of the organisation's financial and human resources;

- setting-up an anti-corruption compliance programme, with the designation of a compliance officer, as well as the implementation of an internal whistle-blowing system;
- control mechanism, to ensure its effectiveness, both with internal and external controls. A report on such verification must be presented to management bodies;
- communication, training and follow-up of the anti-corruption compliance programme; and
- setting-up a sanction policy, without prejudice to the ability to report incidents to police services and to the prosecutor.

Numerous French major companies already apply these kinds of internal controls, given the extraterritorial reach of some foreign legislation and in order to limit the exposure to the risk of a potential conviction for corruption, with the help of external auditors and certification bodies.

Proposed reforms / The year ahead

Various reforms were proposed by the CSPC, the High authority for public life transparency and by the United Nations Office on Drugs and Crime (the UNODC) and may lead to legislative change in the forthcoming years.

Here are the most significant proposals made by these authorities:

- setting up an actual status for whistle-blowers: as stated before, the current regime only protects, through disparate provisions, employees that denounce criminal facts. The CSPC and UNODC call for the setting up of a general status for whistle-blowers, with a broader protection that encompasses every kind of retaliation (such as end of contracts for suppliers or customers, physical pressure on the whistle-blowers or their relatives) and which provides fair and comprehensive compensation to its beneficiaries;
- improving the civil servants' reporting system, by the creation of a French authority similar to the UK's Serious Fraud Office, called the High authority for public life transparency;
- setting-up an impeachment process by allowing each legislative body to exclude one of its members in case of serious breach;
- ensuring that every conviction for breach of probity will be systematically sentenced by the ineligibility of the perpetrator; and
- expanding the limitation period from three to five years (for offences punishable by an imprisonment period of less than three years) or three to seven years (for offences punishable by an imprisonment period over three years) in order to bring the French limitation periods in line with those in most other European countries.

* * *

Endnotes

1. Cass. Crim. May 6th, 2009, n°08-84107.
2. Cass. Crim., March 19th, 2008, n°07-82.124.
3. Cass. Crim., October 22nd, 2008, n°08-82.068.
4. Cass. Crim. March 19th, 2014, n°14-90.001.
5. Vote of the National Assembly on January 22nd, 2015, on the law proposal to "facilitate the exercise, by the local elected representatives, of their mandate".
6. Cass. Crim., December 16th, 2014, n°14-82.939.
7. Cass. Crim., October 27th, 1999, n°98-85.757.
8. OECD, Phase 3 report on implementing the OECD anti-bribery convention in France, December 2014.
9. http://www.justice.gouv.fr/include_htm/pub/Lignes_directrices_EN.pdf, for an English-language outline.

Emmanuel Marsigny
Tel: +33 153 712 000 / Email: emarsigny@marsigny.eu
Emmanuel Marsigny has been a member of the Paris Bar since 1995.
Since then he has developed a recognised expertise in criminal defence, and is regularly ranked as one of the leading criminal defence lawyers in France in the leading directories.

He is the founder of Emmanuel Marsigny Avocats, a French boutique law firm specialised in white-collar crime, financial and business criminal law including tax fraud, market abuse, insider trading, embezzlement, bribery, bankruptcy crimes, recovery of assets, as well as general criminal law including manslaughter (notably large-scale disasters, e.g. air accidents and health and industrial catastrophes).

The firm also provides assistance in the course of transnational criminal proceedings, including extradition, freezing of assets, multi-jurisdictional investigations, embargoes and international sanctions, as well as international corruption and money laundering cases.

Emmanuel Marsigny obtained a law degree from Panthéon-Sorbonne University in criminal law and criminal policy in Europe.
He speaks French, English and Spanish.

EMMANUEL MARSIGNY AVOCATS

203 bis, boulevard Saint-Germain, 75007 Paris, France
Tel: +33 1 5371 2000 / URL: http://marsigny.eu

Germany

Hans-Peter Huber
Knierim | Huber

Brief overview of the law and system concerning sanctions

Without exploring its historical development too in-depth, the following is a summarised insight of the history of German criminal law, which may be helpful.

The law that came into force on 15 May 1871 during the former German Empire has a uniform criminal code. It was essentially that of the Prussian Penal Code of 1851, which first started development in 1826. The origin of this has helped to shape and develop the classification of laws against bribery and corruption until today. A key aspect of the success of the Prussian state in the 19th century and the rise of the German Empire in the second half of the 19th century was the existence of an excellent management system of civil servants. It was most characterised by the fact that it was almost free of corrupt elements, in contrast to many other administrations. Criminal law applied strict professional rules for the conduct and operation of public office holders, which are absolutely essential for such roles.

Under present German law, it is a punishable offence for a public official, pursuant to § 331 of the Criminal Code, to allow himself to be promised or to accept a benefit as an advantage for himself or for a third party for the discharge of an official duty. In accepting such advantages, a sentence includes imprisonment up to three years or a fine. A public official involved with bribery under § 332 of the Criminal Code is punishable if he in turn receives a benefit for himself or a third party as compensation, for carrying out an official act which additionally violates his official duty. The penalties here are much higher, namely imprisonment from six months to five years. The party who provided the advantage to the public official is also liable for prosecution. § 333 of the Criminal Code defines the criminal offence of the so-called "granting of advantages", and seeks punishment of imprisonment of up to three years or a fine. This offence corresponds with § 331, which focuses on the exchange of the advantage with the officials, without causing a breach of official duties. If, in addition, the bribed official violated his official duties, the bribing person is punishable under § 334 of the Criminal Code. Such party now faces imprisonment for a minimum of three months and a maximum of five years.

In any case, the term 'benefit' is to be understood in a very broad sense in relation to the aforesaid provisions. All benefits may be tangible or intangible in form. It must seek to improve the economic, legal, or even personal situation of the official as a main objective, and be considered an advantage.

Practical problems with these rules frequently arise on the question of who qualifies as a public official. A definition can be found in § 11 of the Criminal Code, which provides a description of the terminology, but relates in particular to modern forms of public administration, in which there is a departure from the traditional notion of officials originally defined by the legislature; such a change has caused arguments about its certainty, which in turn casts doubt. It must be noted that the provision in § 331 para. 3 of the Criminal Code excludes punishment if the perpetrator allows himself to be promised or accepts a benefit which he did not demand and the competent public authority, within the scope of its powers, either previously authorises the acceptance, or the perpetrator promptly reports it and it authorises the acceptance.

Bribery under § 332 StGB states that such approval comes naturally out of the situation at hand. Bribery of Foreign Public Officials in Germany had not been an offence for a long time. The granting of benefits to foreign officials was in 1999 made a criminal offence in Germany through the Act of Combating International Bribery of 10 September 1998. Please note that the strict regulations of §§ 331 and 333 concerning the acceptance and granting of advantages in carrying out an official duty are not covered by this Act, which only targets (active) bribery of foreign public officials. Up to this point of time, funds which had been used for the bribery of foreign public officials were deductible under German tax law.

It took some years until the German economy had adjusted to the new legal reality that it is today. A variety of large and publicised criminal proceedings on corruption in Germany have their origins in the period of transition from the old to the current law. The most significant case is probably the one that concerned the investigations against managers of Siemens AG, which in 2006 drew considerable attention and, as a consequence, many companies in Germany had their compliance situation and practice concerning corruption improved.

Corruption in a business transaction is easily explained through its history, which initially received no special attention in Germany. The current provision in § 299 of the Penal Code originally concerned free competition backed by UWG (Unfair Competition Law). It was only by the Anti-Corruption Act of 1997 that these provisions were included in the core criminal law of Germany, contained in the Criminal Code to be exact.

The current version of § 299 determines that an employee or agent of a business, which can be in trade, demands, allows himself to be promised, or accepts a benefit for himself or another in a business transaction as consideration for giving a preference in an unfair manner to another, commits a criminal act and is punishable. This penal provision continues to protect and allow free and fair competition concerning the financial interests of a business. Furthermore, the provision of § 299 of the Penal Code is also written to not only protect national but also international competition.

In the summer of 2014, Germany finally committed to the fulfilment of requirements of the United Nations. This concerns the bribery of Members of a Parliament (§ 108e of the Criminal Code). Due to the soft wording of this Act, any conviction of a member appears to be questionable. The legislature has clearly sought to make the rules as risk free as possible for MPs.

A presentation of the basics of the German legal system concerning bribery and corruption would be incomplete without an insight into German Procedural Law. The law enforcement agencies, prosecutors and police, are subject to the so-called principle of legality, which is found in § 152 of the German Code of Criminal Procedure. It states that the prosecution will take action against any suspects, provided the sufficient factual indicators are satisfied. The legislature wants to put forth through this law that equality and justice prevail to the fullest extent possible. Unlike many other countries, the investigating authorities in Germany have no discretion as to whether they want to actively become aware of circumstances that may indicate a crime or not. Investigations have to be carried out and they must examine each of these cases individually. Other special features of the German criminal procedural law will be examined later.

Overview of prosecution and political considerations during the past two years

A case that took on considerable attention among the general public this summer was the trial involving the head of Formula 1 management, Bernie Ecclestone. This process had a connection that led back to the earlier conviction of the former bank *board member*, Gerhard Gribkowsky, in 2012. In Germany there are a number of banks that are owned by a German state or states collectively (held directly or indirectly by the public sector). Gribkowsky was Chief Risk Officer of Bayerische Landesbank at the time.

In 2005 he had led the negotiations for the sale of rights and interests in the Formula 1 business. He was sentenced in June 2012 to a prison term of eight-and-a-half years for taking bribes in the amount of US$ 50m. The court had then assumed that the head of Formula 1 management, Bernie Ecclestone, had paid this sum. It was determined that Ecclestone was involved with bribery of a public official. The indictment by the Munich public prosecutor had been approved by the court by public hearing.

During the ongoing process, problems surfaced that required the defendant to prove that he had known that the payment of the sum to Gribkowsky had been to a public official; the implications that the Bayerische Landesbank is a state-owned bank may have been unknown or unclear to him. To shorten the process, Ecclestone was willing to pay a fine of US$ 100m and the process was stopped. Ecclestone subsequently has no criminal record and may further continue to direct Formula 1.

At present there is considerable attention over allegations against several German companies within the defence sector, of alleged bribery of Greek officials concerning the purchase of arms. Three companies are involved in the proceedings: Krauss-Maffei Wegmann *re* the production of 170 Leopard 2 main battle tanks and some Howitzer 2000 tanks. As to a period of limitation of five years for bribery but of 10 years for criminal tax fraud this investigation focuses on the issue that corruptive payments are not deductible. One manager is under custody and indictment is expected during summer 2015.

Atlas Ltd. is under investigation *re* the contracts for submarines and submarine modernisation. No details of this ongoing proceeding are available.

Rheinmetall Defence Electronic Ltd. was under investigation *re* an anti-aircraft missile defence system and has settled the case for the company. Individual proceedings continue.

Factually all these cases are under investigation in Greece as well; we may have the chance to learn about the practice of how to deal with the restriction of double jeopardy under European Law (Art. 50 of the Charter of Fundamental Human Rights).

In a similar sector of the economic system, there are also allegations against the aircraft manufacturer EADS, involving rogatory letters from the Austrian authorities.

Overall, Germany has somewhat emerged with a wider range of economic crime. The focus is not only on corruption and bribery. Many companies have recurring problems because of tax charges for alleged fraud, in violation of antitrust laws.

Law and policy relating to issues of facilitation of payments and hospitality

There are two areas that give rise to much discussion and confusion in Germany. These include the so-called 'facilitation of payments' (Facilitation Payments, Grease Payments) and the area of 'invitations and sponsorship'. As described above, all parties and public officials involved in such benefits for legitimate service are liable to be prosecuted under German law. So far, no exceptions exist. The law has certainly made some limitations in that it requires an agreement with the wrongdoer. It says that there must be a link between the reason of service exercised on the one hand, and the benefit provided on the other.

This issue is not seen as an advantage in the realm of social adequacy. The limits of what is permissible here are, however, often difficult to find. Surely much will be allowed in terms of courtesy and kindness. The same problem is also found in cases in which officers are invited to cultural, sporting, and culinary or other social events. Also, generally speaking, the invitation to wine and dine in order to maintain a professional exchange of ideas within a relaxed atmosphere can often be viewed as problematic. One should note that there exist in the area of social adequacy (social appropriateness) a variety of parameters to be considered. One should take into account the status of the person being invited, the activity of the company and the company declaring the invitation in connection with general cultural etiquette. Namely, whether it is an invitation based on tradition, or a non-traditional and surprising action for the promotion of gains. The Federal Authorities have gravitated away from fixed amounts of money as a settlement for purposes of social adequacy. The question whether an invitation qualifies as "socially adequate" is not determined by a fixed amount, but depends on the individual case. For example, an invitation valued at €10.00 may already be considered an unjust agreement, but a generous invitation to an entire group with a value of several hundred euros, depending on the circumstances, can still prove to be within the realm of social adequacy.

While it is correct to view each individual case separately and not to rely on general rules, it remains important for each firm to provide clear internal guidelines for basic awareness of such potentially dangerous situations. Everyone in an organisation should, however, be given the opportunity in situations of doubt to contact its Compliance Department to find out if they would become a criminal in particular cases when crossing such borders.

It is regrettable to observe that public debates, professional legal discussions and even investigating authorities are becoming more and more inclined to transfer the strict rules of the Civil Service on to private businesses. This does not coincide with legal standpoints, but shows a worrying trend towards longer sentences. The same applies to the erroneous assumption that the area of facilitation payments and invitations with cultural elements would follow German rules. Given that in Germany, bribery of foreign public officials is only criminal when the bribed official violates his official duty, questions of social adequacy never play a role in this context. The question is what may be considered appropriate in other cultural and social systems.

The periodic excessive zeal of the implementation of laws regarding compliance requirements of a company unfortunately leads many employees to recognise the utter impracticability of compliance rules concerning the hospitality sector. This shows such compliance rules to be unfeasible. Of course, the warning seems appropriate for certain volumes when equivalent indications exist, but it is the granting of benefits that is expected to mean an unlawful official act.

Key issues relating to investigation, decision-making and enforcement procedures

A key element of German Procedural Law has already been presented above: the principle of legality in criminal prosecution. It has been made clear that if there exists suspicion of offences concerning bribery or corruption, the German authorities have to perform an assessment. As for the practical conduct of the investigation, it is clear that there is a general distinction between the traditionalists and the modernists, in particular on the part of the defence in Germany.

The traditional criminal defence in Germany either does not recognise modern forms of co-operation with law enforcement authorities or rejects them. The traditional defence counsel relies on the right of silence of the accused and waits until the prosecution has pursued its investigations as far as it can, and has granted access to the file of the accused. It often lasts for many months and can exceed one year.

The traditional teachings are based on the idea that the economic criminal investigating authority considers a very extensive load of documents and experiences problems with developing a concrete criminal accusation. However, some things are often overlooked that modernists have already taken up with defence lawyers. The modern processing of data allows searches, even through millions of documents, to find those passages that are relevant to the alleged offence. The relationship and often the systematic pattern of corrupt behaviour within an organisation is recognised very quickly when it comes to email screening by the investigating authorities or through a mandate by the companies' internal investigators. The idea that one might hide in a 'solid castle', until the prosecutor can remove the besiegers, is no longer true. Modern information technology is the weapon that breaks through every castle's wall. It is only that the behaviour of the defence changes slowly in economic criminal matters. In addition, the quality of internal investigations conducted by forensic investigators in Germany is highly variable. The thrust of such investigations is often tempted to follow that of the alleged defence interests of their clients. Deceptions are sometimes successful, but they often fail – with dire results for the company.

Although the duties of the Institute of Internal Investigation were acquired by the United States, mandatory rules for such investigations are still missing; a predicament which has not yet affected the legislature. The representatives of law enforcement agencies in Germany shy away from giving appropriate publications on a reliable set of rules concerning the matter. In addition, German Criminal Law is aimed at punishing individuals and not at penalising shortcomings in business. This aspect will be explored below in more detail.

Regarding investigation against individuals, it is important to note that it is not necessarily a public accusation that must be levied in all cases where the result to be determined is to prove criminal behaviour. In Germany, it is a principle that criminal behaviour is presented to the court by the prosecution for a decision; however, the Code of Criminal Procedure has developed some exceptions over time. A very important provision is § 153a of the Code of Criminal Procedure. Here, if the accused person is viewed as having a low level of guilt, the possibility exists to resign from the eventual indictment if the person balances the unjust act by satisfying the "public interest" and if the "weight of guilt is notwithstanding"; notably by the payment of a fine.

As much as this provision is criticised time and time again, it greatly helps the practice of criminal procedure to arrive at fair and equitable solutions.

This provision was used in the case of Bernie Ecclestone, described above. The question was whether the defendant knew of Gribkowsky's status as an office-bearer or minister and had followed through with the act of bribing an office-bearer or minister. To have resolved the matter completely would have been a lengthy process that would likely have continued for at least one year without a reliable verdict in sight.

If one had reached the conclusion that the defendant had certainly known it, one could view his behaviour to be on account of his cultural and economic intention and therefore in a mild light, and one would also consider it to be a low-level fault. However, German criminal proceedings maintain a certain level of consideration which cannot be concluded entirely as 'cut-and-dry'. Purely for the reason of the high caseload of penal justice, § 153a of the Code of Criminal Procedure is an acceptable possibility for the termination of proceedings in such cases.

The German Code of Penal Procedure was introduced in its basic form in the second half of the 19th century, on the basis that no formalised method of plea-bargaining was to be permissible. Under pressure from the Federal Court in 2009, the legislature was prompted to introduce a new provision concerning the regulation of plea-bargaining, which is defined in § 257c of the Code of Criminal Procedure. The new standard has already caused fierce debate about the practicality and whether it fully encompasses justice in such matters.

Only by the summer of 2014 did the constitutional court of the Federal Republic of Germany feel obliged to give it unequivocal borders, but meanwhile allow very free interpretation of the legal norm by the courts. It should be noted that the issue of plea-bargaining in Germany is still new and not part of a well-established legal culture. In that regard, further practical developments remain to be seen.

Cross-border issues

As pointed out above, fundamental changes in the German legal view on corruption were introduced by the IntBestG in 1999. Two debatable topics have recently arisen concerning problematic cross-border areas in the field of corruption. If a company is under an internal investigation for suspected corruption, it is often asked what rules these investigations have to follow in Germany or abroad. The internal investigations always experience tension concerning the right of privacy. However, one should not overlook that in private investigations it is often easier to dispense with formal requirements of legal assistance to achieve quick results in acquiring an explanation. A point that received attention in recent months by a decision of the European Court of Justice (ECJ) was the question of whether the principle of the prohibition of double jeopardy within the European Union in its entirety is valid. The current regulation within the European Union narrowed down the applicability of double jeopardy when it came to the same convicted offence in another country and an execution of the sentence has to have already begun, at the very least (C 129/14 Spasic).

This regulation has been declared compatible with the rules governing the protection of fundamental rights in Europe. Connected to this should be the notion that the legal assistance between the European States within the EU has been greatly simplified and a quicker acceleration of criminal prosecutions can be conducted.

Corporate liability for bribery and corruption offences

Corporate responsibility concerning corruption in German criminal law is characterised by the so-called principle of guilt. Only the person who bears the blame for an individual offence shall be punished in Germany. Now, by definition of a company, it cannot take on an individual debt unto itself. Thus, a company falls outside the scope of criminal law in this aspect.

Of course, the lack of a company's organisational measures concerning compliance, such as inadequate precautions, for example, can give way to sanctions in Germany. This would be governed by the Code of Administrative Offences under the Administrative Offences Act. § 30 provides that international offences committed by a governing body of the company can be given a fine of up to €10m. This provision must be viewed in conjunction with § 130 of the same Act, whereby breaches of duty by the business owner, particularly in the context of supervisory measures, can also lead to a fine of up to €1m. Additionally skimming of the profits may be ordered as the law rules that there shall not remain any advantage caused by illegal behaviour. The purpose of these regulations is on the one hand to impose high fines upon the responsible individuals, and on the other hand to obtain tax profits derived from criminal offences at a company. The rules may seem a bit complicated in theoretical representation, but they have proven to be an effective method for many years now.

Those that do not follow the political influence in this matter will be able to manage their affairs well under the given legal conditions of the Administrative Offences Act concerning the term "corporate criminal". One need only recall that based on these legal instruments, companies like Siemens, MAN or Ferrostaal paid hundreds of millions in penalties. These amounts would run parallel under American authorities, but no higher. This area leads on to the final section.

Proposed reforms / The year ahead

Political discussion about the so-called corporate criminal law has become more calm and factual. But many politicians still hold the mistaken belief that improvement can be achieved by renaming company sanction law concerning offences on administrative penalties in corporate criminal law. This will hardly be the case. Above all, it can be seen that investigations are nowhere close to political approaches to internal regulations. This is seen as a reliable approach, which could relieve the investigative bodies who are heavily burdened with such work. Discussions concerning the "privatisation of the prosecution" favour the need to revert to German tradition, and the notion that only the state draws up criminal charges. The legal reality is something quite different, and the need for clear and reliable rules for an internal investigation is great.

But the Federal Ministry of Justice and Consumer Protection is working hard to integrate the rules of the IntBestG from 1998 into the German Criminal Code simultaneously sharpening the scope of the rules, especially of Section 299, for business transactions. These new ideas will force the public prosecutors in Germany to investigate a case where a business man from Australia during a stopover at a German Airport offered a payment to a Chinese official. Experts still hope this draft will never pass through parliament.

Hans-Peter Huber
Tel: +49 30 887 2839 0 / Email: huber@knierim-huber.com
Senior Partner Hans-Peter Huber studied law at Ludwigs Maximilians University in Munich. From 1980 to 1992, Huber held various positions within the judiciary, including a post as prosecuting attorney and judge in Munich. He later headed the press and public relations section of the Bavarian Ministry of Justice. Subsequently, he served as the first head of the criminal law department of the newly established Thuringian Ministry of Justice in Erfurt. Following this period of public service, Huber returned to Munich to serve as chief editor of the Beck and Vahlen publishing houses. From 2000 to September 2012, he served as General Counsel for the legal department of the KPMG AG accountancy firm in Berlin. Hans-Peter Huber was made Senior Partner at the Berlin Office of Knierim | Huber in October of 2012. Furthermore, Huber is the co-editor of the Corporation Law journal, *Neue Zeitschrift für Gesellschaftsrecht* (NZG).

Knierim | Huber

Meierottostraße 1, 10719 Berlin, Germany
Tel: +49 30 887 2839 0 / Fax: +49 30 887 28 39 29 / URL: http://www.knierimhuber.com

Ghana

Esi Tawia Addo-Ashong
Ashong Benjamin & Associates

Introduction

Ghana's criminal justice system is currently mired in a bribery and corruption scandal. A private investigator has published video evidence of 34 judges, hundreds of judicial services officials, seven attorneys and five police officers receiving or brokering bribes to influence the exercise of judicial discretions. Clearly the fight against corruption in Ghana is facing serious challenges. It is important, as a contribution to fixing this problem, to develop a full understanding of the anti-corruption regime and its workings. This article seeks to do that.

Over the years, Ghana has employed a full range of strategies to combat corruption. These have included public executions, passage of Draconian decrees, the imposition of custodial sentences, confiscation of properties from public servants, passage of numerous anti-corruption laws, embarking on public sector reform, ratification of international conventions, strengthening and resourcing anti-corruption agencies such as the Commission on Human Rights and Administrative Justice (CHRAJ) and the Economic and Organised Crime Office (EOCO) and more recently the publicity and support being given to investigative journalism in the bid to name and shame perpetrators.

Overview of the law and enforcement regime

The 1992 Constitution

The 1992 Republican Constitution addresses corruption in a number of respects.
*   Article 35 (8) obligates the State to take steps to eradicate corrupt practices and the abuse of power.
*   Article 37 (2) establishes a role for citizens in development and the right to form associations without interference from the State. This is important in the context of activism around corruption issues.
*   Chapter 18 establishes a Commission on Human Rights and Administrative Justice (CHRAJ) (discussed further below).
*   Article 284 provides that: "A public officer shall not put himself in a position where his personal interest conflicts or is likely to conflict with the performance of the functions of his office."
*   Article 286 requires specified public officials to submit a written declaration of their assets and liabilities to the Auditor General upon assumption of office, periodically during service and upon termination of appointments.
*   Articles 126(3) and 127(2) – Independence of the Judiciary.

The effect of these constitutional provisions is to create the foundation from which the anti-corruption fight can be waged. To fulfil these constitutional provisions, the state, through the legislature, has enacted various pieces of legislation to combat bribery and corruption.

Even though the law enforcement regime seems comprehensive, the most current country review by the United Nations Office on Drugs and Crime (UNODC) makes a number of recommendations for the amendment and enhancement of a number of laws.

Legislation

Ghana has passed a number of laws whose primary aim is to deal with corruption, whiles others have provisions that relate to corrupt activity. In no particular order, these are:
*   Anti-Money Laundering Act, 2008 (Act 749).
*   Anti-Money Laundering Regulations, 2011 (L.I. 1987).
*   Anti-Terrorism (Amendment) Act, 2012 (Act 842).
*   Anti-Terrorism Regulations, 2012 (L.I. 2181).
*   Audit Service Act, 2000 (Act 584).
*   Banking Act, 2004 (Act 673).
*   Credit Reporting Act, 2007, (Act 726).
*   Criminal Offences (Amendment) Act, 1993 (Act 458).
*   Commission on Human Rights & Administrative Justice Act, 1993 (Act 456).
*   Customs, Excise & Preventive Service (Management) Law, 1993 (PNDCL 330).
*   Economic and Organized Crime Act, 2010 (Act 804).
*   Economic and Organized Crime Office (Operations) Regulations, 2012 (L.I. 2183).
*   Electronic Transaction Act, 2008 (Act 772).
*   Financial Administration Act, 2003 (Act 654).
*   Financial Administration (Amendment) Act, 2008 (Act 760).
*   Internal Audit Agency Act, 2003 (Act 658).
*   Internal Revenue Act, 2000 (Act 592).
*   National Identity Register Act, 2008 (Act 750).
*   Payment System Act, 2003 (Act 662).
*   Political Parties Act, 2000 (Act 574).
*   Public Office Holders (Declaration of Assets & Disqualification) Act, 1998 (Act 550).
*   Public Procurement Act, 2003 (Act 663).
*   Representation of the People Act, 1992 (PNDCL 284).
*   Value Added Tax Act, 1998 (Act 546).
*   Whistleblower Act, 2006 (Act 720).

Relevant policies
*   Code of Conduct for Public Officers of Ghana.
*   Anti-Corruption Manual (Gap Analysis).
*   National Anti-Corruption Strategy.
*   MOU by Key Accountability Institutions.
*   Government White Paper on CRC Report.
*   Ghana is a party to the African Union Convention on Preventing and Combating Corruption (signed 31/10/2003, ratified 13/06/2007, deposited instrument of ratification 20/07/2007).
*   In 2012, Ghana developed a National Anti-Corruption Action Plan.

Additional initiatives to fight corruption include the adoption of the United Nations Convention against Corruption (UNCAC) in 2003. The African Union (AU) convention against corruption and the ECOWAS protocol on the fight against corruption were adopted at the regional and sub-regional level.

Legal regime – are bribery and corruption criminal or civil offences?

Bribery and corruption as defined under Ghanaian law are purely criminal offences committed by or with a public official. Commercial bribery between private individuals is not recognised under Ghana law. It is, however, possible for a civil action to be instituted for restitution, against an official who has been convicted for bribery.

Historically, the first pieces of legislation in the fight against corruption were enacted in 1960 at the time of the formation of the first Republic. The Criminal Offences Act, 1960 (Act 29) criminalises active and passive bribery, extortion, exploitation of a public office and the use of public office for private gain, irrespective of the nationality of the bribe payer/taker. Acts of direct and indirect acts of corruption are illegal, as well as is attempting, preparing or conspiring to bribe both agents and principals.

Bribing governments or state-related officials

Chapter 5 of Act 29 creates offences relating to public officers and to public elections. Sections 239(a) and (b) of that Act make the paying and receiving of a bribe, oppression and extortion misdemeanours.

While Act 29 lists the prohibited acts that amount to corrupt practices, the Criminal and Other Offences (Procedure) Act, 1960 (Act 30), is the tool by which the prohibited practices can be punished and criminal prosecutions carried out. This statute not only complements Act 29, but also other statutes that create criminal offences, including corruption. Sections 240 and 241 of Act 29 define what amounts to corruption: (1) **by** a public officer as well as what would amount to corruption; and (2) **of** a public officer. An interesting provision is section 242 which guards against a person receiving such gifts prior to or in anticipation of assuming a public office, provided there is a reasonable expectation of the person assuming that office at the time of receiving the "gift".

Legislation relating to bribery and corruption

Several other statutes have been enacted to enhance the legal regime for the protection of public funds against corruption. Among these is the Public Procurement Act, 2003 (Act 663), which seeks to bring transparency to the issue of government procurement by making it compulsory to institute a tender process in the award of government contracts.

Others are the Customs and Excise and Preventive Service (Management) Law, 1993 (PNDCL 330), the Financial Administration Act, 2003 (Act 654), the Audit Service Act, 2000 (Act 584), and the Internal Audit Agency Act 2003, (Act 658). Each of these laws specifically criminalises the act of using one's public office for any form of private gain, actually given or promised.

Ghana has also passed into law an Anti-Money Laundering Act, 2008 (Act 749) as amended by the Anti-Money Laundering (Amendment) Act 2014 (Act 874). This act seeks to prevent persons from hiding or diluting proceeds from illegal activities through their use in a legitimate enterprise. Sections 1 and 2 thereof create the offences of money laundering and abetment, while section 3 places a punishment of either a fine of 5,000 penalty points or a custodial sentence of between 12 months and 10 years for the offence.

The Ghana Political Parties Law, 2000 (Act 574) requires all political parties and their office holders to periodically declare their personal assets, sources of funds, liabilities and expenditure in relation to elections in the Gazette. It also disqualifies persons who have been found by a competent authority to have acquired assets unlawfully, defrauded the State or abused his or her office.

The Whistleblowers Act was passed to provide an enabling environment for people to come forward and report corrupt practices without fear of repercussions. It grants them the protection they need from the persons they are reporting. Most importantly, it regulates conduct in both private and public sectors by encouraging employees to come forward with information on improprieties conducted by their employers, other employees or institutions. This statute makes provision for the protection of the whistleblower, as well as rewards them in the appropriate cases.

The Holders of Public Officers (Declaration and Disqualification) Act 1998 (Act 550), provides for the declaration of assets and liabilities by public office holders in conformity with Chapter 24 of the Constitution, to provide for disqualification from holding specified public offices as a result of an adverse finding made or a criminal conviction against an individual and to provide for related matters.

In addition to the above, various successive governments have set up Commissions of Inquiry, Public Tribunals, Citizen Vetting Committees, conducted House Cleaning Exercises, and established the National Anti-Corruption Strategy and Plans. Between the years 2001 and 2010, a Zero Tolerance for Corruption policy was launched, CHRAJ instituted Guidelines on Conflict of Interest to assist public officials to identify and manage conflict of interest situations, a Code of Conduct for Public Officers was launched, an Anti-Corruption manual was produced by the Ministry of Justice and a working group to develop the National Anti-Corruption Action Plan (NACAP) was inaugurated.

Process for whistleblowers

Under Part 2 of the Whistleblower Act, sections 4 to 11 provide the procedure for reporting an unlawful or illegal conduct or corrupt practices. The whistleblower is required to make a report to a person in authority where they have witnessed any wrongdoing or have information that such an infraction has occurred. The person receiving the report, where it is not the Attorney-General, is required to submit a written report to the A-G within seven (7) working days. The law requires certain investigative procedures be followed before a determination is made. Where these procedures have led to an acceptance of the findings, the whistleblower will be protected by the Act (**s. 12**).

Bodies involved in investigating and enforcing corrupt activities

For the purposes of enforcement, the most relevant bodies responsible for the fight against corruption are the Ghana Police, the Commission on Human Rights and Administrative Justice (CHRAJ), the Economic and Organised Crime Office (EOCO), the Attorney General's Office, the Financial Intelligence Centre (FIC), the Auditor General's Office, the Internal Audit Agency, the Public Procurement Authority, the Controller and Accountant-General's Department, the Bureau of National Investigations and the Public Accounts Committee of Parliament. Special Financial and Economic Crime Courts have also been established within the Judicial Service.

Commission for Human Rights and Administrative Justice (CHRAJ)

The functions of the Commission established by the Commission for Human Rights and Administrative Justice, 1993 (Act 456), include the duty to investigate, corruption, abuse of power and unfair treatment of any person by a public officer in the exercise of his official duties and taking all necessary steps including reports to the Attorney General (AG) and the Auditor General resulting from such investigations. It has special investigative powers, which allow it to issue subpoenas, but does not have the power to prosecute cases.

Internal Audit Agency

The Internal Audit Agency was established by the Internal Audit Act, 2003 (Act 658). The object of the Agency is to co-ordinate, facilitate and provide quality assurance for internal audit activities within the Ministries, Departments and Agencies (MDA) and the Metropolitan, Municipal and District Assemblies (MMDA) (Section 2 of Act 658). The functions of the Agency include ensuring that the financial activities of MDAs and MMDAs are in compliance with laws, policies, standards and procedures.

Economic and Organised Crime Office (EOCO)

The EOCO, formerly known as the Serious Fraud Office, was created by the EOCO Act, 2010 (Act 804). The EOCO was given enhanced powers in the prevention and detection of organised crime and generally to facilitate the confiscation of the proceeds of crime. EOCO has the power to seize currency and property if there are reasonable grounds to suspect that the currency is the proceeds of crime, or the currency is intended by the person for use in the commission of a serious offence, or if the holder of the currency is unable to account satisfactorily for the source of the currency (Section 23 Act 804). EOCO also has a duty to provide assistance to foreign agencies to locate or seize property in the country suspected to be property obtained from the commission of a serious offence (Section 32 of Act 804) and may conduct its investigations in conjunction with the security agencies.

Bureau of National Investigation

The Bureau of National Investigation is an integral part of the National Security Council and is the internal intelligence agency of Ghana. This force is more restricted in their investigative powers than the EOCO and was created under the Security and Intelligence Agencies Act, 1996 (Act 526). It investigates acts, which have caused or have the potential to sabotage the economy of Ghana.

The Financial Intelligence Centre

The Financial Intelligence Centre was established by the Anti-Money Laundering Act 2008 Act 749 (Section 4). The Centre has as its object the duty to assist in the identification of proceeds of an unlawful activity and the combat of money laundering activities. Money Laundering is an extraditable offence Under the Extradition Act 1960 (Section 45 of Act 749).

The Office of Accountability

The Office of Accountability was established by the President in 2003 as a watchdog agency for close monitoring of ministers and other executives.

With the exception of CHRAJ, these institutions generally prosecute, if at all, on the authority of the Attorney General, who is the chief legal officer of the state. Some of the investigative bodies have powers of prosecution, like the Police, BNI and EOCO. However, the offences that they can prosecute are generally restricted and larger cases, especially involving corruption issues, are referred to the Attorney General's department for review and prosecution where necessary.

Sanctions

Sanctions for corrupt acts vary. The Criminal Code categorises a corrupt act as a misdemeanour; a category of offence that attracts a sentence of not more than a three-year imprisonment. Section 296 (5) of the Criminal and Other Offences (Procedure) Act, 1960 (Act 30), however, imposes a term of imprisonment of not more than 25 years for specific sections in Act 30 including: Section 239 – Corruption of and by a public officer or juror; Section 252 – Accepting or giving bribe to influence a public officer or juror; Section 253 – Corrupt promise by a judicial officer or juror; and Section 260 – Withholding of public money by a public officer. These offences, even though categorised as misdemeanours, may attract much higher sentences under the Act. Under Section 179C of the same Act, a person commits a crime if, while holding public office, he or she uses his or her office for profit. In this instance the penalty is a fine of not less than 250 penalty units or a term of imprisonment not exceeding 10 years or both.

Other specific offences such as money laundering, bribery by a person or employee connected with the collection or disbursement of public money, a member of the Audit Service who commits a corrupt act, attract sanctions which range from fines to imprisonment between 12 months and 10 years.

Overview of enforcement activity within the last two years

There have been a series of matters prosecuted related to corruption.

(i) THE REPUBLIC v SELORMEY [2001-2002] 2 GLR 424

Even though this is a 2002 matter, I refer to it because it resulted in the incarceration of a Minister of State. It involved certain transactions that the then Deputy Minister for Finance entered into on behalf of the state and for which he approved payments of about **$1,297,500** to an entity he should not have made those payments to. He was found guilty and sentenced to eight years' imprisonment (consisting of two four-year terms to run consecutively). This was in addition to several fines as well as an order for the reparation of the monies embezzled.

(ii) OKUDZETO ABLAKWA (NO 2) & ANOTHER V. ATTORNEY-GENERAL & OBETSEBI-LAMPTEY (NO 2) [2012] 2 SCGLR

This case involved the grant of a lease of a government-owned house to a sitting government official. An action was commenced in the Supreme Court of Ghana by some Ghanaian citizens for a declaration that the disposal, lease or outright transfer of the disputed property to the second defendant, a Minister of State, smacked of cronyism and the same was arbitrary, capricious, discriminatory and a gross abuse of discretionary power vested in a public officer under the Constitution. While the Supreme Court held that the action could be brought by citizens, it was dismissed on the grounds that no evidence had been adduced to prove the allegations of corruption. The Supreme Court held that: "Where the plaintiffs would want those illegalities and improprieties to be tagged on to specific officers, they should be in the position to establish the facts which would support that belief and the basis of that belief in the illegalities and improprieties on the one hand, and the nexus which would amount to truth and justification for the accusations. The necessity to adduce proof would become even more imperative where, as in the instant case, the accusers had invited the court to declare the actions as tainted with cronyism, corruption, arbitrariness, capriciousness, conflict of interest and abuse of discretionary power vested in a public officer."

(iii) IN THE MATTER OF THE COMMISSION ON HUMAN RIGHTS AND ADMINISTRATIVE JUSTICE AND IN THE MATTER OF INVESTIGATIONS INTO ALLEGATIONS OF CORRUPTION, CONFLICT OF INTEREST AND ABUSE OF POWER AGAINST HON. DR. RICHARD ANANE (MP) AND THE MINISTER FOR ROADS TRANSPORT

In 2009, CHRAJ instituted corruption and abuse of power investigations against Dr. Anane, a Member of Parliament and Minister for Health based solely on media allegations.

One of the allegations levelled against Dr. Anane was that under the colour and by virtue of his public office, he improperly and corruptly paid or remitted directly as well as through several persons and some institutions and officers of state, monies in an amount totalling at least US$126,560.00 to one private person by the name Miss Alexandra O'Brien, a woman with whom he was reputed to have had an amorous relationship.

CHRAJ found that the evidence available showed the payments came out of his personal sources, through a friend and family. On the construction of the provisions of the Criminal Code, the evidence did not support the offence of corruption. The Commission accordingly found that the allegations were not proven.

The second allegation related to abuse of power. Dr. Anane, without due diligence and proper authority, purported to commit the nation to a project sponsored by the WHMP in which Miss O' Brien was involved. The Commission found that the Minister was in a conflict of interest situation as he had begun an intimate relationship after he opened negotiations/discussions with Miss O'Brien who was representing the said WHMP project.

The Commission, *inter alia*, recommended that the President of the Republic severely sanction the respondent by relieving him of his post as Minister of State for abusing his power and bringing his office and government to disrepute.

The respondent, after the CHRAJ decision, sought the intervention of the Supreme Court, challenging the "jurisdiction" of the CHRAJ to proceed with an investigation in a matter without the lodging of a formal complaint by an identifiable claimant. The Supreme Court upheld his objection and ruled that under 218 (e) of the Constitution, for CHRAJ to investigate complaints of violation of corruption and abuse of power, there must be a complaint from an identifiable complainant. The CHRAJ decision was consequently quashed, with significant implications for the ability of the Commission to initiate actions in matters of alleged corruption by public officials.

Significant cases currently under investigation

(i) THE GYEEDA MATTER

This concerns the Ghana Youth Employment and Entrepreneurial Development Agency (GYEEDA). The former National Co-coordinator of GYEEDA and a representative of Goodwill International Group (GIG) respectively, are facing various charges of causing financial loss of GH¢41.1 million to the state. The National coordinator is accused of making false claims for securing a $65 million facility from the World Bank. Another person stands accused of conspiring with the Coordinator to cause financial loss to the State. This matter is currently being prosecuted.

(ii) ALLEGATIONS OF BRIBERY IN THE JUDICIAL SERVICE

In August 2015, a private investigative team, Tiger Eye Private Investigations, published video evidence of 12 High Court judges, 22 lower court judges, hundreds of court clerks, seven attorneys and five police officers receiving bribes for the disposition of judicial outcomes. The video evidence was in at least some cases, secured by agents of the private investigator posing as interested parties and offering the officials involved bribes to secure bail and other rulings for their protégés. The video evidence has been aired publicly in Accra. A subsequent proposed airing in Ghana's second city, Kumasi, was blocked by court order.

These individuals implicated in this video are under investigation by their respective employers: the Attorney-General's Department; the Judicial Service; and the Ghana Police Service.

The current findings have placed the investigative journalist under the protection of the Whistleblowers Act and has been said to have been granted "immunity". Section 18 of the Act states that: "***A whistle blower is not liable to civil or criminal proceedings in respect of the disclosure unless it is proved that that whistle blower knew that the information contained in the disclosure is false and the disclosure was made with malicious intent.***"

The case has raised a huge amount of public interest and has started, at all levels, a public debate as to whether there was entrapment, whether the administrative procedures or prosecutorial processes should have precedence and has also raised concerns about the impact of the ongoing trial by the media and the public after a public airing of the videos.

There are questions regarding what "immunity" is about in this context and who has the power to grant it. The Whistleblowers Act does not empower the AG to grant immunity. It simply enables the whistleblower to apply to CHRAJ for protection against victimisation, request for police protection and offers protection from civil and criminal proceedings in respect of the disclosure.

The Whistleblowers Act protects people who come across evidence of corrupt acts. Does it protect those who suborn corruption?

Was Tiger Eye acting as an agent of the state? The Attorney General can ask a Whistleblower to conduct further investigations after an initial report is made. Does this somehow circumvent the normal rules on entrapment?

These are just some of the legal issues that are being raised in respect of this matter.

Law and policy relating to facilitating payments

The OECD defines a facilitating payment as a payment made to a government employee to speed up an administrative process where the outcome is already pre-determined. It is not intended to influence the outcome of the official's action, but its timing.

In Ghana, there is no specific legislation relating to facilitation payments. As discussed above, any payment, promise to pay or non-pecuniary assistance, which will benefit a public official personally regardless of amount, may be defined as a corrupt act.

The CHRAJ has published a Code of Conduct for Public Officers which seeks to provide guidance on how to manage conflict of interest situations, recruitment and employment, abuse and misuse of office, accepting gifts, gifts and gratuity checklist, use of public property, etc. Even though the terminology "facilitation payments" is not used in Ghanaian law, the payment of cash of any amount is categorically prohibited.

In relation to hospitality and entertainment, not much guidance is given. The Code does however permit a public official to accept social invitations under certain circumstances. The Constitutional Review Commission has made recommendations to pass the Code of Conduct into law. It is hoped that facilitation payments, entertainment and travel will be dealt with in more detail in this legislation.

Overview of cross-border issues

The Mutual Legal Assistance Act, 2010 (Act 807), was passed to assist in the implementation of agreements and other arrangements for collaboration with foreign jurisdictions and entities in relation to criminal matters. It gives the Attorney General and Minister of Justice the power to enter into an administrative arrangement with a foreign entity or state for mutual legal assistance in respect of an act, which if committed in Ghana would be a serious offence.

The Anti-Money Laundering Act, 2008 (Act 749), amended by the Anti-Money Laundering (Amendment) Act 2014 (Act 874), sets up the Financial Intelligence Centre (FIC) which is required to inform, advise, co-operate and exchange information in relation to money laundering and similar activities with their foreign counterparts. Act 874 clarified the original Act and sought to make the law more consistent with international standards and best practices. It also clarifies and strengthens, *inter alia*, the provisions on sharing of information with its foreign counterpart agencies.

Section 45 makes money laundering an extraditable offence under the Extradition Act, 196 (Act 22), as amended by the Extradition (Amendment) Decree, 1966 (NLCD 65).

The Extradition Act and its amendment were enacted to allow the surrender of fugitive criminals from countries with which Ghana has reciprocal arrangements.

How are overseas bribery and corruption laws impacting Ghana?

A number of countries, particularly the OECD countries, have passed laws on bribery and corruption of foreign officials. For various reasons, of particular relevance to Ghana are the FCPA and the UK Bribery Act. These two pieces of legislation have particularly far-reaching consequences for their citizens and corporations and for foreign companies listed on their stock exchanges. The FCPA, for example, criminalises the use of telephone, email or banking services in the United States, for the purpose of bribing a foreign official. A number of large international companies from these jurisdictions have attempted to satisfy these requirements by implementing fairly detailed anti-corruption policies, which their staff must comply with. The strict controls and policies imposed in relation to employment requests from government officials, facilitation payments, the handling of gifts, entertainment, corporate donations, the giving of hampers during holidays and travelling with government officials have had a direct impact on the way they conduct business in Ghana.

One of the impacts of these laws is in the area of petroleum. With the recent discovery of oil and gas in commercial quantities, the government passed laws to ensure the participation of Ghanaians in the industry. Under the Petroleum (Local Content Participation) Regulations 2013 (L.I. 2204), preference is given to indigenous companies and to joint ventures between foreign and indigenous companies in the granting of petroleum agreements, licences and provision of services to the petroleum industry. The direct consequence is that foreign companies operating in the Ghanaian petroleum industry must invest in joint ventures with local companies.

As a result, these entities become directly impacted by the US and UK legislation on corruption and may be required to demonstrate the existence of adequate anti-corruption procedures and policies if they are to attract the desired partners.

The new model agreements for petroleum blocks also require specific commitments by the parties regarding corruption.

Can a body corporate be found liable for bribery and corruption offences?

Section 192 of Act 30 allows a corporation to be charged singularly or jointly with any other persons, with an indictable offence. This Act applies to the corporation as it applies to any other accused. In view of the fact that bribery and corruption of a public official is categorised as a misdemeanour, it would appear that a body corporate cannot be charged for this offence.

Proposed reforms to legislation, guidelines or policies

A National Anti-Corruption Action Plan (NACAP) was prepared in 2011. It is a document which constitutes Ghana's national framework to drive anti-corruption activities for the next ten years. The plan offers a framework to mobilise public support and resources for a sustainable anti-corruption programme. It is intended that its action plans be integrated into national development plans and programmes for both public and private institutions.

Ghana has a number of bills pending that are relevant to the matter of corruption:
* Extradition Bill.
* Public Officers (Code of Conduct) Bill.
* Whistleblower (Amendment) Bill.

- Witness Protection Bill.
- Right to Information Bill.

Relevant policies under development include:
- Code of Conduct for Public Officers of Ghana.
- Anti-Corruption Manual (Gap Analysis).
- National Anti-Corruption Strategy.
- MOU by Key Accountability Institutions.
- Government White Paper on CRC Report Ghana is a party to the African Union Convention on Preventing and Combating Corruption (signed 31/10/2003, ratified 13/06/2007, deposited instrument of ratification 20/07/2007).

The impact of these laws when passed is intended be to bring Ghana to par with current trends in other jurisdictions in combatting corruption. For example, the protection that the Witness Protection Bill will bring would provide the confidence to whistleblowers that the current Whistleblowers Act does not provide.

The Public Officers (Code of Conduct) Bill is also expected to bring more clarity and transparency into the conduct of public officers. This bill, and the Right to Information Bill, should make it theoretically easier to access important data from public officials.

The government accepted some recommendations, *inter alia*, made by the Constitutional Review Commission, which was inaugurated in January 2010. It accepted recommendations to strengthen the judicial council to curb corruption in the judiciary, accepted proposals for new legislation on ethics and anti-corruption on "gifts" and what constitutes "conflict of interest" to assist the CHRAJ in determining complaints made against public officers. Further, in response to the Supreme Court decision in the Anane case, the government accepted the recommendation that the CHRAJ should be empowered to initiate investigations without a formal complainant in all aspects of its mandate and that all its decisions should be directly enforceable by the courts.

Conclusion

In spite of all the laws, policy guidelines and international conventions, Ghana continues to be plagued by bribery and corruption incidents. A review of the policies, legislation, amendments and formal institutions represent layer upon layer of *ad hoc* responses rather than a comprehensive and cohesive plan that can attempt to tackle the roots of corruption.

There is a need for a more holistic and comprehensive public policy review leading a restatement on the corruption laws. There is also a need for a greater focus on socialisation and consensus building at all levels on standards of public decency and ethics.

Sources

1. National Anti-Corruption Plan – www.chrajghana.com/wp-content/uploads/2012/08/nacap.pdf.
2. UNODC Review by Rwanda and Swaziland of the implementation by Ghana of articles 15 – 24 of Chapter III. "Criminalisation and law enforcement" and articles 44-50 of Chapter IV. "International Cooperation" of the United Nations Convention against Corruption review cycle 2010-2015.

Esi Tawia Addo-Ashong
Tel: +233 244 325436 / Email: tawia@ashongbenjamin.com

Tawia is the Managing Partner for Ashong Benjamin & Associates, a private law practice and partnership based in Accra, Ghana, recently founded by three lawyers of national and international repute. The firm offers legal services in energy (upstream and downstream), power, banking and finance, corporate and commercial, mergers and acquisitions, natural resources, tax, corporate governance and compliance and land transactions. Tawia's practice areas are mining, labour and employment, anti-bribery and corruption training programmes, offering specialised assistance to clients navigating the Ghanaian regulatory environment, and developing and maintaining communications between private enterprise and governmental departments. Tawia was, until the end of December 2014, Director for Legal and Government Relations in Newmont Ghana Gold Limited. She spearheaded the creation of the Ghana Business Integrity Forum, which brought together organisations under the auspices of the Ghana Anti-Corruption Coalition to collaborate and strengthen corporate anti-corruption policies in Ghana.

Ashong Benjamin & Associates

6 4th Norla Street, Labone, Accra, P.O. Box CT 6265, Cantonments, Accra, Ghana
Tel: +233 302 774378 / URL: http://www.ashongbenjamin.com

Hong Kong

Kareena Teh & Fabian Roday
Dechert

Brief overview of the law and enforcement regime

Introduction

Hong Kong has a reputation for having strong anti-corruption laws and an effective enforcement regime. In the recent past, Hong Kong's track record has suffered, however, as high-ranking executives of the Hong Kong government and the business community have been involved in corruption investigations. Over the last four years, Hong Kong has been dropping in its ranking in the Transparency International Corruption Perception Index (CPI). While it is still ranked as one of the least corrupt jurisdictions in the world in the CPI, it was ranked 17 out of 175 countries in 2014,[1] dropping from 12 out of 183 in 2011.[2]

The enforcement bodies

Hong Kong's main government body responsible for the investigation and prevention of corruption is the Independent Commission Against Corruption (ICAC) which was established in 1974 and had its 40-year anniversary in 2014. It was set up not only to investigate and prosecute corruption offences, but also to educate the public about corruption and work with relevant government departments to improve processes. For that purpose, the ICAC has three separate departments:

- the Operations Department;
- the Corruption Prevention Department; and
- the Community Relations Department.

The Operations Department is responsible for investigating corrupt practices under the Prevention Of Bribery Ordinance, Cap. 201 (POBO), the Elections (Corrupt and Illegal Conduct) Ordinance, Cap. 554 (E(CIC)O), and the Independent Commission Against Corruption Ordinance, Cap. 204 (ICACO), the Corruption Prevention Department for reducing the opportunities for corruption occurring within the Hong Kong government and other public bodies (by, for example, examining the practices and procedures of the government), and the Community Relations Department for educating the public on issues of corruption and obtaining public support for the work of the ICAC.

The ICAC is an independent body accountable and subject only to the Chief Executive of Hong Kong's orders and control. It is led by a Commissioner who is directly appointed by the Chief Executive.[3]

The ICAC is assisted by other government departments, such as the Hong Kong Police and the Department of Justice, as well as regulatory bodies such as the Securities and Futures Commission (SFC). Several departments of the Hong Kong Police, including the Commercial Crime Bureau, regularly assist the ICAC in its investigations, while the Department of Justice provides legal advice from time to time or as requested by the ICAC.

The SFC assists the ICAC in the investigations of listed companies and listed company personnel, and also refers its cases to the ICAC for further investigation and provides expert evidence to the ICAC as required.

The legal regime

Hong Kong's main law including relevant bribery and corruption offences is the POBO. It regulates both the public and private sectors. The public sector covers government departments, public bodies, prescribed officers[4] and public servants.[5] Prescribed officers include the civil service while public servants extend beyond employees of the government. The private sector covers anyone in a principal and agent relationship.

The POBO does not define the term "bribery". Rather, it creates offences that proscribe the soliciting, accepting or offering of an advantage.

The offences

There are seven specific offences under the POBO that relate to bribery in the public sector and one which has general application to both the public and private sectors.

Official bribery

The seven specific public sector offences are set out in Part II of the POBO in sections 3 to 8 and 10.

Sections 3 and 10 solely target prescribed officers. Section 3 makes it an offence for such prescribed officers to accept or solicit an advantage without the general or special permission of the Chief Executive, while section 10 makes it an offence for prescribed officers and the (current or former) Chief Executive to maintain a standard of living or be in control of wealth or property which is beyond their present or past emoluments, which they cannot satisfactorily explain.

Section 4 applies to public servants generally, and the Chief Executive, and makes it an offence to, without lawful authority or reasonable excuse, offer an advantage to a public servant or the Chief Executive for the performance of an act in the capacity of that public servant or the Chief Executive or to influence the transaction of any business with a public body. This section applies to the solicitation or acceptance of such advantage by a public servant or the Chief Executive in a similar manner. It is worth noting that section 4 is the only provision in the POBO that expressly applies extra-territorially and makes it an offence to offer, solicit or accept an advantage "whether in Hong Kong or elsewhere".

Section 5, 6 and 7 cover public sector contracts, tenders and auctions respectively. Section 5 makes it an offence to, without lawful authority or reasonable excuse, offer an advantage to a public servant or the Chief Executive for assistance in influencing the promotion, execution, or procuring of any contract with a public body or the payment of moneys provided in such contract. This section of the POBO also applies to the solicitation or acceptance of an advantage by a public servant or the Chief Executive in a similar manner. Sections 6 and 7 respectively make it an offence for any person to, without lawful authority or reasonable excuse, offer, solicit or accept an advantage for the withdrawal of a tender or a bid at an auction of a public body.

Section 8 makes it an offence for any person – while having dealings with the government or public bodies – to, without lawful authority or reasonable excuse, offer an advantage to any prescribed officer of the government or public servant employed by such public body.

Apart from the seven specific public sector bribery offences created by sections 3 to 8 and 10 of the POBO, section 9 (which covers both the public and private sectors) makes it an offence for an agent to accept an advantage for doing (or forbearing to do) any act or showing favour or disfavour to any person in relation to the business of that agent's principal.[6] It supplements the specific public sector offences, for example, by making it an offence for a public servant to use falsified documents to deceive his principal (i.e. the relevant public body), which is not covered by the other specific public sector offences. It has also been used by the Hong Kong courts to target bribery of foreign officials, who are not covered by the specific public sector offences. Relying on the broad definition of the term "agent" in section 2 (1) of the POBO, i.e. "including a public servant or any person employed by or acting for another", the courts have applied the section 9 offence to bribery of foreign officials where the *actus reus*, i.e. the offer, solicitation or acceptance of an advantage, is carried out in Hong Kong[7] (see also the section on 'Cases involving aspects of extraterritorial application of POBO' for a discussion on the relevant cases and the section below on 'Commercial bribery' for further discussion of this offence).

It is noteworthy that sections 3 and 8 of the POBO differ from sections 4 to 7 and 9 in that they do not require the advantage to be paid for a corrupt purpose, i.e. the offences under those sections do not require a quid-pro-quo, such as any act undertaken by the public servants in exchange for the advantage. Additionally, sections 4 and 9 of the POBO also differ from sections 3, 5 to 8 and 10 in that they expressly provide that no offence is committed if the solicitation or acceptance of the advantage is made with the permission of the public servant and/or agent's employer and/or principal (see also the section below on 'Statutory defences').

Hong Kong also maintains the common law offence of misconduct in public office. The elements of this offence include that a public official culpably misconducts himself in the course of or in relation to that public official's public office. The relevant misconduct has to be wilful and intentional. Hong Kong courts have used this offence to complement the provisions of the POBO and deal with situations not proscribed by the POBO.

Commercial bribery

Section 9 of the POBO which targets "corrupt transactions with agents" covers commercial bribery as well as official bribery (see section above on Official Bribery).

Under Section 9, it is an offence for an agent to accept an advantage without lawful authority or reasonable excuse for doing (or forbearing to do) any act or showing favour or disfavour to any person in relation to the business of that agent's principal.[8] In the same manner it is an offence for any person to offer an advantage to an agent to undertake the relevant conduct set out above.[9] While the POBO does not include provisions imposing requirements on companies to make and keep accurate books and records,[10] Section 9 makes it an offence for any agent to use falsified receipts, accounts or other documents for the purpose of misleading his or her principal.[11] It is worth noting that the offences under section 9 do not apply in cases where the agent has the principal's permission for the acceptance of the advantage (see section below on 'Statutory defences'). This means that section 9 mainly targets secret commission earned by an agent without the knowledge of his or her principal.

Conspiracy

Many of the recent bribery cases involve several defendants who have been charged with conspiracy to commit the bribery offences set out in Part II of the POBO. The offence of conspiracy is set out in section 159A of the Crimes Ordinance, Cap. 200, and requires that a person agrees with any other person on a course of conduct, which if the conduct is carried out will necessarily amount to the commission of an offence (by one or more parties of the agreement). It follows that a conspiracy under section 159A of the Crimes Ordinance is not an independent offence but requires the commission of a separate offence (even though this separate offence does not have to be carried out). Section 159A of the Crimes Ordinance also explicitly states that the separate offence that is the subject of the conspiracy has to be an offence triable in Hong Kong. This means that for cases involving the bribery of a foreign official, it is not enough when the agreement to bribe such foreign official is reached in Hong Kong (i.e. the conspiracy occurs in Hong Kong). For there to be a triable offence in Hong Kong, the relevant *actus reus* of the offence has to occur in Hong Kong, i.e. the offer of the bribe has to be made in Hong Kong. If the offer is made abroad then there is no triable offence under the POBO and therefore not all required elements for the conspiracy are present (see discussion in section below on 'Cases involving aspects of extraterritorial application of POBO').

Definition of bribery

The relevant provisions in the POBO include the term "advantage" rather than bribe or bribery when setting out the relevant corruption offences. As the use of the neutral term "advantage" would suggest, the scope of benefits offered or solicited that could fall within this term is very wide. According to the definition of "advantage" included in section 2 of the POBO, the following benefits are covered: property (defined in section 2 as "any gift, loan, fee, reward or commission consisting of money or of any valuable security or of other property or interest in property of any description"); employment; discharge of a debt; any other service or favour (other than entertainment); the exercise or forbearance from the exercise of any right, power or duty; and any offer or promise of any of the above benefits.

While the definition of "advantage" specifically excludes "entertainment", "entertainment" is narrowly defined as "the provision of food or drink, for consumption on the occasion when it is provided, and of any other entertainment connected with, or provided at the same time".[12] As such, the exemption of entertainment is limited to meals/drinks and other forms of entertainment that occur with such meals/drinks (e.g. music that is provided alongside a meal). Any entertainment provided outside of this narrow scope could still constitute an advantage under the POBO and lead to an exposure. In addition, according to guidelines on conduct and discipline of civil servants, a civil servant must avoid "lavish, or unreasonably generous or frequent entertainment, or any entertainment that is likely to give rise to any potential or real conflict of interest, put the officers in an obligatory position in the discharge of their duties, compromise their impartiality or judgement, or bring them or the public service into disrepute bearing in mind public perception".[13] There are also specific guidelines for officials appointed under the political appointment system that deal, *inter alia*, with entertainment and set out that politically appointed officials should not accept entertainment if the entertainment (for example, due to its excessive nature) may lead to embarrassment in the discharge of the official's function or bring the public service into disrepute.[14]

Statutory defences

The bribery offences in sections 4 to 9 of the POBO provide a statutory defence if there is "lawful authority or reasonable excuse" for the offer, solicitation or acceptance of the advantage. According to Section 24 of the POBO the burden of proof (that there was such lawful authority or reasonable excuse) lies with the accused. The standard of proof is the balance of probabilities. The POBO itself provides such lawful authority in sections 4 and 9, which allow a public servant (other than a prescribed officer) and/or agent to solicit and accept advantages with the permission of their employer and/or principal).

For prescribed officers, the Acceptance of Advantages (Chief Executive's Permission) Notice 2010 was put in place to, *inter alia*, limit the very broad application of section 3 of the POBO which prohibits the acceptance of any advantages. The Notice gives general permission for prescribed officers to accept advantages that fall outside four restricted categories (namely gifts, discounts, loan of money, and passage). For the restricted categories, the Notice sets out some narrowly defined limits within which advantages can be accepted by prescribed officers, including for example low value gifts on specific occasions such as weddings (up to HKD1,500 (US$195 / €175) and on any other occasion (up to HKD250 (US$32 / €30) provided that the person making the gift has no official dealings with the prescribed officer or his or her department.[15] Any advantages that do not fall within the exceptions provided by the Acceptance of Advantages (Chief Executive's Permission) Notice 2010 require the special permission of the relevant approving authority for such prescribed officer.[16]

Threshold for enforcement

The POBO does not include a *de minimis* exemption and even advantages of a very minor amount or value could potentially lead to exposure under the applicable provisions (see discussion of case involving "red envelopes" in section below on 'Enforcement activity' and discussion in section below titled 'Facilitation payments').

Other relevant anti-corruption laws

The ICAC is also responsible for enforcing the E(CIC)O. The E(CIC)O sets out offences related to corruption occurring during elections including for example cases where an advantage is paid to influence a person to stand or not stand as a candidate in elections[17] or where an advantage is paid to influence votes.[18]

The Banking Ordinance, Cap. 155, prohibits the receipt of commission by staff of relevant financial institutions for the procurement of any advance, loan, financial guarantee, credit facility, etc. from that financial institution.[19]

Penalties and legal consequences

Apart from the section 3 bribery offence which is a summary offence and carries a maximum prison term of one year,[20] the other bribery offences under Part II of the POBO are indictable offences and on indictment can lead to imprisonment of up to 10 years for offences under sections 5, 6 and 10 and imprisonment of up to seven years for all other offences.[21] On indictment, section 10 carries a maximum fine level of HKD 1 million (US$130,000 / €115,000) while all other offences carry a maximum fine of HKD500,000 (US$65,000 / €57,500) (with the exception again being section 3 with a maximum fine of HKD100,000 (US$13,000 / €11,500). In addition, an offender may be ordered to disgorge the advantage received (or for section 10 a sum not exceeding the unexplained property).[22]

Under section 12A of the POBO, an offender who is convicted of conspiracy to commit a bribery offence under Part II of the POBO shall be sentenced as if he or she is convicted of the bribery offence itself.

The offences under the E(CIC)O described above are indictable offences and carry a maximum prison term of seven years and a maximum fine level of HKD500,000 (US$65,000 / €57,500). The offence of receiving commission under the Banking Ordinance is also an indictable offence and carries a maximum prison term of five years and a maximum fine level of HKD200,000 (US$26,000 / €23,000).

Overview of enforcement activity and policy during the past two years

The ICAC processes a large number of corruption complaints each year. The ICAC receives such complaints ("Corruption Reports") through its whistle-blowing hotline and the ICAC offices. Once a Corruption Report is received, the ICAC assesses internally whether the Corruption Report is "pursuable" or "non-pursuable". If the Corruption Report is pursuable, the investigations section of the ICAC will commence investigations.

In recent years, the number of Corruption Reports received by the ICAC has declined and the total annual Compliance Reports hit a four-year low in 2014. While the ICAC received 3,868 Corruption Reports in 2011, this figure has gradually declined, and in 2014 it only received 2,236 Corruption Reports. This figure represents a decline of 58%. In 2015, this trend is likely to continue albeit the decrease is much less pronounced: The ICAC received 1,116 Corruption Reports for the period of January to June 2015, which is a decrease of 0.3% compared with the same period in 2014.[23] Of these 1,116 Corruption Reports, those on suspected corruption in the government and public bodies have decreased, while those on suspected corruption in the private sector have increased by 8% when compared with the figures for 2014.

Important cases

Despite the downward trend in the numbers of Corruption Reports, the ICAC has investigated a number of high-profile corruption cases in the recent past which have resulted in the prosecution and conviction of high-ranking officials and members of Hong Kong's business community.

Former Chief Secretary and business tycoon

In December 2014, the ICAC case against the former Chief Secretary for Administration in Hong Kong, Rafael Hui Si-yan, concluded, after a trial lasting 128 days, with his conviction on five counts of misconduct in public office and bribery. Hui was sentenced to seven-and-a-half years in jail and ordered to return bribes in the amount of HKD 11,182,000 (US$1.4 million / €1.3 million). As the Chief Secretary for Administration heads the Government Secretariat, Hui was second only to the Chief Executive in terms of seniority within the lines of the government officials in Hong Kong, and the highest ranking government official to date to be convicted for corruption-related offences.

For his involvement in payments made to Hui, Thomas Kwok, co-chairman of a leading property developer in Hong Kong, was found guilty of one count of conspiracy to commit misconduct in public office, sentenced to a prison term of five years and fined HKD500,000 (US$65,000 / €57,500). Kwok's brother Raymond Kwok, the other co-chairman of the relevant property development was acquitted. Thomas Chan Kui-yuen, an executive of the property developer, and Francis Kwan Hung-sang, a former senior staff at the Hong Kong stock exchange, were both convicted and sentenced to prison terms of six and five years respectively for their roles in facilitating the transfer of bribes to Hui.

Hui, the Kwok brothers, Chan and Kwan were first arrested in March 2012 and officially charged by the ICAC in July 2012. The ICAC based its charges on a number of payments made to Hui by companies and middlemen connected with the Hong Kong property developer run by the Kwok brothers, and on the rent-free use of two expensive apartments owned by and granted to Hui by the property developer. In exchange for the various payments and the free-of-charge use of the apartments Hui was not expected to conduct any particular act on behalf of the property developer or the relevant persons involved in the matter. Rather, Hui received these benefits in exchange for his favourable disposition and goodwill as Chief Secretary towards the property developer and its subsidiaries and associated companies. As of September 2015, Hui, Kwok, Chan and Kwan have appealed their verdicts, with the hearing to commence in November 2015.

Former Chief Executive

In October 2015, the former Chief Executive of Hong Kong, Donald Tsang Yam-kuen, was charged with two counts of misconduct in public office, contrary to the law. The charges relate to a luxury residential unit in Shenzhen, China (the "Residential Unit") leased by Tsang. The charges cover, *inter alia*, Tsang's alleged concealment from, or failure to declare or disclose to:

1) the Executive Council (ExCo) – his negotiations with the majority shareholder of a radio station to lease the Residential Unit and a related payment, when the ExCo was considering and approving the radio station's various licences or related applications, and

2) the then Permanent Secretary for the Chief Executive's Office, the Development Bureau and the Honours and Non-Official Justices of the Peace Selection Committee – his interest in the Residential Unit and his engagement of an interior designer for interior design work for the Residential Unit, when he proposed that the designer be referred for consideration for nomination under Hong Kong's honours and awards system.

Tsang was released on bail pending the hearing of the charges.

The ICAC commenced its investigations into allegations against Tsang in February 2012 when Tsang was still in office as the Chief Executive. Apart from the above charges, the ICAC also investigated other allegations relating to Tsang's acceptance of complimentary or cheap rides in private yachts or jets owned by members of the Hong Kong business community to various travel destinations during Tsang's tenure as Chief Executive from 2005 to 2012. When Tsang was charged in October 2015, the Department of Justice confirmed that there is insufficient evidence to justify the commencement of criminal prosecution in respect of the other allegations against Tsang.

Former ICAC Commissioner

The ICAC has launched a criminal investigation into the conduct of its former Commissioner, Timothy Tong Hin-ming. Following media reports on the former Commissioner's handling of official entertainment, gifts, and duty visits, the Chief Executive announced the establishment of the Independent Review Committee on the ICAC's Regulatory Systems and Procedures for handling Official Entertainment, Gifts and Duty Visits on 2 May 2013. After its review, the committee presented its report[24] in September 2013 and identified several non-compliances and short-comings in relation to entertainment, gifts and official visits during Tong's term as ICAC Commissioner. The report highlighted, *inter alia*, occasions where during meals, alcoholic beverages were procured separately in order to comply with the per person expenditure limit for meals, multiple occasions where such expenditure limits for lunches or dinners were exceeded, instances where official gifts given exceeded expenditure limits, and official duty visits that involved excessive activities that were not related to official duty. As some of the lavish dinners involved officials from China, and Tong was appointed as a delegate to the Chinese People's Political Consultative Conference, an influential political advisory body in China, following the end of his tenure as Commissioner, one of the specific criticisms is that Tong may have used public funds to advance his own career. In response, the government in January 2014 published new guidelines regulating gifts and entertainment for government departments. Under the new guidelines, gifts should only be given when "necessary" or "unavoidable", and extravagant gifts should be avoided. As of October 2015, the ICAC has not published any outcome of its criminal investigation against Tong.

Red envelopes/gifts of trivial value

While the ICAC has investigated high-profile cases in the recent past and obtained convictions against high-ranking officials, it also continues to investigate and prosecute smaller corrupt acts that occur in the regular course of business. One such case from 2014 confirms that under the POBO there is no *de minimis* exemption for bribery in low or trivial amounts. In an appeal from a Magistrate Court's decision, the Court of First Instance confirmed that low value gifts given in the form of "red envelopes" containing cash can lead to an exposure under the POBO. In the relevant case, the appellant was convicted for having given "red envelopes" to supermarket managers on three occasions in exchange for information on the super market's sales performance and stock of milk powder. The red envelopes contained cash gifts that ranged from HKD100 (US$13 / €11) to HKD800 (US$100 / €90). The Magistrate Court had sentenced the appellant to a six-month prison term for a violation of section 9 of the POBO (corrupt transactions with agents). On appeal, the Court of First Instance confirmed the sentence of the Magistrate Court.

Cases involving aspects of extraterritorial application of the POBO

Offer of a bribe to a foreign official made outside of Hong Kong

In a landmark decision, the Court of Appeal (CACC 99/2012, 18 December 2013)[25] held that section 9 of the POBO does not apply extraterritorially to an offer of a bribe made outside of Hong Kong aimed at inducing acts of a foreign official, and any agreement made in Hong Kong to make such an offer is not triable in Hong Kong as a conspiracy under section 159A of the Crimes Ordinance, Cap. 200. The decision was confirmed by the Court of Final Appeal on 1 August 2014 (FAMC 1/2014) when the prosecution's leave to appeal application was dismissed.

In the relevant case, two executives of a Macau waste management company (majority owned by a Hong Kong-based company) devised a plan in Hong Kong to bribe a Macau public official to obtain a renewal and award of government contracts for the waste management company. However, the actual offer to the public official was only made at a later stage and outside of Hong Kong. The two defendants were convicted of conspiracy to offer advantages to an agent, contrary to section 9 (2) (a) of the POBO and section 159A of the Crimes Ordinance. Each was sentenced to three years and three months' imprisonment.

The Court of Appeal reversed the convictions. In doing so, it held that an offence under section 9 of the POBO is only complete when the offer of the bribe is communicated to the recipient. As the offer was communicated in Macau and not Hong Kong, it was not triable as an offence under section 9 of the POBO. Additionally, as a conspiracy under section 159A of the Crimes Ordinance is not a separate offence but requires the commission of an offence that is triable in Hong Kong, the acts of planning that were made in Hong Kong were also not triable in Hong Kong.

Offer of Bribe to Foreign Official made in Hong Kong

Prior to the above case involving the offer of a bribe in Macau, the Court of Final Appeal considered a case (FACC 6/2009, 19 January 2010)[26] with similar facts but where the foreign official was offered the bribe in Hong Kong. In that case, the Court of Final Appeal found that the definition of "agent" under the POBO was broad enough to include a public official of a place outside Hong Kong, and that section 9 of the POBO applies where an advantage is offered in Hong Kong, even if the offeree is a public official of a place outside Hong Kong and the act or forbearance concerned is in relation to his public duties in that place outside Hong Kong. As such, an agreement made in Hong Kong in respect of the offer is a conspiracy under section 159A of the Crimes Ordinance and therefore triable in Hong Kong.

Law and policy relating to issues such as facilitation payments and hospitality

Facilitation payments

Some jurisdictions such as the USA provide for narrow exceptions in their anti-bribery laws for "facilitating payments". In the U.S. Foreign Corrupt Practices Act (FCPA), this exception applies only for cases where a payment is made to further "routine governmental action" involving non-discretionary acts.[27] The POBO does not include any similar exception for facilitation payments. Instead, the text of the relevant bribery offence explicitly includes advantages offered for "expediting" the performance of an act by a public servant.[28] As set out above, there is also no *de minimis* threshold under the POBO that excludes small payments from prosecution. As such, any payment including to facilitate or expedite a routine government act would *prima facie* constitute an offence under the POBO (unless any of the statutory defences set out above applies).

Hospitality

The POBO excludes entertainment from the relevant definition of an "advantage". This exemption is however narrowly defined and only applies to "the provision of food or drink, for consumption on the occasion when it is provided, and of any other entertainment connected with, or provided at the same time".[29] As such, any entertainment provided outside of a meal or drinks would potentially fall within the relevant definition of 'advantage' under the POBO. For public servants, it is worth noting that specific guidelines apply that prohibit lavish entertainment (see also the above section on 'Definition of bribery').

Key issues relating to investigation, decision-making and enforcement procedures

Investigation powers

The ICAC has far-reaching investigative powers that it exercises independently of any other government body. According to section 12 of the ICACO, the Commissioner has the duty to investigate:
- complaints alleging corrupt practices as he considers practicable;
- alleged or suspected offences under the POBO / E(CIC)O or conspiracies to commit such offences;
- alleged or suspected offences of blackmail or conspiracy to blackmail by or through the misuse of the office of a prescribed officer; and
- any conduct of a government officer that is connected with or conducive to corrupt practices.

To assist ICAC officers in their investigations, the ICACO provides a right in section 10 for ICAC officers to arrest without a warrant any person the officers reasonably suspect to be guilty of an offence under the POBO, E(CIC)O and ICACO, or of an offence of blackmail committed by or through the misuse of office (if the relevant suspect is a prescribed officer). This section also gives the ICAC officers a right to arrest without warrant a suspect whom the officers reasonably suspect to be guilty of other offences that are revealed during their corruption investigations.

Part III of the POBO also sets out various measures aimed at assisting the ICAC in its investigations of suspected corrupt practices. It provides ICAC officers with the power to:
- inspect and take copies of accounts, books, documents or other articles which may be required for the purpose of investigations (it is worth noting that no court order is required before this power can be exercised);[30]
- make an *ex parte* application to the Court of First Instance for production or access to particular material held by the Inland Revenue Department;[31]
- make an *ex parte* application to the Court of First Instance for the provision of information by any suspect in relation to, for example property, expenditures, etc. of such suspect or any other person believed to be acquainted with relevant facts,[32] including attending an interviews with the ICAC officers;[33]
- make an application to the Court of First Instance[34] for a restraining order to be imposed on relevant property in the control of a suspect;[35]
- make an *ex parte* application to the Court of First Instance for a search warrant;[36] and

- make an *ex parte* application to a magistrate for the surrender of travel documents held by a suspect.[37]

An ICAC officer may also apply to any public servant for assistance with ongoing investigations into an alleged or suspected offence.

It is an indictable offence for persons to refuse to comply with what the ICAC requires them to do or produce, or to make a false statement. The relevant offences carry a maximum prison term of one year and a maximum fine of HKD20,000 (US$2,600 / €2,300).[38]

Safeguards

While the ICAC operates independently when exercising its broad investigation powers, there are a number of safeguards that ensure a suspect's rights are not prejudiced.

As set out above, most of the ICAC's investigative powers (apart from section 13 of the POBO) require an application to the court and are therefore subject to judicial oversight.

Additionally, section 14 (1) (d) of the POBO provides that statements compelled by the ICAC in the exercise of its investigative powers are not admissible in prosecutions against the person making such statement.

Section 15 of the POBO and section 18 of the ICACO also expressly safeguard legal professional privilege. In order to avoid a waiver of privilege, it is important for legal advisers to claim privilege on behalf of their clients over any privileged information that is seized by the ICAC officers. If the ICAC disputes the claim of privilege, they will seal the information. The owner of the information will then have to establish privilege by way of an application to the Court of First Instance. On such an application, the judge can examine the documents seized by the ICAC to determine whether the documents are privileged. In some cases, the warrants authorising the seizure of the relevant information prescribe a timeframe for bringing the application. The ICAC will have recourse to the information seized if no application is made within the timeframe specified in the warrant or if the Court of First Instance rules that the information is not legally privileged.

Whistle-blowers

In detecting possible corruption offences the ICAC relies heavily on information provided by the general public. For that purpose, the ICAC maintains a whistle-blower hotline as well as a Report Center, both of which are staffed with duty officers and are active around the clock. To protect the identity of whistle-blowers and the information provided, section 30A of the POBO provides, *inter alia*, that the name and address of any informer are kept confidential and any documents that may lead to a disclosure of such informer's identity will have to be redacted prior to any disclosure of the same in civil or criminal proceedings. The ICAC also offers witness protection programmes, established and maintained in accordance with the Witness Protection Ordinance, Cap 564, which provide protection and other assistance for witnesses whose personal safety or well-being may be at risk as a result of being witnesses for the ICAC.

Despite the ICAC's heavy reliance on information provided by the public there is no positive duty under the POBO to report corruption to the ICAC. Such a duty exists, however, under the Organized and Serious Crimes Ordinance, Cap. 455 (OSCO): Section 25A (1) of the OSCO imposes a duty to report on any person who knows or suspects that any property was used in connection with or represents the proceeds of an indictable offence (including bribery and corruption). Failure to make a disclosure under section 25A (1) is an offence, and is punishable by imprisonment for three months and a fine of level 5 (currently equivalent to HKD50,000 (US$6,500 / €5,750), according to Criminal Procedure Ordinance, Cap. 221, Schedule 8).

Confidentiality of investigations

All investigations are confidential. The POBO makes it an offence to tip-off a possible subject of an ICAC investigation, and offenders could be liable for a prison term of up to one year and a fine of HKD20,000 (US$2,600 / €2,300).[39] Similarly, the OSCO also makes it an offence to tip-off. Any person who discloses to any other person any matter which is likely to prejudice any investigation which might be conducted following a disclosure under section 25A of the OSCO could be liable upon conviction on indictment for a fine of up to HKD500,000 (US$65,000 / €57,500) and imprisonment for up to three years.[40]

Enforcement

On concluding its investigations, the ICAC has to prepare the evidence and submit it to the Secretary of Justice (i.e. the head of the Department of Justice) for consideration. This is because under section 31 (1) of the POBO prosecutions for offences under Part II of the POBO shall be instituted only with the consent of the Secretary for Justice. This consent requirement reflects the separation of investigation and prosecution within the common law criminal justice system and provides for an independent assessment through the Secretary of Justice whether a prosecution is in the best interests of the public.

If the Secretary of Justice is of the opinion that the evidence is sufficient to warrant a prosecution but in the particular case such prosecution may not be in the best interest of the public, the Secretary of Justice can decide to "caution" the subject provided that the subject has admitted his or her guilt. The caution, if administered, will be kept on record and can be taken into consideration for future cases for the decision of whether to prosecute or on sentencing. Factors that the Secretary of Justice may take into account in arriving at his decision include the seriousness of the offence, the likely penalty upon conviction, the effect on the accused, etc.

Overview of cross-border issues

Extraterritorial application of the POBO

As set out above the only bribery offence under the POBO that expressly applies extraterritorially is section 4 which regulates the bribery of public servants (which is limited by its definition to Hong Kong public servants). The extraterritorial application of section 4 stems from the words "whether in Hong Kong or elsewhere" which qualify the relevant conduct, i.e. the offer, solicitation or acceptance of the advantage found in the offences set out in section 4, making offers of advantages to public servants and/or solicitations and/or acceptances of advantages by public servants offences whether they take place in Hong Kong or outside Hong Kong. As such, offenders cannot escape the scope of section 4 by offering the bribe and/or soliciting or accepting the bribe in a place outside Hong Kong.

As confirmed by relevant case law (see discussion on 'Cases involving aspects of extraterritorial application of the POBO' above), all the other bribery offences under the POBO require the relevant conduct, i.e. the offer, solicitation or acceptance of the advantage to occur in Hong Kong, otherwise the relevant conduct does not constitute a triable offence in Hong Kong.

Foreign public officials

The POBO applies to the bribery of foreign public officials albeit to a very limited extent. The Hong Kong Court of Final Appeal has confirmed that section 9 of the POBO can apply to the bribery of foreign public officials as a foreign public official can fall within the definition of "agent" under the POBO. However, as section 9 of the POBO does not have an extraterritorial effect, the bribery of a foreign official is only covered by section 9 of the POBO if the relevant conduct of offering, soliciting or accepting of an advantage occurs in Hong Kong.

International cooperation

Hong Kong provides mutual legal assistance to other jurisdictions under the United Nations Convention against Corruption (UNCAC) and via a number of bilateral treaties.

Hong Kong, as a special administrative region of China (which is a signatory of the UNCAC), is required to provide mutual legal assistance in investigations, prosecutions and judicial proceedings in relation to the offences covered by the UNCAC.[41] The Secretary for Justice of the Department of Justice is China's designated authority in Hong Kong for receiving requests for mutual legal assistance and cooperation on surrender of fugitive offenders under the UNCAC. The ICAC is designated as the relevant authority in Hong Kong responsible for assisting other signatories of the UNCAC in developing and implementing specific measures for the prevention of corruption. Since the UNCAC came into force in Hong Kong on 12 February 2006, the ICAC has received more than 20 requests for assistance under the UNCAC.[42] For its support with extradition and mutual legal assistance under the UNCAC, the ICAC relies on the Fugitive Offenders Ordinance, Cap. 503, and the Mutual Legal Assistance in Criminal Matters Ordinance, Cap. 525, which as a result of legislative amendments in 2007 apply as between Hong Kong and the States Parties of the UNCAC.

Hong Kong has also signed bilateral agreements for mutual legal assistance with 29 jurisdictions.[43] The statutory framework for implementing these bilateral agreements (as in the case of the UNCAC) is the Mutual Legal Assistance in Criminal Matters Ordinance. Similar to the designation under the UNCAC, the Department of Justice is responsible for coordinating requests for international extraditions and mutual legal assistance, and does so through its Mutual Legal Assistance Unit. In addition, the INTERPOL Division of the Hong Kong Police's Liaison Bureau works closely with the Mutual Legal Assistance Unit in executing international extraditions and mutual legal assistance requests. In 2014, the ICAC handled 34 requests from overseas jurisdictions for investigative assistance and received assistance for eight requests it placed with its overseas counterparts including in Japan, the Republic of Korea, Malaysia, New Zealand, Singapore and the United States of America.[44]

Corporate liability for bribery and corruption offences

Prosecutions of corporates are extremely rare under Hong Kong's applicable corruption laws. In general, the ICAC's investigations and prosecutions target individuals (see case examples set out in the section on enforcement activity that primarily deal with individuals).

The POBO does not include strict liability offences for corporates. Corporates can, however, be prosecuted under the POBO for bribery offences because they apply to any "person", which is defined under Hong Kong laws to include both natural persons as well as any public body and any body of persons, corporate or unincorporated.[45] In determining if a corporate is liable, the courts apply the common law, and in particular the "identification principle" which holds a corporate liable for the acts of its officers who are in control of the corporate and who commit the offences in question.

Proposed reforms / The year ahead

Hong Kong's reputation as one of the least corrupt places in the world has suffered in recent years. Media reports of corruption within the highest echelons of Hong Kong's administration and business community (see the discussion in the above section on 'Important cases') have impacted the previously good reputation of Hong Kong, its government and business community. This is evident from Hong Kong's four-year slide on the Corruption Perception Index of Transparency International (from rank 12 in 2011 to rank 17 in 2014)[46] and the progressive four-year decline in Corruption Reports that the ICAC received from the general public in the same timeframe.

In response, criminal investigations were undertaken by the ICAC which led to successful convictions of the former Chief Secretary Hui and the business tycoons Kwok, Chan and Kwan at the end of 2014, and the prosecution of the former Chief Executive Tsang in October 2015. Independent reviews were also undertaken in relation to the conduct of the former Chief Executive Tsang and the former ICAC Commissioner Tong. While an outcome of the investigation against former ICAC Commissioner Tong is still pending, the government has already implemented several recommendations of the independent reviews conducted in connection with the independent reviews and further reforms are likely to follow.

One of the recommended reforms under consideration relates to a "fundamental defect" in the present system regulating the solicitation or acceptance of advantages under sections 3 and 8 of the POBO which was identified by the Independent Review Committee for the Prevention and Handling of Potential Conflicts of Interests set up on 26 February 2012 in its report presented in May 2012.[47] Presently, sections 3 and 8 apply to officials under the political appointment system and civil servants, but not the Chief Executive. The committee recommended that both sections be amended to include the Chief Executive within their scope. On receipt of the committee's report, the Government stated it generally agreed with the findings and considered how to implement the recommendations. In October 2015, the Government stated that it is still considering the implications of the recommended changes to the POBO. At this stage, it is unclear when the relevant amendments to the POBO will be implemented.

The proactive criminal investigations, independent reviews and reforms undertaken so far demonstrate that Hong Kong, through the government and the ICAC, is actively addressing the issues that have led to Hong Kong's downward slide on the Corruption Perception Index of Transparency International. Going forward, provided the criminal investigation and prosecution are resolved properly, and the recommended amendments to the POBO are implemented to help ensure that similar cases are less likely to occur in the future, Hong Kong will be well placed to continue its successful history of fighting corruption and eventually regain its favourable ranking on the Corruption Perception Index of Transparency International.

* * *

Endnotes

1. Transparency International, CPI Results 2014: http://www.transparency.org/cpi2014/results.
2. Transparency International, CPI Results 2011: http://www.transparency.org/cpi2011/results.
3. See Article 57 of the Basic Law of the Hong Kong Special Administrative Region.
4. A prescribed officer includes mainly persons holding an office of emolument under the Government, officials of the Monetary Authority, members of the ICAC, judicial officers and the Chairman of the Public Service Commission (Section 2 (1) POBO).
5. A public servant includes prescribed officers and employees of public bodies (Section 2 (1) POBO).
6. Section 9 (1) POBO.
7. Hong Kong Court of Final Appeal, *B v Commissioner of the Independent Commission Against Corruption* [2010] HKEC 122.
8. Section 9 (1) POBO.
9. Section 9 (2) POBO.
10. Other laws in Hong Kong include such requirement, for example, the Companies Ordinance, Cap. 622, which provides in section 380 that a company has to maintain annual financial

statements for a financial year that give a true and fair view of the financial position of the company and the financial performance of the company for the financial year.
11. Section 9 (3) POBO.
12. Section 2 (1) POBO.
13. See publication of the Administration of the Civil Service, Summary of the Regulatory Regime on Acceptance of Advantages and Entertainment by Civil Servants: http://www.csb.gov.hk/english/admin/conduct/files/aae_e.pdf.
14. Chief Executive's Office, Code for Officials under the Political Appointment System, Chapter 5.10, http://www.cmab.gov.hk/doc/issues/code_en.pdf.
15. Acceptance of Advantages (Chief Executive's Permission) Notice 2010. http://www.csb.gov.hk/hkgcsb/rcim/pdf/english/central/aan_e.pdf.
16. The relevant approving authorities are set out in section 1 of the Acceptance of Advantages (Chief Executive's Permission) Notice 2010.
17. Section 7 E(CIC)O.
18. Section 11 E(CIC)O.
19. Section 124 Banking Ordinance.
20. Section 12 (2) POBO.
21. Section 12 (1) POBO.
22. Section 12 (1) (2) (3) POBO.
23. Number of Corruption Complaints received by the ICAC, published on the ICAC website at: http://www.icac.org.hk/en/useful_information/cr/index.html.
24. Report of the Independent Review Committee on ICAC's Regulatory Systems and Procedures for handling Official Entertainment, Gifts and Duty Visits, dated September 2013. http://www.gov.hk/en/theme/irc-icac/pdf/irc-icac-report.pdf.
25. Court of Appeal, *HKSAR v Lionel John Krieger & Tam Ping Cheong James* [2013] HKCU 2898.
26. Hong Kong Court of Final Appeal, *B v Commissioner of the Independent Commission Against Corruption* [2010] HKEC 122.
27. US Department of Justice, Securities Exchange Commission, A Resource Guide to the U.S. Foreign Corrupt Practices Act, page 25.
28. Section 4 (1) (b) POBO.
29. Section 2 (1) POBO.
30. Section 13 POBO.
31. Section 13A POBO.
32. Section 14 POBO.
33. Section 14 (1) (d) POBO.
34. Section 14C (7) POBO
35. Section 14C POBO.
36. Section 17 POBO.
37. Section 17A POBO.
38. Sections 13 (3) (4) and 14 (4) (5) POBO.
39. Section 30 POBO.
40. Section 25A (5) and (9) OSCO.
41. Article 46 (1) UNCAC.
42. ICAC publication, "40 years in the Operations Department", page 119 (available at: http://www.icac.org.hk/en/about_icac/p/index.html).
43. Department of Justice, List of Mutual Legal Assistance Agreements (Legislative References): http://www.doj.gov.hk/eng/laws/table3ti.html.
44. ICAC, Annual Report 2014, page 45 (available at: http://www.icac.org.hk/en/about_icac/p/index.html).
45. Interpretation and General Clauses Ordinance, Cap. 1, section 3.
46. Transparency International, Corruption Perception Index, Result 2014: http://www.transparency.org/cpi2014/results. Result 2011: http://www.transparency.org/cpi2011/results.
47. Independent Review Committee for the Prevention and Handling of Potential Conflicts of Interests, Report dated May 2012 http://www.legco.gov.hk/yr11-12/english/panels/ca/papers/ca0604-rpt20120531-e.pdf.

Kareena Teh
Tel: +852 3518 4755 / Email: Kareena.Teh@dechert.com
Kareena Teh advises multinational, Hong Kong and PRC clients in governance, regulatory and compliance matters, contentious government, regulatory and internal investigations, and corporate and commercial disputes. Ms. Teh's experience in these areas includes representing companies and individuals in cross-border fraud, corruption, money laundering and market misconduct investigations. She also represents such clients in actions involving directors' and officers' liability, joint venture disputes, shareholders' remedies, insolvency, asset-tracing and recovery, insurance and enforcement of judgments and arbitration awards. Ms. Teh was the first female solicitor in Hong Kong to be granted higher rights of audience, a designation permitting select, highly qualified litigators to represent clients in civil matters in all levels of Hong Kong's judicial system.

Ms. Teh was recognised by the 2015 edition of *The Legal 500 Asia Pacific* and was profiled in the 2015 edition of *Global Investigations Review*'s "Women in Investigations" that highlights 100 remarkable women from around the world for their accomplishments in this area of law.

Fabian Roday
Tel: +852 3518 4706 / Email: Fabian.Roday@dechert.com
Fabian Roday is an associate in the litigation group of Dechert's Hong Kong office. Mr. Roday focuses his practice on government and internal investigations, commercial litigation and international arbitration. He has assisted multinational clients with government and internal compliance investigations involving cross-border fraud, corruption and customs violations in various jurisdictions. Mr. Roday regularly provides clients with compliance advice covering a wide range of topics, including the design of compliance programmes, policies and procedures as well as the implementation of government-mandated monitoring requirements. He has also assisted clients with complex cross-border litigation involving legal issues in various jurisdictions and international arbitration of disputes. Mr. Roday has represented clients in various industries, including automotive, food & beverage, life sciences, paper and packaging, and solar energy.

Mr. Roday is qualified as a lawyer in Hong Kong and New York. He is fluent in English, German and Mandarin.

Dechert

27/F Henley Building, 5 Queen's Road, Central, Hong Kong
Tel: +852 3518 4700 / Fax: +852 3518 4777 / URL: dechert.com

Indonesia

R. Suharsanto Raharjo & Pamela Kiesselbach
Hiswara Bunjamin Tandjung in association with Herbert Smith Freehills

Overview of the Indonesia anti-corruption law and enforcement regime

Corruption is a topical and a nationwide issue in Indonesia. On the one hand, providing gifts is a culture in Indonesia. On the other hand, Indonesia's anti-corruption regime is overarching and there is a gap between what is often still considered customary behaviour and what is written in the law. Indonesia's anti-corruption legislation has been introduced with the hope of eradicating the corruption problems affecting the government. Although, over the past decade, a number of corruption cases have been investigated and prosecuted in Indonesia, the expected effect on corruption trends in Indonesia has fallen short of expectations.

Indonesia's anti-corruption regime has an extensive scope, ranging from bribery to money laundering. Law No. 31 of 1999 on the Eradication of the Criminal Act of Corruption, as amended by Law No. 20 of 2001 ("**Anti-Corruption Law**") and Law No. 11 of 1980 on the Criminal Act of Bribery ("**Anti-Bribery Law**"), comprise the primary anti-corruption legislation in Indonesia.

The Anti-Corruption Law establishes a series of offences which relate to corruption, embezzlement, extortion, conflict of interest, fraud and bribery of public officials. The term "Public Officials" is very broadly defined and includes employees of an enterprise which receives state funding or "*use[s] capital or facilities from the state or from the public*". This will include employees of State Owned Enterprises (SOEs), as well as of private companies which receive state funding or assistance.

The Anti-Bribery Law establishes offences in respect of bribery which involve matters of public interest. The concept of "public interest" is broad and will involve bribery in the private sector which impacts upon public interest. Although the Anti-Bribery Law does not provide a definition of "public interest", the term has been interpreted as referring to the interest of the country or community or the people in general.

Corruption offences under both laws are drafted broadly. For example, although an element of corrupt intent is usually required, an offence is committed where an advantage is provided to a public official on account of the public official's position (Article 13 Anti-Corruption Law).

Other than the Anti-Corruption Law and Anti-Bribery Law, the following are also relevant to the anti-corruption regime in Indonesia:
1. The Indonesian Criminal Code ("**ICC**"): sets out the basic principles of the criminal offence of corruption. The provisions of the Anti-Corruption Law expand upon the ICC.
2. Law No. 8 of 2010 on the Prevention and Eradication of Criminal Acts of Money Laundering: classifies a range of criminal acts as money laundering offences and sets out penalties.

3. Law No. 28 of 1999 on Good Governance: sets out the basic principles of good governance and transparency in government institutions.
4. Law No. 30 of 2002 on the Commission for the Eradication of Corruption ("**KPK Law**"): established the Commission for the Eradication of Corruption (*Komisi Pemberantasan Korupsi* – the "**KPK**"). The KPK is the main body in Indonesia responsible for anti-bribery investigation and enforcement.
5. Law No. 46 of 2009 on the Corruption Tribunal: established the corruption tribunal. The Corruption Tribunal is established to examine corruption cases only and is separate from the district court.
6. Law No. 5 of 2014 on Civil Servants ("**Civil Servants Law**"). The Civil Servants Law provides guidance on who may be considered as a civil servant.
7. Presidential Decree No. 37 of 2009 on the establishment of the Legal Mafia Eradication Task Force. The Task Force is tasked with tackling corruption within law enforcement bodies.

The Anti-Corruption Law and the Anti-Bribery Law set out a range of penalties (usually imprisonment and/or a fine) for those found guilty. These vary widely in severity depending on the nature and extent of the corruption. Under the Anti-Corruption Law and the Anti-Bribery Law, the fines range from IDR 50m and IDR 1bn, and prison sentences are up to 20 years. In certain circumstances, life imprisonment or the death penalty can be imposed.

Besides fines and imprisonment, the Anti-Corruption Law also provides for additional sanctions such as: (i) confiscation of assets obtained from a corrupt practice; (ii) payment of compensation at an amount equal to the amount of money obtained from a corrupt practice; (iii) temporary or permanent closure of business; and (iv) revocation of permanent or temporary rights that have been previously granted to the defendant.

Companies found guilty of corruption are subject to the maximum fine plus an additional one-third. It is not clear whether the additional one-third is discretionary or will always apply, although the latter view prevails. This view is also supported by the KPK.

There are a number of institutions that are empowered to investigate corruption. These are the State Police, the Public Prosecutor and the Financial Transaction Reports and Analysis Centre (*Pusat Pelaporan Dan Analisis Transaksi Keuangan*) which deals with money laundering offences and the KPK.

Overview of enforcement activity

The KPK is the main body which handles high-profile corruption cases. More recently, the Attorney General's Office also has been more active in investigating corruption cases since the establishment of an Anti-Corruption Task Force within the Attorney General's Office.

To date, the investigation and prosecution of corruption has almost entirely focused on corruption and bribery involving high-profile government officials and large amounts of money. Often there will be phases during which there will be a particular sector focus. For example, presently, the KPK is focusing on corruption and/or bribery within the law enforcement sector (e.g. the police, lawyers, prosecutors and the judiciary), although there are also prosecutions related to other sectors.

By way of an example, in October 2013 the KPK arrested Akil Mochtar (the former Chairman of Indonesia's Constitutional Court) for receiving bribes in relation to various disputes relating to provincial elections that were brought in the Constitutional Court. Akil Mochtar was tried and Indonesia's Supreme Court sentenced him to life imprisonment in February 2015.

Another example is an investigation initiated against a very senior litigation lawyer, O.C. Kaligis. In early July 2015, the KPK caught an associate of O.C. Kaligis & Partners bribing three judges and a clerk from the Medan Administrative Court. The case is being examined by the KPK and O.C. Kaligis is being held in detention at the KPK detention centre.

A similar case happened in 2013, when a lawyer was caught bribing an employee of Indonesia's Supreme Court. The lawyer was sentenced to four years' imprisonment and fined IDR 200 million (approximately USD 15,000).

To date, prosecutions have been directed towards individuals, instead of corporations, although the Anti-Corruption Law also provides for the liability of corporations and, indeed, a corporation's management. A recent publication from the KPK suggests that in future the KPK will focus more on pursuing corporations.

Overview of gifts, travel, entertainment and facilitation payments

The Indonesian Anti-Corruption Law prohibits providing gratification to government officials where the gift is provided in consideration of the government officials' position or authority. The Anti-Corruption Law defines "*gratification*" broadly as being anything of value, which includes money, gifts, travel, accommodation, entertainment, sports membership, etc. To provide a better understanding of the provision of gratification, the KPK have issued a non-binding guideline which provides examples and case studies of what will be considered as prohibited gratification. In addition to the KPK's guideline, several government institutions have issued their own internal guidelines in relation to the giving of gratification to their officials.

Indonesian corruption laws do not provide for an exception for facilitation payments. Under the Anti-Corruption Law, a facilitation payment constitutes a bribe. However, certain "speed payments" may be allowed if there is a legal basis for them. For example, in the immigration office it is now possible to expedite a passport application for a one-day service by paying a special fee. This fee is provided for in the regulation set out by the Directorate General of Immigration for the "one-day service" programme. However, there are very few cases where governmental institutions in Indonesia provide for a legal speed payment.

Overview of investigation and enforcement procedures

As discussed earlier, an investigation of a corruption or bribery offence can be initiated by the police, the public prosecutor, or the KPK. The investigators can commence their investigation based on a report from the public or on their own initiative.

In carrying out an investigation, the KPK have broader powers than the police and/or the public prosecutor. For example, the KPK is authorised to tap phone conversations, while the public prosecutor generally does not have that power. In exchange for these broad powers, the KPK is not permitted to drop an investigation. This is why the KPK is known for its record of winning all of the cases it investigates.

It is also worth noting that the Anti-Corruption Law does not recognise formal concepts of whistleblowing, plea bargaining or leniency. Although in practice these can be implemented by the KPK, the implementation will largely depend on the discretion of the investigator, and the criminal court will have a broad discretion to decide whether or not it will accept any plea bargain that the KPK has entered into.

Overview of cross-border issues

Under the Anti-Corruption Law, any individual located outside Indonesia who bribes or facilitates a bribe to an Indonesian official may be punished. The Anti-Bribery Law also contains provisions regarding extraterritoriality. If a bribe involving an Indonesian civil servant and/or state administrator takes place outside Indonesia, the Anti-Bribery Law may apply. However, neither the Anti-Corruption Law nor the Anti-Bribery Law extend to the bribery of foreign public officials by Indonesian nationals. Although Indonesia has ratified the United Nations Convention against Corruption which prohibits the bribery of foreign public officials, this prohibition has not (yet) been implemented in national Indonesian laws, and there do not appear to be any plans to implement this prohibition in the near future.

Indonesia is party to the United Nations Convention against Corruption which requires signatories to cooperate in fighting corruption. Further, the KPK Law specifically provides for cooperation between the KPK and foreign investigation bodies in carrying out an investigation. For example, the KPK cooperated with the United States Department of Justice in a corruption investigation involving an Indonesian parliament member in a tender for a power plant project in Indonesia. The cooperation was conducted in the form of exchanging examination results.

The above cooperation was an example of how foreign legislation on anti-corruption and anti-bribery (i.e. the Foreign Corrupt Practice Act – "**FCPA**" and the UK Bribery Act – "**UKBA**") may impact the enforcement of anti-corruption and anti-bribery cases in Indonesia. As a result of the broad extraterritorial reach of the FCPA (and the UKBA) investigations involving bribery in Indonesia may be initiated by foreign enforcement agencies with the KPK becoming involved subsequently.

Overview of corporate liability

As mentioned above, the Anti-Corruption Law allows for corporations to be held liable for corruption and bribery. Corporations can be held liable for corruption if the corruption is conducted by or on behalf of the corporation, either by an employee or another person acting on behalf of the company.

Members of the management may be held personally liable if they themselves are involved in the corrupt activity.

Corporations that are found guilty of corruption and bribery are subject to the maximum fine given to individuals plus an additional third. It remains to be seen, however, how this provision will be implemented because to date prosecutions have primarily been targeted at individuals.

Acknowledgment

The authors would like to thank Narendra Adiyasa for his assistance in the preparation of this chapter. Narendra is a Partner with Hiswara Bunjamin & Tandjung with over a decade of experience in relation to commercial dispute resolution and contentious regulatory matters.

R. Suharsanto Raharjo, S.H.
Tel: +62 215 744 010 / Email: suharsanto.raharjo@hbtlaw.com

Suharsanto has been a litigation lawyer for more than 8 (eight) years with extensive experience in commercial disputes, arbitration, employment law, corporate criminal and internal investigation cases, competition law and anti-bribery and corruption cases. He has dealt with various litigation processes and is licensed to practise law across Indonesia.

During his tenure with Hiswara Bunjamin & Tandjung, he had the opportunity to work for Herbert Smith Freehills, on a secondment programme, in their Singapore office. He has also been seconded to BHP Billiton's subsidiary in Indonesia dealing with compliance with anti-bribery and corruption laws.

Pamela Kiesselbach
Tel: +65 686 89 826 / Email: pamela.kiesselbach@hsf.com

Pamela has over 20 years' experience in assisting multinational and regional clients engaged in high value, cross-border disputes involving Asian, Australian, European, UK and US companies. She has advised energy and telecommunication companies, banks, airlines and manufacturing companies on a variety of investigations, disputes and other contentious matters involving proceedings in Asia-Pacific, Europe and the US.

Pamela transferred to Hong Kong in 2012 where she joined the Corporate Crime and Investigations team. Since that time she has led teams on some of the largest, and most complex, cross-border internal investigations currently underway anywhere in the world. Pamela relocated to Singapore in late 2014 where she now leads the South East Asia Corporate Crime and Investigations team. She has assisted clients of the firm with the drafting of their regional compliance programmes and with compliance training with particular focus on local requirements.

Hiswara Bunjamin Tandjung in association with Herbert Smith Freehills

BRI 2 Building, Jl. Jend. Sudirman Kav. 44-46, Jakarta 10210, Indonesia
Tel: +62 21 574 4010 / Fax: +62 21 574 4670 / URL: http://www.hbtlaw.com

Ireland

Jamie Olden, Brendan Hayes & Caitríona Harte
Ronan Daly Jermyn

Introduction

Until very recently, the primary source of law on anti-corruption and bribery in Ireland were rules developed in the 1890s which had, over the intervening century, been subject to a number of non-substantive amendments. However, over the past two decades Ireland has endured an economic and banking crisis, well-publicised tribunals of inquiry concerning matters of public importance and increasing international pressure to bring Ireland's anti-corruption law into line with international best practice, which has served as an impetus for legislative reform.

Irish law on combatting corruption is focused on the elements of the offences and does not distinguish as to the type of gift when determining whether an offence has been committed. The principal statutory sources of bribery law in Ireland are the Public Bodies Corrupt Practices Act, 1889 (as amended)[1] and the Prevention of Corruption Acts, 1906-2010. A widespread reform of anti-bribery law has taken place in Ireland over recent years, including legislative reform on whistleblower protection,[2] the lobbying of public officials,[3] a general consolidation and reform of company law[4] and a proposed consolidation of anti-corruption laws.[5] Prior to considering those reforms, it is necessary to understand the myriad nature of the existing legal framework and the means of enforcement of those laws in Ireland.

The legal regime

The principal bribery offences

Public Bodies Corrupt Practices Act, 1889 (as amended)

Scope: The Public Bodies Corrupt Practices Act, 1889 (as amended) prohibits bribery and corruption, inside or outside of the State, of a "public official":[6] members and agents of "public bodies".[7] Under these Acts, it is an offence for a member of a public body to solicit, receive or agree to receive, for him/herself or another, any "inducement"[8] to do or refrain from doing something in which the public body is concerned.

Penalties: On summary conviction for offences (being minor offences), an individual may be liable to a fine and/or imprisonment for up to 12 months. On indictment (being more serious offences which must be tried before a judge and jury), an individual may be liable to conviction or a fine and/or imprisonment for up to seven years. In addition, an individual convicted of such an offence can also be ordered to pay his employer the value of the gift received by him.

Prevention of Corruption Acts, 1906-2010 (the "POC Acts")

Scope: The Prevention of Corruption Act, 1906 (the "1906 Act") prohibits three offences in relation to "public officials":[9]

(i)   corruptly accepting a gift;
(ii) corruptly giving a gift; and
(iii) the making of a false statement with the intent to deceive.[10]

These offences also extend to agents acting on behalf of their principals. The Prevention of Corruption Act, 1916 (the "1916 Act") extends the remit of the prohibition on corruption of, or by, a third party, with the intention of influencing the conduct of an agent. The 1916 Act also introduced a rebuttable presumption of corruption in relation to offences under the POC Acts, where the donor of the gift had an interest in the public body/official granting a relevant licence or contract, for example where that public body exercises its function under the Planning and Development Act, 2000 or the National Asset Management Agency Act, 2009.

The Prevention of Corruption (Amendment) Act, 2001 (the "2001 Act") introduced a specific offence of corruption in public office, which provides that a public official can act alone for his/her own benefit, without the need for a second person for the commission of the offence. This offence is punishable by a fine and up to 10 years' imprisonment. In addition, further to section 9 of the 2001 Act corporate bodies will be deemed to have committed an offence under the POC Acts through the consent or neglect of its officers, members or agents, such that both the body corporate and the person(s) responsible are liable.

The Criminal Justice Act, 2011 prohibits the aiding, abetting, counselling, procuring, conspiring to commit or inciting the commission of an offence under the 1906 Act and the 2001 Act punishable by a prison sentence of up to five years.

The Criminal Justice (Corruption) Bill, 2012 in its current form proposes to retain the above offences and to introduce an additional offence of corruptly threatening harm to a person with the intention of influencing any person to do or omit to do something in relation to his/her public function (and we have considered this in further detail below).

Penalties: A person found guilty of a corruption offence under the POC Acts is liable on summary conviction to a fine not exceeding €4,000 and/or imprisonment for a term not exceeding 12 months. A person convicted on indictment is liable to an unlimited fine and/or imprisonment for a term not exceeding 10 years. An employer summarily convicted of an offence under the whistleblower protections contained in the POC Acts can be fined up to €5,000. Upon conviction on indictment, an employer can be fined up to €250,000 and imprisoned for up to three years.

Ethics in Public Office Act, 1995[11] *(the "1995 Act")*

Scope: The 1995 Act purports to prevent corruption in public office but obliging designated "public officials"[12] to disclose details of prescribed conflicts of interest and hospitality, which could materially affect their role. There are also rules on the surrender of certain gifts and payments by senior members of the public service, which include the imposition of an obligation on office holders to surrender gifts that exceed €650 in monetary value on the basis that they are deemed gifts to the State.

A statutory body, the Standards in Public Office Commission (SIPO), has been established to monitor and publish findings under the 1995 Act. SIPO have published guidelines on the area, which extend beyond "office holders" and provides for the disclosure but not surrender of gifts in excess of €650. In addition, further to the Electoral (Amendment) (Political Funding) Act, 2012, there are requirements and restrictions on the acceptance of political donations and SIPO has published a series of new Guidelines under the Electoral Act, 1997 concerning these recent changes.

In its 2014 report, published in July 2015, SIPO noted that a total of €25,500 of donations had been disclosed by 239 individuals.[13] The report also stated that a total of 12 complaints had been received and deemed valid by SIPO in respect of breaches of the 1995 Act, one example being two former local councillors who were found to have contravened a code of conduct pertaining to claims for travel and subsistence expenses.[14]

Penalties: SIPO may refer reportable offences to the Director of Public Prosecutions. A recent example of such reporting is the case of a former Minister of State who was jailed for five months in 2014 when he fraudulently claimed €4,207.45 expenses based on forged mobile phone invoices.[15]

Criminal Justice (Theft and Fraud Offences) Act, 2001 (as amended)[16] *(the "TFO Act")*

Scope: The TFO Act introduced into Irish law rules on 'active' and 'passive' corruption, pursuant to the EC Convention of the Protection of European Communities Financial Interests, 1995. The offences set out in the TFO Act overlap with those listed above, albeit the TFO Act is focused on the corruption of officials of institutions of the European Union (or member states), which damages the financial interests of the EU.

Penalties: An individual convicted on indictment of corruption under the TFO Act can be subject to an unlimited fine and/or imprisonment for a term of up to five years. An auditor who fails to refer reportable offences to the appropriate authorities may be found guilty of an offence and will be liable on summary conviction to a fine and/or imprisonment to a term not exceeding 12 months.

Regulation of Lobbying Act, 2015 (the "Lobbying Act")

Scope: The Lobbying Act introduces new registration and disclosure obligations for those involved in "lobbying activities" in Ireland. The new rules commenced as of 1 September 2015. "Lobbying" is defined as including the making of any communication to a "designated public official"[17] in relation to a "relevant matter".[18] Certain communications are not subject to these requirements, such as those relating to the implementation of a policy, a technical query and communication seeking factual information. It is important to note that all individuals who make relevant communications are subject to these requirements, not just those who lobby professionally. SIPO will maintain an online, publicly available register of lobbyists. Where the publication of lobbying activity is adjudged as potentially having an adverse effect on the financial/business interests of the State, or the person to whom the lobbying relates, the registration of that lobbying activity may be delayed for up to six months.

Penalties: It is an offence for those carrying out lobbying activity not to make a return, to provide inaccurate or misleading information to SIPO, and failing to comply with or obstructing an investigation. However, a defence may be raised if the subject took "all reasonable steps" to avoid the commission of the offence. Persons convicted of an offence may be fined between €200 and €5,000 and/or imprisonment for a maximum of two years. It shall be a defence for the person to prove that they took all reasonable steps to avoid the commission of the offence.

The Companies Act, 2014

Scope: The Companies Act, 2014, which came into effect in June 2015, has sought to consolidate a plethora of company-related legislation. The Act includes a reaffirmation of the role of the Office of Director of Corporate Enforcement in investigating and prosecuting breaches of company law and the introduction of a codified set of directors' duties.

Penalties: There are four categories of penalties that apply to offences which arise under the Act, ranging from a "Class A" fine (being fines not exceeding €5,000) for minor offences up to the most serious offences, which may result in a term of imprisonment of up to 12 months and/or a €500,000 fine. In addition, where an individual is convicted of an indictable offence in relation to a company, or convicted of an offence involving fraud or dishonesty, that individual may be prohibited from being in any way concerned with a company, whether directly or indirectly.

Protected Disclosures Act, 2014 (the "Protected Disclosures Act")

Scope: The Protected Disclosures Act was enacted on 15 July 2014 and brings Ireland into line with international best practice in providing for the reporting of suspicions of illegality, otherwise known as "whistleblowing".[19] Under this Act, all public bodies must introduce whistleblowing polices, and private bodies should review pre-existing policies, to ensure compliance with the Act.

The Protected Disclosures Act ensures that a "worker"[20] may disclose information which they "reasonably believe" evidences a "relevant wrongdoing",[21] which came to their attention during the course of their employment. The motivation for making the protected disclosure is irrelevant provided that the worker reasonably believes there is a reportable circumstance. An employer may not penalise a worker due to their making a protected disclosure and furthermore, the employer may not disclose information, which may identify the person who made the disclosure. Employers and employees are prohibited from contracting out of the provisions of the Act.

On 25 September 2015, the Minister for Public Expenditure and Reform (the "Minister") issued draft guidelines to assist public bodies in the performance of their functions under the Protected Disclosures Act.[22] The draft guidelines contain a sample protected disclosures procedure and members of the public have until 23 October 2015 to comment on the proposed guidelines before the Minister finalises and publishes the final set of guidelines.

Penalties: Where an employer negatively treats a worker due to a protected disclosure, the employer may be required to pay the worker compensation of up to 260 weeks' remuneration and the worker may also bring an action in tort for detriment experienced.[23] However, where a worker makes a disclosure knowing or being reckless as to whether that the information was false, they may be subject to a claim in defamation and/or compensation in an unfair dismissal claim may be reduced by up to 25%.

Civil remedies

Employers may seek to recover damages from employees who have caused loss to their business by virtue of a corrupt act and the employees may be made accountable for unauthorised profits made by him/her.

Enforcement framework

Investigating and prosecuting authorities

It is useful to understand how the above offences are investigated and prosecuted. In Ireland, offences are distinguished between minor/summary offences and serious/indictable offences. Whilst regulatory bodies are generally authorised to prosecute summary offences, the prosecution of the majority of offences is carried out by the Office of the Director of Public Prosecutions (ODPP). By and large it is the ODPP that decides if a charge should be brought against an accused and then prosecuting that charge.

Minor company law offences are prosecuted in the District Court by the Office of the Director of Corporate Enforcement (ODCE), the Registrar of Companies or the ODPP. The role of the ODCE has been afforded a wide variety of investigative powers under the

Company Law Enforcement Act, 2001,[24] including powers of entry, search and seizure and the power to compel the production of specific documents that are of material assistance to an investigation. Revenue Commissioners can prosecute certain offences (such as market abuse) and it has extensive investigation and prosecution powers, taking an active role in investigating tax evasion and, similar to the ODCE, Revenue Commissioners may prosecute summary offences and refer indicatable offences cases to the ODPP for prosecution. In respect of certain "regulated entities" (such as financial institutions), the Central Bank of Ireland ("CBI") has investigatory and regulatory powers, including powers of inspection, entry, search and seizure, in respect of financial institutions under the Central Bank Act, 1942 (as amended).

As explained above, SIPO is responsible for the investigation of breaches of the Ethics Act, 1995 (as amended) and where following an investigation, SIPO takes the view that a relevant has committed an offence, it may refer the matter to the ODPP. An Garda Siochána (Irish police force), or in the case of complex fraudulent crime the Garda Bureau of Fraud Investigation (GBFI), are responsible for investigating crimes. Furthermore, the Office of the Ombudsman, an independent office established by Statute, may investigate complaints from individuals who believe they may have been treated unfairly by designated public bodies. The ability to pursue complaints through the Ombudsman's office further strengthens the accountability of those in the public service.

The structure described above can be contrasted with the position in England, where the Serious Fraud Office (SFO) was set up to investigate and prosecute complex white-collar crimes which have an international dimension with an alleged value of over £1 million. The establishment of SFO has resulted in successful prosecution on a large scale, such as the 2014 successful prosecution of a £23 million biofuel scam involving Sustainable AgroEnergy plc.

Seizure of proceeds of crime

There are a number of legislative provisions relating to the seizure by An Garda Siochána of goods deemed to be the "proceeds of crime",[25] for example further to the Criminal Justice Act, 1994 (as amended), the Proceeds of Crime Act, 1996 (As amended), the Public Bodies Corrupt Practices Act, 1889 (as amended) and the POC Acts. Depending on the legislative provision being relied upon, seizure of goods may not require a Court Order. However, it is an arm of An Garda Siochána, the Criminal Assets Bureau, which is principally involved in the management of assets that are deemed the proceeds of criminal activities.

Recent enforcement activity

Courts

It is very difficult to identify and monitor trends in the sentencing of prosecuted financial crimes, given that there is no one body dealing with the prosecution of such crimes. In Ireland, indictable offences are tried before a lay jury and an issue that often attracts commentary is the ability of jurors to understand issues arising in the trial of complex white-collar crimes.

However, there have been a number of cases in recent years, which suggest that juries are well placed to reach decisions even absent expert knowledge in white-collar crime. In 2013, Thomas Byrne, a former solicitor who was charged with more than 50 counts of theft, deception and forgery, was found unanimously guilty of all charges.[26] This followed a complex 27-day trial before a jury. In 2014, in a case which involved alleged breach of financial assistance rules by certain former officers of Anglo Irish Bank plc.,[27] a vast amount of technical and factual evidence was put before the jury, including a reported 800 witness statements and due to a then recent legislative change, the jury were able to be supplied with charts, diagrams, graphics and summaries of evidence to help its deliberations. At the end of deliberations, and perhaps as evidence of the diligent approach taken by them, the jury found two of the accused guilty and a further accused not guilty of the alleged offences. A more recent example is a July 2015 conviction of three former bank officials for defrauding Revenue (currently under appeal), whose trial involved the hearing of a large amount of technical evidence on how financial transactions are processed and how information systems are managed.[28]

CBI investigations

The CBI is entitled, pursuant to the Central Bank Act, 1942 (as amended), to investigate a "regulated entity" and/or persons concerned with such a regulated entity. This process, known as the Administrative Sanctions Procedure ("ASP"), provides for significant monetary penalties and restrictions. It is also open to the CBI to agree settlements with regulated entities the subject of investigation, as has occurred in the case of Quinn Insurance Limited (2013) and Irish Nationwide Building Society (2015). Where a matter is not settled, it is open to the CBI to launch a formal Inquiry into the alleged misconduct and it was announced in August 2015 that the first Inquiry arising out of an ASP investigation will be held into the conduct, during a specified period, of certain individuals concerned with the affairs of Irish Nationwide Building Society.

Tribunals, inquiries and commissions

Tribunals: Over the past two decades, a number of temporary fact-finding tribunals were established by Government to investigate certain issues of controversy/dispute of public importance and chaired by judges or senior lawyers under the Tribunals of Inquiry (Evidence) Acts, 1921-2004. A small number of convictions have arisen as a result of the findings of the tribunals of inquiry, notably the conviction of Government politicians, a planning official, and a former Government minister who pled guilty to two charges of making false tax returns.

These tribunals are publicly funded and have proved inordinately expensive. For example, the renowned Mahon/Flood Tribunal, which ran for 15 years and concerned alleged inappropriate payments concerning the rezoning of land in the Dublin region, is reported to have cost the State approximately €247 million. A constitutional amendment to provide that the Houses of the Oireachtas (the Irish Parliament) could conduct inquiries was proposed, but ultimately rejected in 2011. A further Bill, the Tribunals of Inquiry Bill 2005, which seeks to consolidate and modernise the law regarding tribunals of inquiry, remains a proposed reform but it appears to have stagnated in recent times.

Public Inquiries: The system of public inquiries was reformed in 2013 with the enactment of the Houses of the Oireachtas (Inquiries, Privileges and Procedures) Act, 2013, which allows Oireachtas committees to inquire into certain matters. The first such inquiry was the 'Banking Inquiry', which is presently in session and it is anticipated that it will present its final report in late 2015.

Commissions of Investigations: The Commissions of Investigation Act, 2004 provides for the establishment of commissions of investigation, which may investigate a matter of "urgent public concern". These are more streamlined fora than tribunals of inquiry but they have fewer powers. Examples of such commissioners are the 2010 Nyberg Report which considered the reasons for the Irish banking crisis and, more recently, a Commission of Investigation on "Certain matters concerning transactions entered into by Irish Bank Resolution Corporation (formerly Anglo Irish Bank)".

Pertinent enforcement issues

Self-reporting

Further to section 19 of the Criminal Justice Act, 2011, there now exists a positive obligation on all individuals and companies to report to An Garda Siochána (Irish police force) as soon as practicable, any information which that person believes may be of "material assistance" in preventing the commission of a corruption offence or securing the arrest, prosecution or conviction of another person for a corruption offence.

As stated above, the TFO Act also provides that auditors are under an obligation to report suspected offences to the appropriate authorities and further to the Companies Act, 1990,[29] a similar obligation rests on auditors for suspected breaches of company law. Additionally, under the Criminal Justice (Money Laundering and Terrorist Financing) Act, 2010, designated persons are also obliged to report suspected offences of money laundering or terrorist financing. Furthermore, senior personnel of regulated entities are obliged to disclose to CBI as soon as practicable, information relating to a suspicion of financial service-related offences.

Plea agreements/deferred prosecution agreements

The Irish system does not provide for plea-bargaining, which is a common feature in the United States. This is primarily due to the requirement that Courts must have exclusive jurisdiction over sentencing matters. This means that where an accused wishes to plead guilty to an offence, they do so without an assurance from the prosecutors as to the severity of the sentence, given that sentencing is solely at the discretion of the judge.

However, in practice the conduct of an accused, such as an event of self-reporting, is often a mitigating factor in leniency exercised by a judge when sentencing. Moreover, the ODPP is entitled to grant immunity in any case, often subject to an agreement to provide evidence in prosecutions against other individuals/companies. An example of such immunity is that provided for in the Cartel Immunity Programme, the most recent version of which came into effect in January 2015 and which sets out the criteria for an application for immunity to be successful. The ODPP may also direct that a matter be disposed of summarily in the District Court which would result in a lower penalty being imposed. The conduct of the subject of a CBI ASP investigation may be considered by the CBI when deciding on the sanctions to be applied. The 'deferred prosecution agreement', another feature of the US criminal justice system, is not known to the Irish jurisdiction.

Jury trials

Minor, summary offences come before the District Court, which is a judge-only forum. However, more serious offences, being indictable offences, come before the Circuit or Central Criminal Courts, in the presence of a jury. One of the key issues affecting juries, which are made up of non-legal persons, is the availability of the jurors. In the past, once a panel of 12 individuals was identified, grave difficulties could arise if it turned out that some of those jurors were unable to continue to act on the jury due to work, health or other reasons. Such was this concern, that the legislature introduced reforms to the Juries Act, 1976 by way of Courts and Civil Law (Miscellaneous Provisions) Act, 2013 (together the "Juries Act").

The Juries Act provides for the empanelling of 15 individuals so as to circumvent the risk of a trial collapsing if the number of available jurors fell below 10. The first jury of 15 individuals to be empanelled under the new rules was the 2014 prosecution of three former officers of Anglo Irish Bank plc[30] (which is discussed above), during which the barrister for the State noted that the jurors were "making history". During that trial, the jurors heard all of the evidence at the end of the evidence; 12 of the jurors were selected at random to reach a verdict.

Burden of proof/strict liability offences

There is a long-accepted rule that an accused enjoys the presumption of innocence and, on that basis, prosecutors must prove every aspect of an offence, including showing that the accused had the *mens rea* to commit the crime, i.e. that the accused intended, or was reckless as to the outcome of his/her actions. However, the concept of the reversal of the burden of proof is not uncommon in Ireland. This dictum is such that Statute may provide that where certain facts are proved, a rebuttable presumption arises that the offence has been committed, subject to the accused being able to rebut the presumption or successfully raise a defence. This reversal of the burden of proof is merely evidential in nature and a Statute requiring a court to convict an individual due to the existence of certain facts, may be found unconstitutional.

Separately, for certain regulatory offences, where the sanction is minimal (such as littering which is punishable by fine only), the courts have affirmed that there is no need to evidence *mens rea* on the part of the accused. These are known as strict liability offences. For more serious crimes however, the same principle will not be applied.

Cross-border issues

Legal framework

Ireland has signed and ratified seven international anti-corruption conventions,[31] and Irish legislation must be interpreted in light of those conventions, albeit the conventions may not supplant national law. Certain provisions of the conventions have been specifically included on the Irish statute book, such as the prohibition on the bribery of a foreign official, further to both the POC Acts and the TFO Act.

Cross-border prosecution arises in two instances. Firstly, an offence arises where an Irish person or company does something outside of Ireland which, if done within Ireland, would constitute an offence under the relevant legislation; that person is liable as if the offence had been committed in Ireland. Secondly, if a relevant offence is committed in both Ireland and the foreign jurisdiction, a person may be prosecuted in Ireland for that offence. Whilst there are no reported instances of Irish persons or companies bribing foreign officials, the OECD noted in 2013 that there were at that point three allegations of bribery of foreign officials at a pre-investigation stage, and one allegation was under investigation by the Irish authorities.

International cooperation

The primary piece of legislation governing mutual legal assistance between Ireland and other countries is provided for in the Criminal Justice (Mutual Assistance) Act, 2008.[32] The extradition of individuals for suspected offences is governed by the European Arrest Warrant Act, 2003 and the Extradition Act, 1965 (as amended). In addition, Ireland has entered an Inter-Governmental Agreement with the United States in relation to the exchange of information in relation to accounts held in Irish financial institutions by US persons and *vice versa*. This is on foot of the Foreign Account Tax Compliance Act, 2013. On this basis, it is important that Irish businesses consider reporting requirements in their anti-corruption policies and procedures.

International assessment

Praise: By virtue of the recent Protected Disclosures Act, 2014, the OECD regard Ireland as having the highest level of protection available to whistle-blowers in the EU, and in 2014, Transparency Ireland ranked Ireland well in the Corruption Perceptions Index, wherein out of 175 countries Ireland ranked 17th. This means that Ireland is perceived as one of the least corrupt countries in the world. Furthermore, the European Commission commended Ireland in 2014 for the introduction of new rules on the disclosure of contributions to political parties, which was on foot of a 2009 recommendation by the Group of States against Corruption (GRECO), a body established by the Council of Europe. The Implementation Group of the United Nations Convention against Corruption has also praised Ireland in June 2015, for the non-existence of immunity from investigations of "public officials" and the fact that Irish anti-bribery law goes beyond the requirements of the Convention in the application of laws to both domestic and international public officials.

Criticism: Whilst the impending introduction of a consolidated legal framework on anti–corruption is to be welcomed, Ireland has been criticised in the past for a lack of enforcement of anti-corruption laws. For example, according to GRECO, between 2005 and 2008 there were just 17 prosecutions directed under the POC Acts. Moreover, GRECO advised in late 2014 that there should be reforms of the systems of ethical standards and conduct of members of the Oireachtas, the system of appointment and promotion of judges, and the structure to receive and the handling of complaints in relation to the ODPP and An Garda Siochána. In addition, Transparency International reported in late 2014 that Ireland was ranked as conducting 'little or no enforcement' of the OECD Convention on Combating Bribery of Foreign Public Officials in International Business Transactions and was one of 22 countries with this ranking out of the 40 signatory countries to the Convention. The inability of SIPO to commence investigations without a complaint from a third party was criticised by the European Commission in a February 2014 report.

Corporate liability for bribery and corruption offences

Pursuant to the Interpretation Act, 2005, references to "persons" in Irish legislation are interpreted as including corporate entities. Moreover, further to the POC Acts, an officer of a company that commits a relevant offence will also be guilty of an offence, if that offence is proved to have been committed with the consent or neglect of the company's officers. Under common law, a company may be found liable for the criminal acts carried out by its agents (including employees and officers), by way of vicarious liability. However, this principle appears confined to a civil context and the same concept has not adopted within a criminal context. Proposed reforms of corporate liability are dealt with in the next section.

Proposed reforms

Criminal Justice (Corruption) Bill, 2012

The legislation governing corruption in Ireland is disjointed despite attempts in recent years at ensuring that Ireland meets its international obligations. However, there is a draft piece of legislation currently before the Irish Parliament, which seeks to consolidate all anti-corruption legislation – the Criminal Justice (Corruption) Bill, 2012. The new legislation will, according to the Minister for Justice, benchmark Ireland's laws with the United Nations Convention against Corruption and take into consideration certain recommendations made by tribunals of inquiry in recent years.

The Heads of the Bill were published in 2012 and the draft legislation was listed for publication in the Government's legislative programme for Spring/Summer 2015. On 6 October 2015, the Minister for Justice announced that she intended to bring a revised Bill to Cabinet before the end of 2015, with the intention that the Bill would be published and enacted in early 2016. When the Bill is finally enacted, not only will it seek to consolidate existing legislation, it is proposed that it will also introduce new concepts to the Irish legal system, some of which include:

(a) offences:

- expansion of the definition of "corruption";[33]

- a new rebuttable presumption of corruption in the case of enrichment of an Irish public official (for example where a public official maintains a standard of living "above that commensurate with official remuneration" or has control of a disproportionate amount of property) albeit there is some doubt as to whether this will form part of the final wording given constitutional concerns; and

- a new offence of 'making reckless payments' whereby an individual is guilty of an offence if he provides gifts to a designated person while knowing, or being reckless as to whether such a gift would constitute a bribe;

(b) corporate liability:

- the introduction of liability for companies for corruption caused by persons concerned with the company where there is an intention by those persons to obtain/retain business for the company;

- for the purpose of the above, agents are deemed concerned persons and this will place a significant onus on businesses to conduct due diligence on those who could fall within this undefined term; and

- a new defence available for companies where it can be shown that "all reasonable steps" were taken and "all due diligence" was exercised to prevent the corruption occurring;

(c) penalties:

- the ability of the courts to remove public officials from office and to exclude them from holding office for up to 10 years; and

- the majority of summary offences are to be punishable by a fine not exceeding €5,000 and/or imprisonment for a term not exceeding 12 months, whereas penalties on indictment will be include a term of imprisonment of up to 10 years and/or a fine and/or forfeiture of any gift;

(d) whistleblowers: the draft scheme also contains protections for whistleblowers, but it is as yet unclear what form the final wording will take given the enactment of the extensive Protected Disclosures Act, 2014; and

(e) cross-border issues:

- the ability to prosecute offences committed overseas by companies or individuals with Irish nationality; and

- an expansion of extra-territorial provisions concerning corrupt acts committed outside Ireland by certain categories of person.

Best practice for businesses

With recent and impending reforms, it is important that businesses update their policies and procedures to ensure compliance and minimise risk. The most significant development will be the enactment of the Criminal Justice (Corruption) Bill, 2012, which provides that Irish companies with foreign subsidiaries will have a responsibility to ensure the ethical behaviour of its servants, officers and agents. To counter this, a company may raise a defence to certain corporate offences where it took "all reasonable steps" and exercised "all due diligence" to prevent the corruption taking place. It is unclear whether guidelines will be issued on what "reasonable steps" and "due diligence" a company should take so as to ensure it can avail of this new statutory defence. In the meantime it may be useful for companies who wish to establish anti-bribery policies, to consider the principles issued in the UK in connection with similar statutory defences, for example:

- *training*: anti-corruption polices should form part of the employee handbook and training, tailored to the respective roles which employees take within a business, should be rolled out;

- *management*: compliance with the anti-bribery policy must 'come from the top' and senior management should proactively ensure that the policies are rolled out;
- *contracts*: contractual arrangements with third parties should include anti-corruption provisions, incorporating anti-corruption disclosures and related warranties;
- *monitor*: there should be an ongoing review of anti-bribery policies to ensure their effectiveness;
- *risk assessment*: a risk analysis should be carried out by the business to identify risks, particularly risks involving agents both domestic and cross-border;
- *due diligence*: there may be a need to enhance due diligence carried out prior to entering transactions or engaging agents;
- *penalties*: where an employee or agent does not conform with the best practice policies, there should be clear rules on appropriate sanctioning of the affected person(s); and
- *lobbying:* given the extent of requirements to disclose lobbying activity (under the Lobbying Act), best practice policies should also seek to ensure that all business personnel are aware of reporting obligations.

Conclusion

As is evidenced above, over the past 20 years Ireland has undergone a significant transformation of its legislation on anti-corruption and anti-bribery. A loss of public confidence in public officials due to allegations emerging out of tribunals of inquiries, international criticism of Ireland's tardiness in ratifying and introducing into law core principles of international anti-corruption conventions and a number of high-profile criminal prosecutions arising out of the banking and economic crisis, have been the catalyst for the significant legislative reforms. The enactment of the Registration of Lobbying Act, 2014, the Protected Disclosures Act, 2014, amendments to the Juries Act, 1976, and the consolidation of company law through the Companies Act, 2014, have all been important milestones in recent Irish legislative reform. However, the anticipated enactment of the Criminal Justice (Corruption) Bill, 2012 could well be the most significant reform to-date, and businesses should now take the opportunity to put appropriate policies and procedures in place to ensure they are compliant with impending changes in legislation.

* * *

Endnotes

1. As amended by the Prevention of Corruption Act 1916 and the Ethics in Public Office Act 1995 (the Public Bodies Act).
2. The Protected Disclosures Act 2014.
3. The Regulation of Lobbying Act 2015.
4. The Companies Act 2014.
5. Criminal Justice (Corruption) Bill 2012.
6. "Public official" is defined as: a person who is an office holder, director or employee of, a "public body".
7. "Public body" itself is defined as: any county, town or city council, any board, commissioners or other body which has power to act under any legislation relating to local government or the public health or otherwise to administer money raised by taxes.
8. Further to section 1(1) of Public Bodies Corrupt Practices Act 1889. "Inducement" requires only the intention to induce, not that the inducement be acted upon, and it also includes facilitation payments to carry out existing duties.
9. There is a non-exhaustive list of public officials set out in section 1 of the POC Acts.
10. The definition of "corruptly" has been significantly widened from the definition contained in the Prevention of Corruption (Amendment) Act 2010.

11. As amended by the Standards in Public Office Act 2001.
12. The Ethics Act applies only in respect of "public officials". There is no single definition of public officials and the rules pertaining to a public official varies depending on the nature of their role – for example, a Minister of Government faces more stringent oversight than public servants such as principal officers in the civil service.
13. The individuals comprised 165 TDs (being Irish members of Parliament), 60 Senators, 11 Members of the European Parliament, two former Members of the European Parliament and one former TD.
14. http://www.irishtimes.com/news/politics/councillor-contravened-standards-with-expense-claims-1.1835564, and http://www.irishexaminer.com/ireland/alan-kelly-blitz-on-council-travel-expense-claims-begins-today-310204.html.
15. http://www.irishtimes.com/news/politics/ivor-callely-sentenced-to-five-months-in-prison-1.1880454.
16. The TFO Act defines "public officials" as either: an official of the European Community, itself defined as including an official or contracted employee of the European Communities, or a secondee to the European Communities; or a national official, including any national official of another member state. This is generally understood as being a national official, as defined by the national law of the member state in which the official resides.
17. "Designated public official" includes: Ministers, members of the Houses of the Oireachtas, Irish M.E.Ps, members of local authorities, special advisors, and servants of "public service bodies" which will be designated in due course by the designated Minister.
18. "Relevant Matter" means: the initiation, development or modification of any public policy or public programme; or the preparation or amendment of an enactment; or the award of any grant, loan or financial support, contract or other agreement, or of any licence or other authorisation involving public funds.
19. Whistleblower protection also continues to exist under specific pieces of legislation, where the 2014 does not apply, including the Prevention of Corruption Acts 1889-2010. Other pieces of legislation offering whistleblower protection include the Protections For Persons Reporting Child Abuse Act 1998, Standards in Public Office Act 2001, Competition Act 2002, Communications Regulation Act 2002, Health Act 2004, Employment Permits Act 2006, Consumer Protection Act 2007, Chemical Act 2008, Charities Act 2009, National Asset Management Act 2009, Inland Fisheries Act 2010, Criminal Justice Act 2011, Property Services (Regulation)) Act 2011, Protection of Employees (Temporary Agency Work) Act 2012, Further Education and Training Act 2013 and Central Bank (Supervision and Enforcement) Act 2013.
20. "Worker" includes: employees (including temporary and former employees); interns; agency staff; trainees; contractors; members of An Garda Síochána; and consultants. Volunteers are excluded from the definition of "employee".
21. "Relevant wrongdoing" includes: the commission of an offence; non-compliance with a legal obligation (except one arising under the worker's employment contract); a miscarriage of justice; endangerment of health and safety; damage to the environment; misuse of public funds; mismanagement by a public body; or concealing or destroying information relating to any of the above.
22. See http://www.per.gov.ie/en/protected-disclosures-act-2014/.
23. "Detriment" includes: coercion; intimidation; harassment; discrimination; disadvantage; adverse treatment in relation to employment or prospective employment; injury; damage; loss; or threat of reprisal.
24. The Company Law Enforcement Act, 1990, has been repealed and was replaced with the Companies Act, 2014, which was a piece of legislation that consolidated company law in Ireland.

25. "Proceeds of crime" are defined as: any property obtained or received by or as a result of, or in connection with, the commission of an offence; and include the proceeds of corruption.
26. http://www.irishtimes.com/news/crime-and-law/thomas-byrne-guilty-on-all-50-counts-of-fraud-theft-1.1598737.
27. http://www.irishtimes.com/news/crime-and-law/mcateer-and-whelan-spared-jail-in-anglo-case-1.1777520.
28. http://www.rte.ie/news/2015/0731/718364-anglo/.
29. The Companies Act, 1990, has been repealed and was replaced with the Companies Act, 2014, which was a piece of legislation that consolidated company law in Ireland.
30. http://www.irishtimes.com/news/crime-and-law/anglo-irish-bank-trial-the-numbers-the-charges-the-witnesses-1.1765328.
31. (1) The EU Convention on the Protection of the European Communities Financial Interests (and Protocols) – entered into force on 17 October 2002; (2) the OECD Convention on Combating Bribery of Foreign Officials in International Business Transactions – entered into force on 21 November 2003; (3) the Council of Europe Criminal Law Convention on Corruption – entered into force on 1 February 2004; (4) the Convention of the Fight against Corruption involving Officials of the European Communities or Officials of Member States of the European Union – entered into force on 28 September 2005; (5) Additional Protocol to the Council of Europe Criminal Law Convention on Corruption – entered into force on 1 November 2005; (6) the UN Convention against Transnational Organized Crime – entered into force on 17 July 2010; and (7) the UN Convention against Corruption – entered into force on 9 December 2011. Ireland signed the Council of Europe Civil Law Convention on Corruption on 4 November 1999 but has not yet ratified it.
32. Examples of mutual assistance include: the ability to take evidence in connection with criminal investigations or proceedings in another country; search for and seizure of material on behalf of another country; serve a summons or any other court process on a person in Ireland to appear as a defendant or witness in another country; and transfer a person imprisoned in Ireland to another country to give evidence in the foreign criminal proceedings.
33. To include: acting in breach of duty; acting without due impartiality; acting without lawful authority; acting in breach of a relevant code; acting in pursuit of undue benefit; and acting in a deceitful, dishonest or misleading manner.

Jamie Olden
Tel: +353 1 605 4200 / Email: jamie.olden@rdj.ie
Jamie Olden is the Partner in Charge of the Dublin office of Ronan Daly Jermyn. Jamie specialises in commercial litigation and in particular in professional indemnity defence work. He has handled a wide range of commercial disputes and has extensive experience in High Court, including Commercial Court, and Supreme Court litigation, Irish and large-scale multi-jurisdictional disputes and mediation. He has also acted for companies who have faced product liability claims and has carried out regulatory advisory work. Jamie is an Accredited Mediator (CEDR) and a member of the Irish Taxation Institute.

Brendan Hayes
Tel: +353 21 233 2884 / Email: brendan.hayes@rdj.ie
Brendan Hayes is a solicitor specialising in commercial litigation. He recently completed a secondment with Irish Bank Resolution Corporation Limited (in Special Liquidation), where he held the position of Interim Head of Legacy. During his time on secondment, Brendan was responsible for the co-ordination of a number of significant civil proceedings against former advisors to, and officers of, Anglo Irish Bank and Irish Nationwide Building Society. Through his involvement with a number of regulatory and criminal investigations, Brendan is familiar with the procedures of the Garda Bureau of Fraud Investigation, the Director of Public Prosecutions, the Central Bank of Ireland and the Office of the Director of Corporate Enforcement.

Caitríona Harte
Tel: +353 21 480 2700 / Email: caitriona.harte@rdj.ie
Caitríona Harte is a trainee solicitor with the firm's Commercial Litigation department. She holds an LL.B. in Law, French and Politics from the University of Limerick and an LL.M. in International Law from the University of Edinburgh. Prior to joining RDJ, Caitríona worked with the International Bar Association in London as a programme administration manager and as a paralegal with the National Asset Management Agency.

Ronan Daly Jermyn

2 Park Place, City Gate Park, Mahon Point, Cork, Ireland. Tel: +353 21 480 2700 / Email: cork.rdj.ie
28th Floor, 30 St Mary Axe, EC3A 8BF, London, United Kingdom. Tel: +44 20 7337 6178 / Email: london@rdj.ie
URL: http://www.rdj.ie

Italy

Roberto Pisano
Studio Legale Pisano

Brief overview of the law and enforcement regime

Bribery of both domestic and foreign public officials is prohibited as a criminal offence under the Italian Criminal Code (ICC). On November 28, 2012, by Law no. 190/2012, a significant reform of the Italian anti-corruption system entered into force, introducing, *inter alia*, new bribery offences, increasing the punishments for existing offences, and generally enlarging the sphere of responsibility for private parties involved in bribery.

<u>Domestic bribery</u>

The bribery offences relating to domestic public officials are provided for by articles 318-322 ICC and by article 346 *bis* ICC, and in principle their sanctions apply equally to the public official and the private briber (article 321 ICC). In particular, the ICC provides for the following forms of domestic bribery, the essence of which is the unlawful agreement between the public official and the briber:

(i) 'proper bribery', which occurs when the public official, in exchange for performing (or having performed) an act conflicting with the duties of his or her office, or in exchange for omitting or delaying (or having omitted or delayed) an act of his or her office, receives money or other things of value, or accepts a promise of such things (article 319 ICC). Punishment is imprisonment from six years to 10 years, and it can be increased due to 'aggravating circumstances';

(ii) 'bribery for the performance of the function', which occurs when the public official, in connection with the performance of his or her functions or powers, unduly receives, for him/her or for a third party, money or other things of value or accepts the promise of them (article 318 ICC). It should be noted that Law no. 190/2012 has significantly broadened the reach of this offence, which now relates to the receiving of money or other things of value, by the public official, either in exchange for the carrying out of a specific act not conflicting with the public official's duties (as it was also in the previous version), or for generally putting the public office at the potential availability of the briber, even in the absence of a specific public act being performed in exchange for a bribe. Punishment is imprisonment from one year to six years, and it can be increased due to 'aggravating circumstances';

(iii) 'bribery in judicial acts', which occurs when the conduct mentioned under the first two points above is taken for favouring or damaging a party in a civil, criminal or administrative proceeding (article 319-*ter* ICC). Punishment is imprisonment from six years to 12 years, and it can be increased due to 'aggravating circumstances';

(iv) the offence of 'unlawful inducement to give or promise anything of value', introduced by Law no. 190/2012, which punishes both the public official and the private briber, where the public official, by abusing his or her quality or powers, induces someone to unlawfully give or promise to him/her or to a third party, money or anything of value

Studio Legale Pisano

Italy

(article 319-*quater* ICC). Punishment is imprisonment from six to 10 years and six months for the public official, and up to three years for the private briber, which can be increased due to 'aggravating circumstances'. It should be noted that, under the previous regime, only the public official was responsible for the mentioned conduct, in relation to the differing offence of 'extortion committed by a public official' (article 317 ICC), whilst the private party was considered the victim of the crime. In the new system, the offence of 'extortion committed by a public official' (article 317 ICC) only applies to the residual cases where the private party is 'forced' by the public official to give or promise a bribe: in relation to such cases, the private party is still considered the victim of the crime, and the offence entails the exclusive criminal liability of the public official;

(v) the offence of 'trafficking of unlawful influences', introduced by Law no. 190/2012, which punishes anyone who, out of the cases of participation in the offences of 'proper bribery' and 'bribery in judicial acts', by exploiting existing relations with a public official, unduly makes someone giving or promising, to him/her or others, money or other patrimonial advantage, as the price for his/her unlawful intermediation towards the public official, or as consideration for the carrying out of an act conflicting with the office's duties, or for the omission or delay of an office's act. Criminal responsibility also equally applies to the private party who unduly gives or promises money or other patrimonial advantage (article 346-*bis* ICC). Punishment is imprisonment from one year to three years, and it can be increased due to 'aggravating circumstances'; or

(vi) 'instigation to bribery', which occurs when the private party makes an undue offer or promise that is not accepted by the public official, or when the public official solicits an undue promise or payment that is not carried out by the private party (article 322 ICC). Punishments provided for 'proper' bribery and for 'bribery for the performance of the function' apply, reduced by one-third.

Mental element

The mental element required for bribery offences is always intent (including, for the private party, knowledge and will to carry out an undue payment to a public official).

Foreign bribery

The bribery offences relating to foreign public officials are provided for by article 322-*bis* ICC (introduced by Law no. 300/2000, which implemented into the Italian legal system both the EU Anti-Corruption Convention of Brussels of 1997 on European Officials, and the OECD Anti-Bribery Convention of Paris of 1997 on Foreign Officials).

EU officials

As far as bribery relating to public officials of the EU institutions and of EU Member States is concerned, article 322-*bis* (paragraphs 1 and 2) ICC extends to such public officials, and to the private briber, the same bribery offences provided for domestic public officials indicated above.

Foreign and international officials

With respect to bribery relating to public officials of foreign states, and of international organisations (such as the UN, OECD, European Council, etc.), article 322-*bis* (paragraph 2) ICC extends to these situations the application of the mentioned domestic bribery offences, but with the following two significant limitations:

(i) only active corruption is punished (namely, only the private briber, on the assumption that the foreign public officials will be punished according to the laws of the relevant jurisdiction); and

(ii) on condition that the act is committed to obtain an undue advantage in international economic transactions or with the purpose of obtaining or maintaining an economic or

GLI - Bribery & Corruption Third Edition

143

www.globallegalinsights.com

financial activity (this last part of the prohibited conduct was recently introduced by Law no. 116/2009, which has implemented the UN Convention against Corruption of 2003).

Council of Europe Conventions

It should be noted that Italy recently ratified both the Council of Europe Criminal Law Convention against Corruption, signed in Strasbourg on January 27, 1999, through Law no. 110/2012, which came into force on July 27, 2012 and the Council of Europe Civil Law Convention on Corruption, signed in Strasbourg on November 4, 1999, through Law no. 112/2012, which came into force on July 27, 2012.

Entities

As far as entities/corporations are concerned, as of 2001 prosecutions can be brought against them also for bribery offences (article 25 of Legislative Decree no. 231/2001). In that respect, it is necessary that a bribery offence is committed in the interest or for the benefit of the corporation by its managers or employees.

The corporation's responsibility is qualified as an administrative offence, but the matter is dealt with by a criminal court in accordance with the rules of criminal procedure, in proceedings which are ordinarily joined with the criminal proceedings against the corporations' officers/employees.

Where the bribery offence is committed by an "employee", the corporation can avoid liability by proving to have implemented effective "compliance programs" designed to prevent the commission of that type of offence (article 7 of Legislative Decree no. 231/2001).

Where the bribery offence is committed by "senior managers", the implementation of effective "compliance programs" does not suffice, and the corporations' responsibility is avoidable only by proving that the perpetrator acted in "fraudulent breach" of corporate compliance controls (article 6 of Legislative Decree no. 231/2001).

Sanctions

Individuals. As previously mentioned, the sanctions for bribery offences (domestic and foreign ones) vary depending on the nature of the offence. In particular:
(i)   for 'proper bribery', punishment is imprisonment from four years to eight years, and it can be increased due to 'aggravating circumstances';
(ii) for 'bribery for the performance of the function', punishment is imprisonment from one year to five years, and it can be increased due to 'aggravating circumstances';
(iii) for 'bribery in judicial acts', punishment is imprisonment from four years to ten years, and it can be increased due to 'aggravating circumstances';
(iv) for the offence of 'unlawful inducement to give or promise anything of value', punishment is imprisonment from three to eight years for the public official, and up to three years for the private briber, and they can be increased due to 'aggravating circumstances';
(v)   for the offence of 'trafficking of unlawful influences', punishment is imprisonment from one year to three years, and it can be increased due to 'aggravating circumstances'; or
(vi) for 'instigation to bribery', punishments provided for 'proper' bribery and for 'bribery for the performance of the function' apply, reduced by one-third.

In addition, in case of conviction, confiscation of the "profit" or "price" of the bribery offence has to be applied (even "for equivalent", on assets of the offender for a value corresponding to the profit or price of the offence; art. 322-*ter* ICC).

Entities. As far as corporations are concerned, they are subject to sanctions represented by fines, disqualifications and confiscation.

Disqualifications can be particularly damaging, because they can include the suspension or revocation of government concessions, debarment, exclusion from government financing, and even prohibition from carrying on business activity (articles 9-13 of Legislative Decree no. 231/2001).

Such sanctions can also be applied at a pre-trial stage, as interim coercive measures. In case of conviction, confiscation of the "profit" or "price" of the offence has to be applied, even by confiscating "for equivalent" the assets of the corporation (article 19 of Legislative Decree no. 231/2001).

At a pre-trial stage, prosecutors can request the competent judge to grant freezing of the "profit" or "price" of the bribery offence (article 45 of Legislative Decree no. 231/2001).

Private commercial bribery

Until 2002, bribery offences were only applicable to the bribery of 'public officials' or 'persons in charge of a public service'. In 2002, an offence related to the corruption of private corporate officers has been introduced by article 2635 of the Italian Civil Code, punishable by imprisonment for up to three years, for both the briber and the corporate officer, on the condition that the corporation suffers damage from it and that the bribe is given or offered to its directors, general managers, internal auditors, liquidators or external auditors. Law no. 190/2012 has extended the reach of the offence to bribery of managers in charge of the accounting books and to bribery of ordinary employees, who are subject to the direction or supervision of the top managers: in this latter case, punishment is imprisonment up to one year and six months. A pre-condition for prosecuting the offence is a criminal complaint filed by the victim, unless the crime generates a distortion of competition in the acquisition of goods or services. The punishments are doubled in relation to corporations listed in Italy or in the European Union. No relevant case law has been developed yet on this offence.

Overview of enforcement activity and policy during the past two years

Main bodies responsible for the investigation of corruption offences

The main bodies responsible for the investigation and prosecution of corruption offences are the Public Prosecutors, who are assisted by the Public Forces, which include the State Police, the Carabinieri and the Financial Police.

Italian Public Prosecutors are not related to the government, but are professional magistrates. Their duties to bring criminal actions are compulsory and not discretionary (article 112 of the Constitution): such that where there is a "notice of crime" (a notice regarding specific facts potentially constituting a crime), the Public Prosecutor has a duty to open a formal criminal proceeding, to start investigations, and subsequently – if he assesses that the requirements of a crime are met – to bring a criminal prosecution, by requesting the "committal for trial" of the suspect. In the event the Public Prosecutor assesses that the "notice of crime" against a certain suspect is ungrounded, he has to request the dismissal to the competent judge (the so-called Judge for the Preliminary Investigations).

Enforcement

In relation to bribery offences, several investigations and prosecutions have been conducted by Italian authorities in recent years, also involving foreign companies. The following cases can be mentioned.

Domestic bribery (relating to Italian public officials)

(i) *The Enipower case*

This case concerns an investigation started in 2003 by the Milan Prosecution's Office for the alleged payment of bribes by several private parties to officers of the companies Enipower

Spa and Snamprogetti Spa (controlled by the state-owned company ENI), for the obtaining of public contracts and supplying. Some of the defendants, individuals and companies, have been sentenced by court decisions or entered into plea bargaining according to court authorisation.

(ii) *The Siemens AG case*

This case started in connection with the Enipower case mentioned above, and concerned the alleged payment of bribes by Siemens' officers to Enipower's officers for the obtaining of public contracts and supplying. The great significance of the case relates to the fact that, in April 2004, the Milan court applied for the first time the provisions on corporate criminal responsibility to a foreign corporation, and even at a pre-trial stage as interim coercive measures (Siemens was prohibited from entering into contracts with the Italian public administration for one year). The conviction of Siemens AG and of its officers has been subsequently confirmed by the Milan court.

(iii) *The G8 case*

The G8 case concerns allegations of corruption against government members in connection with the adjudication of public tenders regarding restructuring and building projects, in connection with the G8 held in Italy in June 2009. In October 2012, in a relevant leg of the prosecution, the Rome court of first instance sentenced both the public officials and private parties involved to punishments ranging from two years' to four years' imprisonment. In another leg of the prosecution, in September 2013, the judge of the preliminary hearing in Rome ordered the committal for trial for some relevant individuals charged with corruption and conspiracy. The first instance trial started in January 2014.

(iv) *The Lombardy Region case*

Investigations and prosecutions are pending against top politicians and officers of the Lombardy region, for allegedly having facilitated the obtainment of public health-care funds by certain private hospitals, in exchange for money or other patrimonial advantages. On November 27, 2014, the Court of first instance of Milan sentenced, in a separate relevant leg of the proceeding, the alleged intermediary of the bribe to five years' imprisonment. As far as the proceeding against the former President of the Lombardy Region is concerned, the trial is currently pending before the Court of first instance of Milan, section X.

(v) *Expo*

On May 2014, the Prosecutor's Office of Milan started an investigation in relation to the adjudication of public tenders in the context of the 2015 Universal Exposition of Milan. A relevant leg of the proceeding has already ended with plea bargaining by the main defendants, granted by the Judge of the Preliminary Hearing. The most severe sentence given was three years and four months' imprisonment,

(vi) *Mose*

In 2014, the Prosecutor's Office of Venice started an investigation against top politicians of the Veneto Region and business men for corruption relating to public funds used for the so-called *Mose project*, a huge dam aimed at protecting Venice from the high tide. On October 16, 2014, a relevant leg of the proceeding ended with plea bargaining of 19 defendants, granted by the Judge of the Preliminary Hearing. The most severe sentence was two years and 10 months' imprisonment and the confiscation of €2.6 million.

(vii) *Mafia Capitale*

In 2014, the Prosecutor's Office of Rome started investigations against top politicians of the Municipality of Rome and business men for corruption and conspiracy, in relation to the adjudication of public tenders concerning assistance services to be carried out by the Rome

Municipality (in particular assistance services for immigrants and refugees). Forty-four people were arrested in December, 2014 and the investigations are still pending.

<u>Foreign bribery (relating to foreign public officials)</u>
(i) *The Oil-for-Food programme*

With respect to the mismanagement of the Oil-for-Food programme, on March 10, 2009 the Milan court of first instance sentenced to two years' imprisonment three Italian individuals acting, directly or indirectly, for an Italian oil company, for the offence of foreign bribery, under the assumption that they paid bribes to a state-owned Iraqi company. On April 15, 2010 the Milan court of appeal acquitted all co-defendants owing to the time bar of the charges.

(ii) *ENI-Nigeria*

The ENI-Nigeria case concerns an investigation conducted by the Milan Prosecution's Office against the companies ENI Spa and Saipem Spa in relation to the offence of foreign bribery allegedly committed by the companies' officers (in the frame of the international consortium Tskj, involving the US company KBR-Halliburton, the Japanese Igc, and the French Technip), and allegedly consisting of significant payments to Nigerian public officials between 1994 and 2004 in order to win gas supply contracts. On November 17, 2009, the Milan judge for the preliminary investigations rejected the prosecutors' application to apply to ENI Spa and Saipem Spa the pre-trial 'interim measure' of prohibition from entering into contracts with the Nigerian National Petroleum Corporation, owing to lack of Italian jurisdiction. The case against ENI Spa was subsequently dismissed, and the case against five officers of Saipem Spa was also dismissed on April 5, 2012 due to the time bar. By contrast, in July 2013, Saipem Spa was sentenced by the Milan court of first instance in relation to this case, and appellate proceedings are currently pending.

(iii) *Finmeccanica-AgustaWestland/India*

The *Finmeccanica-AgustaWestland* case concerns an investigation conducted by the Prosecution's Office of Busto Arsizio (an area close to Milan) against the companies Finmeccanica and AgustaWestland, and their top managers, in relation to the offence of foreign bribery allegedly committed in 2010 in connection with the supply to the Indian government of 12 helicopters. In summer 2014, the Prosecutor discontinued the investigations against Finmeccanica, in the light of the assessment that the company was not involved in the alleged wrongdoing, and had implemented adequate compliance programmes to prevent corruption offences. In the same period, AgustaWestland Spa and AgustaWestland Ltd. entered into a plea bargain with the Prosecution's Office. In October 2014, the court of first instance acquitted on the merits the top managers of both companies for not having committed the bribery offences, but convicted them to about two years' imprisonment for the offence of tax fraud.

(iv) *New investigations*

New investigations for alleged foreign bribery are currently pending against the companies ENI and Saipem, and their managers, in relation to the adjudication of licences and/or public tenders in Nigeria and Algeria. In particular:
(a) with respect to Nigeria, in November 2013, the Milan Prosecution's Office started a new criminal investigation against the company ENI Spa, its top managers and some Italian and foreign intermediaries, in relation to the alleged offence of bribery of Nigerian public officials, in relation to the granting in 2011 by the Nigerian government to the subsidiaries of Eni and Shell of the oil-prospecting licence of an oil field located in the offshore territorial waters of Nigeria. The proceeding is still at the stage of investigations; and

(b) with respect to Algeria, the Milan Prosecution's Office started in recent years a criminal investigation against the companies ENI Spa and its subsidary Saipem spa, some of their top managers and foreign agents, in relation to the alleged offence of bribery of Algerian public officials, with respect to the adjudication of several tenders in Algeria in the period 2007-2010. On February 11, 2015, the Prosecutor's Office of Milan requested the committal for trial for all the defendants and the proceeding is pending the stage of the Preliminary Hearing.

Hot topics

<u>Facilitation payments</u>

Facilitation payments are prohibited by Italian law. Payments amounting to bribery offences are prohibited whether they are carried out directly or indirectly, through intermediaries or third parties. In the event of payments made through intermediaries, Italian prosecutors should prove, and Italian courts should assess, that the payment to the intermediary was made with the knowledge and intent of the intermediary subsequently bribing the Italian or foreign public official.

<u>Gifts/Hospitality</u>

Criminal provisions. Italian criminal provisions do not expressly restrict the providing of gifts, meals, entertainment, etc., either to domestic or foreign officials. However, all these advantages could potentially represent "undue consideration" for a public official, prohibited as a criminal offence by Italian law.

In particular, with respect to the offence of "bribery for the performance of the function", the consolidated case law excludes *tout court* criminal relevance with regard to gifts/hospitality of objective "small value", and which could be considered as "commercial courtesy" in the concrete case. Therefore, in the event no act conflicting with the duties of the office is carried out, and the two mentioned criteria are satisfied ("small value", to be considered as "commercial courtesy" in the concrete case), criminal responsibility should in principle be excluded.

On the contrary, in relation to the offence of "proper bribery" (act of the public official conflicting with the duties of his office), the consolidated case law maintains that the "small value" of the gift/hospitality never excludes, as such, the criminal responsibility. A crucial criterion for affirming or excluding criminal liability is therefore the relation of "*do ut des*" between the gift (or other advantage) and the "act" of the public official, in terms that the gift (or other advantage) represents the consideration for carrying out the mentioned "act".

Non-criminal provisions. Some Italian non-criminal regulations provide for specific restrictions about providing Italian officials with gifts and other benefits.

In particular, the Decree of the Prime Minister of December 20, 2007, entered into force on January 1, 2008, provides that Italian government members and their relatives are prohibited from keeping for their personal possession so-called "entertainment gifts", received on official occasions, for a value higher than €300 (article 2). Gifts having a value higher than €300 shall remain in the possession of the administration, or could be kept by the government members, on condition they pay the related difference (for the amount higher than €300).

Furthermore, on June 19, 2013, a new code of conduct for employees of the public administration entered into force (incorporated into Presidential Decree no. 62 of April 16, 2013), specifically aimed at preventing corruption and ensuring compliance with the public officials' duties of impartiality and exclusive devotion to the public interest. Pursuant to this code of conduct, the limit on the permissible value of "gifts of courtesy of small value" is equivalent to a maximum of €150.

A similar prohibition on receiving gifts or hospitality of any kind, with the exception of ones considered to be "commercial courtesy of small value", is ordinarily contained in most of the ethical codes implemented by the various state-owned or state-controlled corporations.

Notion of public officials

Bribery offences apply not only to "public officials" but also, with some exceptions, to the so-called "persons in charge of a public service" (article 320 ICC).

As far as the definitions of "public officials" and "persons in charge of a public service" are concerned, according to Italian criminal law:
(i) "public officials" are such persons "who perform a public function, either legislative or judicial or administrative" (for criminal law purposes, "[it is public] the administrative function regulated by the rules of public law and by acts of a public authority and characterised by the forming and manifestation of the public administration's will or by a procedure involving authority's powers or powers to certify"; article 357, paragraphs 1 and 2, ICC); and
(ii) "persons in charge of a public service" are "the ones who, under any title, perform a public service" (for criminal law purposes, "a public service should be considered an activity governed by the same forms as the public function, but characterised by the lack of its typical powers, and with the exclusion of the carrying out of simple ordinary tasks and merely material work"; article 358, paragraphs 1 and 2, ICC).

In accordance with the above definitions, the notion of "public officials" includes members of parliament, judges and their consultants, witnesses (from the moment the judge authorises their summons), notaries public, police officers, etc. By contrast, the notion of "persons in charge of a public service" includes state or public administration employees lacking the typical powers of a public authority (i.e. electricity and gas men, etc.).

With respect to employees of state-owned or state-controlled companies, they are not expressly included within the law definition, but they implicitly fall within the relevant "public" categories mentioned above, on condition that the activity effectively carried out by them is governed by public law or has a public nature.

Key issues relating to investigation, decision making and enforcement procedures

Plea bargaining

Under certain conditions, plea bargaining with prosecuting authorities is recognised by Italian law (article 444 of the Italian Code of Criminal Procedure). It has to be approved by the competent judge, the punishment agreed upon cannot be more than five years' imprisonment, and it is substantially considered as a conviction sentence (although with lower weight, because there is no assessment of responsibility further to a trial).

Furthermore, under certain conditions, a civil settlement with the person injured, aimed at compensating damage, can qualify as a 'mitigating circumstance' to reduce the criminal sentence.

Self-reporting and/or co-operation with prosecuting authorities

Italian law, with the exception of mafia or terrorism crimes, does not provide express benefits for voluntarily disclosing criminal conduct. However, it can be stated that, on a case-by-case basis, a certain degree of co-operation with the prosecuting authorities can produce positive effects, especially if joined with the compensation of damage in favour of the injured party (this could qualify as one or more "mitigating circumstances" able to reduce the subsequent sentence).

In particular, co-operation with the prosecuting authorities before trial (in terms of removal of the officers/body members allegedly responsible for the unlawful conduct, implementation of compliance programmes aimed at preventing the same type of offences, compensation of damage, etc.) can have a significant impact in reducing the pre-trial and final sanctions to be applied to a corporation (article 17 of Legislative Decree no. 231/2001).

Overview of cross-border issues

Jurisdiction

The governing principle of Italian law, also applicable to bribery offences, provides that Italian courts have jurisdiction on all offences committed within Italian territory; namely, when at least a segment of the prohibited conduct takes place in Italy (e.g., in relation to the bribery of foreign public officials, the decision to pay a bribe abroad). Italy has not established a general extra-territorial jurisdiction. A derogation in favour of extra-territorial jurisdiction applies only to a limited extent (e.g., presence in Italy of the suspect, and request of proceedings by the Italian Minister of Justice; see articles 9-10 ICC).

Jurisdiction over non-nationals for offences committed within Italy

Italian courts have jurisdiction over all offences committed within Italian territory (namely, when at least a segment of the prohibited conduct takes place in Italy), regardless of the offender's nationality (or corporate offender's main seat) (article 6 ICC).

Jurisdiction over Italian nationals for offences committed abroad

Italian courts have jurisdiction to prosecute a bribery offence involving Italian public officials even if the offence is committed abroad (article 7, no. 4, ICC). In this respect, therefore, the Italian courts have extra-territorial jurisdiction over Italian nationals (and also over non-nationals, in the limited cases where they have the quality of public officials of the Italian state).

In addition, Italian law has limited extra-territorial jurisdiction over corporations whose main seat is in Italy, for a bribery offence committed abroad, where the bribery offence is not prosecuted by the state where it was committed, and all the other requirements for establishing Italian extra-territorial jurisdiction over the corporations' officers/predicate offenders are fulfilled (e.g., presence of the suspect in Italy, request of proceedings by the Minister of Justice, etc.).

Jurisdiction over non-nationals for offences committed abroad

With respect to bribery offences committed abroad by offenders lacking the quality of Italian public officials (e.g., the private briber), Italian extra-territorial jurisdiction applies only to a limited extent, and under stringent requirements (e.g., presence in Italy of the suspect, and a request of proceedings by the Italian Minister of Justice; see articles 9-10 ICC).

Co-operation with foreign authorities

Italian Public Prosecutors do co-operate with foreign authorities. Where there is an international treaty in force with the relevant foreign country, this governs the mutual legal assistance to be provided. In the absence of a treaty, co-operation is governed by the specific provisions of the Italian Code of Criminal Procedure (article 696 ff. ICCP).

A request to a foreign authority for gathering evidence abroad (i.e., interview of suspects and witnesses, search and seizure, etc.) can be made by Italian Public Prosecutors, usually through the Italian Minister of Justice. In turn, where a request for assistance is made from foreign authorities to the Italian ones, both the Italian Minister of Justice and the competent Italian court of appeal usually have to approve it, and the latter delegates the execution of the request to the Italian Judge for the Preliminary Investigations.

Proposed reforms / The year ahead

The recent Law no. 190/2012 has provided for a reshaping of the functions and powers of the so-called Anti-Corruption National Authority (ANAC), in the frame of new compliance procedures within the public administration aimed at improving transparency in the decision-making process, at avoiding conflicts of interest and essentially at preventing the causes of corruption. In order to concretely implement the new philosophy and procedures, most of the efficiency of the system is linked to new decrees and regulations at present only partially issued by the government.

By Law Decree no. 90 of June 24, 2014, significant new powers have been attributed to ANAC, providing for the effective coordination and exchange of information of that body with the various Prosecution's Offices investigating cases of corruption, and for the effective powers of supervision of ANAC about the relevant public tenders. This is a concrete and positive step in the right direction.

Roberto Pisano
Tel: +39 02 7600 2207 / Email: robertopisano@pisanolaw.com
Roberto Pisano obtained a law degree, *summa cum laude*, from the State University of Milan in 1992, and a Ph.D. from the University of Genoa in 1999. Between 1993 and 1997 he was a research associate at Bocconi University of Milan where, since then, he has worked as a contract professor on business and tax crimes. Mr Pisano was co-chair of the business crime committee of the IBA in 2007-2008, and vice-chair of the ECBA in 2008-2009. He is the author of several publications on the subject of business crime and mutual legal assistance. Roberto Pisano is the founder and managing partner of Studio Legale Pisano, an Italian boutique firm which specialises in all areas of white-collar crime including corporate criminal responsibility, corruption, market abuse and false accounting, tax crimes, fraud and recovery of assets, bankruptcy crimes, environmental and health and safety crimes and money laundering. The firm also provides assistance in the course of regulatory investigations and specialises in transnational investigations and related aspects of mutual legal assistance and extradition. The firm benefits from the expertise of specialists in criminal and international law and interacts daily with counsel of various jurisdictions to successfully represent defendants during white-collar criminal and regulatory proceedings. The firm has a history of representing prominent individuals and entities in high-profile Italian criminal proceedings, and in the frame of foreign proceedings for judicial review of search and seizure orders, assets' confiscation, extradition and surrender according to the European Arrest Warrant regulations.

In the course of his practice, Mr. Pisano has successfully represented prominent individuals and entities in high-profile Italian criminal proceedings, including: various cases of corruption and money laundering involving international corporations and their top officials (including alleged corruption of Algerian officials by major international oil companies, with multiple investigations in US, Italy, France, etc.); various cases of extradition (including the recent FIFA investigation by the US authorities); three cases alleging international tax fraud involving the Italian prime minister, in which Mr. Pisano represented a well-known US movie producer; a case involving a claim for restitution of antiquities by the Italian Ministry of Culture, in which Mr. Pisano represented a prominent US museum; a case alleging a fraudulent bankruptcy of managers and contractual parties of Parmalat SpA, including foreign banks, in which Mr. Pisano represents a prominent external counsel of a US bank; a case alleging multiple homicide of employees of a multinational company manufacturing hazardous products, in which Mr. Pisano was a member of the defence team; various appeals in foreign jurisdictions (e.g. the USA, Hong Kong, Switzerland, Monaco, etc.) against seizure and confiscation of assets. Mr. Pisano is also an advisor and represents relevant foreign governments.

Studio Legale Pisano

Via Cino del Duca no. 5, Milan, 20122, Italy
Tel: +39 02 7600 2207 / Fax: +39 02 7601 6423 / URL: http://www.pisanolaw.com

Japan

Daiske Yoshida & Junyeon Park
Latham & Watkins

Background

Japan is widely perceived to be one of the least corrupt countries in the world. Transparency International ranked Japan as the 15th least corrupt country out of 175 in the most recent Corruption Perceptions Index – the second-highest in Asia – and Japanese companies as the fourth-least likely to pay bribes overseas.[1] Global Integrity reported Japan's overall anti-corruption and rule of law performance as "very strong",[2] and the U.S. State Department has characterised the direct exchange of cash for favours from Japanese government officials as "extremely rare".[3]

However, corruption was a prevalent feature of Japan's postwar economic boom, which was built on a close-knit alliance known as the "iron triangle" between Japanese businesses, politicians of the ruling Liberal Democratic Party ("LDP"), and elite bureaucrats.[4] This close coordination guided Japan to its growth as the world's second-largest economy, but it also created a culture of secret, backroom dealings which, when exposed, shocked the public. Some of the most notorious scandals of that era include: the Lockheed case (1976), which led to the conviction of former Prime Minister Kakuei Tanaka (and was partly responsible for the creation of the U.S. Foreign Corrupt Practices Act); the Recruit case (1989), which brought down the administration of Prime Minister Noboru Takeshita; the *Zenecon* (general contractors) cases (1993-1994), which resulted in several prefectural governors along with dozens of others being convicted, and one governor committing suicide; and the Bank of Japan/Ministry of Finance cases (1997-1998), which led to the arrests, resignations and suicides of several high-ranking finance officials.[5]

The type of conduct in these cases included firms seeking to win lucrative contracts through massive cash payments (Lockheed, *Zenecon*); firms offering highly lucrative insider stock information to win influence (Recruit); and officials receiving lavish entertainment, sometimes of a sexual nature, in exchange for favours (BoJ/MoF).[6] Japan's economic downturn through the 1990s soured the public's patience for such behaviour, and increasingly became the focus of blame for the nation's woes.[7] In particular, one type of entertainment – "*no-pan shabushabu*" (referring to an establishment where a type of hot pot was served by women wearing no underwear) – became synonymous in the public imagination with high-level corruption.[8]

In response, the Japanese government enacted various reforms, including requiring disclosure of politicians' assets,[9] bringing more transparency to political contributions,[10] and imposing stricter ethical rules on public officials.[11] In addition, especially over the past 10 years, Japanese companies have begun instituting codes of conduct that prohibit giving or receiving inappropriate payments, gifts or entertainment, not only to government officials, but in business transactions generally.[12] Today, the websites of nearly every listed Japanese company trumpet their commitment to compliance and corporate social responsibility. As a result, while some issues remain, as discussed in the "Current issues" section below, bribery is now widely understood in Japan to be impermissible, and corruption is no longer as prevalent a feature of the Japanese political and business landscape as it was 20 years ago.[13]

Since July 2013, an LDP-led coalition under the leadership of Prime Minister Shinzo Abe has dominated the Japanese government. His administration has pushed for an aggressive economic agenda, dubbed "Abenomics", based on the "three arrows" of fiscal stimulus, quantitative easing, and structural reforms. While the first two arrows have shown positive effects, there has been little progress in actual structural reforms in the Japanese economic system and corporate culture.

Legal overview

Bribery of Japanese public officials

Article 197 of Japan's Penal Code[14] prohibits a public official, defined as "a national or local government official, a member of an assembly or committee, or other employees engaged in the performance of public duties in accordance with laws and regulations",[15] from accepting, soliciting or promising to accept a bribe in connection with his or her duties.[16] It also prohibits a person who is to be appointed as a public official to do likewise, in the event that he or she is appointed.[17] Furthermore, it is an offence to give, offer or promise to give a bribe to a public official or a person to be appointed a public official.[18] Legal persons (*i.e.*, firms and organisations) are not liable for bribery under the Penal Code. Non-Japanese nationals are liable for bribery under the Penal Code only if the crime is committed within Japan.[19] Japanese public officials are liable for accepting bribes outside Japan.[20]

The punishment for the acceptance of a bribe by a public official (or a person to be appointed a public official) is imprisonment with work for not more than five years,[21] plus confiscation of the bribe or its monetary value.[22] Where a public official agrees to perform an act in response to a request, the sanction is imprisonment with work for not more than seven years.[23] Further, where such public official consequentially acts illegally or refrains from acting in the exercise of his or her duty, the sanction is imprisonment with work for a period within a range of one to 20 years.[24] The sanction for offering or promising to give a bribe to a public official is imprisonment with work for not more than three years, or a fine of not more than 2.5 million yen.[25]

As part of the reforms of the late 1990s, the Japanese government established the National Public Service Ethics Board, which provides a website with the ethics code applicable to bureaucrats, as well as detailed guidelines.[26]

"Deemed public officials" and other prohibitions against bribery of employees in public services

Under various laws specific to formerly or predominantly state-owned enterprises, employees of such entities have the status of "deemed public officials" (*minashi koumuin*), and it is expressly forbidden to give bribes to such persons, or for such persons to accept bribes.[27] Also, while not using the term "deemed public officials," certain laws in relation to specific companies that perform public services prohibit the bribery of employees.[28]

Bribery of foreign public officials

Japan has been a member of the Organisation for Economic Co-operation and Development ("OECD") since 1964. It implemented the 1997 OECD Anti-Bribery Convention in 1998, by amending the Unfair Competition Prevention Law ("UCPL")[29] to add Article 18, which criminalised bribery of foreign public officials.[30] Additional law was enacted in 2004 to broaden the jurisdiction of Article 18 to cover conduct by Japanese nationals while abroad.[31] Also, the Tax Law was amended in 2006 to prohibit the deduction as business expenses of bribes paid abroad.[32] Unlike the Penal Code, the UCPL expressly imposes criminal liability on legal persons (firms and organisations).[33]

Article 18 was intended to track the language of the Anti-Bribery Convention, and provides as follows:

> No person shall give, offer or promise any pecuniary or any other advantage, to a foreign public official, in order that the official act or refrain from acting in relation to the performance of official duties, or in order that the official, using his position, exert upon another foreign official so as to cause him to act or refrain from acting in relation to the performance of official duties, in order to obtain or retain improper business advantage in the conduct of international business.[34]

Originally, the penalty for bribery of a foreign public official was imprisonment with work for not more than three years or a fine of not more than 3m yen, or both, and the statute of limitations for natural persons had been three years; but in response to the OECD's recommendations, the penalties were increased to five years and 5m yen, and the limitations period was also extended to five years.[35] In addition, if an individual bribed a foreign official in connection with the business of a legal person, such legal person may be subject to a fine of not more than 300m yen.[36] The law does not provide for confiscation of the proceeds of bribing a foreign public official. The OECD Working Group recently recommended establishment of the legal authority to confiscate the proceeds of foreign bribery, which is required by the OECD Convention, and punish those who launder such proceeds.[37]

The Ministry of Economy, Trade and Industry ("METI") administers the UCPL, including Article 18, but prosecutions under Article 18 are handled by the Public Prosecutors Office. METI's website includes a section dedicated to the prevention of bribery of foreign officials,[38] and provides detailed "Guidelines to Prevent Bribery of Foreign Public Officials" that explains the law, as well as what companies can do to prevent bribery.[39]

Facilitation payments

The original METI Guidelines issued in 2004 indicated that the UCPL does not explicitly exempt "small facilitation payments", but that such payments would not be a criminal offence under the OECD Anti-Bribery Convention. The OECD criticised this (and METI's attempts to explain its interpretation) as confusing,[40] and METI updated the Guidelines in September 2010 to clarify that facilitation payments would be illegal under Japanese law if their purpose was "to obtain or retain improper business advantage in the conduct of international business".[41] The OECD criticised this guidance as misleading, so a revision in July 2015 clarified that demand for bribes from foreign public officials must be rejected as a rule, even if Japanese companies face cases in which they would be forced or extorted to pay bribes in order to avoid being treated unreasonably and unfairly by the foreign public officials.[42]

Commercial bribery

At least theoretically, commercial bribery is prohibited under Article 967 of the Companies Act.[43] Under that statute, if certain specified types of corporate executive or employee, or an accounting auditor, accepts, solicits or promises to accept property benefits in connection with such person's duties, in response to a wrongful request, it is punishable by imprisonment with work of up to five years or a fine of up to 5m yen.[44] In addition, the bribe or its monetary value may be subject to confiscation.[45] Giving, offering or promising to give a commercial bribe is punishable by imprisonment with work of up to three years or a fine of up to 3m yen.[46] This statute is analogous to Article 197 of the Penal Code, and the analysis of what constitutes a bribe is virtually the same.[47] However, this statute has been unused, with prosecutors instead preferring to go after managers who accept bribes based on "aggravated breach of trust" against the company, under Article 960 of the Companies Act.[48] There is no corporate liability for commercial bribery under the Companies Act.

Current issues

Kansei dango

Despite the reforms discussed above, one type of corruption that remains deeply entrenched in Japan is government-led bid-rigging on public projects (kansei dango): a type of bid-rigging scheme in which a public official acts as an organiser to determine which company will win.[49] Typically, the official is a representative of the government entity that issued the bid request, who wishes to dole out favours to firms (especially in construction) which are major sources of political funds, or are potential sources of work after the official leaves government. This type of conduct had been long accepted, but started to be prosecuted in the 1990s as part of the general trend towards anti-corruption. As the widespread nature of the practice became apparent, legal reforms were instituted in the early 2000s, including the passage of a law specifically prohibiting kansei dango[50] and amendments to the Anti-Monopoly Law.[51] But a flood of major bid-rigging incidents in 2005 and 2006, including those resulting in the arrests of three prefectural governors,[52] resulted in an accelerated passage in 2006 of amendments to the existing law against kansei dango.[53] Additionally, in 2006, shareholders began suing corporate executives on the theory that their participation in the bid-rigging schemes damaged the company.[54]

Despite these changes, new kansei dango cases continue to emerge. In 2010, it was reported that Air Self-Defense Force officials were involved in rigging procurement contracts.[55] In 2012, Ground Self-Defense Forces employees were found to have improperly provided information to a firm about a development bid for a next-generation helicopter.[56] In June 2013, Kagoshima police launched an investigation of a prefectural official in connection with a rigged hospital construction bid.[57] In March 2014, the Japan Fair Trade Commission ("JFTC") filed a criminal accusation relating to a bid-rigging case concerning snow-melting equipment engineering works for Hokuriku Shinkansen involving executives of Japan Railway Construction, Transport and Technology Agency, an incorporated administrative agency of the Ministry of Land, Infrastructure and Transportation ("MLIT").[58] In June 2015, the Metropolitan Police Agency raided the offices of MLIT's Tokyo Regional Civil Aviation Bureau in connection with a bid for inspection of sprinkler equipment.[59]

Further, the JFTC found in three separate cases (2007, 2009 and 2012) that officials of MLIT were involved in bid-rigging, requiring the JFTC to demand improvements by MLIT.[60]

Amakudari

A related issue is amakudari, which literally means "descent from heaven", and refers to the practice of government officials retiring into lucrative positions in businesses they used to regulate.[61] This practice has been identified as a significant cause for kansei dango, because bidders are populated by former officials of agencies requesting the bids, or provide future job opportunities for such officials.[62] It has been reported that, for example, 68 bureaucrats retired from METI into top positions at Japan's 12 electricity suppliers, which METI oversees,[63] and that between 2007 and 2009, 1,757 bureaucrats got jobs at organisations and firms that received subsidies or government contracts during 2008.[64]

In the wake of the *kansei dango* scandals of the mid-2000s, in which collusion was found to have occurred between current and former government officials, the National Public Service Act ("NPSA")[65] was amended in 2007.[66] The amendment prevented ministries from finding post-retirement jobs for their officials, limited job-hunting by officials while still in government, and prohibited former officials from recruiting activities.[67] However, the reform has not been particularly effective, with many officials still being hired by firms and organisations they used to oversee. During the administration of the Democratic Party of Japan ("DPJ") from 2009 to 2012, further attempts to amend the NPSA made no headway. In July 2013, the "Headquarters for Promotion of Reform to the National Public Service System", which was founded in 2008 to implement the 2007 amendment, formally disbanded after its five-year term expired; in fact, it was virtually non-operational during the DPJ years. The LDP included the eradication of *amakudari* as one of its campaign promises, but has not yet pressed for new legislation on this issue.

Low enforcement of UCPL Article 18

In the 17 years since its enactment in 1998, UCPL Article 18 has been enforced only four times:[68]

- In March 2007, two Japanese individuals were found guilty of bribing two senior Filipino officials with about 800,000 yen (approximately US$6,600) worth of golf clubs and other gifts, in an effort to win a government contract. They failed to win, but the bribes were reported by a whistleblower. The individuals were fined 500,000 yen (approximately US$4,100) and 200,000 yen (approximately US$1,700), respectively. It appears that the company they worked for (the Philippines subsidiary of a Japanese company) was not prosecuted.

- In January and March 2009, four Japanese individuals were found guilty of bribing a Vietnamese official in connection with a highway construction project that was partly financed by official development assistance ("ODA") from Japan. The value of the contract was approximately US$24m, and the total amount given to the official was about US$2.432m, but the court specified the amount of the bribes at US$820,000, partly because the statute of limitations had run on some of the earlier conduct. The four individuals were sentenced to imprisonment for 2.5 years, 2 years, 1.5 years, and 20 months, respectively, and all of their sentences were suspended for three years. The company they worked for was fined 70 million yen (approximately US$580,900), and also temporarily delisted by the Japan Bank for International Cooperation and the Japan International Cooperation Agency.

- In September 2013, a former executive of a Japanese automotive parts manufacturer was fined 500,000 yen (approximately US$4,100) for bribing an official in China to ignore an irregularity at a subsidiary's factory in Guangdong Province.

- In February 2015, the Tokyo District Court found a railway consulting firm and its three former executives guilty of violating the UCPL by bribing government officials of Vietnam, Indonesia and Uzbekistan with approximately US$1.2m in order to obtain consulting contracts related to ODA projects in the three countries. The court sentenced the three individuals to imprisonment for two years suspended for three years, three years suspended for four years, and two-and-a-half years suspended for three years, and fined the consulting firm 90 million yen (approximately US$747,000).[69] In the meantime, the Japanese government agency in charge of ODA said that Japan will resume providing ODA funds after Vietnam returns the bribe.[70]

The OECD has criticised this low level of enforcement activity, issuing a news release in January 2012, both in English and Japanese, stating: "Japan is still not actively detecting and investigating foreign bribery cases and, as a result, the enforcement of Japan's anti-bribery law remains low."[71] In February 2014, the OECD recommended that Japan establish and implement an action plan to address these concerns, and to report orally in March 2014 and in writing in June 2014.[72] The scheduled reports are not publicly available as of this writing, but the OECD released a critical statement in June 2014, specifically noting the action plan's failure to rectify misleading information on facilitation payments and to establish a legal authority to confiscate the proceeds of foreign bribery.[73]

The greatest challenge for increasing enforcement of this law is creating incentives for companies to self-report, or for whistleblowers to come forward. The type of whistleblower award programme instituted by the U.S. Securities and Exchange Commission will be difficult to implement in Japan, considering the smaller potential recovery available; the amount of the potential reward is unlikely to offset the downsides of reporting on one's employer. Instituting a leniency-type system to reduce potential fines in exchange for cooperation may encourage some companies to self-report, but the maximum corporate exposure of 300 million yen (approximately US$3m) may not be large enough to justify the trouble. Also, to the extent that the four decided cases so far provide any guidance, they seem to indicate that courts will impose a fine that is roughly equivalent to the amount of the bribe.

An interesting point of comparison may be the JFTC's cartel leniency programme, which is modelled on similar programmes in the US and the EU. When the programme was first proposed, many doubted that it would succeed in a group-oriented culture like Japan. But to the contrary, Japanese firms immediately began filing applications. Between 2006 and 2014, there have been a total of 836 filings, resulting in 102 publicised actions against a total of 245 firms.[74] Its success indicates that measures initially viewed as unlikely to succeed in Japan may still be worth implementing.

Daiske Yoshida is a partner and Junyeon Park is an associate in the Litigation Department of Latham & Watkins, Tokyo Office. This article reflects the views of the authors only.

* * *

Endnotes

1. Transparency International, *Corruption by Country: Japan* (http://www.transparency.org/country#JPN).
2. Global Integrity Report, *Japan: 2008* (https://www.globalintegrity.org/global/the-global-integrity-report-2008/japan/).
3. U.S. Department of State, Bureau of Economic and Business Affairs, *2015 Investment Climate Statement – Japan* (May 2015) (http://www.state.gov/e/eb/rls/othr/ics/2015/241609.htm).
4. *See* Takehiko Sone, "*Sei-kan-gyo no yuchaku wo meguru kozo oshoku: Nyusatsu dango ni okeru oshoku jiken wo chushin to shite*" ("Structural Corruption Concerning the Collusion of Politicians, Bureaucrats and Businesses: Focusing on Corruption Cases Involving Bid-Rigging"), *Kikan Kigyo to Houseizou* (*Quarterly Review of Corporation Law and Society*) vol. 3 (Nov. 2004), 149, 151 (http://www.win-cls.sakura.ne.jp/pdf/3/14.pdf) (in Japanese); *see also*, Velisarios Kattoulas, "Corruption Scandals Rack Tokyo's 'Iron Triangle': Struggle for Power in Japan," *New York Times*, Dec. 7, 1996 (http://www.nytimes.com/1996/12/07/news/07iht-scandal.t.html); David Holley "Bank of Japan Exec Arrested in Deepening Scandal," *Los Angeles Times*, Mar. 12, 1998 (http://articles.latimes.com/1998/mar/12/business/fi-27998).
5. Sone, *supra*, at 149 endnote 5, 6.
6. *See* Andrew Horvat, "MoF fries in 'no pan shabu shabu'," *Euromoney*, Mar. 199? (http://www.euromoney.com/Article/1005671/MoF-fries-in-no-pan-shabu-shabu.html)

7. *See* Alan C. Miller, "Japan's Money in the Mists," *Los Angeles Times*, Nov. 24, 1998; "Japan: Away with the Rogues," *The Economist*, Sep. 21, 2000.

8. *See* Horvat, *supra*.

9. Act No. 100 of 1992.

10. Act No. 5 of 1994, Act No. 106 of 1994.

11. Act No. 129 of 1999.

12. *See, e.g.*, Honda Conduct Guideline (http://world.honda.com/conductguideline/); Mitsui & Co., Ltd. Business Conduct Guidelines for Employees and Officers (http://www.mitsui.com/jp/en/company/governance/disclosure/); Toshiba Group Standards of Conduct (http://www.toshiba.co.jp/csr/en/policy/soc.htm).

13. There are still some cases, but they tend to be more regional and at a lower level. In June 2014, Hiroto Fujii, the mayor of Minokamo City in Gifu prefecture and widely known as the youngest mayor in Japan, was arrested on charges of receiving hundreds of thousands of yen in bribes from a businessman in 2013 while he was still a member of the city council. In March 2015, Fujii was found not guilty by the Nagoya District Court. "Nation's youngest mayor acquitted of bribery in Gifu", *The Japan Times*, Mar. 6, 2015 (http://www.japantimes.co.jp/news/2015/03/06/national/crime-legal/nations-youngest-mayor-acquitted-bribery-gifu/#.VgYaH5P55-8).

14. Act No. 45 of 1907.

15. Penal Code, art. 7. Unless otherwise noted, translations of Japanese laws in this article are from the "Japan Law Translation" website of the Ministry of Justice (http://www.japaneselawtranslation.go.jp/).

16. *Id.* art. 197(1).

17. *Id.* art. 197(2).

18. *Id.* art. 198.

19. *Id.* arts. 1(1), 3-2.

20. *Id.* art. 4(iii).

21. *Id.* art. 197.

22. *Id.* art. 197-5.

23. *Id.* art. 197.

24. *Id.* art. 197-3(1).

25. *Id.* art. 198.

26. http://www.jinji.go.jp/rinri/eng/index.htm (English website).

27. *See* Act No. 165 of 1947 (Japan Post); Act No. 89 of 1997 (Bank of Japan); Act. No. 205 of 1949 (bar association); Act No. 112 of 2003 (national universities); Act No. 185 of 1951 (driving schools); Act No. 141 of 1959 (National Pension Fund Association). This list of "deemed public officials" is not exhaustive.

28. *See* Act No. 69 of 1984 (Japan Tobacco); Act No. 85 of 1984 (NTT); Act No. 88 of 1986 (Japan Railways); Act No. 132 of 1950 (NHK); Act No. 124 of 2003 (Narita Airport); Act No. 37 of 2007 (International Criminal Court). In April 2015, employees of Japan Freight Railway Company and electrical equipment seller Kanaden Corporations have been arrested by Tokyo police on charges of taking and giving bribes in connection with warehouse construction projects in violation of the Act No. 88. "Officials of JR Freight, Kanaden arrested over bribes", *The Japan Times*, Apr. 12, 2015 (http://www.japantimes.co.jp/news/2015/04/12/national/crime-legal/officials-of-jr-freight-kanaden-arrested-for-bribery).

29. Act No. 47 of 1993.

30. Act No. 111 of 1998.

31. Act No. 51 of 2004; *see also* Penal Code, art. 3 and UCPL art. 21(6).

32. Act No. 10 of 2006, amending Article 45-2 of the Tax Law.

33. UCPL art. 22(1).
34. UCPL art. 18(1); translation from METI, *Guidelines to Prevent Bribery of Foreign Public Officials* (rev. Sep. 21, 2010) (http://www.meti.go.jp/policy/external_economy/zouwai/pdf/Guidelines%20to%20Prevent%20Bribery%20of%20Foreign%20Public%20Officials.pdf) ("Guidelines"). As of this writing, METI's official English translation of the current Guidelines (rev. July 30, 2015) is not yet available, but METI's English summary of the July 2015 revision is available at METI – July 2015 News Releases – Revision of Guideline to Prevent Bribery of Foreign Public Officials (http://www.meti.go.jp/english/press/2015/0730_03.html).
35. UCPL art. 21(2)(vii); OECD Working Group on Bribery, *Japan: Phase 2bis Report on the Application of the Convention on Combating Bribery of Foreign Public Officials in International Business Transactions and the 1997 Recommendation on Combating Bribery in International Business Transactions* (June 2006), at 11 (http://www.oecd.org/daf/anti-bribery/anti-briberyconvention/37018673.pdf).
36. *Id.* art. 22(1).
37. Statement of OECD on Japan's Efforts to Increase Foreign Bribery Enforcement, June 12, 2014 (http://www.oecd.org/corruption/statement-of-oecd-on-japan-efforts-to-increase-foreign-bribery-enforcement.htm).
38. http://www.meti.go.jp/policy/external_economy/zouwai/index.html (in Japanese).
39. http://www.meti.go.jp/policy/external_economy/zouwai/shishin.html (in Japanese).
40. OECD Working Group on Bribery, *Japan: Phase 2 Report on the Application of the Convention on Combating Bribery of Foreign Public Officials in International Business Transactions and the 1997 Recommendation on Combating Bribery in International Business Transactions* (March 2005), at 40-41 (http://www.oecd.org/daf/anti-bribery/anti-briberyconvention/34554382.pdf).
41. METI press release, "Revision of 'Guidelines to Prevent Bribery of Foreign Public Officials'", Sep. 21, 2010 (http://www.meti.go.jp/english/press/data/20100921_01.html); Guidelines, *supra*, at 16. The OECD Working Group on Bribery criticised that the Guidelines failed to rectify misleading information on "facilitation payments" and suggested METI to make clear that "facilitation payments" are not exempted by Japan's foreign bribery offence. Endnote 37 *supra*.
42. METI – July 2015 News Releases – Revision of Guideline to Prevent Bribery of Foreign Public Officials (http://www.meti.go.jp/english/press/2015/0730_03.html).
43. Act. No. 86 of 2005.
44. *Id.* art 967(1).
45. *Id.* art. 969.
46. *Id.* art. 967(2).
47. Seiichi Ochiai, ed., *Kaishaho Kommentar* (*Companies Act Commentary*) (2011), vol. 21 § 967, at 125 (in Japanese).
48. *See* Masaki Nagamine, "*Fusei no seitaku: Jitsu wa minkan kigyo nimo aru 'shuwaizai' towa*" ("Illegal solicitation: 'Bribery' also exists in the private sector"), *President*, Mar. 15, 2010 (http://president.jp/articles/-/1658) (in Japanese). Companies Act Article 960 is a broader statute with a greater potential penalty (10 years' imprisonment or 10 million yen).
49. *See* Sone, *supra*; Miyuki Takazawa, "*Kansei dango no omo na jirei to boushi taisaku*" ("Major cases and preventive measures for *kansei dango*"), *National Diet Library Issue Brief*, No. 543 (Jun. 13, 2006) (http://www.ndl.go.jp/jp/data/publication/issue/0543.pdf) (in Japanese); Reiji Yoshida, "How Japanese tax-payers' money is lost in bid-rigging," *The Japan Times*, Jul. 3, 2007 (http://www.japantimes.co.jp/news/2007/07/03/reference/how-japanese-tax-payers-money-is-lost-in-bid-rigging/#.UhWX5htcXis).

50. Act No. 101 of 2002.

51. Act No. 35 of 2005.

52. *See* Mariko Sanchanta, "Japan bid-rigging scandal widens," *Financial Times*, Jun. 29, 2005 (http://www.ft.com/intl/cms/s/0/d49230b0-e88f-11d9-87ea-00000e2511c8. html#axzz1N3kxCebs) (Japan Highways case); "Two held over Narita bid-rigging," *The Japan Times*, Dec. 6, 2005 (http://www.japantimes.co.jp/news/2005/12/06/news/ two-held-over-narita-bid-rigging/#.UhWO6BtcXis) (Narita Airport case); "Governor of Fukushima steps down over brother's bid-rigging arrest," *The Japan Times*, Sep. 28, 2006 (http://www.japantimes.co.jp/news/2006/09/28/national/governor-of-fukushima-steps-down-over-brothers-bid-rigging-arrest/#.UhWTTBtcXis) (Fukushima Prefecture case); "Builder allegedly governor's payoff conduit," *The Japan Times*, Nov. 17, 2006 (http://www.japantimes.co.jp/news/2006/11/17/national/builder-allegedly-governors-payoff-conduit/#.UhWU1xtcXis) (Wakayama Prefecture case); "Ex-governor arrested over bidding scandal," *The Japan Times*, Dec. 9, 2006 (http://www.japantimes. co.jp/news/2006/12/09/national/ex-governor-arrested-over-bidding-scandal/#. UhWSjxtcXis) (Miyazaki Prefecture case).

53. Act No. 110 of 2006 (amending Act No. 101 of 2002).

54. *See* Steel Bridge Cartel Shareholder Litigations (2006).

55. "ASDF chief sacked, 49 disciplined for Chiba supply depot bid-rigging", *The Japan Times*, Dec. 16, 2010 (http://www.japantimes.co.jp/news/2010/12/16/national/asdf-chief-sacked-49-disciplined-for-chiba-supply-depot-bid-rigging/#.UhYLRBtcXis).

56. "*Kawaju wo shimei teishi e: Boueicho, heli dangou jiken uke*" ("Kawasaki Heavy delisted by MOD, based on helicopter bid-rigging case"), *Nihon Keizai Shimbun*, July 29, 2013 (http://www.nikkei.com/article/DGXNASDG2903U_Z20C13A7CR8000/) (in Japanese); "*Kawaju kabunushi ga yakuin teiso seikyu: Rikuji heli dango, 46 oku songai*" ("Kawasaki Heavy shareholders seek to sue management; GSDF helicopter bid-rigging, 4.6 billion in damages"), *Kobe Shimbun*, July 23, 2013 (http://www.kobe-np.co.jp/news/shakai/201307/0006185433.shtml) (in Japanese).

57. "*Kagoshima kenritsu byoin to shicho sosaku; Amami Oshima kansei dango jiken*" ("Kagoshima prefecture hospital and government office investigated; Amami Oshima bid-rigging case"), *MSN/Sankei News*, June 9, 2013 (http://sankei.jp.msn.com/affairs/ news/130609/crm13060920030003-n1.htm) (in Japanese).

58. "The JFTC Filed a Criminal Accusation on Bid-Rigging Concerning Snow-Melting Equipment Engineering Works for Hokuriku Shinkansen Ordered by the Japan Railway Construction, Transport and Technology Agency," Mar. 4, 2014 (http://www.jftc.go.jp/ en/pressreleases/yearly-2014/March/140304.html).

59. "*Tokyo Koukukyoku wo Sosaku: Seibitenken de Dango Yougi: Keishicho*" ("Metropolitan Police Investigating Tokyo Aviation Bureau, Suspicion of Bid-rigging on Equipment Inspection"), *Asahi Shimbun Digital*, June 5, 2015 (available at http:// digital.asahi.com/articles/DA3S11791997.html?rm=150) (in Japanese).

60. "*Kochi de kansei dango nintei: Kotorii, Kokukosho ni kaizen sochi youkyu*" ("Government-led bid-rigging found in Kochi: JFTC demands improvements by MLIT"), *Nihon Keizai Shimbun*, Oct. 17, 2012 (http://www.nikkei.com/article/ DGXNASDG1703Y_X11C12A0CR8000/) (in Japanese).

61. *See* U.S. Department of State, *supra*; Hiroko Nakata, "'Amakudari' too entrenched to curb?" *The Japan Times*, May 29, 2007 (http://www.japantimes.co.jp/news/2007/05/29/ reference/amakudari-too-entrenched-to-curb/#.UhWczxtcXis).

62. *See* "1,757 got jobs via 'amakudari' from '07 to '09," *The Japan Times*, Aug. 24, 2010 (http://www.japantimes.co.jp/news/2010/08/24/national/1757-got-jobs-via-amakudari -from-07-to-09/#.UhWk2BtcXis); Takazawa, *supra*.

63. "Utilities got 68 ex-bureaucrats via 'amakudari'," *The Japan Times*, May 4, 2011 (http://www.japantimes.co.jp/news/2011/05/04/news/utilities-got-68-ex-bureaucrats-via-amakudari/#.UhWjsRtcXit).

64. See endnote 60, *supra*.

65. Act No. 120 of 1947.

66. Act No. 108 of 2007.

67. *Id.*; *see also* Kimio Kobayashi, "*Kokka komuin no amakudari konzetsu ni muketa kinnnen no torikumi*" ("Recent Efforts Towards Eliminating 'Amakudari' by Government Officials"), *National Diet Library – Reference* (August 2012), 27, 32 (http://dl.ndl.go.jp/view/download/digidepo_3525594_po_073902.pdf?contentNo=1) (in Japanese).

68. *See* Guidelines, *supra*, at 28; OECD Working Group on Bribery, *Phase 3 Report on Implementing the OECD Anti-Bribery Convention in Japan* (Dec. 2011), at 10-11 (http://www.oecd.org/daf/anti-bribery/anti-briberyconvention/Japanphase3reportEN. pdf); "*Futaba sangyo no moto senmu, bakkin 500,000 en chugoku koumuin-e zouwai*" ("Former Senior Managing Director of Futaba Industrial, fined 500,000 yen for bribing Chinese government officer"), Asahi Shimbun, Oct. 4, 2013 (In Japanese). There have been reports of other investigations that were ultimately dropped. *See* Ministry of Foreign Affairs, "*Tai Mongol ODA wo meguru Mitsui Bussan ni yoru zowai yougi to OECD gaikoku koumuin zouwai boushi jouyaku*" ("Alleged bribery by Mitsui Bussan relating to ODA to Monglia, and the OECD Anti-Bribery Convention") (Sept. 2002) (http://www.mofa.go.jp/mofaj/gaiko/oecd/mongolia.html) (in Japanese); "*Indonesia kokan settai yougi, Sumisho sha-in wo fukiso: Tokyo chiken*" ("Alleged entertainment of high-ranking Indonesia official: Tokyo district prosecutor to not indict Sumisho employees"), *Asahi Shimbun*, July 3, 2012 (http://www.asahi.com/20120703/pages/national.html) (in Japanese).

69. "ODA fusei konsaru maeshachora yuzai Tokyo chizai 'fukouseina kyousou joutaika'" ("For ODA corruption, former consulting firm president found guilty, with the Tokyo District Court finding 'chronic unfair competition'"), *Tokyo Yomiuri Shimbun*, Feb. 5, 2015 (in Japanese).

70. "Vietnam asked to return bribe in Japan's ODA project," *Thanh Nien News*, Apr. 1, 2015 (http://www.thanhniennews.com/society/vietnam-asked-to-return-bribe-in-japans-oda-project-40612.html).

71. OECD news release, "Serious Concerns Remain over Japan's Enforcement of Foreign Bribery Law, Despite Some Positive Developments" (Jan. 12, 2012) (http://www.oecd. org/japan/seriousconcernsremainoverjapansenforcementofforeignbriberylawdespiteso mepositivedevelopments.htm).

72. Japan: Follow-Up to the Phase 3 Report & Recommendations, February 2014, (http://www.oecd.org/daf/anti-bribery/JapanP3WrittenFollowUpReportEN.pdf).

73. Endnote 37 *supra*.

74. JFTC news release, "*Heisei 26 nendo ni okeru dokusen kinshiho ihan jiken no shori joukyou ni tsuite*" ("Regarding the Enforcement of the Anti-Monopoly Law in Fiscal Year 2014"), May 27, 2015 (http://www.jftc.go.jp/houdou/pressrelease/h27/may/150527_1.html) (in Japanese).

Daiske Yoshida
Tel: +81 3 6212 7800 / Email: daiske.yoshida@lw.com
Daiske Yoshida is a partner in the Tokyo office of Latham & Watkins. He has extensive experience in cross-border litigation, arbitration and investigations in a wide range of subject areas, including intellectual property, antitrust, securities, accountant liability, and general commercial litigation. Mr. Yoshida represents clients in US federal and state courts as well as international arbitrations, and supervises large-scale internal investigations in Japan, US and Europe involving anti-trust, anti-corruption and securities law issues. His experience includes cases both at the trial and appellate levels, including appeals before the U.S. Supreme Court and the Second, Ninth and Federal Circuit Court of Appeals.

Mr. Yoshida also has extensive experience in pre-litigation analysis of potential intellectual property and antitrust claims (both defensive and offensive), and advises clients in transactions involving intellectual property rights, antitrust issues, and arbitration agreements.

Mr. Yoshida is qualified to practise before the New York bar and in Japan as *Gaikokuho-Jimu-Bengoshi* (registered foreign lawyer, New York law). He is fluent in Japanese and English.

Junyeon Park
Tel: +81 3 6212 7815 / Email: junyeon.park@lw.com
Junyeon Park is an associate in the Litigation Department of Latham & Watkins' Tokyo office. Her practice focuses on cross-border litigation and international arbitration.

Prior to joining Latham & Watkins, Ms. Park worked in the New York office of a major New York law firm as an associate, where she was a member of the firm's litigation department. Before attending law school, she served as a foreign service officer for the Ministry of Foreign Affairs and Trade of Korea. During law school, Ms. Park served as Senior Articles Editor of the NYU Journal of International Law and Politics.

Ms. Park is fluent in English, Japanese, and Korean.

Latham & Watkins

Marunouchi Building, 32nd Floor, 2-4-1 Marunouchi, Chiyoda-ku, Tokyo 100-6332, Japan
Tel: +81 3 6212 7800 / Fax: +81 3 6212 7801 / URL: http://www.lw.com

Mexico

Luis F. Ortiz
OCA Law Firm

Historical overview

Corruption in Mexico dates back to when the Spanish took over in around the 16th century; in those times, public officials and governors were appointed by the king and had to pay the Crown.

Since the late 1950s, Mexico has a documented history of bribery and there have been several attempts to fight it by former presidents while in office. Corruption has accompanied more than 70 years of the PRI Party (*Partido Revolucionario Institucional*), now back in office after two consecutive six-year terms when the PAN party (*Partido Acción Nacional*) had a chance to tackle corruption but failed to do so.

In the Congressional arena, deputies and senators have constantly recognised the threat corruption and money laundering pose to growth, how they affect poverty and how they distort the Mexican economy, among other real threats.[1] Corruption has been around long since, and is widespread in the business sector as well as the justice system and police groups.

"The most striking issue in Mexico is the extent to which the drug war has negatively influenced the country's anti-corruption and transparency efforts… The drug war also has affected the autonomy and physical safety of Mexican judges and journalists."[2]

Now President Enrique Peña Nieto is in office, and as part of his presidential campaign he has promised to deliver an Anti-corruption Commission, while ending the Ministry of Administration's long-standing position as the agency in charge of governmental and public procurement corruption investigations. This big-budget Ministry has changed its name and been reformed several times without proving to make a difference in tackling corruption. Probably one of its legacies will be the elimination of more than 16,000 rules and norms in order to standardise administrative processes and thus provide good-quality services to citizens and eliminate all unnecessary rules (the so-called 'guillotine of administrative regulations').

In the late '90s, Mexico reinforced its legal framework towards combatting bribery and corruption. Since then, significant changes and legal reforms have been part of its social and economic development agenda including the fight against and prevention of money laundering.

On December 2nd 2012, the main political parties signed a national political agreement called the Pact for México in Mexico City's historical Chapultepec Castle. The document comprises specific agreements to reform the education, telecoms, justice and security, as well as transparency and anti-corruption sectors.

This agreement provides the creation of the National Anti-corruption Commission and local commissions, with specific emphasis on the oil and gas giant Pemex and Energy CFE (*Comisión Federal de Electricidad*) (Agreement No. 85), as well as the National Ethics Council aiming at aspects such as transparency and government spending (Agreement No.86). These two agreements should have been public and functional by the second semester of 2014 and second semester of 2015, respectively. The Anti-corruption Commission never came into effect and instead, legislators decided on the creation of the National Anti-corruption System which supposedly increases investigative and sanctioning powers to Superior Audit Office and the Federal Tribunal of Administrative Justice; the details of the changes will be proposed and discussed in secondary laws that must be passed in the next year.

Mexico is a member of: the OAS Inter-American Convention against Corruption; the OECD Convention on Combating Bribery of Foreign Officials in Business Transactions; and the United Nations Convention Against Corruption, and has been assessed by OECD on a second round by Spain and Slovenia, along with OECD officials, for 2011.[3]

Following such assessments Mexico has decided to comply with its recommendations, while taking into consideration reforms in the areas of the anti-corruption legal framework, transparency and prosecution topics.

Consequently, in accordance with OECD and OAS Convention principles, since the 1990s Mexico has assumed its obligation to legislate on bribery and money laundering too.

Current laws related to anti-bribery and corruption:
- Federal Criminal Code.
- Federal Anti-corruption Law on Public Procurement.
- Federal Law of Administrative Responsibilities of Public Officials.
- Agreement that aims to issue the Code of Ethics of civil servants of the Federal Government, the integrity rules for the exercise of public functions and general guidelines to foster the integrity of public servants and to implement permanent measures to encourage their ethical behaviour through the Ethics Committees and the Prevention of Conflicts of Interest (2015).
- Agreement that issues the protocol on public contracts, granting and renewal of licences, permits, authorisations and concessions (2015).

Competent authorities on bribery and corruption in Mexico:
- Ministry of Public Administration.
- Attorney-General's Office.
- Superior Audit Office.
- Federal Tribunal of Administrative Justice.
- Ethics Council for Government Spending (pending and agreed upon as part of the political instrument, Pact for México).

Recent cases and enforcement actions and clean-up campaigns

Since former President Felipe Calderon's mandate, Mexico has started to react to crime and corruption. An open war against drug lords and a clean-up of the police has taken place since then.

Before this war was declared on warlords, cartels fought one another, inefficient police were not able to react accordingly due to lack of will, inferior weaponry and, of course, corruption. In 2011 a big clean-up of corrupt public officers occurred in the police sector, and many had their employment terminated. Official reports state that 600 policemen were removed, 600 were reassigned and 20,000 PGR (Attorney General's Police Corps.) were to be vetted through drug tests, lie detectors and psychological exams.[4]

Both during and after the campaign, just like one of his predecessors, Vicente Fox, Enrique Peña Nieto has promised to catch "the untouchables"; after three years in office this has not yet happened. Enforcement on bribery and corruption scandals has been slow and certainly inaccurate, leaving Mexican citizens with a sense of distrust and affecting foreign direct investment decision-making. Civil society has prudently and respectfully demanded President Nieto to unfreeze proposed legislation currently in Deputies' drawers[5], the Anti-Corruption Commission Bill; the surprise was that the bill was not put into action, but instead Congress decided to pass the National Anti-corruption System.[6]

The most interesting case is the commemorative monument of the Mexican Independence Bicentenary Pillar of Light (official name, *Estela de Luz*) known as the 'Monument to Corruption' by locals, and the Maestra case (Elba Esther Gordillo) where Mexicans saw the entire criminal apparatus like never before. On February 26th, Mexican authorities arrested Elba Esther Gordillo Morales, one of Mexico's most prominent political figures. Known in Mexican politics as "The Teacher" (a.k.a. La Maestra), she was apprehended and charged with organised crime[7] and the embezzlement of union funds from the National Syndicate of Education Workers (*Sindicato Nacional de Trabajadores de la Educación*, SNTE), which she has headed or controlled indirectly since 1989.[8] She is still in jail for money laundering and tax evasion charges.

According to the Federal Superior Audit Office (ASF) report, the cost of the commemorative memorial of the Mexican Independence Bicentenary was three times more expensive than its initial budget. ASF detected 400 million pesos in unjustified payments. Some arrest warrants were issued to public officials, most of them from the corporation called *Triple i Servicios* (a Pemex subsidiary).

Mexicans are struggling with a new enemy: conflict of interest and a lack of solid regulation to end it. Leading reporter Carmen Aristegui and her team pointed out a potential conflict of interest between a company associated with the country's first high-speed rail contract and a mansion (valued at about $7m/£4.4m)[9] apparently designed for the presidential family. Immediately after this scandal was brought to light, Finance Minister Luis Videgaray additionally had to explain about a weekend mansion also related to public contracts. Recently appointed federal comptroller (PRI-friendly) Virgilio Andrade's investigation concluded that there was no conflict of interest behind the president and Mr. Videgaray's decisions to award contracts to companies that sold homes to him and the president's wife. This decision left Mexicans in a state of shock and bigger distrust.

Authorities

Anti-corruption Office of the Attorney General

In 2014, the Office of the Mexican Attorney-General published in the official gazette the creation of the Specialized Anti-corruption Prosecution Office, which will address public officials' wrongdoings as well as investigative work related to federal corruption crimes.

Ministry of Public Administration.

After the announcement of the Anti-corruption Commission in a Federal Decree, the Presidency announced the dissolution of the Ministry of Public Administration in order to create the Commission. With the creation of the Anti-corruption System, this office was reborn and is now functioning; its first big project was to investigate President Peña for conflict of interest accusations. While creating a bigger problem with a conflict of interest itself, the Ministry cleared the President, arguing that there was no conflict of interest behind the president and his finance minister's actions to award contracts to companies that sold homes to the president's wife (white house scandal).

Criminal aspect of anti-bribery laws in Mexico and foreign bribery

Since 5th January 1983, bribery has been contemplated in the Criminal Code (*Código Penal*) (art. 222) and sanctions any public officer or any third party who in their representation accept, ask for or receive any bribe, accept a promise to do or stop doing something related to their capabilities or acts in a wrongful manner according to their functions, or where spontaneously someone gives or offers money to a public officer for that same purpose. The sanctions may reach 14 years of imprisonment and fines of up to US$2,800 plus a 14-year prohibition on working as a public official.

The said code also provides for (art. 222-*bis*) foreign bribery and will sanction with the same fines and terms of imprisonment anyone found guilty of bribing a foreign official by promising, offering, or delivering money or gifts to a public official or a third party so that the public official will either act or not act in his or her official capacity in order to secure or retain an advantage regarding public contracts.

Administrative aspect of anti-corruption laws in Mexico

In June 2012, the Mexican Congress enacted the Federal Law Against Corruption in Public Procurement (*Ley Federal Anticorrupción en Contrataciones Públicas* or the Anti-Corruption Law – FCPA).

This is not an FCPA law *per se*, yet some similarities may arise from its reading; the law gathers into a single statute and codifies the actions or omissions that constitute corruption.

This anti-corruption law has an administrative nature rather than a criminal one and holds accountable individuals and companies for offering money or gifts to obtain or maintain a business advantage in the procurement of public contracts with the Mexican government – but it has no municipal or state-contracting jurisdiction, only federal.

Provisions of the anti-corruption law

The law applies to Mexican and non-Mexican corporations as well as individuals engaged in federal government contracting. It is also applicable to any transactions including the preparation process for bidding, and lists what the law may consider to be an intermediary or agent including bidders, participants in tenders, request for proposal recipients, suppliers, contractors, permit holders, concessionaires and their shareholders and agents.

Prohibitions. The acts and omissions prohibited by the law may include the following:
- Promising, offering, or delivering money or gifts to a public official or a third party so that the public official will either act or not act in his or her official capacity, in order to secure or retain an advantage regarding public contracts.
- Influence peddling (traffic of influence).
- Submitting false or altered documentation.
- Engaging in acts or omissions with the purpose or effect of participating in federal public contracting when prohibited from participating under the law or relevant regulations (i.e. debarment).
- Engaging in acts or omissions with the purpose or effect of evading the rules or requirements established in federal contracting procedures (i.e. false declarations or representation).

The Anti-Corruption Law also criminalises bribery of non-Mexican government officials and enables the Ministry of Public Administration to investigate and sanction directly those found guilty.

Economic sanctions are calculated according to the minimum wage but may reach more than US$10m plus a potential debarment from public contracting in Mexico for two to 10 years. The law provides for plea bargaining as an acceptable method of resolving a case, as follows: if the plea is entered during the investigation phase, the monetary penalty may be reduced by up to 70%; if a plea is entered after the sanctions phase has commenced, the monetary penalty may be reduced by up to 50%. For a sanction reduction to happen, the individual or corporation would need to prove: i) wrongdoing to have ceased; ii) no repeated misconduct; and iii) full cooperation. There are no disgorgements of profits in our law.

FCPA international effect

Among multinationals, FCPA seems to be more of a law to focus on than the existing local or federal ones. Mexico has been hit by foreign bribery provoked by US subsidiaries while doing business in Mexico. Some of those corporations have paid more than US$7m to settle allegations with the Department of Justice (DOJ) or Securities and Exchange Commission (SEC); the bribe recipients in recent US enforcement actions involving Mexico have included customs officials, veterinary inspectors and doctors at public hospitals.[10] Some of those investigated have accepted their guilt; some have paid without denying or accepting charges; and some have signed Deferred Prosecution Agreements.[11]

Either way, these situations have raised awareness in Mexico among international corporations' legal staff. Some corporations have taken these public cases as a warning for their corporations. Since the Siemens case, or the Wal-Mart and recently the HP investigations, Mexican corporations are putting in place controls and corruption–prevention tools, and have paid more attention to third party investigations or their KYC systems and protocols. Third party due diligence and assessments have increased dramatically, and are raising awareness.

Foreign bribery

Although there is no special law prohibiting or sanctioning foreign bribery from Mexican citizens and corporations, other legal bodies do provide for this topic. There are administrative and legal provisions that deal with this international crime.

The Criminal Code (article 222-*bis*) prohibits to offer, promise or give, directly or through an intermediary, money or any other gift constituting either goods or services with the purpose to obtain or retain for oneself or for another person illegal advantage while developing or conducting international business transactions; this activity is sanctioned with fines and up to 14 years' imprisonment.

Also, from an administrative standpoint, the Anti-Corruption Law (art. 9) prohibits and sanctions any activity made by individuals or corporations, nationals or foreign corporations that offer to pay, promise to pay, or deliver money or gifts to a public official or a third party so that the public official will either perform or omit an act in his or her official capacity, in order to secure or retain an advantage regarding public contracts in international transactions. The said law also provides for coordinated international cooperation activity. This action between Mexican and one or more foreign administrations, by means of a formal petition made by foreign governments' competent authority, will allow both administrations to coordinate actions, and the means to prosecute and sanction.

USA and AML compliance standards in Mexico

In comparisons of global GDP, Mexico has the 53rd highest, and its economy is predicted to grow by 4% this year. The Mexican automotive industry generated more revenue in the country last year (US$23bn) than tourism or oil, a sign of manufacturing resurgence.[12]

Currently, energy corporations in the US are seeking legal advice from Mexican compliance experts in preparing and strengthening their compliance teams. Foreign corporations doing oil and gas business should help bring to Mexico high standards of compliance.

On 23rd December 2013, President Peña Nieto signed the Senate-amended version of the constitutional energy reform bill into law (ending a 75-year-old state monopoly in the oil sector and a 53-year-old one in the electricity sector). Since the secondary laws were introduced into the Senate on 30th April 2014, intense discussions have taken place with both potential investors and Pemex.[13] On August 12th 2014, a package of energy reform legislation became law in Mexico, which includes nine new laws as well as amendments to existing laws.

According to PricewaterhouseCoopers (cited by ICC), in 2014: 47% of Mexican corporations surveyed consider corruption as the biggest risk of doing business; 25% report having asked for a bribe in order to do business; and 33% say they have lost business due to bribery by their competitors.[14] The energy field is no exception, and state oil company Pemex may be something to watch and blame if meaningful reform does not occur.

President Peña Nieto also signed into law new rules for the telecommunications and broadcasting industries that, according to experts and press, are designed to curb the power of billionaire Carlos Slim's America Movil and broadcaster Televisa.[15] The legislation, approved by Congress, will allow new players into the Mexican telecoms market which will also will face temptation in terms of bribery and probably also extortion; thus their compliance programmes and training should be top priority.

Extortion

Extortion has played a significant role in corporations' stability in Mexico and has been a headache too for citizens and local governments, especially in Michoacán State and some of its most traditional municipalities.

In order to continue the ordinary course of business, owners have been approached by leaders of delinquent groups such as *Los Zetas* or *The Familia* asking for a monthly payment, which if declined then threaten to burn down their business, scare their employees or hurt their families should they notify the authorities.

Locals have illegally armed themselves and publicly threatened to confront these groups in an apparently legitimate but extra-judicial activity. The government has reacted strongly and appointed special government officials to negotiate and avoid further consequences.

Conflict of interest

Mexico lacks an office of conflict of interest, and precisely in the telecoms field of discussions at the Senate, there was a recent case that illustrates well where Mexico stands on this ethical issue.

With the use of telecom spying tools, Senator Purificación Carpinteyro was taped and caught talking about how lucky "they" may get (in a personal business) should the telecom bill be passed, while naming a top-notch game player's brand. When confronted by the media, Senator Carpinteyro argued she "would invest in [the] telecom business as soon as the bill passed", and that in her view, there was no conflict of interest. She faced tough criticism on social media as well as political pressure when she stepped down from the telecom commission at the Senate due to her alleged conflict of interest.[16] Later, Senator Carpintyero was interviewed and gave a list of more than 15 Congressmen who, in her opinion, had a personal or indirect interest in the soon-to-be-approved telecom bill.[17]

In Mexico, public officials are subject to the Ethics Code of Public Officials that encourages them to act with honesty, impartiality and integrity. These principles are also found in the **Federal Administrative Responsibilities Law** but are rarely enforced by authorities on the basis of absolute impunity or violation of the rule of law.

Whistleblowing against public officials

The Federal Administrative Responsibilities Law (art. 10) provides that administrative entities will have specific units with general public access to denounce or submit complaints against public officials when they have failed to comply with their duties. Whistleblowers must provide enough evidence for the Ministry of Public Affairs to proceed; the law expressly forbids anonymous denunciations.

If found guilty, public officials may be sanctioned with a warning; suspended of duty for a period no longer than a year but never less than three days; relieved of their charge; or given a fine or barred from public service.

Civil society and law associations

As part of the OECD 2011 recommendations, civil society must be part of the fight against corruption. The Ministry of Public Administration has recently decided to open its doors to civil society and talk or give training to the general public and officials. The National Corporate Counsel Association College of Law (*Asociación Nacional de Abogados de Empresa Colegio de Abogados, A.C.*) or ANADE,[18] by means of its Anti-corruption Committee, played an important role in the first successful workshop.

Unfortunately, these types of workshops have not continued with the resolve they should, and this is due to the bizarre administrative stasis the Ministry of Administration has fallen into while having no secretary in office for the time being.

Soon, Mexico is likely to receive foreign direct investment due to energy and telecom reforms; in a co-responsibility gesture, government and civil society must pay attention to the bribery area and update their legal framework to investigate and sanction corrupt public officials and discourage corporations from accepting kickbacks or promoting bribery of local officials.

In Mexico, whistleblowing and anti-retaliation laws are missing, and could prove useful in times when corruption has struck at the heart of democracy by corroding institutions; trust in public officials and our leaders is nil.

* * *

Endnotes

1. Sources: i) Forward notes and Law justification for the Anti-Corruption Commission Law enactment process; and ii) State of Reasons Forward Document, Proposed Anti-corruption Law.
2. Global Integrity Report 2011, Source: http://www.right2info.org.

3. Joint Press Release by PGR and SFP on May 2011, www.pgr.gob.mx.

4. Morris, Stephen D., Corruption, Drug Trafficking and Violence in Mexico, Summer Report, Brown Journal of World Affairs Volume XVIII, Issue II, USA 2012.

5. http://www.elfinanciero.com.mx/politica/leyes-anticorrupcion-deben-ser-prioridad-en-el-congreso-pan.html.

6. http://www.reuters.com/article/2015/04/22/us-mexico-anticorruption-idUSKBN0ND1F320150422.

7. Source: http://www.bbc.com/news/world-latin-america-21597680.

8. Source: http://mexico.cnn.com/nacional/2013/02/26/la-pgr-detiene-a-elba-esther-gordillo-por-presunto-desvio-de-recursos.

9. http://www.theguardian.com/world/2014/nov/10/mexico-president-enrique-pena-nieto-mansion-explain.

10. F Joseph Warin and Michael M Farhang and associate Elizabeth H Goergen: "Understand the Risks" Gibbson Dunn: http://www.gibsondunn.com/publications/Documents/WarinFarhangGoergen-UnderstandtheRisks.pdf.

11. http://www.justice.gov.

12. https://www.mapi.net/system/files/PA-110_0.pdf.

13. http://www.brookings.edu/research/articles/2014/08/14-mexico-energy-law-negroponte.

14. Anti-corruption Commission of the International Chamber of Commerce 2014 *Prioridad en México: Combate a la Corrupción 2014*, June 2014.

15. http://www.reuters.com/article/2014/07/14/us-mexico-reforms-idUSKBN0FJ2DU20140714.

16. http://www.forbes.com/sites/doliaestevez/2014/07/07/ignoring-charges-of-conflict-of-interest-mexicos-senate-passes-anti-monopoly-law-against-billionaire-slims-telecom-empire/.

17. http://m.cnnexpansion.com/economia/2014/07/01/prd-exige-salida-de-senadores-de-telecom.

18. http://anademx.com.

Luis F. Ortiz de la Concha
Tel: +52 55 5251 2156 / Email: luisortiz@ocalawfirm.com / @luisfortizc /
@ocalawfirm

Luis is one of the founding partners at OCA Law Firm and a member of the Bioethics Council in Mexico (www.coebio.org). He is responsible for international training and investigations in Mexico and Central and South America on bribery and money laundering. He manages more than 14,000 third parties' audits via OCA's third party exclusive software for Mexico and the LATAM region. He has been involved in third party multijurisdictional due diligences and investigations for US and Mexican corporations related to the energy, public procurement, beverages, pharma and automotive industries. He has studied and graduated at top universities in the USA (University of Florida), Mexico and Europe, currently teaches anti-corruption and AML at two top Mexican universities and is part of the working group on the financial compliance expert certification process in Mexico.

Luis has participated in the representation of civil society with the Mexican government on OECD *in situ* visits to his country and Anti-corruption Training for Mexican Companies. He has worked with Canadian and Mexican Governments on related legal topics. He is the former head of the National Anti-corruption Committee of National Corporate Lawyers Association (ANADE), former President of the Ethics and CSR Committee Mexican Financial Executives Institute – IMEF and Chairman of the Anti-corruption Committee at the IAFEI.org, among other associations. He is a member of the Anti-corruption Committee of the International Bar Association, and of the Bioethics Council for the Corporate Bioethics Prize 2013-2016.

OCA Law Firm

Bosque de Ciruelos 304, p. 4, Bosques de las Lomas 11700, México, D.F., Mexico
Tel: +52 55 5251 2156 / URL: http://www.ocalawfirm.com

New Zealand

Ben Upton
Simpson Grierson

Overview of the law and enforcement regime

<u>Sources of law</u>

New Zealand law treats bribery and corruption as criminal matters. Two principal statutes apply:
- the Crimes Act 1961 (Part 6, sections 99 to 106) (**Crimes Act**); and
- the Secret Commissions Act 1910 (**Secret Commissions Act**).

The Crimes Act contains criminal offences related to, among other things, the corrupt use of official information and the corruption and bribery of the Judiciary, Ministers of the Crown, Members of Parliament, law enforcement officers and public officials. Penalties include terms of imprisonment of up to 14 years for the most serious cases.

The Secret Commissions Act contains bribery and corruption-style offences relevant to the private sector. Penalties range from NZD2,000 to two years' imprisonment.

New Zealand law also contains many other offences covering corruption-style crimes. These include money laundering (under the Crimes Act) and fraud (under the Serious Fraud Office Act 1990), as well as civil sanctions under the Securities Market Act 1978 relating to insider trading and market manipulation. There is also an offence under the Income Tax Act 2012, which is targeted at the bribery of local and foreign tax officials. Electoral laws also require disclosure of donor support to politicians.

Certain international treaties to which New Zealand is a signatory require New Zealand's law makers (Parliament) to ensure that local statutes are consistent with international norms. International treaties may also impose obligations on New Zealand to assist other nations in criminal and non-criminal investigations and proceedings. Relevant treaties to which New Zealand is a signatory are:
- The OECD Convention on Combating Bribery of Foreign Officials in International Business Transactions (signed 1997, ratified 2001).
- The United Nations Convention Against Corruption (signed 2003, not yet ratified, but see proposed reforms below which should enable ratification soon).
- The United Nations Convention Against Transnational Organized Crime (signed 2000, ratified 2002).

This commentary will focus on the principal local law offences under the Crimes Act and Secret Commissions Act.

<u>Bribery and corruption under the Crimes Act</u>

The offences under the Crimes Act essentially cover the corrupt bribery of judges, parliamentarians and other public officials (**Public Servants**) and foreign officials, and the corrupt use of official information.

Bribery of Public Servants

In relation to bribes, it is an offence for a Public Servant to corruptly accept or obtain, agree or offer to accept or attempt to obtain any bribe for himself or any other person in respect of any act done or omitted, or to be done or omitted by him in his capacity as a Public Servant.

It is also an offence for any person to corruptly give or offer or agree to give any bribe to any person with intent to influence any Public Servant in respect of any act or omission by that Public Servant in his capacity as a Public Servant.

"*Bribe*" is defined to mean "*any money, valuable consideration, office, or employment, or any benefit, whether direct or indirect*".

Bribery of foreign public officials

With regard to a foreign public official, it is an offence to corruptly give or offer or agree to give a bribe to a person with the intention of influencing a foreign public official in respect of any act or omission by that foreign public official in his or her official capacity in order to obtain or retain business, or obtain any improper advantage in the conduct of business. This applies whether or not the bribery of the foreign public official occurs within or outside of New Zealand. However, if the act is lawful in the country of the foreign public official involved, it is not an offence.

It is not an offence if the primary or sole purpose of the act or omission was to ensure that a routine government action was performed by that foreign public official and if the value of the benefit was small. Note that this 'facilitation payment' defence only applies to foreign public officials, not Public Servants (see more on this below).

There is a reform underway which should repeal this dual criminality exclusion and also make it an offence for a foreign public official to pay or offer to pay a bribe. At present the law only deals with the acts of people towards such officials, not the acts of the foreign public official himself (see below).

Corrupt use of official information

In relation to the corrupt use of official information, it is an offence for a public official to corruptly use or disclose any information acquired by him in his official capacity, to obtain, directly or indirectly, an advantage or a pecuniary gain for himself or any other person. Similarly, it is an offence for any person to use information obtained in this way in order to gain an advantage or pecuniary gain.

Bribery and corruption under the Secret Commissions Act

The Secret Commissions Act covers bribery offences in the private sector. Under that Act it is an offence (in general terms) to:
* corruptly give a gift to an agent (and for an agent to accept such a gift) without the consent of the principal, where the gift (or other consideration) is an inducement or reward for doing or forbearing to do something in relation to the principal's affairs or business;
* fail to disclose (as an agent) to the agent's principal a pecuniary interest in a contract;
* give an agent a false receipt or invoice (or for an agent to deliver a receipt or invoice he or she knows is false to his or her principal); and
* advise any person to enter into a contract with a third person and receive or agree to receive, without the person's knowledge, a gift or consideration from that third person as an inducement or reward.

The maximum penalty for such offences is two years' imprisonment.

'Corruptly'

The word 'corruptly' is common to most bribery offences. New Zealand's highest court (Supreme Court) opined on the meaning of that word in *Field v R* [2011] NZSC 129. This case involved a prosecution against a Member of Parliament (Mr Taito Philip Field) for corruptly receiving a bribe. There was evidence that he had benefitted through unpaid work undertaken by Thai immigrants on his private properties after he had provided assistance to those Thai immigrants in relation to applications for New Zealand residency. Mr Field's defence was that the unpaid work undertaken by the Thai immigrants was a gift and not a *quid pro quo* for his activities on their behalf. That defence failed.

The Supreme Court, perhaps somewhat simplistically, resolved the matter by saying that Mr Field had acted corruptly because "*... it is simply wrong for an official to accept money or like benefits in return for what has been done in an official capacity*".

This approach would suggest that receipt of any benefit other than salary will – save only for the exception about to be noted – always be received 'corruptly' because it is 'simply wrong' to receive the benefit.

The Supreme Court did, however, introduce a *de minimis* defence. That is one "*in relation to gifts of token value which are just part of the usual courtesies of life*" or where some "*unexceptional ... other benefit*" was received. The Supreme Court opined that in such an instance the transaction would be 'innocent' and therefore not corrupt. The example considered in the case was a Member of Parliament being given an item of sports club attire in return for attending the opening of that sports club's premises.

There has been academic criticism of the Supreme Court's approach as being circular and unclear. There has also been criticism that the *de minimis* defence amounts to an attempted amendment by the Court of the statute or the creation of a form of facilitation payment defence by stealth. Furthermore there will always be doubt as to what is *de minimis* and therefore permissible, and what is not.

OECD reporting has also commented that New Zealand legislators should consider removing reference to the term 'corruptly' from the offence provisions. They argue that this term is unnecessary given the 'intent to influence' element to the offences, and the possibility that the word 'corruptly' increases the evidential burdens placed on prosecutors.[1]

The Serious Fraud Office, for its part, adopts an approach which defines corruption as: "*Behaviour on the part of officials in the public or private sector in which they improperly and unlawfully enrich themselves or those close to them, or induce others to do so, by misusing the position in which they are placed.*"[2]

Overview of enforcement activity and policy during the past two years

New Zealand is a small country (4.6 million people approximately) and has a reputation for a low level of local corruption.[3] It follows that prosecutions in New Zealand for bribery and corruption are few.

The only relevant statistics available (which only show the position up until December 2012[4]) are as follows:
- Between 2006 and 2012 there have been 32 prosecutions for domestic bribery offences. These resulted in 17 convictions.[5]
- There have been no local prosecutions for foreign bribery offences.[6]
There have been prosecutions under the Secret Commissions Act.

Prosecutions tend to receive a good level of publicity and certain high-profile matters have been highlighted in the media and in wider public debate of recent date.[7]

Recent regulator statements and a recent 2013 OECD report,[8] however, have suggested that there may be an under-reporting of bribery, particularly in relation to foreign bribery. This is largely because whereas other foreign nationals, from the United States and United Kingdom in particular, are being caught and prosecuted in jurisdictions where New Zealanders actively trade (such as China), no New Zealanders appear to have been caught or prosecuted.[9] This has led to the following comment by OECD lead examiners:[10]

> "... lead examiners ... are still seriously concerned that the level of foreign bribery enforcement actions remain low. They are also very concerned that outdated perceptions held by some individuals, including in the public sector, that New Zealand individuals and companies do not engage in bribery, may undermine detection efforts. The lead examiners recommend that New Zealand significantly step up efforts to detect, investigate and prosecute foreign bribery."

The OECD report does indicate that certain cases have been investigated. Four are listed in the report. None have led to prosecutions, however.

A 2015 report by Deloitte,[11] which focused on Australia and New Zealand, revealed that of those organisations surveyed, 23% had experienced one or more known instances of domestic corruption within the last five years. The survey also revealed that 40% of the organisations surveyed had operations in high-risk jurisdictions, with 35% of those having experienced some form of bribery or corruption incident within the last five years. A large number of organisations who did have overseas operations in high-risk jurisdictions did not, however, have formal compliance programmes and many had not conducted risk assessments in this area.

There is some concern that the rebuilding of Christchurch (New Zealand's second largest city), after devastating earthquakes in 2010 and 2011, could increase corruption. This is due to the large amount of insurance money that has flooded into that region and the large amount of building and other service work that will be required over the next decade to rebuild the city.[12]

Notwithstanding these matters, there has been no indication from regulators or the Government that major policy changes are envisaged in the near term. Some law reform has been introduced, however (see further below).

Law and policy relating to issues such as facilitation payments and hospitality

Foreign public officials

In the case of the bribery of a foreign public official, the Crimes Act provides that there will be no bribery offence where the benefit given or offered was "*committed for the sole or primary purpose of ensuring or expediting the performance by a foreign public official of a routine government action and the value of the benefit is small*",[13]

'Routine government action' is defined to include any decision about whether to award new business or whether to continue existing business, or the terms of new or existing business.

This provision appears to permit small or nominal facilitation payments or hospitality when it comes to the provision of benefits to foreign officials, even if that official is responsible for determining the award or continuation of business.

The OECD has been critical of this provision and has suggested that this facilitation payment exception make clear that it will not cover instances where the benefit provides undue material benefit to the person making the payment, or undue material disadvantage to any other person.[14] There is no proposed reform in this area, however.

Local bribery offences

The facilitation payment exception available in respect of foreign public officials does not apply to New Zealand Public Servants.

What a local Public Servant can rely on is the *de minimis* defence suggested by the Supreme Court in *R v Field*. That is one "*in relation to gifts of token value which are just part of the usual courtesies of life*", or where some "*unexceptional ... other benefit*" was received.

However, this defence does not strictly refer to 'facilitation payments'. Rather 'thank you' gifts, albeit that such a gift might facilitate an appearance or attendance at an event.

Key issues relating to investigation, decision-making and enforcement procedures

Investigation and enforcement process

Bribery and corruption offences will usually be investigated and prosecuted by either the New Zealand Police (if it is a low level of criminal behaviour) or the Serious Fraud Office (for more serious, complex or high-profile matters).

The Office of the Ombudsman can also look into complaints about corrupt behaviour.

Prosecutions will be dealt with through the criminal courts. The Crimes Act offences will usually be dealt with by the High Court (the superior first instance court), although prosecutions can also be determined through the lower, first instance courts (District Courts).

Prosecutorial guidelines

Decisions to prosecute crimes in New Zealand are made by the Police or Serious Fraud Office with the Solicitor General's Prosecution Guidelines in mind. These guidelines state that prosecutions are to be initiated or continued only where:
- the evidence that can be adduced in Court is sufficient to provide a reasonable prospect of a conviction; and
- prosecution is required in the public interest.

One aspect that is relevant to the public interest test is 'where there is any element of corruption'.

It is expected, therefore, that where there is a case that has a reasonable prospect of conviction on the admissible evidence gathered, a prosecution will be brought against a person for a bribery and corruption offence. There are, however, further hurdles in terms of actually bringing a prosecution to trial. These are addressed in the next section.

Restrictions on prosecutions

Bribery and corruption under the Crimes Act involving judges, judicial officers, law enforcement officers, official information or foreign public officials cannot be prosecuted without the permission of the Attorney General who, before giving such permission, may make such enquiries as he thinks fit.

A prosecution against a senior (High Court) judge must also only be pursued if Parliament so resolves.

Where a prosecution involves a Minister of the Crown or Member of Parliament, then leave of the High Court must be obtained. The application for leave must be on notice to the proposed defendant who must have an opportunity to be heard against the application. In determining such matters, the High Court will apply the following guidelines:[15]
- Is prosecution being brought in good faith?
- The court will examine the strength and sufficiency of the evidence.
- Whether the public interest required a prosecution in the circumstances of the case.
- Are there other considerations that are relevant?

Extraterroriality and international co-operation

Extraterroriality

Even if the acts or omissions relevant to a bribery offence under the Crimes Act were committed wholly outside of New Zealand, proceedings may be brought against a person in New Zealand provided that person is a citizen or New Zealand incorporated company, ordinarily resident in New Zealand, or that has been found in New Zealand and not extradited.[16]

The New Zealand courts will also have jurisdiction to determine prosecutions where any act or omission forming part of an offence occurs in New Zealand or, alternatively, any event necessary to the completion of any offence occurred in New Zealand.[17] In respect of the former, the act or omission must form part of the *actus reus* of the offence.[18]

Bribery outside of New Zealand of foreign public officials is specifically covered by provisions in the Crimes Act. It will not be an offence in New Zealand, however, if the act done outside of New Zealand was not, at the time of its commission, an offence under the laws of the foreign country where the foreign official influenced was located. That provision is the subject of proposed reform (see below).

Foreign cooperation

New Zealand law has provision for mutual legal assistance, as required by the OECD Convention on Combatting Bribery of Foreign Officials in International Business Transactions. This is covered by the Mutual Assistance in Criminal Matters Act 1992. Recent reporting records that no mutual legal assistance requests received by New Zealand up until 2013 concerned bribery or corruption offences.[19]

New Zealand also has a relatively developed extradition process which is covered by the Extradition Act 1999 and numerous international treaties.

Corporate liability for bribery and corruption offences

Bribery and corruption offences can be brought against both natural and corporate persons. A "person" under the Crimes Act includes both incorporated and unincorporated bodies of persons.[20]

In relation to corporate liability, the New Zealand courts had previously tended to follow the English law approach established in *Tesco Supermarkets Limited v Nattrass* [1972] AC 153 (HL). That is, where the courts will look at whether the natural persons involved were the 'directing mind and will' of the corporation involved.

However, the Privy Council decision in the New Zealand appeal concerning *Meridian Global Funds Management Asia v Securities Commission* [1995] UKPC 5 has most likely extended the identification theory, such that the Court is also encouraged to look at the purpose of the provisions creating the relevant offence. That case involved a regulatory offence where certain executives were delegated a reporting task, which was not complied with. In that instance, that delegation permitted the court to find the company liable for the non-reporting by reference to the purpose of the provisions and, due to the general principles of agency and vicarious liability, the knowledge of the employees was attributed to the company.

Such principles may be difficult to apply to bribery and corruption-type offences. It has to be expected that only where very senior levels of management or directors are involved in bribery that a company might also be charged. As such, the 'directing mind and will' test will most likely still remain relevant in this area.[21]

Proposed reforms discussed below, however, will, if introduced, clarify that if an employee commits an offence under the foreign public official provisions, then his corporate employer can be liable if the offence fell within that employee's scope of authority, the employer benefitted and the employer did not take reasonable steps to prevent the offence.

Proposed reforms / The year ahead

On 25th June 2014, the Organised Crime and Anti-Corruption Legislation Bill was introduced. The Bill is at the second of three stages required before being passed into law. Being a Government-backed Bill with cross-party support, it should be passed into law within the year.

The Bill, insofar as it deals with bribery, introduces amendments to the foreign bribery offences in the Crimes Act. It seeks to address recommendations from the OECD Working Group on Bribery, to include clarifying the circumstances in which a company is liable for foreign bribery.

More particularly, the proposed amendments would have the following effect if made law:
*   A company will be liable for bribing a foreign public official if an employee of that company pays or offers to pay a bribe when acting within the scope of their authority as an employee, with the intent to benefit the company. There is a defence available to the company if it has taken reasonable steps to prevent the offence. The onus of proof in that respect is on the company.
*   The creation of a new offence to criminalise the acceptance of a bribe by a foreign public official. At present the law is limited to the payment or offer of a bribe to such an official.
*   The removal of the dual criminality requirement in relation to the corruption of or by foreign public officials. There is a provision which makes clear however, that if the defendant is a foreign public official, then he or she can still rely on any immunity laws that may apply in New Zealand.
*   The creation of a new offence to criminalise the acceptance of a bribe in return for using one's influence over an official.
*   An increase in the penalties for bribery and corruption in the private sector under the Secret Commissions Act (from two to seven years' imprisonment), to bring those offences into line with public sector bribery.
*   The 'facilitation payments' defence in respect of the foreign public official's offences is updated to prevent abuse. Relevant definitions to this offence are also updated to ensure that foreign bribery offence applies to bribery in relation to the provision of foreign aid.
*   Any small facilitation payments must now be disclosed by companies.
*   There is reform to the Income Tax Act 2007 to make clear that no bribes are tax-deductible.

If passed, the above-mentioned amendments will allow New Zealand to ratify the United Nations Convention Against Corruption.

Select Committee reporting (which was published in 2015) has only suggested minor amendments to the Bill as introduced. Principal recommendations relate to the introduction of penalties which would allow fines to be imposed in addition to imprisonment; the only current option being to impose a fine or a prison sentence, not both. One minority political party (the Green Party) has expressed the strong view that any type of 'facilitation' payment should be outlawed. It is unlikely that the Bill will be changed to accommodate that view, although this cannot be ruled out at this time and does have support given OECD findings in respect of New Zealand's current laws.

* * *

Endnotes

1. This recommendation has not been followed in the proposed law reform (as to which see the last section of this chapter).
2. See Serious Fraud Office website (http://www.sfo.govt.nz) – "What is Corruption?" This definition is used by the Asia Development Bank.
3. New Zealand often features in reporting as one of the world's least corrupt countries. It ranks as the World's second least corrupt country (behind Denmark) in the Transparency International Corruption Perceptions Index 2014. New Zealand was previously ranked as the least corrupt country.
4. There are no other available statistics.
5. Phase 3 Report on Implementing the OECD Anti-Bribery Convention in New Zealand, October 2013 (**OECD Report 2013**), page 18, paragraph 42.
6. OECD Report 2013, page 16, paragraph 36.
7. Recent cases or prosecutions which have been publicised have involved several high-profile matters. These include: alleged attempts to bribe a local authority consenting office (*SFO v Li*); alleged bribery in the obtaining road maintenance contracts from a local body organisation (*SFO v Borlaze, George & anr.*); and receipt of a bribe by an immigration official (*R v Meng Tam & Kai Leng Pan*). There have also been matters before the courts involving alleged failures to declare political donations (*R v Banks*) and defrauding of local government bodies (*R v Sweney*), which whilst not strictly corruption matters, did highlight allegations around the probity of public officials. A recent scandal involving payments to a Saudi businessman by the New Zealand government has also attracted public debate around corruption issues.
8. OECD Report 2013.
9. OECD Report 2013, page 8, paragraph 8.
10. OECD Report 2013, page 8, paragraph 9.
11. Deloitte Bribery and Corruption Survey 2015 – Australia and New Zealand. The survey was conducted in November and December 2014. 269 respondents were involved, including some from listed companies.
12. This fact is also noted in the OECD reporting at page 8, paragraph 8. At the time it was reported that the Christchurch earthquakes represented one of the largest insurance events since 2000.
13. Crimes Act 1961, section 105C(3).
14. OECD Report 2013, page 12, paragraph 23.
15. *Burgess v Field*, HC Auckland, CIV-2007-404-3206, 5 October 2007, Randerson J.
16. Crimes Act 1961, section 7A.
17. Crimes Act 1961, section 7.
18. *Tipple v Pain* [1983] NZLR 257.
19. OECD Report 2013, page 39, paragraph 115.
20. Crimes Act 1961, section 2.
21. The OECD Report 2013 makes the same observation. See page 15, paragraph 30.

Ben Upton
Tel: +64 9 977 5207 / Email: ben.upton@simpsongrierson.com
Ben Upton is a partner in Simpson Grierson's Banking and Finance Litigation team. He regularly appears in all levels of the New Zealand courts and also practises in a number of Pacific Island jurisdictions. He advises many banks, financial institutions and listed companies.

He specialises in banking disputes, securities and debt enforcement, insolvency, money laundering and crisis management. He has also practised in England and Hong Kong where he was involved in several bribery and corruption investigations where his firm acted for local and international clients.

He is admitted as a barrister in the Cook Islands.

Simpson Grierson is New Zealand's largest law firm and is a member of Lex Mundi.

Simpson Grierson

Lumley Building, 88 Shortland Street, Auckland, New Zealand
Tel: +64 9 358 2222 / Fax: +64 9 307 0331 / URL: http://www.simpsongrierson.com

Portugal

Paulo de Sá e Cunha, Marta Saramago de Almeida & Carolina Mouraz
Cuatrecasas, Gonçalves Pereira

Brief overview of the law and enforcement regime

The Portuguese legal framework has a large range of provisions prohibiting corruption. First and foremost, the Portuguese Criminal Code sets out various forms of corruption as offences, namely *passive bribery of a public official, active bribery* and *undue receipt of advantage*. There are also a number of other crimes that are generally treated as corruption offences in Portugal: *trading in influence*; *voter bribery*; *misappropriation of public funds by a public official*; *embezzlement of public funds*; and *misappropriation of public property*. Corruption is among the preceding offences of *money laundering*. This means that corruption is one of the offences included in the *money laundering* legal frame, but both offences are punishable simultaneously.

Additionally, some specific sectors have their own legislative anti-corruption frameworks, such as politicians (Law no. 34/87, of 16 July), international commerce and the private sector (Law no. 20/2008, of 21 April) and sports (Law no. 50/2007, of 31 August) (all last amended by Law no. 30/2015, of 22 April).

Furthermore, Law no. 36/94, of 29 September (last amended by Law no. 32/2010, of 2 September) and Law no. 5/2002, of 11 January (last amended by Law no. 55/2015, of 23 June), set out measures to fight corruption and other forms of economic and financial crimes, the latter being applicable whenever *bribery* is conducted in a criminally organised fashion.

Under Portuguese law, both the act of paying the bribe in order to obtain a lawful or unlawful benefit, and the act of receiving a bribe oneself, either on his own behalf or on behalf of a third party, are punishable as acts of *bribery* with a penalty of up to eight years' imprisonment. The exact penalty for these crimes may be increased by a quarter if the bribe amounts to a high value (approximately €5,100), or by one-third if the bribe amounts to a considerably high value (approximately €20,400), or if the perpetrator acted in his capacity as a representative of a corporate entity or individual.

In case of *money laundering*, the penalty may rise to a maximum of 12 years' imprisonment, which can also be increased by one-third if the offences are carried out on a regular basis.

Based on a conversion of imprisonment penalties determined by Portuguese law, corporate entities charged with *bribery* may be sentenced to pay fines in the maximum amount of €12,800,000 (or €19,200,000 for *money laundering*) and may also be sentenced to further penalties such as a formal warning by the court, payment of a good-conduct security, prohibition to enter into agreements or to receive state subsidies, prohibition to exercise activity, dissolution, etc.

Concerning the Portuguese Criminal Code, *passive bribery* may only be committed by public officials, *i.e.*, agents or employees working in the public sector, in the judicial administration or for public companies. This also includes, namely: i) judges, prosecutors, officials and staff of public international organisations, regardless of their nationality or place of residence; ii) foreign public officials, should the offence be committed wholly or partly in Portuguese territory; iii) judges, prosecutors and officials of international courts; and iv) foreign jurors and arbitrators, should the offence be committed wholly or partly in Portuguese territory.

In this respect, holders of political offices (*i.e.*, President of the Republic and President of the Portuguese Parliament, members of the Portuguese Parliament or of the European Parliament, members of the Government or of a representative body of local government), as well as "High Public Offices" (such as public managers, holders of decision-making bodies of semi-public companies, whenever appointed by the Government, members of executive bodies of companies of local enterprise sectors, members of governing bodies of public institutes, members of independent public entities and members of first degree high executive bodies or equivalent) are not included in this definition, since they are covered by special provisions set out by Law no. 34/87, of 16 July. For the purposes of these statutes, political office-holders of public international organisations, as well as political office-holders of foreign countries regardless of their nationality or place of residence, should the offence be committed wholly or partly in Portuguese territory, are also treated as national holders of political offices.

In relation to *bribery harmful to the international commerce*, such an offence may be committed by a Portuguese national or a foreign public official or by a public official of an international organisation, as well as by a political office-holder, whether Portuguese or not. The aim of this specific type of *bribery* is to obtain or retain a business, contract or other undue advantage in the conduct of international commerce, by giving or promising to give any advantages to national or foreign public officials, public officials of international organisations or political office-holders.

Portuguese law also provides the crime of *bribery in the private sector*, which may be committed by a private-sector employee, empowered with managing or supervising a private entity, even if temporarily or unpaid, and whether working under an individual employment contract, a services' supply agreement or other form of agreement.

Concerning *bribery in sports*, it may be committed by any sports agent, such as sports managers, coaches, trainers, fitness coaches, doctors, referees, as well as public limited sports companies, sports associations, clubs, federations or professional leagues. The briber's goal must be to cause the sports agent to perform an act or omission aimed at misrepresenting or distorting the result of an incoming sporting event.

Overview of enforcement activity and policy during the past two years

In the last few years, Portuguese Governments have implemented several legal and institutional measures to combat corruption.

GRECO, UN and OECD have addressed recommendations to Portugal regarding corruption, because of evaluations conducted within the framework of conventions to which Portugal is part. As a consequence of such recommendations, the Portuguese Parliament enacted Law no. 30/2015, of 22 April, which amended the Criminal Code, the law on crimes of responsibility of political offices and high public offices, the law regarding *bribery harmful to the international commerce* and *in the private sector*, the law regarding *bribery in sports* and the law regarding support to whistleblowers in corruption-related matters (Law no. 19/2008 of 21 April).

Also, since the beginning of its mandate, Government has been trying to criminalise *illicit enrichment*. In 2012, the Portuguese Parliament set forth an amendment to the Portuguese Criminal Code, by which it would be deemed as unlawful and punishable with a penalty of up to three years' imprisonment the act of acquiring or holding wealth which was not compatible with the suspect's legitimate income and assets, based on the information which was presented to the tax authorities, should the origin of the wealth under investigation be undetermined. However, the Constitutional Court considered the law to be unconstitutional, deciding that this formulation of the new type of crime of *illicit enrichment* infringed the principle of the presumption of innocence (innocent until proven guilty) and the defendant's right to silence.

This year, another attempt has been made to legislate this issue. The Parliament approved a new amendment to the Criminal Code criminalising *unjustified enrichment*, with a different name and a different wording, but, once again, the Constitutional Court rejected it on the same basis and for the same reasons.

On the other hand, investigations of high-level corruption have increased, namely in the public procurement, in the defence procurement and in the financing of political parties.

Several corruption investigations of high-ranking officials are currently ongoing, such as the criminal investigation of Portugal's former Prime Minister, José Socrates, who has remanded in preventive detention for almost one year, on suspicion of *bribery, tax fraud* and *money laundering*. Another important ongoing criminal investigation pertains to resident permits to wealthy non-Europeans (golden visas). In this case, the head of Portugal's border enforcement agency (*Serviço de Estrangeiros e Fronteiras*), the president of the country's registration and notary institute and the former interior minister of the current Government are under investigation for corruption crimes.

Law and policy relating to issues such as facilitation payments and hospitality

Portuguese legislation does not expressly establish what might be deemed as a bribe. In fact, within certain strict boundaries, all gifts, entertainment, hospitality, advantages may be acceptable and there is no quantitative limit to their permissible value.

It is generally accepted that a crime of *bribery* occurs whenever the value of the bribe or bonus is not insignificant, or is not in accordance with the habits and customs of each economic sector. In this respect, it is also not necessary that the "undue advantage" be proportional to the value or importance of the action that is intended to be performed. Even mere endowments, which cannot be in any other way justified, according to common experience, for their frequency or high value, may be punishable as bribes.

In any case, the general rule to identify legitimate conducts remains within the boundaries of what may or may not be understood as pertaining to "*proper social conducts complying with social conventions and customs*".

In this regard, according to the Portuguese Committee for the Prevention of Corruption, public officials, holders of political offices and even private-sector employees are allowed to accept only "institutional offers", deemed to be those which are offered or accepted in the course of their duties, based on a designated "committee relationship". However, the acceptance of such offers must be reported to the beneficiary's superior or competent bodies.

Key issues relating to investigation, decision-making and enforcement procedures

Portuguese Criminal Investigation has several specialised services responsible to investigate corruption cases – the Central Bureau of Investigation and Prosecution of the Central Public Prosecutor's Office (DCIAP), the National Unity Against Corruption of the Judiciary Policy and, also, the Court of Auditors.

Concerning investigation, it should be noted that the Portuguese Criminal Procedural Code provides that public officers be obliged to report corruption crimes, which come to their knowledge in the course of their duties.

To prevent retaliation and to guarantee freedom of speech, for public (and also private sector) employees, Law no. 19/2008 of 21 April provides for some protection mechanisms for whistleblowers – the right to remain anonymous until the person suspected is formally charged, the right to be transferred after the person suspected is formally charged, and the right to benefit from witness protection schemes.

The procedure to investigate corruption has special rules regarding the collection of evidence, breach of professional secrecy and seizure of assets. This special regime was set out by Law no. 5/2002, of 11 January, which determines the lifting of professional secrecy for tax, credit institutions and financial companies' employees, as well as the monitoring of bank accounts, which requires banks to report, within 24 hours, any suspicious movement. This ruling also provides that in the event of a conviction, the court may order seizure of the defendant's assets, which are considered to be incompatible with their income.

Investigation of corruption cases can last 14 months, but this time-limit shall be extended to 18 months, whenever the special complexity of the proceedings is declared. However, the duration of investigations has gradually been decreasing, as major investigations of banks such as Banco Português de Negócios (BPN) and Banco Privado Português (BPP) have demonstrated, since, in some cases, they took less than two years to investigate.

According to the statistics provided by the Ministry of Justice, between 2007 and 2013, investigations of corruption crimes have been decreasing. The number of such crimes has reduced more than half, from 122 (in 2007) to 58 (2013). Concerning corruption crimes subject to trial, the numbers also show a significant decrease (59 to 37). Nonetheless, Portuguese statistics show that the number of defendants convicted for corruption crimes has slightly increased. In 2007, Portuguese courts sentenced 52 defendants and, in 2013, 55.

Overview of cross-border issues

As referred above, Portuguese penal law may apply extraterritorially in certain circumstances. In relation to corruption, the same offences as set out above will apply if committed anywhere in the territory of Portugal or, if abroad, when carried out by: (i) Portuguese nationals who habitually reside in Portugal; (ii) foreign nationals who reside in Portugal; or (iii) companies with headquarters in Portugal.

This also applies to political office-holders of the European Union, irrespective of their nationality or place of residence, as well as political office-holders of other Member States of the European Union, should the offence be committed wholly or partly in Portuguese territory.

The elimination of borders between European Union Member States facilitates, among other things, the activities of criminal organisations in Europe. The scourge of organised crime has developed in particular thanks to technological advances, but also due to freedom of movement within the European Union.

Therefore, it is important that the Portuguese competent bodies against bribery and corruption cooperate with foreign entities. The Judiciary Police cooperate with foreign entities, under various international police cooperation instruments, and also cooperate with INTERPOL and EUROPOL. Under the law for International Judiciary Cooperation in Criminal Matters, the Attorney General is the central authority for all communications, although in urgent matters there can be direct contact between authorities. This reciprocal cooperation includes, subject to certain limits, extradition requests, exchange of criminal proceedings and sentences, transfers of convicted individuals, monitoring convicted or paroled persons, and mutual assistance, which includes taking testimony from witnesses, suspects or experts, detention and other preventive measures, sending documents or objects, obtaining evidence, conducting searches, arresting individuals and conducting interviews, providing information about foreign law and criminal records, receiving foreign investigators, receiving denunciations and intercepting communications.

Corporate liability for bribery and corruption offences

Private sector bribery is also criminalised, as indicated above. Private companies and businessmen must also prevent corruption by adopting codes of ethics and conduct, requiring employees to inform them of any issues, keeping records of all income and expenses, cooperating promptly with any public authority if asked to do so and informing the latter of any suspicion involving corruption that may arise, regardless of the fact that the law does not provide a penalty for failure to do so. Any corrupt conduct which harms international commerce or is carried out in the private sector is also criminalised.

In certain cases, prosecutions can be brought against a corporate entity (except the State and public bodies). This includes offences of corruption and money laundering, provided the offence has been carried out in the corporate entity's name and in its interests by someone with directing powers (directors, managers, etc.) or someone under an officer's authority who is acting with a lack of vigilance, unless such persons acted against express orders on the contrary. Such liability does not exclude the liability of the agent himself, nor is it dependent on his being held responsible. Those directors may be deemed, in some cases, subsidiarily liable for the payment of fines and indemnities.

Prosecutions against a corporate entity are also possible for money laundering where the offence has been carried out by any director or employee exercising his official functions or by the corporate entity's representative (acting in its name and interest). The liability of the corporate entity does not prevent the individual who acted as a member of its statutory body or as its director or manager from being individually liable as well.

Corporate entities may, in addition, be sentenced to further penalties, such as a prohibition from entering into agreements, receiving subsidies, carrying on its business, etc.

Moreover, according to the Portuguese law, there is no transfer of responsibility between companies in the same group. This means that the liability of a parent company does not follow a subsidiary company and *vice versa*. Each individual company will be charged individually provided that, as stated above, each of the offences has been committed by their respective governing bodies or representatives acting on their behalf.

Proposed reforms / The year ahead

In this respect, the development of Portuguese reforms of anti-corruption and bribery has not been enlightening due to some events occurring in recent years, in particular the fact that the Constitutional Court considered the criminalisation of *illicit enrichment* unconstitutional, and the recent amendments to the Criminal Code (none of them related to anti-corruption and bribery).

Furthermore, in the beginning of October of this year, there will be legislative elections which may affect the proposed measures on anti-corruption followed by the current Government.

Following the amendments to the Public Contracts Code, in order to improve the award of public contracts, to ensure a more transparent and competitive process, it is expected that public authorities continue to develop anti-corruption best practices manuals.

Paulo de Sá e Cunha
Tel: +351 21 355 38 00 / Email: paulo.sa.cunha@cuatrecasas.com
Law Degree, the School of Law of the University of Lisbon, 1988.
Languages: Portuguese, English, Spanish and French.
Associate lawyer of Cuatrecasas, Gonçalves Pereira since 2006. Partner since 2008. Head of the Legal Department of SUCH – *Serviço de Utilização Comum dos Hospitais* (1998-2002). Head of the State Department Office for Health Administration from 1989 to 1990. Recommended by several directories, including Chambers Europe, for his work in Dispute Resolution. Member of the Portuguese Bar Association, since 1988. He is a founding member of APDI – *Associação Portuguesa de Direito Intelectual* (Portuguese association of intellectual property law) and of Gestautor – *Associação de Gestão Colectiva do Direito de Autor* (association for copyright management). He is also a member of ACEGE – *Associação Cristã de Empresarios e Gestores* (Christian association of business executives). He is a founding member and former vice-president of OSCOT – *Observatório de Segurança, Criminalidade Organizada e Terrorismo* (Portuguese Observatory on Security, Organised Crime, and Terrorism). He was an associate lecturer of criminal law at the Faculty of Law of the University of Lisbon from 1993 to 1997. Junior assistant of criminal law, introduction to the law, and labour law at the Faculty of Law of the University of Lisbon (1986-1993), and of 'Introduction to the Law' at the Law Department of *Universidade Lusíada* from 1992 to 2000. He is a member of the jury of the final exams of the training centre of the Lisbon District Bar Association. Member of the Lisbon District Council of the Portuguese Bar Association (2010-2013). Founder and Chairman of Fórum Penal – *Associação dos Advogados Penalistas* (Criminal Lawyers Association).

Marta Saramago de Almeida
Tel: +351 21 355 38 00 / Email: marta.saramago.almeida@cuatrecasas.com
Law Degree from the University of Lisbon Law School, in 2001.
Languages: Portuguese, English, Spanish, Italian and French.
Associate lawyer of Cuatrecasas, Gonçalves Pereira since 2009. Admitted to the Portuguese Bar Association in 2002. Associate lawyer of Barros, Sobral, G. Gomes & Associados from 2002 to 2006. Attended a postgraduate course in European and Economic Criminal Law at the University of Coimbra, in 2003.

Carolina Mouraz
Tel: +351 21 355 3800 / Email: carolina.mouraz@cuatrecasas.com
Law degree from the School of Law of Nova University of Lisbon, in 2007.
Associate lawyer of Cuatrecasas, Gonçalves Pereira since 2010, working in the Criminal Law Department where she practises law in the areas of business criminal law and international criminal law. Admitted to the Portuguese Bar Association in 2007. Postgraduate degree in Criminal Law (Property and Financial Crime) from the University of Lisbon Law School, in 2009. Intensive Course on Accounting from the University of Lisbon Law School, in 2015.

Cuatrecasas, Gonçalves Pereira

Praça Marquês de Pombal, n.º 2 (e 1, 8.º), 1250-160 Lisboa, Portugal
Tel: +351 21 355 38 00 / Fax: +351 21 353 23 62 / URL: www.cuatrecasas.com

Romania

Mihai Mares
Mares / Danilescu / Mares

Brief overview of the law and enforcement regime

In Romania, during the last year, the anticorruption fight appears to have intensified so much that, according to the activity report of the **National Anticorruption Directorate** (DNA, from its Romanian name) – the main authority in the field – in 2014 the most criminal complaints were recorded, the most indictments were issued and it seems to be the year with the most high-ranking officials investigated.

DNA's activity in 2014-2015 covered a wide spectrum of high-level corruption involving public officials and public figures from different political parties. Sent to court and subject to investigations have been former and current ministers, parliamentarians, mayors, judges and prosecutors with important management positions.

An increase in corruption cases among magistrates was noted, which is a highly corrosive form of corruption. According to DNA, this high figure does not reflect an increase in corruption acts in the judiciary system, but rather an increasing number of complaints from the population. Such cases are complex and a new unit was established within DNA, which is responsible for investigating these cases.

Legal regime

Although we have a relatively new criminal legislation – which came into force last year – there have already been several attempts to amend the Criminal Code and Criminal Proceedings Code within the Parliament. Some of them have partially succeeded, others have just passed certain stages.

The last attempt to change the Romanian criminal law, both material and procedural, included no less than 22 amendments, but having received a negative opinion from the Superior Council of Magistracy, these amendments have been postponed until the autumn of 2015.

On the other hand, Romania is still under the Cooperation and Verification Mechanism of the European Commission supervision which provides, *inter alia*, the stability of anticorruption legislation, penalising attempts by lawmakers to change it.

During the last year there have not been any newly adopted legislative amendments affecting bribery legislation or DNA's functioning. Therefore, corruption offences remain subject to the main legislative acts presented in the previous edition: the Romanian Criminal Code; Law no. 78/2000 on the prevention, discovery and punishing of corruption acts; Law no. 656/2002 on the prevention and sanctioning of money laundering; and Law no. 82/1991 on accounting registrations.

Romanian criminal law distinguishes four categories of corruption offences as stipulated in the Criminal Code in Title V, Chapter I ("Corruption offences"): bribery (art. 289); bribe-taking (art. 290); influence peddling (art. 291); and buying influence (art. 292).

Law no. 78/2000 regulates three categories of offences which fall within the sphere of acts of corruption, plus a fourth that covers offences against the financial interests of the European Community. As amended and supplemented, Law no. 78/2000 refers to the following three categories of crimes: corruption offences; offences assimilated to corruption offences; and offences directly related to corruption offences or assimilated offences.

The offence of bribery is provided by the Criminal Code and Law no. 78/2000 in a type version, an assimilated version, an attenuated version and an aggravated version.

Therefore, article 289 para. 1 of the Criminal Code incriminates the act of a public servant who, directly or indirectly, for themselves or on behalf of others, solicits or receives money or other undue benefits or accepts a promise of money or benefits, in exchange for performing, not performing, speeding up or delaying the performance of an action which falls under the purview of their professional duties or with respect to the performance of an action contrary to their professional duties.

Any act described in the paragraph above committed by a public servant (as described in article 175, paragraph 1 of the RCC) is considered an offence only when committed in connection with the failure or delay of the fulfilment of their duties regarding a legal act, or in connection with performing an act contrary to these duties.

In our Criminal Code the perpetrator can only be a public servant. Moreover, in the 2nd paragraph of art. 289, bribery is stipulated as an attenuated version of the crime if the author is a person associated with a public servant (as described in article 175 para. 2) and, according to article 308 of the RCC, the punishment is lowered by a third of the period of imprisonment provided for the crime stipulated in article 289 paragraph 1.

The main punishment for acts which fall in the material element of a bribery offence may be imprisonment from three to 10 years. Article 289 para. 3 states that, in addition to the main penalty, a complementary penalty of prohibition from exercising the right to hold public office or to exercise the profession or activity in the performance of which the offender has committed the act, for a period of one to five years. For this offence, considering the gravity of the criminal act, the additional punishment mentioned above is mandatory, the court no longer being required to check, in each case, whether, given the nature and gravity of the offence, the circumstances of the case and the person of the offender, this penalty is necessary. After enforcement of the main punishment or if it is considered as enforced, the same rights will be banned as an accessory punishment.

In the version of the crime stipulated by Law no. 78/2000, the act is punishable with the penalty provided by art. 289 of the Criminal Code, whose severity is increased by one-third, thereby extending the punishment to between four years and 13 years and four months, stressing that the crime has a more serious character for this type of offence.

Correspondent to the offence of bribe-taking, our legislation regulates the bilateral offence of **giving a bribe**. The promise, the giving or the offering of money or other benefits in the conditions provided under Article 289 shall be punishable by no less than two and no more than seven years of imprisonment.

The protected social value is the same as for the offence of bribery, namely the honesty of state officials, who must not seek or accept any additional benefit for exercising a public function nor must sell the benefit of their status to those who are interested in a particular conduct.

Regulating the offence of bribery as a bilateral offence has an important preventive nature; it also represents an effective means for proving offences of bribery. First, the briber is punishable with a milder punishment than the corrupt official. In addition, through self-denunciation the briber has the opportunity to provide a strong probation means that will help authorities to prove bribe-taking.

However, the decreased difference between the penalties of the two crimes leads to the conclusion that the Romanian legislator has considered that the act of giving or offering bribes must be sanctioned about the same as the act of receiving bribes.

Also included in the corruption chapter of our Criminal Code are the offences of **influence peddling**, punished by article 291, and **buying influence**, punished by article 292.

Influence peddling is defined as soliciting, receiving or accepting the promise of money or other benefits, directly or indirectly, for oneself or for another, committed by a person who has influence or who alleges that they have influence over a public servant and who promises they will persuade the latter to perform, fail to perform, speed up or delay the performance of an act that falls under the latter's professional duties or to perform an act contrary to such duties and is punishable by no less than two and no more than seven years of imprisonment. Buying influence is the promise, the supply or the giving of money or other benefits, for oneself or for another, directly or indirectly, to a person who has influence or who alleges they have influence over a public servant to persuade the latter to perform, fail to perform, speed up or delay the performance of an act that falls under the latter's professional duties or to perform an act contrary to such duties and is punishable by no less than two and no more than seven years of imprisonment and prohibition from exercising certain rights.

Law no. 78/2000 regulates offences assimilated to corruption offences, such as:
- deliberately establishing a reduced value, compared to the real market value, of the goods belonging to the economic units in which the state or an authority of the local public administration is a shareholder, committed during a privatisation activity or on the occasion of a commercial transaction, or of the goods belonging to public authorities or public institutions, during a selling activity of these, committed by those holding management, ruling or administrative duties;
- granting subsidies in violation of the law or not monitoring, according to law, compliance with the subsidies' intended destination;
- using subsidies for purposes other than those for which they were granted, as well as other use of guaranteed loans from public funds or to be reimbursed from public funds;
- the act of a person who, having the task to monitor, control, reorganise or liquidate a private economic operator, fulfils for it any task, intermediates or facilitates conducting financial or commercial transactions or participates with capital to such economic operator if the act is capable of directly or indirectly providing an undue advantage; and
- the act of a person who has a leading position in a political party, a trade union or association of employers or in a non-profit legal person, to use influence or authority for the purpose of obtaining for himself or for another money, goods or other undue benefits.

Other legal consequences

Other penalties applicable to corruption offences include those of a pecuniary nature.

For recovering damages in criminal cases in Romania are set out specific procedures, such as
- Special confiscation, provided by article 112 of the Criminal Code, refers to confiscation of assets originating in an offence and involves passing goods into state ownership strictly and exhaustively provided by law. This sanction has personal character and

implies that assets can only be confiscated from the convicted person and does not imply confiscation from a third party – a relative to whom the assets were alienated, for example.

- Extended confiscation provided by article 112^1 of the Criminal Code can be ordered if the following conditions are cumulatively met:

    (a)   the value of assets acquired by a convicted person within a time period of five years before and, if necessary, after the time of perpetrating the offence, until the issuance of the indictment, clearly exceeds the revenues obtained lawfully by the convict; and

    (b)   the court is convinced that the relevant assets originate from criminal activities such as corruption offences, offences assimilated thereto, as well as offences against the financial interests of the European Union.

- Confiscation of unjustified assets – the National Integrity Agency may ask the courts to confiscate property or money if, after verification of their acquisition, modality is found that the person cannot justify their origin.

Regarding corruption offences, our criminal legislation stipulates that money, valuables or any other benefits received shall be subject to confiscation, and when such can no longer be located, the forfeiture of the equivalent shall be ordered.

In case of bribe-taking or influence peddling, article 293 paragraph 3 RCC and article 291 paragraph 2 does not limit the scope of persons to whom confiscation can be applied only to the convicted person, therefore extended confiscation being possible; in the same way, confiscation is not limited to only the equivalent in cash of the received benefits – any property liable to be valued in money may be subject to confiscation.

Also, for giving a bribe or buying influence, money, valuables or any other benefits offered or given shall be subject to confiscation, and when such cannot be located, the forfeiture of the equivalent shall be ordered, except if a denunciation followed the giving of the bribe, in which case these assets shall be given back to the briber who denounced the act of corruption.

In the first stage, the prosecutor conducting or supervising the criminal investigation in the corruption case shall determine, by accounting expertise or a report compiled by accounting specialists, what the amount of damages is, and will order asset freezing – for example seizure – to ensure that the person who is being investigated will not alienate property and if at the criminal proceedings' termination, the state should find it impossible to recover the damage.

Subsequently, as the court can maintain asset freezing during criminal proceedings or can even extend it, a special or extended confiscation might be ordered. Along with the defendant's conviction, the court will also decide on the compensation. According to DNA's abovementioned report of activity, discovering and seizing products obtained from committing crimes has been addressed as an essential part of the investigation carried out last year by the National Anticorruption Directorate. The total money and property acquired as object of corruption offences was worth RON 87.7m, the equivalent of €19.7m – up by 133.24% since 2013 – and the damage created as material benefits amounted to RON 1687.9m, the equivalent of €379.7m – up by 50.04%.

During the criminal investigation, out of 245 cases in which indictments have been issued for offences which generated criminal product, 180 cases of asset freezing were ordered in view of special confiscation or to repair the damage caused by the offence, which amounted to RON 1,477.9m, the equivalent of €332.5m, and RON 974.7m, the equivalent of €219.3m worth of goods were effectively identified and seized.

There is an increasing degree of recovery from the criminal investigation phase and a concern for maintaining effective implementation of precautionary measures as an important component in the criminal investigation activity carried out by the National Anticorruption Directorate.

It should be noted in this context the importance of using the institution of extended confiscation and the practice and development of Romanian judicial bodies in this area.

Recovery of crime products is a constant interest in the activities of the judicial bodies involved in investigating and prosecuting high-level corruption offences and economic crimes producing damages of great value.

A key challenge is the enforcement of court decisions by the institutions involved in the recovery of confiscated assets or damages against the national budget or the EU budget. The institution with the main role in the recovery of damages to the state is the National Agency for Fiscal Administration, being responsible to actually transfer money into state ownership. Given the low percentage of recovery – according to reports that have been conducted lately of 5-8% – make us notice this institution's modest activity and slow method of work.

Main bodies involved

The National Anticorruption Directorate (DNA) is a criminal investigation body specialised in combatting corruption, created as a necessary tool in detecting, investigating and bringing to court cases of medium and high corruption. Through its work, it contributes to reducing this phenomenon, in support of a democratic society closer to European values.

DNA, a structure with clearly defined powers, was created according to a model adopted by several other European countries – Spain, Norway, Belgium and Croatia.

The National Anticorruption Directorate is independent in relation to the courts and to the prosecutor's offices attached to them, as well as in relation to other public authorities, exercising its duties under the law and only for its enforcement.

The offences provided by Law no. 78/2000 with its subsequent amendments and completions, applicable in the circumstances described below, fall under the jurisdiction of the National Anticorruption Directorate:

a) if, regardless of the capacity of the persons who committed them, they caused a material damage higher than the equivalent in RON of €200,000, or if the value of the sum of the goods which represent the object of the corruption offence is higher than the equivalent in RON of €10,000; or

b) if, regardless of the value of the material damage or the value of the sum or of the goods which represent the object of the corruption offence, they are committed by: deputies; senators; Romanian members of the European Parliament; the member appointed by Romania within the European Commission; Government members; state secretaries; under-state secretaries and persons linked to them; counsellors of the ministers; judges of the High Court of Cassation and Justice and of the Constitutional Court; other judges and prosecutors; members of the Superior Council of Magistracy; the president of the Legislative Council and the person who replaces him/her; the Ombudsman and his/her deputies; presidential and state counsellors within the Presidential Administration; state counsellors of the Prime Minister; external public members and auditors from the Court of Accounts of Romania and of the County Chambers of Accounts; the Governor and the First Deputy Governor and the Deputy Governor of the National Bank of Romania; the president and the vice-president of the Council of Competition; officers, admirals, generals and marshals; police officers; the presidents and the vice-presidents of county councils; the general mayor and the deputy mayors of the Bucharest municipality; the mayors and the deputy mayors of the sectors of Bucharest; the mayors and the deputy mayors of municipalities; county counsellors; prefects and sub-prefects; leaders of the central and local public institutions and authorities and the persons filling control positions therein, except for the leaders of public institutions and authorities at the level of towns and communes and of persons with control positions within them; lawyers; commissioners of the Financial Guard; customs employees; persons with leading positions, higher than and including that of a director within the autonomous administrators of national interest, of national companies and firms, of banks and trading companies where the state is a main shareholder, of public institutions having tasks in the privatisation process, and of central financial banking units; and persons provided by articles 293 and 294 of the NCC.

According to Government Ordinance no. 43/2000, the National Anticorruption Directorate is set up as a structure with legal personality, within the Prosecutor's Office attached to the High Court of Cassation and Justice, following the reorganisation of the National Anticorruption Prosecutor's Office.

The National Anticorruption Directorate has its headquarters in Bucharest and exercises its duties on the entire Romanian territory with specialised prosecutors in combatting corruption.

The General Prosecutor of the Prosecutor's Office attached to the High Court of Cassation and Justice leads the National Anticorruption Directorate with its Chief Prosecutor. The General Prosecutor of the Prosecutor's Office attached to the High Court of Cassation and Justice solves conflicts of jurisdiction which arise between the National Anticorruption Directorate and the other structures or units within the Public Ministry.

In accordance with Government Ordinance no. 43/2000, the duties of the National Anticorruption Directorate are the following:

- to conduct criminal investigations under the conditions provided by the Criminal Procedural Code, by Law no. 78/2000 on preventing, discovering and sanctioning corruption offences and by the present emergency ordinance, and for offences provided by the Law no. 78/2000 which fall, according to article 13, under the jurisdiction of the National Anticorruption Directorate;
- to conduct, supervise and control criminal investigation acts, carried out as a result of the prosecutor's orders by the judicial police officers who are under the exclusive authority of the Chief Prosecutor of the National Anticorruption Directorate;
- to conduct, supervise and control the technical activities of criminal investigations, carried out by specialists in the economic, financial, banking, customs and IT fields, as well as in other fields, appointed within the National Anticorruption Directorate;
- to notify the courts for taking the measures provided by law and for prosecuting cases regarding the crimes provided by Law no. 78/2000, with its subsequent amendments, which fall, according to article 13, under the jurisdiction of the National Anticorruption Directorate;
- to take part in trials, under the conditions provided by law;
- to exercise the means of appeal against judges' decisions, under the conditions provided by law;
- to study the causes which generate corruption and the conditions which favour it, to draw up and submit proposals with a view to their elimination, as well as to improve criminal legislation;
- to draw up an annual report on the activity of the National Anticorruption Directorate and to present it to the Superior Council of Magistracy and to the Minister of Justice not later than February the next year, and the Minister of Justice will present to Parliament the conclusions on the activity report of the National Anticorruption Directorate;

- to set up and update the database in the field of corrupt deeds; and
- to carry out other tasks provided by law.

The National Anticorruption Directorate exercises its rights and fulfils its procedural tasks provided by law in matters regarding the offences provided by Government Ordinance no. 43/2000 under its jurisdiction. In performing his/her duties, the Chief Prosecutor of the National Anticorruption Directorate issues orders.

This criminal investigation body is enjoying great appreciation among Romanians, and public confidence in the actions of DNA is significantly increasing among civil society, reaching, in the current context, over 55% – the highest level since its establishment. Thus, the number of complaints of corruption received from citizens has increased by 78% compared to last year.

Under Romanian law, another option is to report corrupt acts to the Prosecutor General's Office. Prosecutors (magistrates) are the lead investigators in corruption cases. This approach is based on the experience and advice of countries with more advanced economies, including the United States, that call for specialised units to deal with corruption. The Romanian law mirrors this approach.

For the trial of crimes of corruption and of associated crimes, specialised panels of judges may be set up, according to article 15 in Law no. 92/1992 on judicial organisation, republished with the subsequent modifications.

In recent years, the **National Intelligence Service** (SRI, from its Romanian name) has become an important pillar in the fight against high-level corruption.

SRI began to cause discomfort in some political circles because of its increasing involvement in the fight against corruption. For example, in previous years, SRI sent criminal investigation bodies less than 650 criminal information and referrals, whereas in 2014 it reached over 3,200. The main beneficiaries are DNA and DIICOT: deeply rooted institutions in the fight against high-level corruption and organised crime.

SRI supports DNA in anticorruption activities through referrals and technical support. However, with all the confidence in the institution, one of the concerns of civil society is that SRI is too involved in the activity of DNA, which could affect the institution.

If a prosecutor investigating the cause deems it necessary that a suspect be listened to/ watched, he must obtain a warrant from a judge to intercept communications or spying on the person, and SRI is legally required to provide technical support to any prosecutor because, according to our legislation, SRI is the only institution which has the interception/ spying right.

Often, DNA releases a statement that says something along the lines of: "In the present cause, prosecutors were supported by the National Intelligence Service."

Overview of enforcement activity and policy during the past two years

As mentioned, one of the most resounding cases of the past year concerns magistrate Mircea Moldovan. It holds the record for the highest conviction intercepted in Romania – 22 years of imprisonment for multiple acts of corruption and six bribery offences (most of them related to cases on the insolvency of several companies). The motivations of the court's decision are related to the fact that "he has cast a shadow of doubt on the justice system" because he considered his position of being a judge as a means of enrichment.

The fact that he claimed material benefits of any kind (timber, luxury watches, hiring of relatives, food, household items and so on) in exchange for favourable solutions, and the fact that the economic interests were made by the defendant in an organised way, using intermediaries, led to the huge sentence.

Further referring to corruption in the Romanian judicial system, another case that captured public attention was that regarding the former Chief Prosecutor of the Directorate for Investigating Organised Crime and Terrorism (DIICOT), Alina Bica. Her actions are not related to her position as prosecutor, but as one of the members of the Central Compensation Committee of the National Authority for Property Restitution.

More specifically, the Central Compensation Committee of the National Authority for Property Restitution, which included Alina Bica (as State Secretary and representative of the Ministry of Justice) and other defendants, approved an assessment report, submitted by an expert evaluator, thereby violating the law.

The members of the Commission, taking the conclusions of the assessment of the real estate concerned, did not find that the valuation expert had overestimated the land from RON 113,954,741 (actual) to RON 377,282,300 (value of similar land located in a central area of Bucharest), but they were aware that the land was overvalued.

By improper fulfilment of duties, it was ruled that the Romanian state would be paid damages worth RON 263,327,559 (equivalent to €62,548,113, representing the overvaluation), while obtaining undue benefits for the beneficiaries of the litigious rights.

As a result of these facts, the former Chief Prosecutor of DIICOT is being investigated for the offence of abuse of office, being under preventive detention for five months and subsequently placed under house arrest.

Following this scandal, the Chief Prosecutor resigned.

Following investigations revealed that Alina Bica had received undue benefits (real estate) in return for approval of the abovementioned, a new criminal file was opened and she was sent to court on bribery charges.

Amongst many other famous cases, there are some ongoing investigations into corruption offences, targeting persons representing ministries. Since the year 2000, over 30 ministers have been convicted or indicted.

Elena Udrea (former Minister of Regional Development and Tourism and leader of two political parties) is accused of committing several crimes of bribery and abuse of office while she was a minister. Given that she was still a deputy, prosecutors had requested the Parliament's approval in order to obtain preventive detention. Following this, she was under preventive detention for 72 days, and later moved under house arrest.

Relu Fenechiu (former Minister of Transport) was sentenced to five years of imprisonment in the *Transformer* case. He was accused of selling old electrical equipment of Electrica Moldova at overvalued prices, the damage being €6m.

Recently, DNA's investigations revealed irregularities in the district city halls (District no. 1 and District no. 5) with sums of tens of millions accepted as bribes by mayors in order to guarantee the conclusion of contracts between various individuals or legal entities and municipalities. Prosecutors claim the defendants had created a bribe-collection system, which in most cases represented 10% of the contracts' value.

Another recent highly publicised case concerned the former Minister of Finance, Darius Vâlcov. He allegedly laundered money obtained from bribes by purchasing expensive paintings (over 100 pieces), involving them in an organisation of art galleries.

In the previous edition of this book we discussed the details on the sentencing of former Prime Minister Adrian Nastase; this year brought DNA investigations into another prime minister, at the time of writing still in office, Victor Ponta. He is accused of forgery, money laundering and complicity in tax evasion. The charges date back to 2007-2008 when he was a lawyer associated with Dan Şova, the former Minister of Transport. They both are now defendants in the same criminal case and, due to their past association, Victor Ponta is now accused of conflict of interest because he later proposed him as a minister.

Law and policy relating to issues such as facilitation payments and hospitality

By devoting a new approach to the fight against corruption, the Romanian legislator decided to sanction the offence of receiving undue benefits (formerly provided as a stand-alone offence) as an act of bribery. This means that, according to Romanian criminal legislation, no distinction is made between bribes and 'facilitation' payments, which are also prohibited. A facilitation payment is a small payment to a low-level public official, which is not officially required, to enable or speed up a process which it is the official's job to arrange.

A bribe includes a benefit given or received in any form, which may include: cash; favours; unfair advantages for family or friends in respect of training or employment opportunities (secondments, work experience, trainee positions, internships or permanent positions); and the provision of services, gifts, hospitality or entertainment.

The giving and receiving of modest gifts and hospitality is acceptable business practice providing that it is proportionate and not done solely in order to gain or retain business or to create a business advantage.

For example, Law no. 78/2000 provides that the persons who exercise a public position, irrespective of the way in which they are invested, within public authorities or public institutions and who carry out control duties according to the law are obliged to declare, within 30 days from receipt, any direct or indirect donation or physical presents received in connection with the exercising of their functions or duties, with the exception of those that have a symbolic value.

Also, the persons who exercise a public position as well as those that hold a management position, from directors included, and up, within the autonomous administrations, national companies, national societies, trading companies in which the state or an authority of the local public administration is a shareholder, the public institutions involved in the carrying out of the privatisation process, the National Bank of Romania, or the banks in which the state is the controlling stockholder – have the obligation to declare their assets under the terms of Law no. 115/1996 on declaration and control of the assets of dignitaries, magistrates, civil servants and of certain persons with management positions. The non-submission of the declaration of assets by the persons stipulated in paragraph 1 brings about the *ex officio* opening of the control procedure of the assets under the terms of Law no. 115/1996.

Key issues relating to investigation, decision-making and enforcement procedures

Self-reporting and whistle-blowers

In Romania, self-reporting is controlled by a particular impunity clause within the offences of giving bribes and buying influence.

According to article 290 paragraph 3 RCC the bribe giver shall not be punishable if he reports the action prior to the criminal investigation bodies being notified thereupon. Likewise, article 292 paragraph 2 stipulates that the perpetrator shall not be punishable if they report the action prior to the criminal investigation bodies being notified thereupon.

The impunity clause will be applicable if the following conditions are met:
- The briber/purchaser of influence reports the criminal act.
- The denunciation is made before the criminal body is notified.

The provisions of article 290 paragraph 3, as well as article 292 paragraph 2, are designed to prevent bribery offences by creating for those who would be tempted to take bribes the fear that they will be denounced.

In this case, the money, valuables or any other assets will be given back to the briber/ purchaser of influence if they were given following the denunciation. For example, in 2014 courts have ruled the refund of money to persons who self-reported paying bribes or influencing purchasers, along with the benefit provided by law of impunity, amounting to RON 4,041,103.54; the equivalent of €909,216.47. It also ordered the return of two cars.

Given the magnitude of the fight against corruption in Romania in the past year and the success DNA enjoys among civil society, many cases of this structure were formed as a result of the wave of denunciations and self-reports made either by suspects already criminally investigated or people who had knowledge of acts of corruption.

The most important case, thought to be the main catalyst for the wave of self-reports, was a self-report and denunciation made by a former senator of the main political party which is currently leading the Government.

He denounced the former Executive President of the aforesaid political party and former Deputy Prime Minister of Romania for committing the offence of forgery and use of forgery in organising the referendum for the dismissal of the former President of Romania: Traian Băsescu.

Following the criminal investigation thus initiated, it appeared that the former deputy, while organising and conducting the referendum of 29 July 2012, had used his influence and authority in the party in order to obtain patrimonial advantages, such as electoral advantages, for the political alliance the party represented by the defendant was part of, to achieve the necessary quorum of votes obtained by means other than legal ones. Recently, he was sentenced to one year's imprisonment, whose enforcement was suspended for a three-year period.

Plea bargain

The guilty plea agreement is provided as the document of initiating proceedings, concluded between prosecutor and defendant, if the defendant (individual or legal person) means to recognise the facts of which he is accused and their legal classification, and agree a punishment and a way of individualisation, namely the type and amount of the punishment and its form of execution.

Judicial bodies shall notify the defendant of the possibility of signing such an agreement, during the criminal investigation phase, as a result of admitting guilt, and it can be initiated either by the prosecutor or by the defendant.

To have concluded such an agreement, the following conditions must be met:
- The criminal action has been initiated.
- The defendant must be over 18 years old and legal assistance is mandatory.
- Law must provide a punishment up to seven years of imprisonment or a fine.
- The evidence administered during criminal investigation must show sufficient data of the existence of the offence and the guilt of the defendant.
- There is written prior approval from the hierarchically superior prosecutor through his consent to the limits of the agreement.
- The case prosecutor and the defendant must generally agree upon the object of the agreement.

Concluding and accepting the plea agreement requires acceptance by the defendant of the incriminating factual basis.

The persons who agree to be convicted using this agreement give up most of the rights they would have during the trial. Thus, for example, they lose the privilege against self-incrimination or the right to remain silent, the right to participate in direct investigation of evidence by the judge or the right to request new evidence, etc. The most important consequence is that this agreement, once accepted by the court, is equivalent to determining the circumstances without the judicial investigation being performed.

On the other hand, at least theoretically, a guilty plea agreement has the potential to diminish the problems brought by the traditional model for awareness of the defendant. The defendant has the opportunity to negotiate an arrangement with the prosecutor in less legalised and technical conditions and, in this way, to become a person who participates in the decision-making process in determining the punishment. Such participation not only promotes the dignity of the individual, but also has an instrumental value, since the defendant may feel morally obliged to honour the compromise that was reached and will be more likely to feel reconciled with the penalty imposed.

Another form of plea bargaining involves a defendant pleading guilty to a charge in return for a reduction of the penalty limits provided by law for the offence committed, also known as simplified trial procedure.

Simplified trial procedure is actually an abbreviated trial which is based on a plea of guilt and can be applied if the requirements are met.

According to article 374 paragraph 4 of the new Criminal Proceedings Code, in cases where criminal proceedings do not concern an offence punishable by life imprisonment, the judge informs the defendant that he may request that judgment be based only on evidence administered during the criminal investigations phase and documents submitted by the parties, if he fully acknowledges the facts incriminating him.

According to legal provisions, the defendant may plead guilty before the beginning of the court investigation, this meaning the defendant must admit the allegations made by prosecutors against him.

The procedure itself, as evident from the definition, applies only at the trial stage, therefore only before the judge, when the defendant is asked whether he wants to make use of these provisions.

In case of an affirmative answer, the defendant should recognise the facts as they were retained in the indictment, following the outcome of the proceedings, to be made only on the basis of evidence given in the prosecution stage. The only permission established by law in accepting new evidence in this case refers to circumstantial documents the defendant may submit at the same time as the trial.

The clear benefits that the law gives to defendants after confessing are quite attractive and are related to punishment, the limits of which are reduced by a third concerning offences punishable with imprisonment or by a quarter in case of offences punishable with a criminal fine. Another benefit of the law is that the judging process is much faster and there is no need for exchange of arguments, because, by confessing, the defendant assumes the evidence administered by the prosecutors, giving up the classical way of defence.

Admission of guilt has been successfully used in ordinary criminal trials since 2010, but in the last year it also began to be used in corruption cases. The latest case is that of a deputy who recognised the facts of corruption, and his case was trialled in a court of first instance in one day.

He was caught in the act while receiving a bribe from a denouncer. He ran from the place of the crime, but was later caught and detained by prosecutors, with DNA asking permission for preventive detention.

At the first hearing of the trial, the court announced that the deputy admitted his deeds and appealed for the accelerated procedure.

This meant that his trial, which could have taken several months or even a year, was judged in one day. Finally, the deputy was sentenced to one year in prison. In this case, the law provides a penalty of one to five years in prison. Through confession, the maximum sentence was reduced by a third to three years and four months in prison.

Overview of cross-border issues

The fight against corruption has achieved a global dimension. Be it global or regional organisations, e.g. the United Nations, the Organization for Economic Cooperation and Development, the World Bank, the Council of Europe; or strictly regional, e.g. the Organization of American States, the African Union or the European Union. The global orientation and determination to counter this phenomenon is evident.

In this regard, during last year, the International Cooperation Service fulfilled, through international relations, the specific role and mission of the National Anticorruption Directorate: to be a specialised structure of the Public Ministry to fight corruption in the central Romanian authority.

To achieve this objective, the international cooperation activity of the DNA has pursued the subsequent main areas:
*   following up the fulfilment of the DNA's commitments and actions towards the Cooperation and Verification Mechanism of Romania's progress in achieving specific goals in the areas of judicial reform and the fight against corruption;
*   providing an accurate reflection of the external view of DNA activity;
*   DNA involvement in assessment and monitoring activities in line with international standards in the fight against corruption in other countries;
*   DNA involvement in the activities of international networks within anticorruption authorities in other states;
*   projects with European funding regarding implementation and monitoring, of which DNA is a direct beneficiary;
*   providing specialised training for the staff of the DNA, in partnership with other organisations;
*   continuing and expanding cooperation with similar institutions in other states and of DNA work performed in groups and networks of international anticorruption authorities; and
*   activities regarding international judicial assistance.

In relation to cross-border cooperation activities which DNA has carried out in the past year, we can include cooperation with the International Anti-Corruption Academy, EAPC EACN (European Partners Anti-Corruption Network – European Network Corruption Authorities), GRECO, and OECD CAN (OECD Anti-Corruption Network for Eastern Europe and Central Asia). These collaborations concern active participation in international conferences and seminars on corruption and hosting foreign delegations.

Among other EU funding programmes that have been proposed or implemented, the National Anticorruption Directorate manages a project on promoting the exchange of good practices in detecting, investigating and sanctioning corruption offences in the EU (CORRDIS). The project aims to assist in identifying best practices through a comparative approach across

Member States. In each of the organised activities, expert practitioners from each Member State of the EU will participate.

During 2014, DNA presence was assured, as a specialised anticorruption investigation body and active partner, in the activities of international organisations, such as the Council of Europe, ONU and OECD, of international anticorruption organisations and networks with the purpose of increasing the degree of implementation by parties of European and international anti-corruption conventions and for promoting judicial cooperation, exchange of information and good practices, as well as exchange of expertise in order to improve anti-corruption legislation and investigative practices in different countries.

The quality and usefulness of DNA participation in these international activities was recognised by its inclusion in the governing structures of some of the organisations and by constant invitations to carry out anticorruption activities.

In the matter of parallel investigation, the Liaison Office, which has similar institutions in other countries, has brought an important contribution to the field of judicial cooperation in criminal matters, conducting specific tasks on:

*   request of international active rogatory letters for the fulfilment of criminal proceedings acts in several countries, such as Saudi Arabia, Austria, Belarus, Bulgaria, China, Cyprus, Switzerland, Egypt, the United Arab Emirates, Greece, Jordan, Israel, Germany, Italy, the Netherlands, Poland, Moldova, Slovakia, Spain, the USA, Hungary, Ukraine and Turkey;
*   conducting, in 13 international passive rogatory letters, criminal proceedings acts requested by foreign judicial authorities, namely Austria, the Czech Republic, France, Germany, Italy, Moldova, Norway, Hungary and the USA;
*   completion of formalities in six procedures of international summons performed in Italy, Moldova, the USA and Turkey;
*   requesting or performing operational verifications on identifying police officers, people and cars, etc. There were three such verifications required in Belgium and the International Police Cooperation Centre, the results being received in due time. Likewise, it has been acted upon five such requests to perform similar checks received from Israel, Germany, Morocco and the USA; and
*   conducting spontaneous exchange of information with the USA and Switzerland.

Corporate liability for bribery and corruption offences

Under Romanian law, legal entities, except state and public authorities, are criminally responsible for crimes committed in achieving the object of activity or interest, or such on behalf of the legal person. Public institutions are not criminally liable for offences committed in the exercise of these activities.

Basically, criminal liability may arise to any legal entity. This rule, by law, provides exceptions regarding public legal entities, namely the state, public authorities and public institutions, but only for crimes committed in carrying out an activity not subject to private domain. These exceptions are justified, because engaging criminal liability for such entities cannot be conceived or would have negative consequences on society.

The conditions of the criminal liability for legal persons are stipulated in article 135 of the RCC. Thus, in order to attract criminal liability of legal persons the offence is necessary to be committed:

*   in achieving the object of its activity, meaning the offence must be directly related to the activities carried out to achieve the core activity of the legal entity or its corporate policy;
*   in the interests of the legal entity, meaning the offence has to be committed in order to obtain a benefit or to avoid a loss or other negative effect;

- on behalf of the legal person, for example by an agent, representative or proxy; or
- further to a resolution issued by a legal entity or because of its negligence, taking into consideration the conduct of the managing bodies of such legal entity.

The Romanian Criminal Code has set out a general criminal liability of legal entities. At least theoretically, a legal person may be criminally liable for any offence provided under criminal law. The provisions of articles 289 – 292 of the RCC also apply to the managers, directors, administrators and auditors of trading companies, national companies and societies, autonomous administrations and to any other economic units.

There are a number of crimes that cannot be committed by legal entities, as a principal perpetrator, such as bribery, given the special quality the person who commits such an offence must meet, which, according to article 175, has to be a public servant. However, its participation in committing the offence as an instigator or accomplice is not excluded.

The other corruption offences – giving a bribe, influence peddling and buying influence – are possible to be committed by a legal entity, subject to the conditions mentioned above.

The statistical analysis of DNA has revealed that 107 legal entities were sent to trial by indictment or by court referral through a plea bargaining agreement in the last year.

Proposed reforms / The year ahead

Corruption and anti-corruption has been a main concern for a long time. Following the thread of history it may be noted that criminality and corruption, in all forms of manifestation, persists from ancient times, with a long tradition, considering that the human tendency toward corruption has always existed, being a permanent and inevitable phenomenon in the existence of society.

In Romania, corruption tends to become an organised phenomenon, specialised and professionalised, appearing as a network of organisations and individuals, who through various means reach corrupt decision-makers at the highest levels of politics, the legislature, the judiciary and the administration. Recently, this practice has seen an increase without precedent, corruption being present in all areas of economic and social life.

The degree of social threat that corruption acts represent has led to controls being imposed which have punished the corrupt by creating an appropriate regulatory framework and effective anti-corruption bodies.

Although corruption offences are far from sporadic and accidental, the fight against corruption in Romania is on the right path. Considering the intense activity of competent institutions and legislative changes created specifically for sustaining efforts to fight corruption, we can say that all the steps and existing resources are used in solving these kinds of cases.

The special importance of this fight is represented by the measures taken in the prevention of this crime. Also, a transparent and fair system in terms of application and verifying the law enforcement is imperative. Joint collective efforts are also needed.

Monitoring and approval offered by equivalent European and international institutions and professional collaborations between such entities must be maintained and materialised.

Mihai Mares
Tel: +40 314 378 324 / Email: mihai.mares@mares.ro
Mihai is one of the founders and the Managing Partner of Mares / Danilescu / Mares.

Prior to this position, he was the managing partner of Garrigues in Romania, which originally merged with Mares & Asociatii in 2008. When Garrigues pulled out of Romania, Mihai joined as an Of Counsel for the Romanian law firm Musat & Asociatii, being in charge of the "Iberian desk", before re-launching his firm in September 2011.

Since 2014, his practice has focused almost exclusively on criminal defence for senior executives, entrepreneurs, major industrial groups, financial institutions and large international and domestic companies, in a wide range of matters involving accounting, financial, securities and tax fraud, and bribery, antitrust and environmental violations.

In addition, he advises clients in internal investigations and audits involving money laundering, fraud and other corporate misconduct. In international criminal law, Mihai acts in international corruption, freezing of assets, multi-jurisdictional investigations and extradition.

Mares / Danilescu / Mares

No. 55- 55bis, Carol I Bld., 2nd District, Bucharest, Romania
Tel: +40 314 378 324 / Fax: +40 314 378 327 / URL: http://www.mares.ro

Serbia

Vladimir Hrle
Hrle Attorneys

Brief overview of the law and enforcement regime

Legal regime

Serbia signed and ratified the UN Convention against Corruption and the Council of Europe Convention (Criminal and Civil) on Corruption. All three conventions came into force by a special decree and thus became part of the legal system of Serbia; however, the full implementation of these conventions is yet to be seen.

In Serbia, there is no specific national anti-corruption legislation. The anti-corruption framework is scattered between various legislation. The principal legislative enactment is the Criminal Code, which recognises both passive and active bribery (which applies both to private/commercial bribery and public bribery) and trading in influence.

Active bribery – bribing public officials or employees, agents or shareholders/owners of private companies with the intention that they act, or omit to act, contrary to/in accordance with their duties.

Passive bribery – where public officials or employees, agents or shareholders/owners of private companies accept advantages in exchange for an act, or the omission of an act, contrary/in accordance with their duties.

Trading in influence – whoever solicits or accepts, either directly or through a third party, a reward or any other benefit for himself or another in order to use his official or social position, or his real or assumed influence, to intercede for the performance or non-performance of an act; or whoever makes a promise or an offer, or gives to another either directly or through a third party, a reward or any other benefit, so that they might use their official or social position, or real or assumed influence, to intercede for the performance or non-performance of an official act.

The main investigating authority is the Public Prosecution, and the sanctions range from six months up to twelve years' imprisonment. In parallel and in order to eliminate circumstances or conditions that may influence the perpetrator to commit criminal offences in future, the court can impose a security measure of prohibiting a certain duty, e.g. directorship. Similarly, the legal consequence of a guilty judgment can be a termination of employment/appointment.

Overview of enforcement activity and policy during the past two years

The corruption ranking for Serbia for 2014, according to Transparency International, is 78th out of 175 countries in the world. This ranking suggests a small improvement of two places in comparison with 2013.

The main corruption issue in comparison with regional countries and the rest of the world is the proportion of firms that expect to give gifts to secure government contracts, according to Enterprise Surveys (http://www.enterprisesurveys.org), The World Bank, for the year 2013.

Cases

In recent years there have been a few big cases relating to corruption in both the private and public sectors, but considerably more corruption cases come from the public sector, as private companies seek to avoid media publicity on corruption issues. Regardless of the sector where corruption occurs, there are no final or binding convictions for high-profile cases.

On the basis of the existing final and binding convictions, mostly cases of smaller and medium corruption, the analysis made by Partners Serbia found the following rate of convictions:

1) For the crime of "Passive bribery", 68% of convictions were prison sentences, 21% of convictions were fines, 8% of convictions were house arrest, and 3% of convictions were conditional sentences.
2) For the crime of "Active bribery", 7% of convictions were prison sentences, 4% of convictions were fines, and 89% of convictions were conditional sentences.

Most final and binding convictions for the crime of "Passive bribery" came from the public (police) sector (45%), construction sector (25%), medical sector (10%) and educational sector (8%). On the other hand, for the crime of "Active bribery", most final and binding convictions came from the judicial sector (14%), medical sector (14%) and educational sector (7%).

It is expected that enforcement activity will be boosted by the proposed new legislation and government strategy, as set below.

Law and policy relating to issues such as facilitation payments and hospitality

A bribe can be monetary or non-monetary and there is no specific monetary limit up to which a person can offer gifts without being held criminally liable. However, under the Anti-Corruption Agency Act, an official can accept a protocol or holiday gift (the gift may not be in money or securities) if its value does not exceed 5% of the value of his/her average monthly net salary in Serbia.

The donor of the benefit who reports the offence prior to becoming aware that it had been detected may be remitted from punishment.

Key issues relating to investigation, decision-making and enforcement procedures

Self-reporting

Self-reporting is relevant in cases of active bribery, meaning that the perpetrator who reports the offence before becoming aware that it has been detected, may be remitted from punishment. In other cases, self-reporting is relevant for mitigation of the sentence.

Also, the Board of Directors, managers and employees are criminally liable if they knew that a criminal offence was being prepared (only offences punishable of five or more years), but failed to report this during the time of the preparation (when its commission could have still been prevented), and the offence is later committed or attempted.

Deferred plea agreements

In principle, deferred plea agreements (DPAs) do exist in a certain form and the prosecution can defer criminal prosecution for certain criminal offences (up to five years) if the perpetrator accepts one or more of the following obligations: 1) to rectify the detrimental consequence caused by the commission of the criminal offence or indemnify the damage caused; 2) to pay a certain amount of money to the benefit of a humanitarian organisation, fund or public institution; 3) to perform certain community service or humanitarian work; or 4) to fulfil other obligation determined by a final court decision.

The prosecution shall determine a time limit during which the perpetrator must fulfil the obligations undertaken, with the proviso that the time limit may not exceed one year and if the suspect fulfils the obligation within the prescribed time limit, the prosecution shall dismiss the charges.

Civil *vs* Criminal

In principle, an aggrieved party (in this case, the state) can seek civil compensation before a criminal court and usually the criminal court further refers the party to seek redress in the civil court, once there is a guilty judgment.

Plea agreement

Generally speaking, this kind of agreement has not yet gained its full scope, as seen in purely adversarial systems. However, according to the Serbian Criminal Procure Code, the court shall, upon written agreement between the parties (the prosecution and the defendant/perpetrator), accept the agreement, if: 1) the defendant has knowingly and voluntarily confessed the criminal offence or criminal offences which are the subject matter of the charges; 2) the defendant was aware of all the consequences of the concluded agreement, especially that he has waived his right to a trial and that he accepts a restriction of his right to file an appeal; 3) the other existing evidence does not run contrary to the defendant's confession of having committed a criminal offence; or 4) the penalty of other criminal sanction or other measure in respect of which the prosecution and the defendant have reached an agreement, was proposed in line with criminal and other law.

Other agreements

Agreement on testifying by a defendant – the agreement may be concluded with the defendant who has confessed in entirety to having committed a criminal offence, provided that the significance of his testimony for detecting, proving or preventing the criminal offence outweighs the consequences of the criminal offence he has committed.

Agreement on testifying by a convicted person – the prosecution and a convicted person may conclude an agreement on testifying if the significance of the convicted person's testimony for detecting, proving or preventing the criminal offences referred outweighs the consequences of the criminal offence for which he has been convicted.

Whistle-blowers

Under the newly adopted whistle-blowers' legislation, whistle-blowers are protected when reporting suspicions relating to corruption, violation of human rights or the exercise of public authority contrary to the entrusted purpose, danger to life, public health, safety, environment, and prevention of major damage.

Disclosure

Those making disclosure within one year from the day he/she learned about the action which is subject to disclosure, and no later than ten years from the performance of such action, are entitled to protection in accordance with the law provided that, at the moment of disclosure, based on available information, an average person with similar knowledge and experience as the whistle-blower would believe that the disclosed information is true.

The employer of a whistle-blower may not, through its actions or omission to act, put the whistle-blower in an unfavourable position due to whistle-blowing (in relation to employment or work engagement, promotion, evaluation, acquisition or loss of vocation, disciplinary measures and penalties, working conditions, termination of employment, salary, etc.).

Judicial protection

The whistle-blower is entitled to file a motion for protection to the competent court and request the court to: declare that damaging action was taken against him/her; ban the damaging action or its repetition; remove the consequences and grant pecuniary and non-pecuniary damages; and publish a court decision in the media.

Unlike regular civil proceedings, the burden of proof lies on the defendant, meaning that the defendant will have to prove (if the whistle-bower initially demonstrated the likelihood that the damaging action was a result of whistle-blowing) that the damaging action is not related to the whistle-blowing.

Overview of cross-border issues

Legal regime

In principle, the Criminal Code of Serbia shall apply to anyone committing a criminal offence on its territory.

However, Serbia is also no stranger to the extra-territorial application of the US Foreign Corrupt Practices Act (FCPA) and, to a lesser extent according to the practice so far, the UK Bribery Act. Recent years have seen the investigation of, and subsequent DPAs on, bribery allegations concerning several multinational pharmaceutical companies.

Bribery and Trading in influence also extend to foreign officials, meaning that the foreign official who has committed the offence shall be liable under the same regime as the domestic official.

Corporate liability for bribery and corruption offences

Serbia recognises corporate criminal liability and a company can be held liable if: (i) the responsible person, acting within their authority, culpably commits a criminal offence with the intention of obtaining benefits for the company; or (ii) the person acting under the control or supervision of the responsible person was enabled to commit a criminal offence due to the lack of supervision or control of the decision-maker.

A compliance programme or compliance defence is considered when determining the punishment within the limits for the particular offence, and serves as mitigation. A private company can be exempted from the punishment if it voluntarily and immediately takes necessary actions to remove harmful effects or returns unlawfully obtained property. In addition, a company may be exonerated from a punishment if: (i) it detects and reports a criminal offence before learning that criminal proceedings have been instituted; or (ii) on a voluntary basis or without delay removes incurred detrimental consequences or returns the proceeds from crime unlawfully gained.

Proposed reforms / The year ahead

The year ahead should see the start of the application of newly adopted whistle-blowers' legislation. It should be noted that the relevant whistle-blower legislation does not see breaches of whistle-blowers' rights as criminal offences, nor misdemeanours. It is yet to be seen whether these will be included in the Criminal Code amendments, as announced.

In addition, the announced Law on Property Origin should secure a more efficient system for the fight against corruption, officials claim.

Further changes of the Criminal Code are also in progress, especially the part referring to criminal actions in economic areas, with a special focus on the crime of tax evasion. Important roles in the implementation of this amendment lie with the Tax Administration, the Administration for Preventing Money Laundering, and the Customs Administration and Prosecution.

Finally, the Government has adopted a Financial Investigation Strategy for 2015-2016 that comprehensively addresses the problem of financial crime and regulates connections between a wide circle of government authorities. Adoption of this mid-term strategy seeks to improve financial investigations overall, and to keep track of money flows and assets for easier identification of criminal offences, and is one of the objectives set by the National Anti-Corruption Strategy for the period 2013-2018.

Vladimir Hrle
Tel: +381 64 110 6335 / Email: vladimir.hrle@hrle-attorneys.rs
Prior to establishing Hrle Attorneys, Vladimir worked with the law firms
Schoenherr and Karanovic-Nikolic, and was actively involved in two high-
profile cases before the UN court (ICTY) in The Hague. Vladimir started his
career with Dragoslav Cetkovic, an esteemed defence attorney, in 2005.

Vladimir is a member of the Serbian and Belgrade Bar Association and one of
the managers of the Anti-Corruption Working Group of the European Criminal
Bar Association. He is active in the Balkans Regional Rule of Law Network
of the American Bar Association (founding member), European Criminal
Justice Observatory (deputy chair) and Fair Trails International. He also
co-heads the Business Crime practice group of the Roxin Alliance (partner
of the World Bank's Global Forum on Law, Justice and Development) and
cooperates as a consultant with the International Finance Corporation of the
World Bank Group.

Vladimir is a certified trainer of the Council of Europe's Human Rights
Education for Legal Professionals Programme, after successfully finishing
the Training of Trainers (ToT) in Strasbourg, France, with the aim of ensuring
high-quality further training on the European Convention on Human Rights
and the jurisprudence of the European Court of Human Rights for legal
professionals.

Vladimir holds a law degree from Belgrade University and an LL.M. degree
from the University of Amsterdam.

Hrle Attorneys

Simina 1, Belgrade, Serbia
Tel: +381 11 3283 295 / URL: http://www.hrle-attorneys.rs

Spain

Fermín Morales Prats & Thea Morales Espinosa
Gabinete Jurídico Fermín Morales

Brief overview of the law and enforcement regime

The public sector is the main sector involved with cases of criminal conduct that can be included under the notion of corruption. Strictly speaking, in Spain, corruption is classified under the criminal offence of active/passive bribery (art. 419 *et seq.* of the Criminal Code). However, at present the concept of corruption extends to other forms of criminal conduct in the public sector engaged in by public officials, often with the connivance, participation or co-perpetration of private individuals. This is why, currently, the idea of corruption encompasses other offences such as influence peddling (art. 428 *et seq.* of the CC) when it comes to decision-making in the public sector, abusive or unfair management of public funds (which in Spain is called misappropriation of public funds) (art. 432 *et seq.* of the CC), fraud against the administration (art. 436 *et seq.* of the CC), negotiations and activities forbidden to public officials and abuse of public office (art. 439 *et seq.* of the CC). This is how an extensive understanding of the concept of corruption in the public sector is structured which, in recent years, has tended to include other criminal offences by public officials, such as prevarication (issuing manifestly unfair administrative resolutions), disloyalty when it comes to the custody of documents or the disclosure of secrets by public officials. Moreover, the Spanish Criminal Code contemplates corruption offences in business (art. 286a of the CC), formerly known as corruption between private individuals and corruption in international economic transactions (art. 286*ter* of the CC) which extends to private individuals and public officials in the list of international economic activities. In the crime of active/passive bribery and that of influence peddling, the corporate criminal liability clause may be applicable.

It should also be mentioned that crimes against the administration of justice perpetrated by judges and magistrates in the exercise of the jurisdictional function (art. 446 *et seq.* CC) should also be included under this extensive notion of corruption.

This broad conception of corruption in the public sector was reflected in the institutional reforms made in 1995, when a special prosecutor's office against corruption and organised crime was created. This special prosecutor's office has gradually extended its authority to finally take on responsibility for the investigation and indictment of financial crimes associated with corruption in the public sector. The jurisdiction of the special prosecutor's office against corruption in financial matters is dependent on the crime under investigation being classified as bearing "special significance". In practice, this concept has been subject to broad understanding, meaning that the investigation and prosecution of several financial crimes (fraudulent acts, tax frauds, money laundering, etc.) has been included under the functional jurisdiction of this prosecutor's office whenever a minimum association with the phenomenon of corruption in the public sector is identified. Similarly, the ties between financial crime and transnational criminal organisations or groups have led to intervention from the aforesaid special prosecutor's office.

This trend of legislative and institutional organisation politics aimed at giving a global criminal response to the phenomenon of corruption has led to the idea of corruption in Spain extending to the private sector. The clearest reflection of this tendency can be found in art. 286*bis* of the CC, introduced by Organic Law 5/2010, of 22 June. This legislative measure, entitled "Corruption in business", classifies corruption between private individuals as a crime, thus transposing the provisions of the Council of Europe Criminal Law Convention on Corruption (CETS no. 173, Strasbourg, 27.01.1999, ratified by Spain on 01.12.2009) to Spanish Law.

Nonetheless, the idea of transparency and control in business and economic activities in the private sector as a preventive guarantee in relation to corruption requires even more ambitious measures. In this respect, Spanish criminal doctrine has expressed its concerns regarding the effectiveness, usefulness and admissibility of said measures when it comes to the cost of legal guarantees. We are referring to the introduction of corporate criminal liability in the Spanish Criminal Code (art. 31*bis* of the CC).

Overview of enforcement activity and policy during the past two years

The approach of legislative policy in Spain to the phenomenon of corruption is structured into two parts: firstly, the criminalisation of bribing public officials and other unlawful conduct by said parties as falling under the notion of crimes against the public administration and, secondly, corruption in the private sector, a field also including the so-called corruption in sport.

In Spanish jurisprudence there are several precedents of convictions owing to corruption offences perpetrated by public officials involving businesspeople or other professionals from the private sector who have acted as corrupters. In recent years, significant convictions have been verified in large litigations such as the so-called *Operación Malaya* (Andalusia) and *Caso Palma-Arena* (Palma de Mallorca), the latter of which has been subdivided into several investigation and prosecution procedures. Some of these procedures have already led to convictions entailing the imprisonment of important figures in the political arena.

Many proceedings are currently underway in Spain that could be placed within the notion of corruption. According to official figures provided by the General Council of the Judiciary (CGPJ), in early 2013 there were 1,661 cases of corruption being followed. The region with the highest number was Andalusia with 656 criminal proceedings being pursued owing to crimes associated with corruption. In second place, the Valencian Community registered 280 cases, followed by Catalonia with 215 proceedings, the Community of Madrid with 185 and Galicia with 110.

According to the statistics of the CGPJ, the crimes most frequently observed in these proceedings are bribery (paying off public officials), prevarication, influence peddling and misappropriation of public funds. Likewise, the most frequent financial crimes associated with corruption are swindling and embezzlement.

Law and policy relating to issues such as facilitation payments and hospitality

Spanish criminal legislation and jurisprudence do not directly address a specific legal treatment of what could be deemed as facilitation payments and hospitality policies.

In terms of corruption, in Spain these concepts should be re-routed under the alleged criminal relevance of so-called hand-outs or gifts to public officials. Indeed, the Criminal Code contemplates the offence of improper active/passive bribery (art. 422 of the CC), which classifies the conduct of acceptance by an authority or public official of a hand-out or gift offered on account of the position held or function exercised as an offence. This is the legal closure stipulation of the incrimination system for bribes in the public sector. This offence entails a problematic delimitation in relation to the idea of social suitability of the gift accepted. In order to determine the criteria of social suitability, the following is taken into consideration: uses and customs in a specific context; the nature of the hand-out or gift; and the value thereof. These are unstable and changing criteria that depend on the interpretation of the judge in each case, which weakens the guarantees of the principle of legality. A famous precedent of acquittal relating to this crime was the so-called *Caso Camps*, where the controversial issue was whether acceptance of a gift in the form of suits by a president of a regional autonomous community could constitute an offence of improper bribery. Ultimately, the jury and the Supreme Court declared a judgment of acquittal.

Key issues relating to investigation, decision-making and enforcement procedures

In Spain, cases of corruption are addressed by means of the ordinary criminal proceedings set out in the Spanish procedural law (Law of Criminal Procedure). Nevertheless, two clarifications should be made specific to cases of corruption. The first refers to the fact that some of the crimes comprised under the concept of corruption lead to the application of jury trial proceedings. Indeed, pursuant to art. 1 of the Organic Law on the Jury Court, offences of active/passive bribery in the public sector, influence peddling, misappropriation of public funds, fraud against the administration and negotiations forbidden to public officials, among others, fall under the jurisdiction of the Jury Court (jury trial presided by a magistrate).

The second clarification refers to the fact that often the individuals accused in cases of corruption in the public sector are members of the Congress of Deputies or the Senate. In these cases, jurisdiction for investigating the case is directly awarded to the Supreme Court, the legal body that will subsequently also be in charge of prosecution, and the magistrate having investigated the case will not form part of the court in the oral proceedings. In this case, the situation arises whereby the right to second-instance trial proceedings by means of an appeal is lost. Members of Congress or Senators are entitled to waive the privilege of *aforamiento*[1] (parliamentary immunity) by withdrawing from their respective positions. In this instance, the case shall be investigated by an ordinary examining judge and then prosecuted by an ordinary court, whereby the right to second-instance trial proceedings by means of an appeal shall be preserved.

Similarly, cases of corruption involving people holding the position of members of regional parliaments have procedural singularities, since these members of parliament are also entitled to the privilege of *aforamiento*. As a result, investigation of the case shall correspond to the High Court of Justice of the respective regional autonomous community. In this case, the problem of losing the right to second-instance trial proceedings by means of an appeal does not apply as the ruling, if applicable, could be challenged before the Supreme Court. Regional autonomous members of parliament can also waive their privileged jurisdiction with the aforesaid effects of submitting the case to ordinary judges.

Regardless of these singularities, cases of corruption in Spain in the public and private sector are investigated by an examining judge, who is responsible for the pre-trial stage. By contrast, in other European countries investigation is incumbent on the Public Prosecution Service. In the Spanish legal system the public prosecutor is a public plaintiff representing the State and society, but it does not have a monopoly of prosecution, as the Spanish system is very open when it comes to admitting other possible parties for the prosecution. Thus, the full prosecution that the private prosecutor representing the victims of a crime can exercise is admitted, in the same way that conceptually it is also possible to pursue public prosecution as it is a mechanism for citizen participation in criminal proceedings, pursuant to the provisions of art. 125 of the Spanish Constitution.

Overview of cross-border issues

Organic Law 1/2014, of 13 March, amended the Organic Law on the Judiciary (art. 23) in relation to the principle of universal justice. This reform has been extremely controversial in the legal field, generating a debate in which more often than not opinions of a political nature have been superimposed or given preference over legal arguments.

Traditionally, in our criminal legal system the principle of universal justice, as an exception to the principle of territoriality of Spanish criminal law, has been broadly shaped subject to few requirements compared with other regulations seen in the comparative law of our European cultural and legal environment. The public prosecution institution had been in place along with this loose configuration of an exception to the principle of territoriality of criminal law. This combination of factors, as expected, turned the National Court of Spain into a legal body with truly exorbitant functions regarding the prosecution of crimes committed abroad without any ties or links to Spanish interests. The judges and magistrates of the National Court of Spain were shrouded in this culture for many years and some publicly regret and criticise the reform of art. 23 of the Organic Law on the Judiciary made in 2014.

Indeed, in this context the Spanish State had seen its international relations with other countries compromised in some cases, not to mention the strong diplomatic tensions suffered and the threats that could affect the international trade relations in which Spain and its interests are immersed.

For those of us who do not champion the public prosecution (an institution with many followers who see in this indictment mechanism a democratic-participative component in the criminal procedure), the problems arising with the previous regulation of the principle of universal justice were largely motivated by this unwonted means (unknown in comparative law) of publicly opening the possibility to prosecute (art. 125 of the Spanish Constitution). This institution generates many problems and its suppression, with the pertinent constitutional reform, is an issue that no one dares to directly address face-on in this day and age. Interpretative subterfuges keep emerging in the jurisprudence of the Supreme Court and the Constitutional Court, aimed at taming the populist and justicialist component of the public prosecution, which thus unveils its history which has its roots in the Holy Office of the Inquisition.

The 2009 reform already introduced a first limitation of the principle of universal justice with the aim of submitting this jurisdictional exception of Spanish law to consolidated parameters and requirements in comparative law. The new regulation stipulated that crimes associated with the principle of universal justice should stem from facts identifying a connection with Spain. Indeed, the 2009 reform offered a balanced regulatory framework which, nevertheless, needed to address the aforementioned expansive inertia deeply rooted in a long tradition.

In the face of this situation, the Government hastily decided to promote a new reform of the principle of universal justice in view of the international tensions arising with some of the major world powers on account of some of the proceedings already under way. Haste makes waste in legislative reforms. However, the Government was compromised on the international stage and chose to carry out an urgent reform of the Organic Law on the Judiciary, paving the way for the huge debate referred to above as a result.

The new 2014 reform binds the principle of universal justice by means of a system of successive demands aimed at assuring a very restrained application of this exception to the principle of territoriality of Spanish law.

Firstly, the new drafting of art. 23 establishes the first parameter of conditions that must be met in order for the extension of Spanish criminal jurisdiction to apply. Accordingly, Spain will be able to hear crimes committed abroad, provided the parties responsible are Spanish nationals or foreigners having acquired Spanish nationality after committing the crime. In addition to this, other requirements may apply in relation to double incrimination (crime punishable in the place where it is committed unless an exception in international treaties or commitments applies), objective prosecutability conditions (the Public Prosecution Service or the aggrieved party should lodge a claim in the Spanish courts) and the principle of double jeopardy and *res judicata* (the offender has not been acquitted, accused or convicted abroad).

Secondly, as is the case traditionally in relation to the principle of universal justice, the 2014 reform limits the scope of the principle to certain crimes and cases. In this case, the 2014 reform has modified the list of crimes (expanding it in some cases), albeit subjecting each crime for which Spanish jurisdiction may apply to a specific system of requirements in order to be prosecuted in this manner. This opens up an interpretative labyrinth when it comes to understanding and applying art. 23 of the Organic Law on the Judiciary which will undoubtedly give rise to interpretative controversy. Therefore, the regulation is complex and sometimes difficult to understand, meaning interpretative contradictions will occur and loopholes will be identified.

Art. 23 of the Organic Law on the Judiciary contemplates extending the jurisdiction of Spanish criminal law to hear crimes committed by Spanish nationals or foreigners abroad which can be classified as crimes committed by Spanish public officials living abroad and, in general, crimes of corruption against the Spanish public administration (art. 23.3 h of the Organic Law on the Judiciary).

Likewise, the principle of universal justice entails application of Spanish criminal law to hear crimes committed by Spanish nationals or foreigners abroad which can be classified as crimes of corruption between private individuals or in international financial transactions. In this case, the extraterritorial application of Spanish criminal law is conditioned by one of the following alternatives:

- The criminal procedure is followed against a Spanish citizen.
- The procedure is followed against a foreign citizen regularly living in Spain.
- The crime is committed by the manager, director, employee or partner of a company, partnership or any other legal entity with its headquarters or registered office in Spain.
- The crime is committed by a legal entity, company, organisation or any other entity with its headquarters or registered office in Spain.

As a result, the crime of corruption among private individuals (art. 286*bis* of the CC), introduced in the Spanish Criminal Code in the reform of 22 June 2010, is added to the list of crimes to which the principle of universal justice applies.

Nevertheless, it should be considered that the scope of the 2014 reform of art. 23 of the Organic Law on the Judiciary is broad with respect to the list of crimes subject to universal justice, as it contemplates the possibility of extraterritorial prosecution of any other crime according to Spanish law, provided said prosecution is mandatory by virtue of the commitments taken on by Spain in international treaties or any other regulatory instrument from an international organisation of which Spain is member.

In any case, in order to ensure the limitation of the principle of universal justice in Spain, the 2014 legislator refers to the principle of subsidiarity as a factor of exclusion of Spanish jurisdiction. Subsidiarity applies when an international court has initiated a proceeding for investigating or prosecuting a crime, as well as when an investigation or prosecution is under way in a State in which the crime has been committed or in the State of which the person accused is a national. Nonetheless, the principle of subsidiarity does not apply when there is an indication or evidence that, outside national territory, the State exercising its jurisdiction is in fact not willing to carry out the pre-trial investigation or cannot actually do so. In these cases, Spanish legal bodies must refer the case to the Second Chamber of the Supreme Court to decide whether or not the principle of subsidiarity is applicable. The 2014 reform also establishes safeguard guarantees to avoid legal fraud pursuant to the principle of subsidiarity.

Lastly, the 2014 reform establishes a strict system of objective prosecutability conditions, whereby crimes subject to the principle of universal justice shall only be prosecuted in Spain following the lodging of a claim by the Public Prosecution Service or the aggrieved party.

The culmination of the reform is the controversial stipulation set out in the Sole Transitional Provision, by virtue of which the formalities and proceedings being processed at the time Organic Law 1/2012 comes into effect shall be dismissed until fulfilment of the conditions and requirements established in the new regulation is certified. There is no precedent in Spain of any similar legal stipulation that calls for the general stay of proceedings from the outset, unless it can be certified that there are regulating standards in a supervening law. It should be noted that the most immediate goal of the reform was to bring the prosecution of some of the proceedings underway to a close.

Corporate liability for bribery and corruption offences

Corporate criminal liability was introduced into Spanish criminal legislation by Organic Law 5/2010, of 22 June, reforming the Criminal Code and the regulation of this liability was established by the recent reform implemented by Organic Law 1/2015, of 30 March, on reform of the Criminal Code. The insertion of this new criminal liability system is not independent from the cultural legal phenomenon of the fight against corruption in the private sector, as the idea of opacity or disorganisation in the way companies and partnerships operate is a critical factor that can contribute to the phenomenon of corruption, the breaching of market operation rules, money laundering, tax fraud and, in short, the violation of the legitimate interests of investors in the economic and financial sector. The legislative technique applied in Spain raises doubts because the reform of the Criminal Code in this area was not accompanied by a reform of Spanish criminal procedural law addressing the complex criminal procedural status of legal entities in detail. As a result, in practice, Spanish courts see corporate liability with apprehension and great caution. This praxis can also be seen in the indictment approaches of the Public Prosecution Service which, to date, has applied a very restricted indictment policy when it comes to using the mechanism of corporate criminal liability. This is not the case with private and public prosecutors (which exist in Spain as indictment mechanisms in their own right compared to other European countries) which in practice usually use the resource of corporate criminal liability in their charges. At present, Spain still has very limited jurisprudence on the issue.

The indictment approach of the Public Prosecution in the case concerning the signing of football player Neymar by Futbol Club Barcelona stands out owing to its prominence and being the first precedent. In this case being followed at the National Court in Madrid, for the very first time the prosecutor's office chose to accuse the legal entity (FC Barcelona) without having previously accused any individuals. This case, still in the preliminary investigation stage at the time of drafting this paper, has subsequently led to other individuals representing the sports entity being accused. There is still not enough data or elements to assess whether this case entails a shift in the policy of the prosecutor's office in Spain.

Notwithstanding the aforementioned practical data, in relation to the grounds for corporate criminal liability in the Spanish Criminal Code, there are several opinions that can be grouped into two lines of reasoning: Spanish criminal doctrine by and large upholds the theory that corporate criminal liability is based on a lack of organisation and transparency enabling the commission of the crime within the legal entity by its managers or employees over whom the pertinent control has not been exercised. This line of reasoning intends to safeguard the principle of guarantee summed up in criminal liability owing to the actual fact that the company would be liable. In addition, this approach also contemplates in the criminal procedure a right to a defence status which is independent from that corresponding to the individuals accused (directors, legal representatives or employees). In relation to this legal construction of the doctrine, the prosecutor's office has expressed its opinion in Circular 1/2011, issued by the State Prosecution Office. According to this document, the prosecutor's office establishes the principle of automatic transfer of liability on legal entities for the crime committed by individuals within the company.

Proposed reforms / The year ahead

As stated above, Organic Law 1/2015 on the reform of the Criminal Code recently came into force, more specifically last July. This meant a major change in the classification of certain crimes and a legal status for the criminal liability of legal persons was introduced for the first time.

As far as active/passive bribery of public officials is concerned, an amendment to the criminal definition of the concept of public official is introduced, adopting functional criteria, whereby any person holding public office can be the perpetrator of the crime. And this can be extended to any person holding positions or public office in a country of the European Union or any other foreign country, as well as people holding public office in the EU or abroad. This definition also encompasses public companies abroad.

One of the most important modifications to the subject examined herein refers to the change of name of the crimes grouped under the heading "Corruption among private individuals", which shall hereafter be called "Crimes of corruption in business activities". This section of the Criminal Code includes typical conduct of payment of bribes to obtain competitive advantage in the private sector (corruption among private individuals) which had already been introduced in the 2010 reform of the Criminal Code. Now the draft reform also incorporates conduct that may constitute corruption of authorities or public officials in carrying out economic activities and international business activities. Obviously, this last provision overlaps with offences of bribery of public officials already laid down in the Criminal Code, and the draft reform includes a stipulation of subsidiarity of the new figure of the crime of corruption in business activities when classic figures of the corruption offence contemplate more severe sentences.

In this section on corruption offences, the new Criminal Code still preserves the criminalisation of the conduct of corruption in sport, pursuant to the provisions set out in the 2010 reform of the Criminal Code.

The new Criminal Code contemplates aggravated crimes in cases of corruption in business activities which "are especially serious" based on the high value of the benefit or the unlawful advantage obtained, the repetition of the conduct of the perpetrator, the commission of the crime within a criminal group or organisation, or the object of business being associated with humanitarian or essential goods or services. These are excessively broad, undetermined liability, aggravation stipulations – which deserve criticism in terms of the guarantees of the principle of legality.

The new Criminal Code also contemplates the extraterritorial application of Spanish criminal law to crimes of corruption in business activities in relation to the new criteria set out in the applicable reform of the principle of universal justice from 2014 (art. 23 of the Organic Law on the Judiciary).

The corporate criminal liability clause is applicable to most crimes of bribery and corruption both in the public and private sectors. Mainly, the reform is aimed at giving legal acknowledgment for the interpretation made by doctrine whereby the basis for corporate criminal liability lies in shortcomings in organisation, oversight and control on companies. The new wording rules out the theory of automatic transfer of liability to legal entities for the crimes committed by individuals. This statement is made inasmuch as a criminal liability exemption system for legal entities is applicable if said parties have previously adopted organisation and management models including suitable oversight and control measures for preventing crime, what is known as Criminal Compliance. The draft reform requires that the supervision of these preventive models be entrusted to a body of the legal entity with powers independent from the board of directors. However, the draft reform releases small and medium-sized companies from meeting this requirement. Accordingly, if a crime has been committed in a legal entity by means of the fraudulent elusion of the effective oversight and control model, provided that model sufficed and was effective, exemption of corporate criminal liability shall be established.

The new Code regulates the requirements of organisation and prevention models so that the aforesaid acquittal pretext may apply. The philosophy of the draft reform focuses on the idea that the organisation and oversight model is a living being that must be regularly reviewed.

The text adopts a model of corporate criminal liability which is independent from that of individuals in line with the 2010 reform.

An aspect discussed in Spain was the initial projection of the exclusion of political parties and trade unions from the corporate criminal liability clause. This shortcoming was already remedied in the 2012 reform of the Criminal Code, which included parties and trade unions in the liability scheme. Now, the scope of corporate criminal liability is extended to public companies executing public policies or providing economic services of general interest.

In direct relation to the corporate criminal liability system, relevance is granted to the oversight and control models. The possibility of introducing a new heading of crimes associated with non-compliance with said oversight or control duty in legal entities and companies was considered. In particular, the draft reform fostered the inclusion of a crime for omission of adoption of oversight or control measures, which are necessary in order to avoid the violation of duties or dangerous conduct that may constitute a crime. This provision was extended to the legal representatives and the *de facto* or *de jure* directors of any legal entity. In our opinion, this new crime presents overly broad scope for incrimination, which could entail the criminalisation of the infringement of merely formal duties, and only incorporates one limitation in relation to the typical scope of unlawfulness when it comes to the requirement of an objective enforcement condition consisting of the initiation of the execution of the crime, which would have been avoided or seriously hindered if due diligence had been exercised. This crime has finally not been introduced in the final text that was approved.

* * *

Endnote

1. Translator's note: this notion does not exist in common law systems. It may be considered as a form of or a privilege coming under parliamentary immunity.

Fermín Morales Prats
Tel: +34 93 2419 820 / Email: info@fermin-morales.com

Fermín Morales is a directing partner of Gabinete Jurídico Fermín Morales, a law firm specialising in Criminal Law, founded in 1997. The company has built up an extensive track record, particularly in the sphere of economic criminal law and it was chosen by Chambers Europe and Best Lawyers in 2008 as one of the best law firms specialising in criminal defence. Moreover, in 2012 Fermín Morales was appointed "Lawyer of the year", the best criminal defence lawyer in Barcelona.

Dr. Morales has been a full professor of Criminal Law at the Autonomous University of Barcelona for 20 years and a doctor in Criminal Law and professor of Financial Criminal Law at ESADE since 1998. He obtained his degree in Law from the University of Barcelona with the bachelor *summa cum laude* and he has been a lecturer at the University of Barcelona, as well as full professor at the University of Cantabria and the University of Lleida. In addition, he has been guest lecturer at the Italian universities of Parma and Trento and researcher at the Max Planck Institut (Germany). He is a member of the bar associations of Barcelona and Madrid and of the Spanish Union of Criminal Lawyers. He has been awarded the medal from Barcelona Bar Association in acknowledgment of his personal and professional track record.

Fermín Morales takes part and gives lectures in various Master's degrees, conferences and seminars in Spain and abroad, and he has contributed to many publications, all in the field of criminal law. In addition, he has taken part as defence lawyer in the main cases of corruption and financial crimes in Spain.

Thea Morales Espinosa
Tel: +34 93 2419 820 / Email: thea.morales@fermin-morales.com

Thea Morales has been a lawyer at the Gabinete Jurídico Fermín Morales since 2012 and has focused the exercise of her profession on criminal law ever since.

She holds a degree in Law from the University of Barcelona. She specialised in criminal law with Barcelona Bar Association and in Economic Criminal Law at Abat Oliva University.

She is a member of the Barcelona Bar Association.

Gabinete Jurídico Fermín Morales

C/ Tenor Viñas no. 4-6, 5º 1ª, 08021, Barcelona, Spain
Tel: +34 932 419 820 / Fax: +34 932 419 822 / URL: http://www.ferminmorales.com

Sri Lanka

Sudath Perera, Deshan Hewavithana & Zahrah Cader
Sudath Perera Associates

Overview of the law and enforcement regime

The execution of even the most mundane or menial tasks in Sri Lanka calls for the involvement of state institutions. Accordingly, in a Sri Lankan context, state mechanisms are heavily embedded in the general public's day-to-day life.

Over the years, the general practice that has been developed by any average citizen is the habit of looking for the so-called "known person" in the event for which they require the urgent attention of a state official or authority in the execution of a particular document or task. Effectively, what this means is that any Sri Lankan's first stop in the process of getting something done would be to either look for a primary connection, or failing which a secondary connection or link, to an employee in the state service. The higher the rank, the more likely that what is required will be successfully completed.

Against such a backdrop, the abuse of power for personal gain is visible in many areas of society and is not uncommon in the average Sri Lankan's life.

The visibility of corruption and bribery is brazen in select public domains. Such domains include:

- in the process of obtaining birth certificates, National Identity cards, certified copies of vital documents, driving licences and passports;
- in the process of admitting children to government schools;
- in competing for government tenders/procurements;
- in the registration of businesses and companies, and immovable properties;
- in the payment of direct and indirect taxes, customs duties and excise duties; and
- in dealing with the police and law enforcement agencies on a day-to-day basis, to name a few.

Historical backdrop

Bribery was an offence punishable under the Penal Code from as far back as 1883. It was during the British rule that bribery made its appearance as a criminal offence into the Sri Lankan Statute Books. In 1954, the Bribery Act was enacted to include and accommodate in its scope bribery in the Public Service. The Bribery Commissioner's Department was established in the year 1958 by virtue of Act No. 40, under the Ministry of Justice. In 1994, Act No. 19 created the Commission to Investigate Allegations of Bribery or Corruption, what is presently known colloquially as the Bribery Commission. The first Commission commenced activities on 15th December 1994.

The Commission to Investigate Allegations of Bribery or Corruption (CIABOC)

The **Commission to Investigate Allegations of Bribery or Corruption (CIABOC)** was established by Act No. 19 of 1994 with the goal and objective of making provision for the establishment of a permanent Commission to Investigate Allegations of Bribery or Corruption and to direct the institution of prosecutions for offences under the Bribery Act and the Declaration of Assets and Liabilities Law No. 1 of 1975.

The initial Commission consisted of three members, two of whom were to be retired Judges of the Supreme Court or of the Court of Appeal and one of whom was a person with wide experience relating to the investigation of crime and law enforcement. Every member of the Commission holds office for a period of five years and is not be eligible for re-appointment.

The Commission is empowered to investigate allegations contained in communications made to it, and where appropriate to initiate proceedings under the Bribery Act or the Declaration of Assets and Liabilities Law No. 1 of 1975.

In such investigations the Commission has wide spread powers at its discretion, *inter alia*: the ability to procure and receive all such evidence, written or oral, and to examine all such persons as the Commission may think necessary; to require any person to be present before the Commission for the purposes of being examined by the Commission and to answer, orally on oath or affirmation to inquiries made by the Commission; to summon any person to produce any document or other thing to the Commission; to direct any bank to produce documents that are relevant to any particular investigation; to direct the Commissioner-General of Inland Revenue to furnish all information available from the Inland Revenue Department by way of written notice; and to direct any government department, state corporation or local authority to produce any documents that are relevant to the investigations.

Subsequent to the investigation procedure and calling for the relevant documentation required as supporting evidence, the Director General of the Commission is empowered by law to initiate criminal proceedings under the Bribery Act or the Declaration of Assets and Liabilities Law, No. 1 of 1975. All affidavits, sworn statements, any book, document, cheques and records that are produced to the Commission in the course of an investigation convert into evidence that is relevant and admissible at the trial.

Therefore, it is clear that the Commission has adequate power throughout the entire process commencing from the initiation of investigations right through to the conduct of proceedings before a court of law.

Undisclosed income and assets that are available in both local or foreign banks, and funds deposits secured outside the island are often the consequence of bribery and corruption. Values/Wealth locked in such undisclosed assets and income may move from place to place, change its form or even be converted into legitimate assets or income. Thus, any legislation/ institutions governing such movements and conversions could be considered as effective tools against bribery and corruption. The toughest challenge in the present Sri Lankan system therefore is the absence of both the legal framework as well as the resources to enable law enforcers to track the widespread disposal of "black money" across the globe. It is self-evident that a country which is recuperating from both financial and legal impacts of a 30-year ethnic conflict is yet to channel its resources and focus into this particular aspect of law.

In the interests of providing a 360-degree background to the established practice, a brief overview of the several other institutions that are encompassed in this category follow.

The Financial Intelligence Unit (FIU)

One such unit is the Financial Intelligence Unit (FIU) of Sri Lanka, which was established in March 2006 under the Financial Transactions Reporting Act No. 06 of 2006 (FTRA). The

FIU was introduced as an autonomous body under the Ministry of Finance and Planning. The FIU was reorganised as a Department in the Central Bank of Sri Lanka in February 2007 and at present it functions as an independent institution within the Central Bank's framework and administrative structure. The scope of work that falls under the purview of the FIU includes:

1. Convention on the Suppression of Terrorist Financing Act, No. 25 of 2005 (CSTFA)

Section 3(1) of the act lists the possible offences under this act. The said offences include an attempt not only to combat terrorism locally but also internationally, as it includes in Schedule 1, all treaties that fall within the purview of the act.

2. Prevention of Money Laundering Act, No. 05 of 2006 (PMLA)

Section 3(1) of The Prevention of Money Laundering Act, No. 05 of 2006 defines the offence of money laundering as:

> "(a) engaging directly or indirectly in any transaction in relation to any property which is derived or realized directly or indirectly, from any unlawful activity (Any offence under the Bribery Act is included) or from the proceeds of any unlawful activity;
>
> (b) Receiving, possessing, concealing, disposing of, or brings into Sri Lanka, transfers out of Sri Lanka, or invests in Sri Lanka, any property which is derived or realized, directly or indirectly, from any unlawful activity or from the proceeds of any unlawful activity".

Interestingly, Section 4 of the PMLA lays down a presumption that:

> "it shall be deemed until the contrary is proved, that any movable or immovable property acquired by a person has been derived or realized directly or indirectly from any unlawful activity, or are the proceeds of any unlawful activity, if such property—
>
> (a) Being money, cannot be or could not have been—
>
> (i) Part of the known income or receipts of such person; or
>
> (ii) Money to which his known income or receipts has or had been converted; or
>
> (b) Being property other than money, cannot be or could not have been—
>
> (i) Property acquired with any part of his known income or receipts; and
>
> (ii) Property which is or was part of his known income or receipts; and
>
> (iii) Property to which is any part of his known income or receipts has or had been converted."

Further, this Act imposes a responsibility on any person who knows or has reason to believe from information or other matter obtained by him in the course of any trade, profession, business or employment carried on by such person, that any property has been derived or realised from any unlawful activity to disclose such knowledge or information to the FIU. All professionals, for example, accountants, lawyers, and investment advisors are obliged to fulfil this requirement and to report any such information or activity to the FIU. There is doubt as to whether, firstly, the said professionals have awareness of such a requirement, and secondly, even if such awareness existed, it is actually practised in each case.

3. Financial Transactions Reporting Act, No. 06 of 2006 (FTRA)

Section 7 and 8 of the act specifically lists out relevant institutions that are required to report select transactions that fall within the defined monetary value to the FIU. Accordingly, authorised money changers, financial institutions and insurance companies are expected to comply with the requirements set out in the act for all transactions above Rs. 1m in cash or the equivalent in foreign currency. The institution handles suspicious transactions via a Suspicious Transaction Report (STR), and is obligated to identify the source of funds and retain copies of all reference documents used to verify the identity of the customer. The act specifies further that there is a requirement for the verification of cash deposits by third parties of over Rs. 200,000, as well as a mandatory reporting requirement of electronic funds transfers in excess of Rs. 500,000 or US$5,000.

However, privileged communications between a client and their attorney-at-law are excluded from transparency obligations with the only exception being for details involving a lawyer's Trust Account.

The table below provides a quick guide to the recorded reports of such activities for the timeline 2009 to 2013. The data and statistics for 2014 are yet to be published. There is a sharp rise in the number of reported cases in the year 2013 which more than tripled the number of reports in 2009, indicating a clear growth in the number of suspicious activities taking place in the country.

Suspicious Transaction Report (STR) Analysis	2009	2010	2011	2012	2013
From reporting institutions	78	87	91	144	272
From law enforcement/regulators	29	156	91	26	88
From the general public	4	3	3	3	6
Total	111	246	185	203	366

(Source: Annual Report 2013 FIU)

Of the abovementioned matters, select matters have been referred to Law Enforcement Agencies including the Bribery Commission for further investigation and initiation of legal action.

Presidential Commission of Inquiry to Investigate and Inquire into Serious Acts of Fraud, Corruption and Abuse of Power, State Resources and Privileges

On 6th March 2015, the President of Sri Lanka appointed the Presidential Commission of Inquiry to Investigate and Inquire into Serious Acts of Fraud, Corruption and Abuse of Power, State Resources and Privileges during the period commencing from 10th January 2010 and ending on 10th January 2015. The establishment was to call for, and receive public complaints, information and other material relating to serious allegations against persons who have held or continue to hold political office and those who have been or continue to be public servants and officers of statutory bodies, regarding acts of corruption, fraud, criminal breach of trust, criminal misappropriation of property, cheating and abuse or misuse of power, state resources and privileges, of which offences and acts of wrongdoing occurred and have resulted in serious loss or damage to state assets and state revenue. The Commission is headed by a sitting Judge and includes two other Judges, a retired Auditor General and a retired Additional Solicitor General.

The Commission has taken up number of high-profile cases which are said to have caused massive financial losses to the state within the above scope and has attracted wide attention from the public.

One such example of the matters taken up by the commission is the case relating to a security services organisation, which entailed the deployment of approximately 500 of its employees in the presidential election campaign which was concluded in January 2015. The same institution is under review for arms deals which were entered into with foreign organisations without following the due procedure.

The Presidential Commission has also inquired into the funds that were allegedly utilised out of the budgetary allocation for the development of the Negambo Lagoon Development Project. The utilisation of the funds were allegedly done by the Ministry of Fisheries under the previous regime, and it is alleged that the funds were used for a public rally that was dubbed the launch of the Development Project.

The commission also launched investigations pertaining to the state-owned television station. The questions arose with regards to select promotional campaigns that were run on the state media in the run-up to the 2015 presidential campaign with an approximate value of Rs. 102m (approximately US$727,000) at no cost being charged.

The Commission has been set a requirement to report its findings and recommendations to the President by 5th March 2016.

Fraud and Corruption Investigations Division (FCID)

The Fraud and Corruption Investigations Division, more commonly known in Sri Lanka as the FCID, is a recently established unit that falls under the purview of the Sri Lankan Police. The division was established under the powers vested with the police and is under the exclusive supervision of the Inspector General of Police. The establishment of the FCID was provided with the approval of the Cabinet and was gazetted in government gazette number 1901/20 dated 13th February 2015.

The circumstances leading to the establishment of the FCID has given rise to a fair share of controversy and questioning over its legitimacy; however, the Sri Lankan government firmly backs the decision and cites several examples of the establishment of various specific units that were established for the combatting of specific offences and addressing targeted issues. For example, the Terrorist Investigation Division, the Environment Protection Division and the Narcotics Bureau have all been established under the provision of Section 55 of the Police Ordinance, the same section that establishes the FCID. The powers granted to these entities are all within the scope of the powers granted to the police in general. The issues arise owing to the nature of the scope of work of the FCID. The transition in the political landscape in Sri Lanka over the past 10 months has resulted in the present government being accused of utilising the FCID to embark on a political witch-hunt against the individuals and entities loyal to the previous regime.

Section 55 states that:

> "The Inspector-General of Police may from time to time, subject always to the approbation of the said Minister, frame orders and regulations for the observance of the police officers who shall be placed under his control as aforesaid, and also for the general government of such persons, as to their places of residence, classification, rank, and particular services, as well as their distribution and inspection, and all such orders and regulations relative to the said police force as he may deem expedient for preventing neglect or abuse, and for rendering such force efficient in the discharge of its duties; and every police officer who shall neglect or violate any such orders or regulations, or any duty imposed upon him by this or any other enactment, shall be guilty of an offence, and be liable to any fine not exceeding fifty rupees (which fine or any part thereof may be deducted from any salary then or at any time thereafter due to such offender), or to imprisonment with or without hard labour for any period not exceeding one month."

The gazette notification established that the FCID aims to fill a gap in the present penal code as per the Inspector General of Police in Sri Lanka. In the wake of allegations of illegitimacy of the FCID, the defence of the body comes in the form of the fact that grievous financial crimes, corruption and massive unauthorised projects which are the focus of the initiative are not particularly specified in the Penal Code. The establishment of the FCID is therefore a turning point in the Sri Lankan legal framework that has progressed from primarily dealing with terrorism-related issues, towards creating a cleaner landscape that will facilitate investment into the country and building confidence in the ease of doing business in Sri Lanka.

The Director of the FCID Senior DIG Ravi Waidyalankara has clarified that the gazette notification publishing the establishment of the FCID was done with the intent of creating awareness in the public domain of its existence as a unit as opposed to complying with a non-existent legal requirement. He also stated that the consequence of providing such information to the public has resulted in 15 cases being filed in the Supreme Court of Sri Lanka questioning the legitimacy of the FCID. The FCID, as part of the Police system of Sri Lanka, works within the framework of the Criminal Procedure Code of Sri Lanka and follows the process set out in Section 109 of the Penal Code for the collection of information and recording thereof.

Anti-Corruption Committee (ACC)

The Anti-Corruption Committee (ACC) is a forum that has been established in the country's quest towards a corruption-free nation. The ACC was set up on 21st January 2015 at a Cabinet meeting and was created with the intention of being a channel whereby the appearance of future large-scale corruption and fraud may be prevented as a result of the recommendations made by the Committee. The Committee, at a very early stage, came out with the recommendation to establish an Anti-Corruption Committee Secretariat that will facilitate the coordination of the investigations of allegations of serious fraud, financial crimes and corruption.

The link between the ACC and the FCID comes in the form of gathering source material. The present set up is such that the ACC accepts complaints from any individual who wishes to report an act that falls within the purview of the FCID. The ACC is meant to weed through the chaff and identify the allegations that require the urgent attention of the FCID. The ACC therefore is the base that channels the various complaints to the relevant department. It directs the traffic in such a manner that results in the most effective clearance of matters or reported cases.

The FCID has come under fire by several politicians and other members of the general public for not being accommodating of complaints; however, the Director of the FCID, Senior DIG Ravi Waidyalankara, in an interview clarified that the FCID has not been established to open the flood gates of corruption-related complaints, but rather that its goal is to gather information that will be utilised to address allegations of corruption.

Overview of cross-border issues

The provisions for the sharing of information with foreign Financial Intelligence Units (FIUs) has been set out in terms of Sections 16 and 17 of the Financial Transaction Reporting Act, No. 6 of 2006 (FTRA). Accordingly, the Sri Lankan FIU can enter into agreements for the exchange of information on a regular basis with any institution or agency of a foreign state. Such agreements may be fostered subject to the approval of the Minister of Finance.

A brief list of the MOUs that have been presently signed by the Sri Lankan FIU are listed herewith along with the relevant foreign counterparts for each agreement.

Date of signature	State	Institution or organisation
17.07.2014	Republic of the Union of Myanmar	The Financial Intelligence Unit
05.06.2014	Republic of Peru	Financial Intelligence Unit
05.06.2014	Republic of Albania	General Directorate of Prevention of Money Laundering
30.09.2013	Denmark	Financial Intelligence Unit
08.07.2013	Costa Rica	Financial Intelligence Unit
03.07.2013	Lebanon	Special Investigations Commission (SIC)
11.03.2013	Japan	Financial Intelligence Center
11.07.2012	Saudi Arabia	Financial Investigation Unit (SAFIU)
11.07.2012	Russian Federation	Federal Financial Monitoring Service
11.07.2012	Mongolia	Financial Information Unit of the Bank
10.07.2012	United States of America	Financial Crime Enforcement Network (FinCEN)
09.08.2011	Slovenia	Financial Intelligence Unit
02.08.2011	Canada	Transaction Reports and Reports Analysis Centre
21.07.2011	Fiji	Financial Intelligence Unit
02.12.2010	South Africa	Financial Intelligence Centre
28.10.2010	Bangladesh	Financial Intelligence Unit
15.07.2010	Solomon Islands	Financial Intelligence Unit
18.06.2010	Belgium	Financial Intelligence Unit
07.05.2010	Australia	Australian Financial Transactions and Analysis Centre
30.03.2010	India	Financial Intelligence Unit
26.10.2009	Cambodia	Cambodian Financial Intelligence Unit of National Bank
09.07.2009	Philippines	The Anti Money Laundering Council
09.07.2009	Nepal	Financial Information Unit of Nepal Rastra Bank
27.05.2009	Indonesia	Indonesian Financial Transaction Reports and Analysis Centre
18.12.2008	Korea	Financial Intelligence Unit
29.02.2008	Slovenia	Financial Intelligence Unit
18.01.2008	Malaysia	Financial Intelligence Unit of Bank Negara

When a foreign national is arrested under the Money Laundering Act, the Sri Lankan government is required to inform the relevant foreign government of the description of the measures that are to be taken against him. Further, such foreign nationals are entitled to communicate with the relevant embassy or the High Commission in Sri Lanka.

The Prevention of Money Laundering Act has made significant changes to the Extradition Law, No. 8 of 1977. Accordingly, the Sri Lankan government has two possible alternatives of either prosecuting such individuals in Sri Lanka or, alternatively, the government could extradite the individual to the country of origin.

Overview of key issues relating to investigation, decision-making and enforcement procedures

Several reports in the recent past indicated the potential dissolution of the Commission to Investigate Allegations, more commonly known as the Bribery Commission in Sri Lanka.

The story broke out in the wake of the inability of the Bribery Commission to present a united front as friction occurred between the Director General of the Commission who was appointed this year and the Chairman of the Bribery Commission. The alleged failure on the part of the Commissioner to sign the requisite documentation for the completion of the relevant reports and filing of cases resulted in the public airing of the dirty laundry of the Bribery Commissioner.

As at September 2015, the Bribery Commission has reportedly initiated legal action against 16 individuals since the beginning of the current year. The individuals include former cabinet ministers, mayors, parliamentarians and former chairmen of state corporations. The investigations leading up to the action has long been ongoing and has ventured into various industries such as mass media, projects, investment and misuse of public funds.

The 19th Amendment to the Constitution, which was passed by parliament on 15th May 2015, established the Constitutional Council which has been provided with the power to make recommendations pertaining to the membership and composition of the Bribery Commission of Sri Lanka. Chapter XIXA of the amendment sets out Section 156A specifying the establishment and powers of the Bribery Commission that is to be established.

Section 156A states:

"(1) Parliament shall by law provide for the establishment of a Commission to investigate allegations of bribery or corruption. Such law shall provide for–

> *(a) The appointment of the members of the Commission by the President on the recommendation of the Constitutional Council;*

> *(b) the powers of the Commission, including the power to direct the holding of a preliminary inquiry or the making of an investigation into an allegation of bribery or corruption, whether of its own motion or on a complaint made to it, and the power to institute prosecutions for offences under the law in force relating to bribery or corruption;*

> *(c) measures to implement the United Nations Convention against Corruption and any other international Convention relating to the prevention of corruption, to which Sri Lanka is a party.*

(2) Until Parliament so provides, the Commission to investigate Allegations of Bribery or Corruption Act, No. 19 of 1994 shall apply, subject to the modification that it shall be lawful for the Commission appointed under that Act, to inquire into, or investigate, an allegation of bribery or corruption, whether on its own motion or on a written complaint made to it".

The 19th Amendment to the Constitution also makes the Bribery Commission one of the entities that are answerable to parliament. It is arguable that such a restriction would result in the hampering of the execution of the duties of the Bribery Commission; however, the practical implication of the inclusion of such a provision has not surfaced as yet.

At the time of writing this report, the Constitutional Council had declared that the recommendations of members to the Bribery Commission will be made by 15th October 2015. The consequence of such appointments is that all present office bearers in the Bribery Commission would lose their positions, thereby providing the Constitutional Council with the opportunity to iron out all alleged kinks and present to the public a Commission of individuals who are likely to cooperate with each other. The hope then becomes that the newly appointed commission will be able to provide the general public with results of its endeavours to combat bribery in the country.

The missing links

There is, at present, a lacuna in the description of the link or relationship between the FCID and the Bribery Commissioner. There is no clear demarcation of each entity's duties and scope of work. The same individuals have been summoned by each of the two bodies for separate purposes and courses of investigations. The fundamental distinction between the two entities is, of course, the fact that the FCID is directly linked to the Police. It is a body established under the Police, whereas the Bribery Commission is an independent body created to investigate corruption. The distinction has been made that fraud is the focus of the FCID, and it is said that it is easier to gather evidence and prove, whereas corruption which falls under the Bribery Commission presents slightly tougher circumstances with regards to evidence. The two bodies have also referred matters that seemingly fall within the scope of the other, to one another.

Overview of enforcement activity and policy

Various special enforcement measures are available at the discretion of the entities and may be acted upon by different enforcement agencies. Such enforcement measures exist apart from the general measures that are available.

1.   Prohibitive orders by the Bribery Commission

The Bribery Commission is specifically empowered to issue a select type of order in the course of any investigation undertaken by it. Accordingly, the Commission can prohibit the transfer of the ownership of, or any interest in, any movable or immovable property and inform the same to the Registrar of Lands, the Commissioner of Motor Traffic and the Registrar of Companies and the Secretary of such company. Furthermore, the Bribery Commission is also able to impound the passport and other travel documents of any individual under investigation, via an Order to the Controller of Immigration and Emigration for three months and prevent the departure of any individual from Sri Lanka via an order to the Police for a period of three months.

2.   Freezing order for seven days under the Prevention of Money Laundering Act

A Police Officer not below the rank of the Superintendent of Police, or in the absence of such an officer, an Assistant Superintendent of Police, may, where there are reasonable grounds to believe that any person is involved in any activity relating to the offence of money laundering and it is necessary for preventing further acts being committed in relation to such an offence, issue an order prohibiting any transaction in relation to any account, property or investment which may have been used or which may be intended to be used in connection with such an offence.

Such orders could be extended by the High Court upon an application.

Brief synopsis of recent case law on bribery and corruption in Sri Lanka

In September 2013, the Assistant Commissioner of Labour attached to the Polonnaruwa District Labour Office in Sri Lanka had solicited a bribe for a private security company as payment for the settlement of a matter that arose pertaining to the settlement of an employment provident fund and employee trust fund payments. The said payments are statutorily required to be made to the relevant bodies on a monthly basis by employers in Sri Lanka. The bribe was requested in exchange for a reduced balance of the remittance owed by the Security Services Company. The arrest of the Assistant Commissioner of Labour was made by the Investigation Officers of the Commission to Investigate Allegations of Bribery or Corruption whilst the bribe for Rs. 50,000.00 (approximately US$400) was being accepted by him.

A complaint was made to the Commission to Investigate Allegations of Bribery or Corruption by an individual who was transporting curd in an unrefrigerated vehicle in June 2014. The Public Health Inspector of the Warallegama who falls within the purview of the Medical Office of Health of the Warallegama area had initially requested a bribe of Rs. 15,000.00 from the individual who was illegally transporting the curd. The transportation of curd without proper temperature control is an offence under section 10(6) of the government gazette (extraordinary) No. 1742/26 dated 26th January 2012. However, upon negotiations the Public Health Officer had reduced the value of the bribe to Rs. 10,000.00. The arrest was made when the Public Health Officer was in the midst of accepting the bribe.

The Commission to Investigate Allegations of Bribery or Corruption made an arrest of an Excise Officer attached to the Special Investigating Unit of the Excise Department of Sri Lanka in 2014. The case concerned the acceptance of a bribe by the said officer in exchange for failing to initiate legal action against the offender for the production and sale of illegally obtained toddy and spirits. The demanded value of the bribe was Rs. 500,000.00 (approximately US$3,600) which was later reduced to Rs. 450,000.00. The arrest of the officer was made in August 2014 whilst the officer was accepting an instalment of Rs. 50,000.00 of the entire value. The bribe was accepted in instalments of Rs. 50,000.00 each.

With the escalation of awareness in the sphere of bribery and corruption, 2015 saw a rise in the number of cases that were brought into the spotlight by the Commission to Investigate Allegations of Bribery or Corruption. The arrests were also of more high-profile individuals. In March 2015, the Private Secretary of the Chairman of the local governing body, Pradeshiya Sabhawa of Panadura, was arrested along with the technical officer of the same office. The arrest was made on the charge of accepting a bribe of Rs. 100,000.00 for the expedition of a plan approval request by an individual. The general process for approving applications for plans is done at a nominal fee that is charged by the office. The initial demanded value of the bribe was Rs. 200,000.00.

Several other complaints have been accepted and investigated by the Commission to Investigate Allegations of Bribery or Corruption over the year. Other complaints include: matters at the International Airport of Sri Lanka by an Indian supervisory officer for the release of a passport that was detained; acceptance of a bribe by an office assistant at the District Court of Homagama for the expedition of the process of tracking a case; and the acceptance of a bribe by the general manager of a private security firm to enable a businessman to carry out his business at a local market without hindrance.

Larger, higher-profile cases under the subject of fraud have already been filed in the magistrate's court by the newly established FCID. For example, on 20th April 2015, the FCID filed a report in the Magistrate's Court of Colombo against an individual who is the former Sports Director General of Sri Lanka. The allegation levelled against her was for granting Rs. 2,400,000.00 to a leading sports broadcasting network in violation of the financial regulations of Sri Lanka. Several other allegations are levelled against the individual for the utilisation of a private company for the purchase of airline tickets for sportsmen and women representing the country in violation of the regulations. As a consequence of this, on 21st April 2015, the Former Chairman of the said sports broadcasting network was summoned to the FCID for questioning.

Where to from here

The FCID is said to be the first step towards covering a wide-open lacuna in the system. The goal, therefore, of the present administration is to create a central multidisciplinary agency that will focus on combatting and addressing matters related to bribery, corruption and fraud. The Director of the FCID states that the present infrastructure has several barriers that complicate the process of collection of evidence and filing of action against the perpetrators. The anticipated goal, therefore, is to provide a mechanism whereby the red tape involved is reduced to a minimum whilst striking a balance between the rights of the accused and the need for justice: a task that is easier said than done. An example of such complications is that in the process of obtaining a warrant for documentation and financial statements, the delay results in providing parties with ample time to conceal the documents or funds comfortably.

The Sri Lankan system is presently in the process of discussing wholesale reform and complete upheaval of the legal framework by adopting globally recognised policies and measures to ensure the best possible framework to combat corruption and bribery.

One of the greatest holes in the present system is the protection provided to whistleblowers. Sri Lanka is yet to match up to international standards in this regard, and if the state is to reach the level of complexity it aspires to in combatting this problem, protection for those who aid the goal is paramount. The present system allows for anonymous tips and for the submission of complaints online via the portal known as "Tell IGP"; however, these are relatively primitive measures in a system that is aspiring to fill larger shoes.

A second obstruction is the question of what becomes of the assets that are seized under the scope of bribery and corruption. Wrongfully appropriated assets that are not state property and assets that are purchased with *black money* are both cause for question with regards to the assets' fate. Furthermore, the question of what measures are applicable in the event that an innocent third party is involved in such a transaction is also unresolved and unaddressed. The future reform, it is anticipated, will address these issues and provide a legitimate framework to channel these assets and funds. At present, the FCID informs the Inland Revenue Department when it is made aware of the availability of any funds or assets that belong to those who are questioned by them. The streamlining of the process is what is required as the next step.

Final remarks

The actual long-term effects and results of the wave of change that has taken over the spectrum of bribery and corruption in Sri Lanka is yet to be reflected in the form of tangible outcomes. The realisation of the general public of the need for social change in the realm of large-scale corruption that takes place in the country has resulted in infrastructure being created for the purposes of combatting an age-old issue that has plagued the nation. What it means in reality, however, is yet to be evaluated. The state anticipates the codification of the framework to combat corruption and bribery, which is presently found in scattered sources, to be concluded in the coming year. Whilst it is admirable that the big fish are being chased, a blind eye is being turned to the small acts of bribery that occur on a daily basis at most state-operated departments and offices. Its existence has become so integrated in the culture of Sri Lanka that little is being done to address it. Small-time efforts are being made, such as the arrests detailed above, and media campaigns have been executed for several years to create awareness on the subject to little, if any, avail. The actual effectiveness of such approaches will only be deduced at the point at which a citizen does not require a 'contact' or 'connection' to assert a right that is legally theirs. So the question still lies, what really has changed?

* * *

Bibliography and references

1. Financial Intelligence Unit of Sri Lanka, 28 September 2015 – 5 October 2015, http://fiusrilanka.gov.lk.
2. The Commission to Investigate Allegations of Bribery & Corruptions, 28 September 2015 – 5 October 2015, http://www.ciaboc.gov.lk.
3. Annual Report – 2013, Financial Intelligence Unit of Sri Lanka Prevention of Money Laundering Act, No. 5 of 2006 and related Regulations, Rules, Circulars and Guidelines issued Financial Transactions Reporting Act No. 6 of 2006 and Related Regulations, Regulations, Rules, Circulars and Guidelines.
4. Extraordinary Gazette No. 1904/57, 6 March 2015 Synopsis of Anti-Corruption and Related Laws.
5. U.S. Agency for International Development, 2007.
6. http://documents.gov.lk/Extgzt/2015/PDF/Feb/1901_20/1901_20(E).pdf.
7. http://www.vertic.org/media/National%20Legislation/Sri%20Lanka/LK_Police_Ordinance.pdf.
8. http://newsfirst.lk/english/2015/02/new-office-anti-corruption-secretariat-declares-open/79119.
9. http://documents.gov.lk/Bills/2015/19th%20Amendment/E.pdf.
10. http://www.dailymirror.lk/36016/pnaruwa-asst-labour-commissioner-nabbed-over-bribe.
11. http://www.cbsl.gov.lk/pics_n_docs/07_af_4epfm/_docs/epf_act_cap623.pdf.
12. http://www.etfb.lk/pdf/ETF%20Act.pdf.
13. http://documents.gov.lk/Extgzt/2012/PDF/Jan/1742_26/G%2015603%20(E).pdf.

Sudath Perera
Tel: +94 777 353 989 / Email: sudath@sudathpereraassociates.com

Twenty-four years' experience as an Attorney has culminated in Sudath Perera being the Founder and Managing Partner of Sudath Perera Associates, a full service law firm. He has branched out his practice to entities such as Legal Base which provides legal services to global clients, IPS Lanka (Pvt) Ltd which is a joint venture with a US-based Company that specialises in compliance auditing and Sapath Lanka (Pvt) Ltd which is an IT solutions company having its parent company in the United Kingdom.

Sudath holds professional membership with the Bar Association of Sri Lanka, the Asian Patent Attorneys Association, the International Trademark Association (INTA), the Anti-counterfeiting Committee (2016-2017) of INTA and the International Association of Outsourcing Professionals. He has also served as a Director on the Export Development Board and currently serves on the Board of the investment firm, Investrust Capital (Private) Limited.

Deshan Hewavithana
Tel: +94 117 559 944 / Email: deshan@sudathpereraassociates.com

Having joined Sudath Perera Associates in 2002, Deshan Hewavithana now holds the position as a Partner of the firm. Deshan specialises over a diverse sphere of areas, with his primary areas of focus being Criminal Law, Brand Protection, Anti-counterfeiting, Anti-piracy and Bribery and Corruption. He serves as one of the firm's most senior members by providing litigation and advisory services to local as well as international clients and has successfully carried out over 300 raids for several global brands.

Deshan was awarded his Bachelor of Laws degree from the University of Colombo, and in 1999 he was called to the Bar of the Supreme Court of Sri Lanka. He is also a life member of the Bar Association of Sri Lanka and his background and areas of practice have made him eligible to be a member of the Center for Monitoring Election Violence of Sri Lanka (CMEV).

Zahrah Cader
Tel: +94 117 559 944 / Email: zahrah@sudathpereraassociates.com

Zahrah Cader plays an integral role at Sudath Perera Associates in dealing with Corporate and Commercial matters including Mergers and Acquisitions as well as advising clients on Foreign Direct Investment. She has been with the firm since 2013 and currently practises as an Associate of the firm. Prior to commencing her career at Sudath Perera Associates, Zahrah worked as a Researcher at the Supreme Court of Sri Lanka. She also practises Real Estate and Immigration Law.

Zahrah graduated with an LL.B. degree from the University of London. She was called to the Bar of the Supreme Court of Sri Lanka in 2013 and is a life member of the Bar Association of Sri Lanka.

Sudath Perera Associates

No. 5, 9th Lane, Nawala Road, Nawala, Sri Lanka
Tel: +94 117 559 944 / Fax: +94 117 559 948 / URL: http://www.sudathpereraassociates.com

Switzerland

Marcel Meinhardt & Fadri Lenggenhager
Lenz & Staehelin

Introduction

In the 2014 "Corruption Perception Index" of Transparency International, Switzerland ranked 5th out of 175 countries. And still, even though Switzerland is perceived to be one of the least corrupt countries in the world, it is still affected by corruption. Switzerland's unique political system, which is governed by the militia system and contains a lot of small decision-making bodies, is vulnerable to nepotism and 'trading in influence'.

Switzerland is also a preferred base for non-governmental organisations. In particular, about 60 sports organisations have their headquarters in Switzerland, e.g. the International Olympic Committee (IOC), the World Football Federation (FIFA), the Union of European Football Associations (UEFA), the International Ski Federation (FIS) and the International Cycling Union (UCI). In connection with awarding big sporting events such as the FIFA World Cup, those organisations are regularly faced with allegations of corruption (see below).

Above all, however, the biggest challenge in the fight against corruption are enterprises based in Switzerland that do business abroad where they are confronted with corruption. The small size of Switzerland and the accordingly restricted opportunities of doing business within its borders impels a lot of small and medium-sized enterprises ('SMEs') to operate abroad. According to a recent study, '40% of Swiss SMEs operating abroad are confronted with bribery of public officials'.

But this problem is not limited to SMEs. The attractive Swiss tax regime, as well as its geographical position in the middle of Europe, has encouraged international companies to relocate their headquarters to Switzerland. When those companies operate in foreign countries, they face the same corruption issues as their smaller counterparts (see below, section 'Cross-border issues and corporate criminal liability').

These challenges are dealt with by a quite comprehensive anti-corruption law set out in the Swiss Criminal Code ('SCC'). The SCC, in turn, is subject to a steady development driven by three multilateral instruments in the fight against corruption of which Switzerland is a part: the OECD Convention on Combating Bribery of Foreign Public Officials in International Business Transactions; the Council of Europe's Criminal Law Convention on Corruption; and the UN Convention against Corruption.

These instruments have already led to three substantial reforms of the SCC. In 2000, provisions regarding the active bribery of foreign public officials and regarding the granting and acceptance of an undue advantage were introduced. In 2003, corporate criminal liability for bribery offences was introduced and, in 2006, the prohibition of bribery was extended to passive bribery of foreign public officials as well as to passive bribery in the private sector (see below section, 'Brief overview of the law and enforcement regime').

Indeed, the next reform is already in the legislative pipeline. The planned reform targets bribery in the private sector (see below, section 'Proposed reforms / The year ahead').

Brief overview of the law and enforcement regime

General legal basis

In Switzerland, bribery of public officials and bribery in the private sector are governed by two different legal acts.

The bribery of *public officials* is governed by the SCC. The SCC defines a public official as a *"member of a judicial or other authority, a public official, an officially-appointed expert, translator or interpreter, an arbitrator, or a member of the armed forces"* (Article 322[ter] SCC), including private individuals who carry out a public function (Article 322[octies](3) SCC). Persons in this category are "foreign public officials" when they act for a foreign state or an international organisation (Article 322[septies] SCC). This includes employees of state-owned or controlled legal entities.

By contrast, bribery of *private individuals* is regulated by the Federal Law against Unfair Competition ('UCA'; Article 4a). Unlike the bribery of public officials, bribery of private individuals is pursued under criminal law only on complaint (Article 23 UCA).

Swiss law sanctions both so-called active and passive bribery. In the case of public officials, *active bribery* is an act by which an official is offered, promised, or granted any undue advantage, for his own benefit or for the benefit of any third party, for the commission or omission of an act in relation to his official duties that is contrary to his duties or depends on the exercise of his discretionary powers (Article 322[ter] SCC). Active bribery in the private sector is described similarly in Article 4a(1)(a) UCA. *Passive bribery* occurs when a person solicits, elicits a promise of, or accepts an undue advantage, for his own benefit or for the benefit of a third person, for the commission or omission of an act that is contrary to his duties or depends on the exercise of his discretionary powers (Article 322[quater] SCC; Article 4a(1)(b) UCA).

In a narrow sense, bribery is defined as an act whereby a person offers, promises or gives a private individual or a public official an undue advantage in exchange for a specific act. In a broader sense, bribery also includes any acts whereby a person offers, promises or gives a person an undue advantage in exchange for a future behaviour which is not directly linked to a specific act (Article 322[quinquies] to 322[sexies] SCC) as well as payments done with the intention to speed up the execution of administrative acts to which the payer is legally entitled ('facilitation payments'). The giving and accepting of undue advantages according to Article 322[quinquies] to 322[sexies] SCC are only punishable when a Swiss public official is concerned. In contrast, facilitation payments may be punishable as bribery (and thus irrespective of whether a Swiss or a foreign official is concerned) if the payment influences the discretion of the public official.

In all cases of corruption, advantages are not undue when allowed by staff regulations or when they are of minor value in conformity with social custom (Article 322[octies](2) SCC). This would typically include small Christmas or thank-you gifts, as long as such gifts are not given with the intention of influencing a public official's performance.

Individuals found guilty of bribing (either Swiss or foreign) public officials are sentenced to prison for a term of up to five years or a monetary penalty up to CHF 1,080,000 (Article 322[ter] and Article 322[septies] SCC). When determining the amount of the monetary penalty, the court takes into account the culpability of the offender and his or her personal and financial circumstances at the time of conviction (Article 34(1) and (2) SCC). Bribery in the private sector results in imprisonment for up to three years or a monetary penalty (Article 23 UCA).

Depending on the circumstances, penalties may also include a prohibition from practising a certain profession (Article 67 SCC), or expulsion from Switzerland for foreigners as an administrative sanction (Article 62(b) and Article 63(1)(a) of the Federal Act on Foreign Nationals). Further, the court can order the forfeiture of assets deriving from corruption or intended to use for corruption (Article 70 SCC). Finally, Swiss criminal procedure law provides for the possibility that the person suffering harm from corruption may bring civil claims as a private claimant in the criminal proceedings.

Corporate criminal liability

In cases of corruption, it is primarily the *individual* ("natural person") who is liable to punishment and is prosecuted.

However, in addition to the liability of the acting individuals, Article 102 SCC establishes corporate criminal liability. Generally speaking, corporate criminal liability exists if, due to an inadequate organisation of the company, it is not possible to attribute a felony or misdemeanour (including bribery) that was committed in the exercise of commercial activities to any specific individual (Article 102(1) SCC). Furthermore, a company may also be punished irrespective of the criminal liability of any natural persons if the enterprise did not undertake all requisite and reasonable organisational precautions required to prevent the bribery of Swiss or foreign public officials or persons in the private sector (Article 102(2) SCC).

In both cases, the company is subject to criminal prosecution and a fine of up to CHF 5m. The amount of the fine is determined taking into account the seriousness of the offence, the degree of the organisational inadequacies, the loss or damage caused and the economic ability of the company to pay the fine.

The exact scope of the organisational measures required under Article 102(2) SCC is not defined by law. Clearly, it is insufficient to merely stipulate compliance rules (e.g. in a code of conduct). Rather, a company is required to show that its employees were made aware of, trained in and monitored regarding such rules. In general, Swiss prosecuting authorities take international good practice standards into account when determining the required compliance measures.

Jurisdiction and procedural issues

Bribery is subject to federal jurisdiction insofar as the offences are committed by a member of an authority or an employee of the Swiss Confederation or against the Swiss Confederation (Article 23(1)(j) Swiss Criminal Procedure Code ('CPC')), or if the offences have to a substantial extent been committed abroad, or in two or more cantons with no single canton being the clear focus of the criminal activity (Article 24(1) CPC).

Criminal investigations regarding bribery cases subject to federal jurisdiction are conducted by the Office of the (federal) Attorney General ('OAG'). All other investigations into bribery cases are handled by the competent cantonal law enforcement authorities; generally the cantonal public prosecutor's office.

Swiss anti-corruption law does not provide for credit or leniency during an investigation. However, cooperative behaviour of the accused person or entity may be taken into account when determining the sentence.

Further, there is no general mechanism to resolve corruption cases through plea agreements, settlement agreement or similar means without trial. However, in all cases of corruption (bribery as well as the giving or accepting of advantages according to Articles 322ter through 322^{septies} SCC), criminal prosecution, judicial proceedings or the imposition of a penalty can be waived in *de minimis* cases (Article 52 SCC). Further, the competent authority shall refrain from prosecuting or punishing an offender if the latter *"has made reparation for the loss, damage or injury or made every reasonable effort to right the wrong that he has caused"* and the interests of the general public and of the persons harmed in prosecution are negligible (Article 53 SCC). In addition, under certain circumstances, there is no need for fully fledged criminal proceedings and they may be substituted by accelerated or summary judgment proceedings.

Overview of enforcement activity and policy during the past two years

In Switzerland, the number of reported corruption cases is rather limited. Statistics show a total of 10 to 20 cases on average per year, the majority of which are relatively minor domestic cases. Cases dealing with transnational corruption (other than in the context of a foreign request for international mutual assistance) are rare. Nevertheless, there are some investigations and decisions that are noteworthy and might be regarded as a sign that foreign and transnational corruption is increasingly under scrutiny by Swiss enforcement authorities.

A leading case in this regard is the 'Alstom' decision (see below, section 'Cross-border issues and corporate criminal liability'). Another interesting case is the 'Ben Aissa' case relating to the bribery payments to Saadi Gaddafi, the son of the former Libyan dictator Muammar Gaddafi.

In October 2014, Mr. Riadh Ben Aissa, the former head of global construction at the Canadian engineering and construction firm SNC-Lavalin, was sentenced to three years in prison on charges of bribery of a foreign public official (Article 322^{septies} SCC), criminal mismanagement (Article 158 SCC) and money laundering (Article 305bis SCC).

The Swiss Federal Criminal Court held that Mr. Ben Aissa paid briberies to Saadi Gaddafi in order to secure construction project and other benefits for SNC-Lavalin.

A particularly interesting aspect of this case is that the Federal Criminal Court characterised Saadi Gaddafi as *de facto* public official and applied Article 322^{septies} SCC by stating that, even though Saadi Gaddafi did not hold any office or official function in the relevant field, he was a member of the ruling family and had the *de facto* power to grant SNC-Lavalin the requested benefits. This decision is of fundamental importance with regard to dictatorial regimes, where *de facto* power is often not congruent with official power. During the investigations the OAG confiscated CHF 40m worth of assets, including properties in Switzerland and France that were used to launder the proceeds of the crimes. The unlawful payments were made from bank accounts in Switzerland. This was the (only) nexus to Switzerland and was sufficient to give rise to the OAG's investigation (see below, section 'Cross-border issues and corporate criminal liability').

In general, there has been a growing public awareness of corruption. As an example, Twint, a subsidiary of Swiss Post (the national postal company), has recently been criticised publicly because it gave journalists at a press conference a credit of CHF 100 to test a newly launched payment application for smartphones.

Cross-border issues and corporate criminal liability

According to Article 3 SCC, anyone who *commits* an offence in Switzerland is subject to Swiss Criminal Law. Article 8 SCC further specifies that an offence is considered to be committed both at the place where the person concerned acts or unlawfully omits to act, and at the place where the offence has taken effects. Even attempts to commit or omit are sufficient. However, mere preparatory acts are not deemed sufficient to trigger jurisdiction in Switzerland. As an example, the opening of a bank account in Switzerland with the intention to use it to pay or to receive bribes in the future, does not yet give jurisdiction to Swiss authorities.

The place of commission is broadly construed. For instance, as the Ben Aissa case mentioned above has confirmed, it may suffice to establish Swiss jurisdiction if the only connection to Switzerland is the existence of a Swiss bank account from which − or to which − the bribe was paid, even though all persons involved were acting outside Switzerland, and all negotiations took place outside Switzerland.

Of particular interest are cross-border issues in the context of corporate criminal liability. In these cases, Swiss authorities may claim a wide jurisdiction.

As mentioned above, a corporation can be held liable under the SCC if specific prerequisites are met. According to Article 102(2) of the SCC, a company is penalised irrespective of the criminal liability of any natural persons and with a fine of up to CHF 5m if:
- the offence committed is, *inter alia*, an active bribery offence; and
- the company is responsible for failing to take all the reasonable organisational measures that were required in order to prevent such an offence.

In cross-border cases, Swiss corporate criminal liability is deemed to be applicable not only when the bribery offence was committed in Switzerland, but also if the only place where the company failed to take all the reasonable organisational measures is within Switzerland. This may be the case, if the lack of organisation occurred (at least partially) in Switzerland. It is not necessary that the company is headquartered in Switzerland. Instead, it may be sufficient if only a branch of an international company group is located in Switzerland.

Corporate criminal liability in combination with the offence of bribery of a foreign official may lead to a very broad jurisdiction of Swiss authorities and even allow for extraterritorial jurisdiction, with the only connection to Switzerland being the lack of organisation.

This constellation was at the core of the recent case of the French-based Alstom Group ('Alstom'). Alstom has its headquarters in Paris, France. It mainly operates in the fields of power generation and the transport markets and is active in over 100 countries. In order to receive construction contracts in foreign countries, in particular in Asian and African countries, Alstom hired so-called "consultants". These consultants acted as intermediaries and were responsible for building up relationships with foreign governments and companies. For their services, the consultants received a 'success fee' that was calculated as a percentage of the mediated contracts.

Alstom was aware of the fact that consultants may be exposed to corruption. Therefore, Alstom implemented specific anti-corruption measures. First, internal compliance rules were adopted. According to those rules, consultants had to show in detail what services they provided for Alstom. Second, Alstom Network Switzerland Ltd ("Alstom Switzerland"), which has its registered office in Switzerland, was established. Alstom Switzerland's purpose was to act as an intra-group compliance service provider, i.e. to ensure that the consultants conformed to the internal compliance rules, and to transfer payments to these consultants via Alstom Switzerland's Swiss bank accounts. However, these anti-corruption measures did not work properly. In at least three cases, the consultants used part of their salaries, which were paid by Alstom Switzerland, to bribe foreign officials in Latvia, Tunisia, and Malaysia, the purpose of which was to win contracts and, in some cases, to avoid claims against Alstom for breaching contracts.

In November 2011, after three years of investigation, Alstom Switzerland was held criminally liable as a company and was convicted for bribery of foreign officials, fined CHF 2.5m and a compensatory claim of CHF 36.4m was imposed. According to the relevant decision, Alstom Switzerland's overall anti-corruption measures were sufficient in theory. However, these measures were not well-implemented or enforced in practice. For instance, it was pointed out that the compliance unit was under-staffed in relation to the overall number of global employees. Furthermore, it was emphasised that the compliance staff were not trained and experienced enough.

Even though only the Swiss-based company Alstom Switzerland was fined, the authority also conducted its investigation against Alstom in France, irrespective of the fact that the parent company has its registered office outside of Switzerland and all bribes were paid outside of Switzerland. The Swiss authority claimed extraterritorial jurisdiction, as **the lack of organisational measures at least partially occurred** in Switzerland.

Criminal liability of companies and the extraterritorial jurisdiction as applied in Switzerland are comparable to the respective provisions in the UK. According to the UK Bribery Act, a company is criminally liable if part of a business of the company is carried out in the UK and the company does not have in place adequate procedures designed to prevent bribery of foreign officials (Sections 7(2) and (5)(b) of the Bribery Act 2010). Thus, the Swiss and the UK provisions are strikingly similar in this regard.

Proposed reforms / The year ahead

As mentioned before, the SCC has already been amended three times recently. The next revision, however, is already on its way as the Swiss Federal Council has proposed to the parliament a further reform of the Swiss anti-corruption law which in particular targets bribery in the private sector.

The current regime regarding private sector bribery is regularly discussed and criticised in Switzerland. This topic received special media attention in the context of the selection process for the FIFA World Cup in Russia (2018) and Qatar (2022), as there have been allegations of bribery. Indeed, in March 2015 the OAG opened criminal proceedings against persons unknown in connection with the allocation of the 2018 and 2022 Football World Cups after a criminal complaint was filed by FIFA in late 2014. The opening of the OAG's investigation was based on information contained in a report commissioned by FIFA as well as on information taken from a mutual legal assistance request from the US Department of Justice DOJ. Based on the latter, several football officials and suspected bribers were arrested in Zurich by order of the Swiss Federal Office of Justice in May 2015 and were placed in detention pending extradition as part of criminal investigations of the US Attorney's Office for the Eastern District of New York.

However, even though the awarding body, FIFA, has its headquarters in Switzerland, the Swiss private bribery provisions were deemed inapplicable and the investigations by the OAG are conducted on the grounds of suspicion of criminal mismanagement and of money laundering, but not of private bribery. As a matter of fact, there is a lack of application of the current provisions. So far, there have not been any convictions for bribery in the private sector.

The reason for this is considered to be twofold. First, the provisions are, as outlined above, part of the Unfair Competition Act and, thus, only apply when private bribery has an effect on a competitive relationship. Therefore, for instance, bribery in a tender process for an international sporting event, such as the FIFA World Cup, does not fall within the scope of the provision. Second, the prosecution of such offences requires a formal complaint from a person who suffered harm due to the bribery act. This requirement of "no plaintiff, no judge" has the effect that certain forms of corruption are typically not punished.

According to the proposed bill, those weaknesses shall be eliminated. Private bribery shall become an *ex officio* crime, i.e. an offence which has to be prosecuted by the authorities whether reported or not. Furthermore, the offence of private bribery shall be transferred to and included in the SCC. Accordingly, all cases of private bribery, notwithstanding their effect on a competitive relationship, would be covered by those provisions. As a consequence, bribery in the tender process of a sporting event would be within the scope of the future provisions. However, irrespective of the introduction of the private bribery offence into the SCC, the offence shall remain a misdemeanour with a maximum penalty of three years' imprisonment (while bribery of a public official and bribery of a foreign public official have a maximum penalty of five years' imprisonment). This may lead to a situation where private sector bribery will still not qualify as a predicate offence for money laundering, as money laundering is only punishable under Swiss criminal law if the assets that are "laundered" originate from a felony (like, for instance, bribery of a public official and bribery of a foreign public official).

The Council of States adopted the proposed bill in June 2015. However, it abolished the requirement for a criminal complaint as a prerequisite to prosecution only in relation to cases of public interest. According to the parliamentary debate, public interest will typically be assumed in matters involving organisations that hold a powerful position in their sector, where a lack of governance could negatively affect a multitude of stakeholders. Another example given was the use of false deeds (e.g., untrue company accounts) to enable or cover up bribery payments, since such behaviour would undermine public trust in the reliability of such instruments. It remains to be seen whether this view will withstand the debate in the National Council which is scheduled to deal with the matter during its session in autumn 2015.

In addition to the proposed reform of private sector bribery, there shall be an amendment to the offences of granting or accepting an undue advantage. In future, those offences shall also cover cases in which the undue advantage is given in favour of a *third party*.

Besides the proposed reforms, further amendments have been discussed but no action was deemed necessary by the Swiss Federal Council. The following two, discussed-but-declined amendments seem noteworthy:

First, the introduction of a specific offence of "trading in influence" (abuse of real or supposed influence with a view to obtaining an undue advantage) was discussed but eventually declined. It was argued that a specific offence is not required as the conduct is already covered by the bribery provisions in place. This does not always hold true. If the intermediary is not a public official and abuses his influence on a public official without giving or promising an undue advantage, the conduct is not penalised under Swiss law.

Second, it was discussed whether the scope of bribery of foreign public officials should be extended and also cover cases in which the foreign public official does not breach the law or a duty. In particular, it was argued that so-called "facilitation payments" to foreign public officials are currently not within the scope of the SCC. However, the Swiss Federal Council argued that an adaption of the offence is not necessary as, according to the Federal Council, facilitation payments could already be penalised under the current provision if construed broadly.

The coming year will show whether the parliament will agree to the proposed bill in this form or another. As of now, it seems that the bill should pass the parliament, with the only disputed point being the transformation of the private bribery into an *ex officio* offence.

Marcel Meinhardt
Tel: +41 58 450 80 00 / Email: marcel.meinhardt@lenzstaehelin.com

Dr Marcel Meinhardt is specialised in handling and managing internal investigations and in advising and representing companies *vis-à-vis* the authorities. He has broad experience in both contentious and non-contentious matters. He heads the practice groups "regulatory and competition law" as well as "internal investigation and white collar crimes".

Marcel holds a degree in law from the University of St. Gallen (1990), a doctor's degree from the University of Zurich (1996), and LL.M. degrees from the New York University School of Law (1994) and the College of Europe (1995). Marcel was admitted to the Bar in 1992.

Fadri Lenggenhager
Tel: +41 58 450 80 00 / Email: fadri.lenggenhager@lenzstaehelin.com

Fadri Lenggenhager is an associate with Lenz & Staehelin in Zurich. His practice focuses on litigation and arbitration as well as regulatory compliance. Fadri also practised as a member of the dispute resolution team in Lenz & Staehelin's Geneva office and the international arbitration practice group of Wilmer Cutler Pickering Hale & Dorr in London. He holds degrees in Political Science (2003), International Management (2003) and Law (2005) from the University of St. Gallen and an LL.M. degree (2011) from the University of California, Davis School of Law. Fadri was admitted to the Zurich Bar in 2007.

Lenz & Staehelin

Bleicherweg 58, 8027 Zurich, Switzerland
Tel: +41 58 450 80 00 / Fax: +41 58 450 80 01 / URL: http://www.lenzstaehelin.com

Turkey

Gönenç Gürkaynak & Ç. Olgu Kama
ELIG, Attorneys-at-Law

Brief overview of the law and enforcement regime

The legislation on combating bribery and corruption in Turkey is as follows:
*   Turkish Criminal Code No. 5237 (Criminal Code);
*   Turkish Criminal Procedure Law No. 5271;
*   Law No. 657 on Public Officers (Law No. 657);
*   Law No. 3628 on Declaration of Property and Fight Against Bribery and Corruption;
*   Law No. 5326 on Misdemeanours;
*   Regulation No. 90/748 on Declaration of Property; and
*   Regulation on Ethical Principles for Public Officers and Procedures and Principles for Application (Regulation on Ethical Principles).

The main legislation criminalising acts of corruption is the Criminal Code, which prohibits acts of bribery, fraud, embezzlement, malversation, malfeasance and bid-rigging. Importantly, under Turkish law, anti-corruption issues are dealt with under the criminal law and there is no civil enforcement. Also of significance, as a result of the "*nulla poena sine culpa*" (no crime and punishment without fault) principle, Turkish criminal law does not recognise strict liability as a form of liability. Therefore, the relevant acts of crime are not punishable unless the perpetrators are proven to have some degree of fault or negligence.

The enforcement of the bribery and corruption legislation is undertaken by the judiciary. So far no special agencies with regard to prosecution of the relevant crimes have been established. Once the judicial proceedings establish that a person is guilty, the perpetrator may be punished with: (i) four to twelve years of imprisonment for bribery; (ii) one to five years of imprisonment and a judiciary fine of up to five thousand days for fraud and two to seven years of imprisonment and a judiciary fine of up to five thousand days for qualified fraud; (iii) five to twelve years of imprisonment for embezzlement; or (iv) five to ten years of imprisonment for malversation. The amount of the penalty depends on the type of malfeasance, as stipulated under the Criminal Code (Articles 255, 257, 259, 260, 261 *et seq*. of the Criminal Code). As per Article 52 of the Criminal Code, the amount of the judiciary fine is determined by taking into account the economic and personal circumstances of the perpetrator, with the lower limit for the daily amount being TL 20, and the upper limit being TL 100.

Turkish criminal enforcement does not allow for any dispute resolution mechanism other than through litigation.

Overview of enforcement activity and policy during the past two years

The enforcement cycle of Turkish anti-corruption legislation which traditionally focused on bid-rigging was broken in December 2013, with the investigation of bribery, money laundering and smuggling allegations against officials of the Housing Development Administration of Turkey (TOKI), the Ministry of Environment and Urban Development, the Municipality of Fatih as well as several business tycoons. The sons of three cabinet ministers were also detained within scope of the investigation, which eventually led to the resignation of the relevant ministers. In October 2014, the public prosecutor issued a non-prosecution decision about the case. Subsequently, the Parliamentary Inquiry Commission investigation into alleged acts also resulted in the acquittal of the suspects.

Notwithstanding the abovementioned incident, as seen from the examples below, in recent years the Turkish enforcement of bribery and corruption legislation has focused on bid-rigging:

- A corruption investigation into the allegedly corrupt acts of 41 persons (including top level executives) working in the Turkish Air Institution culminated in an indictment submitted to the courts in June 2015. According to the indictment, a French firm allegedly bribed the president of the institution to rent certain helicopters from their firm. The illegitimate payments were alleged to be made to a consultancy firm, who then transferred the funds to the accounts of the president's son. Allegedly, the involved persons attempted to launder the illegitimate amounts through purchasing industrial mineral oil. The case is still ongoing.
- Another recent case is a bribery investigation against public authorities working under the Firefighting Department of the Istanbul Metropolitan Municipality and multiple business owners. In October 2014, multiple public authorities and business owners were taken into custody for reasons of soliciting and providing bribes in order for undue work place permits to be provided. Subsequently 13 people were arrested. The investigation is ongoing.
- Another corruption case against the public officials of a municipality is against the officials of the Municipality of Eskişehir, which was initiated in January 2013. The officials of the municipality are charged with bid-rigging, allegedly perpetrated between the years 2006-2008. The case resulted in the acquittal of the suspects.

On the policy side, Turkey issued a letter of intent in 2011, stating their decision to join the initiative and intention to develop an action plan in due time. So far, Turkey has committed to two action plans regarding (i) Increasing Integrity in Public Sphere, and (ii) Improving the Quality of Public Services. In addition, during its G20 Presidency in 2015, Turkey established a separate working group for anti-corruption, resulting in the discussion of cutting-edge anti-corruption policy matters in the public and private sectors.

Law and policy relating to issues such as facilitation payments and hospitality

The Criminal Code does not provide an exception for facilitation payments, as the definition of bribery includes all benefits provided to a public official for the performance by the public official of its duties. Therefore, facilitation, or grease payments, would constitute a crime in Turkey, in contrast with the US Foreign Corrupt Practices Act (FCPA).

Acceptance of gifts by public officials, on the other hand, is prohibited by Law No. 657 and the details of the prohibition are set out in the Regulation on Ethical Principles. According to Article 29 of Law No. 657, public officials are prohibited from accepting or requesting gifts directly or indirectly, and from accepting gifts or borrowing money from business owners with the purpose of providing benefits, even while they are off-duty. The Public Officials Council of Ethics is authorised (i) to determine the scope of the prohibition to accept gifts and (ii) at the end of each calendar year to request a list of gifts received by public officials who are at least at the general director level or an equivalent high-level official.

Article 15 of the Regulation on Ethical Principles sets out that the scope of the prohibition on accepting gifts includes travel and accommodation expenses as well as scholarships, which may be deemed as hospitality payments, received from those who have an interest relationship with the institution in which the public official is on duty. Accordingly, in 2009, the Council of Ethics found that it was a breach of the prohibition when companies paid the accommodation expenses of public officials who were to attend the companies' meetings. Accordingly, the hospitality of commercial partners or government officials could be deemed to breach the prohibition of acceptance of gifts by public officials as put forward in Article 29 of Law No. 657.

Key issues relating to investigation, decision making and enforcement procedures

Turkish criminal enforcement does not allow for any dispute resolution mechanism other than through litigation. This being said, through the leniency procedure provided in Article 254 of the Criminal Code, the perpetrators of the crime of bribery may be exempt from punishment. Accordingly, if the person who has accepted a bribe informs the competent authority about the particular act of bribery before the relevant authority becomes aware of the situation, then that person will not be punished for bribery. The same is true for the person: (i) who has agreed with someone to accept bribery; (ii) who has bribed the public official or agreed with the public official on the bribe; and (iii) who has been complicit in the crime and who informs the competent authority before the relevant authority learns about the situation. However, this rule is not applicable to a person who gives a bribe to foreign public officials (article 254/4). A leniency procedure is also available for the crime of embezzlement if the embezzled goods are returned or the damages resulting from the crime are compensated in full before the investigation commences. In this case, the perpetrator's sentence will be reduced by two-thirds (article 248/1). If the embezzled goods are returned voluntarily or the damages are compensated in full before the prosecution commences, the perpetrator's sentence will be reduced by half. In case the leniency occurs before the verdict, the perpetrator's sentence will be reduced by one-third (article 248/2).

Overview of cross-border issues

Turkey is a signatory to and/or has ratified the following European and international anti-corruption conventions.

Council of Europe
- Council of Europe Criminal Law Convention on Corruption of 27 January 1999 (signed on 27 September 2001; ratified on 29 March 2004);
- Council of Europe Civil Law Convention on Corruption of 4 November 1999 (signed on 27 September 2001; ratified on 17 September 2003); and
- Council of Europe Convention on Laundering, Search, Seizure and Confiscation of the Proceeds from Crime and on the Financing of Terrorism of 8 November 1990 (signed on 28 March 2007).

International
- OECD Convention on Combating Bribery of Foreign Public Officials in International Business Transactions, 17 December 1997 (including OECD Recommendation for Further Combating Bribery of Foreign Public Officials in International Business Transactions) (signed on 17 December 1997; ratified on 26 July 2000) (OECD Convention on Bribery);
- the United Nations Convention against Transnational Organized Crime, 15 November 2000 (signed on 13 December 2000; ratified on 25 March 2003); and

• the United Nations Convention against Corruption, 31 October 2003 (signed on 10 December 2003; ratified on 9 November 2006).

In addition to multilateral treaties, Turkey has also been a member of the Group of States against Corruption (GRECO) since 1 January 2004, the Financial Action Task Force since 1991, and the OECD Working Group on Bribery. The extraterritorial reach of the foregoing conventions require Turkish companies and foreign companies operating in Turkey to comply with local laws in order to avoid being charged and investigated with criminal charges for transacting irregularity. Therefore, Turkey is obliged to cooperate with foreign and international authorities in corruption investigations, in compliance with its obligations under the said conventions.

Among the abovementioned conventions, the OECD Convention on Bribery's open-ended, peer-driven monitoring mechanism has allowed Turkey to make significant progress in its efforts to combat bribery in international business deals. The most recent criticism of the Working Group on Bribery through the Third Phase Report on Turkey generally are: (i) the lack of enforcement of the foreign bribery crime; (ii) the lack of a legal structure for whistle-blower protection; and (iii) the ambivalent nature of the administrative liability arising on legal persons in cases of bribery and bid-rigging.

With the overreaching applications of the FCPA and the UK Bribery Act, the globalisation of anti-corruption legislation has pointed the barrel of the gun at the Turkish subsidiaries of US and UK companies. Accordingly, such companies have been the first to seek legal help in complying with the Turkish anti-corruption legislation as well as the FCPA and the UK Bribery Act.

Corporate liability for bribery and corruption offences

As per Article 20 of the Criminal Code, criminal sanctions cannot be imposed against legal persons. However, in case of a crime, security measures may be imposed against a legal person. In line with this provision, legal persons who receive an unjust benefit due to bribery may face: (i) invalidation of the licence granted by a public authority; (ii) seizure of the goods which are used in the commitment of, or the result of, a crime by the representatives of a legal entity; or (iii) seizure of pecuniary benefits arising from or provided for the commitment of a crime. Law No. 5326 on Misdemeanours holds a legal person liable for misdemeanours committed in the scope of duty by its organs, representatives or persons who are assigned with duties to carry out its activities (Article 8). This provision was added in 2009, within the scope of Turkey's efforts to comply with the OECD Convention on Bribery, Article 43/A, and was inserted into Law No. 5326 with the special purpose of increasing corporate liability for bribery and corruption offences. Accordingly, legal persons risk being fined from 14,969 Turkish Liras to 2,994,337 Turkish Liras if the organs, representatives or persons who are assigned with duties to carry out its activities commit the crimes of bid-rigging and bribery for its benefit. This being said, Turkish law and its enforcement are far from providing for corporate liability similar to that provided under the UK Bribery Act, 2010.

Proposed reforms / The year ahead

Although there is no clear cut agenda for reforms to be realised in the coming years, several areas are at the forefront of criticism in the field of corruption and bribery in Turkey. The first of these issues is that there is no central institution responsible for the enforcement of anti-corruption laws, although there are some public agencies with an anti-corruption mandate, including: (i) the Financial Crimes Investigation Board (MASAK) which works on issues of money laundering; (ii) the abovementioned Council of Ethics, whose main function is promoting transparency in public administration; and (iii) the Prime Ministry Inspection Board, which has the mandate to inspect public bodies. Furthermore, there is no coordination between these existing agencies. Therefore, there is an explicit need for a specialised and coordinated enforcement body in the field of corruption and bribery.

It is also important to note that the previous reforms enacted for the purpose of combating corruption and bribery, lacked sufficient involvement of the civil society and non-governmental actors. Accordingly, in the coming reforms, the greater participation of wider segments of society should be secured.

Gönenç Gürkaynak
Tel: +90 212 327 17 24 / Email: gonenc.gurkaynak@elig.com

Gönenç Gürkaynak, Esq., is a founding partner and the managing partner of ELIG, Attorneys-at-Law, a firm of 55 lawyers based in Istanbul. Mr. Gürkaynak graduated from Ankara University Faculty of Law in 1997 and was called to the Istanbul Bar in 1998. Mr. Gürkaynak received his LL.M. degree from Harvard Law School, while also continuing his academic studies there as an assistant. He is qualified to practise law in Istanbul, New York, Brussels, and England and Wales (as a non-practising solicitor). Before founding ELIG, Attorneys-at-Law in the beginning of 2005, Mr. Gürkaynak worked as an attorney at the Istanbul, New York and Brussels offices of a global law firm for eight years. Mr. Gürkaynak has been practising law for more than 18 years.

Mr. Gürkaynak is the head of Regulatory and Compliance department of ELIG, Attorneys-at-Law. His main areas of practice include the fields of competition law, anti-corruption and irregularities, internet law, freedom of expression and fundamental rights and freedoms, compliance projects, contracts law, administrative law and commercial litigation.

Ç. Olgu Kama
Tel: +90 212 327 17 24 / Email: olgu.kama@elig.com

Ms. Olgu Kama graduated from Istanbul Bilgi University Faculty of Law in 2002, and was called to the Istanbul Bar in 2003. She obtained her first LL.M. degree from Galatasaray University Faculty of Law in 2006, on Law of Economics, and her second LL.M. degree from Fordham Law School, New York, in 2008 on Banking, Corporate and Finance Law. Ms. Kama has been working in the Regulatory and Compliance department of ELIG for over six years and has been a partner in the department since January 2014. She has extensive experience in corporate compliance matters and white collar irregularity projects, contracts law, commercial law, general corporate law and real estate law. Ms. Kama has also authored and co-authored many articles and essays in relation to corporate compliance and white collar irregularities matters.

ELIG, Attorneys-at-Law

Citlenbik Sok., No. 12, Yildiz Mah., Besiktas, Istanbul, Turkey
Tel: +90 212 327 17 24 / Fax: +90 212 327 17 25 / URL: http://www.elig.com

Ukraine

Svitlana Kheda
Sayenko Kharenko

Brief overview of the law and enforcement regime

The Ukrainian anti-corruption legal framework consists of the following major segments:
- the anti-corruption legislation itself;
- provisions of the Code of Ukraine on Administrative Offences (the "**Administrative Offences Code**") and the Criminal Code of Ukraine (the "**Criminal Code**") regulating corruption-related administrative offences and crimes; and
- legal provisions establishing the rules of conduct of Ukrainian governmental officials, including officials representing Ukrainian legislative, administrative and regulatory bodies (the "**Officials**").

Starting from 26 April 2015, the main legislative act dealing with combatting corruption in Ukraine is the Law of Ukraine No. 1700-VII "On Preventing Corruption" dated 14 October 2014 (the "**Anti-Corruption Law**"). The Anti-Corruption Law:
- defines corruption, a corruption offence, an unjustified benefit and, importantly, a gift;
- distinguishes between a corruption offence and a corruption-related offence;
- introduces changes in the groups of subjects of liability for corruption offences;
- provides for an algorithm for preventing acceptance of unjustified benefits and gifts, and for dealing with them when provided;
- introduces several important restrictions aimed at preventing and combating corruption (e.g. restriction on receiving gifts by Officials);
- sets up the rules aimed at preventing corruption in legal entities;
- introduces certain changes related to liability for corruption and corruption-related offences to the Criminal Code and the Administrative Offences Code;
- regulates protection of whistle-blowers;
- emphasises the importance of corporate anti-corruption compliance programmes;
- establishes the ethical conduct rules for certain groups of Officials; and
- tightens the financial control regulation for Officials.

Unlike the U.S. Foreign Corrupt Practices Act (**FCPA**) and the UK Bribery Act 2010 (**UKBA**), the Anti-Corruption Law does not have extraterritorial application. Nor does it use the term 'bribery'; however, the legal meaning of the bribery notion under the FCPA and the UKBA is mostly covered by the corruption-related crimes of the Criminal Code (e.g. corruption payments to the officers of private companies and persons rendering public services, exercising undue influence, giving unjustified benefits to Officials, etc.).

In 2014, Ukraine became a jurisdiction, the legislation of which provides for criminal liability of companies, including for crimes of corruption committed by their authorised representatives (*please see section below, 'Company liability for corruption offences', for more detail*).

Neither the Anti-Corruption Law nor the Criminal Code establish liability of the officers and employees of the company for corruption offences and crimes committed by agents and other third parties, including if they commit them specifically to get business, keep business, or gain a business advantage for this company.

Bribery *vs* Unjustified Benefits

The notable distinction of the Ukrainian anti-bribery and anti-corruption legislation is that it has never clearly distinguished between corruption and bribery. For instance, the Anti-Corruption Law contains provisions directly or indirectly related to bribery (e.g. gifts to Officials, payment of charitable contributions, membership of NGOs, etc.). Moreover, in 2013, the legal notions of 'bribe' and 'bribery' were eliminated from the Ukrainian law and replaced with the notion of 'unjustified benefits', (i.e. the term 'bribery' is no longer used under Ukrainian law). Therefore, the words 'anti-corruption legislation' or 'anti-corruption legal framework' will be a sufficient equivalent of bribery in the meaning of the FCPA and the UKBA.

Under the New Anti-Corruption Law, the unjustified benefits are defined as money or other property, preferences, advantages, services, non-pecuniary assets, and any other benefits of non-pecuniary or intangible nature that are being illicitly promised, offered, delivered, or received. Under the old anti-corruption legislation, the unjustified benefits were defined as money or other property, preferences, advantages, services, non-pecuniary assets being illicitly promised, offered, delivered, or obtained free of charge or at a price lower than a minimum market value. This definition suggested two tests for classifying benefits as unjustified, being their promise, offer, delivery or obtaining (1) illicitly; and (2) free of charge or at a price lower than a minimum market value. In the definition of the unjustified benefits provided by Anti-Corruption Law, the second test (i.e. price) is missing. Considering that the unjustified benefits are the key category of the anti-corruption legislation, its definition in the present wording gives the law enforcement authorities and courts more discretion in applying the anti-corruption laws and deciding on the guilt of the potential subjects of liability for corruption offences.

Subjects of liability for corruption offences, corruption and corruption offence

The term 'Officials' is not defined in the Anti-Corruption Law *per se*. However, it speaks of the 'individuals authorised to perform state or local government functions' and covers government officials, as well as public servants and local government officers.

In addition to Officials, Article 3 of the Anti-Corruption Law lists other groups of individuals who potentially can be held liable for committing corruption offences (the "**Subjects of Liability**"), including:

- persons conferred the same status as persons authorised to perform state or local government functions for the purposes of the Anti-Corruption Law, namely: (i) officers of the public legal entities other than Officials (the "**Public Entity Officers**"); and (ii) individuals, other than public servants or local government officials, rendering public services (e.g. auditors, notaries, experts, and other persons determined by law) (the "**Public Services Officials**"); and
- individuals permanently or temporarily holding positions related to organisational, executive, or administrative and economic responsibilities, or persons specifically authorised to perform such duties in any private company in accordance with the law, as well as other individuals performing works for or rendering services to such companies based on respective agreements (in cases provided by the Anti-Corruption Law) (the "**Private Company Officers**").

The Ukrainian law defines corruption as an activity of Officials and other Subjects of Liability aimed at unlawful use of their powers and related opportunities to obtain unjustified benefits or accept such benefits, or accept a promise/offer of such unjustified benefits for themselves or other individuals, as well as a promise/offer of unjustified benefits to Officials and other Subjects of Liability or provision of unjustified benefits to them or, at their demand, to other individuals or legal entities, aimed at persuading Officials and other Subjects of Liability to unlawfully use their powers and related opportunities.

The Anti-Corruption Law distinguishes between a corruption offence and a corruption-related offence, which is a novelty in the Ukrainian anti-corruption regulation. A corruption offence is the intended act of corruption, for which the law establishes criminal, disciplinary and/or civil law liability, committed by an Official or other Subjects of Liability.

A corruption-related offence is a wrongdoing that does not fall under the characteristics of corruption but violates the requirements, prohibitions and limitations imposed by the Anti-Corruption Law, for which the law establishes criminal, administrative, disciplinary and/or civil law liability, committed by an Official or other Subjects of Liability.

Liability for corruption offences

The Anti-Corruption Law sets forth criminal liability for legal entities (*discussed in section 'Company liability for corruption offences' below*), as well as criminal, administrative, civil and disciplinary liability for corruption offences for responsible Officials and other Subjects of Liability.

In accordance with Ukrainian law, unless a corrupt activity constitutes a criminal offence provided by the Criminal Code (e.g. offering, promising, or providing unjustified benefits to an Official), a responsible Official or other Subject of Liability shall be subject to administrative liability for a committed corruption offence (e.g. for violating statutory restrictions regarding receiving a gift/donation).

The Anti-Corruption Law introduced a new wording to or supplemented several Sections of the Administrative Offences Code resulting in the increased administrative liability for corruption offences. This includes establishing administrative liability for violating the restrictions to:
- engage in other paid or entrepreneurial activities (except for teaching, scientific and creative work, as well as some other activities;
- become a member of governing bodies of profitable companies (except when representing the state interests in the governing bodies of such companies);
- receiving gifts;
- violating the financial control requirements;
- preventing and resolving the conflict of interest;
- unlawful use of information which became known during performance of the official duties; and
- failure to take anti-corruption measures.

Additionally, the Anti-Corruption Law introduced a new Article 188[46] into the Administrative Offences Code, establishing liability for:
- not observing the lawful requirements (orders) of the National Anti-Corruption Agency of Ukraine (the "**Anti-Corruption Agency**");
- failing to provide it with information and documents (violation of the statutory terms of their provision); or
- providing knowingly untrue or incomplete information.

The Criminal Code provides for the following types of corruption crimes:
- receiving unjustified benefits;
- receiving the offer or promise of unjustified benefits;

- promising or providing unjustified benefits;
- corrupt payment[1] to Private Company Officers;
- corrupt payment to Public Services Officials;
- corrupt payment to an employee of an entity, other than the Official, or a person working for the benefit of an entity;
- unlawful enrichment; and
- unlawful influencing Officials performing state duties.

Penalties for individuals convicted of corruption offences

Depending on the degree and type of a particular crime, the corruption crimes committed by individuals are punishable by (as a single penalty or in combination with the below penalties):

- a fine;
- community works;
- confinement or imprisonment; and, as the case may be,
- deprivation of the right to hold certain office or engage in certain activities for up to three years and confiscation of property and/or special confiscation.

Other legal consequences of corruption activities

Under Ukrainian law, information on persons liable for corruption shall be listed in the Unified Register of Individuals Liable for Committing Corruption Offences within three days upon the coming into force of a respective judgment or upon coming into force of a respective judgment, or receiving by the Anti-Corruption Agency of the paper copy of the internal order of the relevant employer on taking a disciplinary action for committing a corruption or corruption-related offence.

Under Article 22 of the Anti-Corruption Law, performance of duties of an Official or other Subject of Liability shall be suspended if formal charges are filed against such person to initiate prosecution for committing a crime within the scope of his/her official duties. Officials brought to criminal or administrative liability for corruption offences shall be subject to dismissal within three days after a respective judgment comes into force, unless otherwise provided by law.

The Anti-Corruption Law supplemented Article 36 of the Labour Code of Ukraine (the "Labour Code") with a new ground for employment termination, namely concluding an employment agreement (contract) contrary to the requirements of the Anti-Corruption Law established for Officials listed in Article 3, part 1 (1) of the Anti-Corruption Law.

According to Article 53 of the Anti-Corruption Law, whistle-blowers cannot be fired or caused to terminate their employment, or brought to disciplinary liability or be otherwise retaliated (be threatened with retaliation) by their employers in connection with reporting by such whistle-blowers of violations of the Anti-Corruption Law committed by other persons. Article 235 of the Labour Code was amended with a new provision aimed at protecting whistle-blowers or members of their families from such retaliation. The new part 4 of this Article 235 provides that in case such whistle-blowers refuse to be reinstated at their job, they shall be entitled to compensation in the amount of their average salary for six months.

Apart from the aforementioned administrative, criminal and disciplinary liability, Officials violating provisions of the Anti-Corruption Law may be held liable for damages. In addition, they can be forced to eliminate the consequences of their corrupt actions by:

- compensating damages;
- annulling unlawful laws, regulations and decisions initially enacted in the course of corruption activities;
- restoring rights of and compensating damages to the offended companies and individuals; and
- seizing the unlawfully gained property.

Anti-Corruption Agency

The Anti-Corruption Law provides for establishing the Anti-Corruption Agency, a central government body having a special status and tasked with forming and implementing the state anti-corruption policy. The Anti-Corruption Agency is authorised to:

- control and verify financial declarations of Officials, keep and publish such declarations, as well as monitor the Officials' way of living;
- maintain the Uniform State Register of Declarations of Individuals Authorised to Perform State Functions or Local Government Functions and the Uniform State Register of Individuals who Committed Corruption and Corruption Related Offences;
- approve the rules of ethics for public servants and local government officials;
- develop a template anti-corruption compliance programme of a legal entity; and
- cooperate with whistle-blowers, ensure their legal and other protection, and bring to liability those guilty in violating the whistle-blowers' rights related to notifying about possible corruption or corruption-related offences.

Corruption activities investigation and law enforcement bodies

Under the Criminal Procedure Code of Ukraine (the "Criminal Procedure Code"), investigation of the abovementioned corruption offences falls within the competence of the Ministry of Internal Affairs of Ukraine, the Prosecutor's Office of Ukraine and the Security Service of Ukraine.

Investigators of the Prosecutor's Office of Ukraine investigate offences committed by the highest Officials (i.e. Officials who hold positions belonging to the first three categories of public servants established by the applicable law (e.g. first deputy ministers, heads of regional state administrations, heads of Administration of the President of Ukraine, etc.), as well as by judges and officers of the law enforcement bodies). Under the Criminal Procedure Code, after creation of the State Investigation Bureau of Ukraine such cases will be investigated by this Bureau.

The Law of Ukraine No. 1698-VII "On the National Anti-Corruption Bureau of Ukraine" provides for establishing the National Anti-Corruption Bureau of Ukraine (the "**Anti-Corruption Bureau**"). This Bureau is a new state law enforcement agency authorised with preventing, detecting, stopping, investigating, and exposing corruption offences within its competence, as well as discouraging from committing new ones. The task of the Anti-Corruption Bureau is fighting corruption crimes committed by high public Officials that threaten the national security of Ukraine.

Overview of enforcement activity and policy during the past two years

Considering that the Anti-Corruption Law became fully effective on 26 April 2015, and other anti-corruption legislation was significantly amended, including recently, that the new legislation introduces a number of new notions and concepts into the Ukrainian law, and that many of the existing legal acts governing this area have to be brought in compliance with the Anti-Corruption Law and other newly enacted anti-corruption laws, the enforcement of the new anti-corruption legal framework remains an issue, while the success of its application will largely depend on interpretation of the new laws by the Ukrainian enforcement agencies and courts.

There have been no significant or policy-shaping court cases in the anti-corruption area during the past two years. On the other hand, court rulings on various corruption-related offences seem to be relatively consistent for many years in a row.

Based on the established court practice, it appears that the most frequently prosecuted corruption-related cases are the crimes punishable under Article 368 of the Criminal Code (i.e. for accepting the offer or promise of unjustified benefits, or for receiving unjustified benefits, or for requesting to provide such unjustified benefits by an Official, as well as for requesting such unjustified benefits for their own or for any other third party for performance (or refusal of performance) by such an Official of any act using his or her official powers or position for the benefit of a person providing unjustified benefits or a third party). Particular punishment ordered by courts normally depends on the circumstances of a committed crime, position held by the Official, amount of the unjustified benefits involved, and the level of the criminal intent's implementation.

The established court practice evidences that law enforcement in the anti-corruption area has been rather subjective in Ukraine. Mainly the prosecution and conviction have been carried out with respect to mid- or low-level Officials (i.e. mostly local government Officials). Even though recently there were several high-profile corruption cases involving high-level Officials (e.g. officials of the State Employment Center and the State Migration Service were incriminated committing a crime envisaged by Section 368 of the Criminal Code, etc.) it is still not clear what the court ruling/outcome of investigation would be in these cases. Among those recently brought to liability were also Private Company Officers and Public Entity Officers.

In 2015, the number of corruption-related criminal proceedings increased, as did the liability for committed corruption crimes established by courts. Notably, the number of special agreements on recognition of guilt (the "**Plea Agreement**") in anti-corruption criminal cases also increased recently.

The Ukrainian legal and business community is anticipating first court rulings related to bringing companies to criminal liability for corruption offences to receive some guidance on the prospective law enforcement in this area.

Law and policy relating to issues such as facilitation payments, gifts and hospitality

Facilitation payments

Unlike the FCPA, facilitation payments are not allowed by Ukrainian legislation. The facilitation or 'grease' payments defence under the FCPA should be carefully considered while doing business in Ukraine. Normally, in Ukraine various central and local government agencies and state and municipal entities officially establish higher fees for the expedited performance of their services. Therefore, any payments other than such official fees may be viewed as corruption under Ukrainian law.

Gifts

Under Article 1 of the Anti-Corruption Law, the notion of 'gift' is defined as money or other property, advantages, preferences, services, intangible assets provided/received free of charge or at a price lower than the minimum market price. This legal definition of the gift is rather broad and the only clear test for distinguishing between the gift and the unjustified benefit seems to be the pecuniary nature of the gift. Analysis of the relevant provisions of the Anti-Corruption Law allows separating another test for differentiating between the gift and the unjustified benefit being the illegitimate ground for providing/receiving unjustified benefits. Finally, a gift is something that can be given/received while an unjustified benefit is something that can also be promised/offered.

Based on the above, a company or an individual presenting a gift to an Official may bear a risk of such gift being treated as a corrupt payment or provision of unjustified benefits (i.e.

commit corruption crimes punishable under the Criminal Code), depending on the value of the gift, intent of the gift giver, circumstances and the timeframe.

Article 23 of the Anti-Corruption Law bans Officials, as well as Public Entity Officers and Public Services Officials (the "**Restricted Individuals**") from demanding, asking and receiving, either directly or through closely associated persons, gifts from legal entities and individuals: (i) with respect to conducting activity related to the implementation of state or municipal government functions by liable individuals; and (ii) from subordinates of such persons.

An Official can be held criminally liable for receiving unjustified benefits only if s/he received those unjustified benefits for performance (non-performance) of actions, which could have been performed only by using his/her powers or duties in his/her capacity as an Official or related to his/her position.

An Official can be charged for committing the act of corruption notwithstanding his/her actual performance or non-performance of any actions (their consequences) for the benefit of a person who provided this Official with the valuables, services, preferences or other benefits (i.e. the mere fact of the receipt of benefits is sufficient for bringing the charges).

Notwithstanding the abovementioned prohibition on Officials and Restricted Individuals receiving gifts from companies and individuals, these individuals may accept personal gifts consistent with the generally recognised ideas for hospitality. The Anti-Corruption Law establishes a value threshold for such gifts. The value of a one-time gift may not exceed the amount of one minimum monthly salary established on the date of a particular gift acceptance (currently constituting €50). The aggregate value of gifts from the same person (group of persons) within a given year should not exceed two minimum subsistence level amounts established for individuals capable of working as of 1 January of the year during which the gifts were received (currently being €100).

The above 'group of persons' notion is a recently introduced amendment. Therefore, there is no official or any commonly accepted interpretation of it yet. The 'group of persons' can mean either several persons visiting an Official and presenting a gift to him/her at the same time, or just people from the same organisation presenting gifts to such Official during a given year. In the latter case, this amendment appears to be a more precise equivalent of the 'same source' notion under the previous anti-corruption statute. Therefore, until there is more clarity on this issue, it is recommended to interpret the 'group of persons' as people from the same organisation.

It should be emphasised that not only the gift's value, but also circumstances under which it is presented are important for determining the corporate policy for giving gifts to Officials. Under certain conditions, even a gift of the equivalent of €20 or a private lunch with an Official could raise the suspicion of the law enforcement authorities and result in allegations of corruption. Therefore, in addition to the value/timeframe established by the Anti-Corruption Law, it is always important to consider circumstances under which each particular gift is presented. Otherwise, there is a significant risk of prosecution against responsible Officials, a company's officers or a company itself.

Hospitality/entertainment

There is no definition of a hospitality/entertainment under Ukrainian law. However, the definition of the gift provided in the Anti-Corruption Law seems to be broad enough to cover hospitality/entertainment (similarly to the FCPA, UKBA, and some other foreign anti-bribery legislation). Therefore, each case of entertaining an Official should be carefully evaluated.

For instance, paying a fee (honorarium) to an Official for speaking at a conference organised or sponsored by a company is not prohibited by the Anti-Corruption Law and, therefore, should not be treated as an act of corruption. On the other hand, compensation of an Official's expenses for his/her travel to the venue of the conference, accommodation, etc. could be viewed as corruption. Furthermore, whereas an invitation of an Official to attend a formal reception might be acceptable, treatment of the same Official to a private dinner might be considered as a corrupt activity. Some Ukrainian companies prefer to extend invitations to government agencies rather than to particular Officials to minimise the risk of being accused of corruption.

Key issues relating to investigation, decision-making and enforcement procedures

Article 96[10] of the Criminal Code directly provides that, while deciding on penalties to be imposed on companies, courts have to consider the following:
- degree of the corruption crime committed;
- level of implementation of criminal intent;
- amount of damage caused by this crime;
- nature and amount of unjustified benefits received or which may have been received by the company; and
- measures taken by the company to prevent the crime.

The Criminal Procedure Code provides that a prosecutor and a suspected or accused person may conclude the Plea Agreement under which they can determine:
- precise wording of the suspicion or accusation and its legal qualification under the appropriate Section of the Criminal Code;
- essential circumstances for the proper criminal proceeding;
- unconditional recognition by a suspected or accused person of his/her guilt in committing the relevant crime;
- obligations of a suspected or accused person in relation to collaboration in investigating the crime committed by another person (in case it was agreed);
- agreed punishment and consent of a suspected or accused person for his/her punishment or for declaring the agreed punishment and his/her further release from serving the sentence on the terms of probation;
- consequences of conclusion and approval of the Plea Agreement provided by the Criminal Code; and
- consequences for a suspected or accused person in case of his/her failure to execute the Plea Agreement.

Under Ukrainian law, it is prohibited to conclude the Plea Agreement with a suspected or accused authorised person of a company in respect of which a criminal proceeding takes place.

Under the Criminal Code, a provider of unjustified benefits responsible for committing certain crimes (e.g. offering, promising or providing unjustified benefits to an Official) provided by the Criminal Code may be released from criminal liability: (i) if unjustified benefits were given due to their extortion; or (ii) in case of his/her voluntary reporting on providing unjustified benefits to the body responsible for commencing criminal proceedings prior to initiation of investigation by such body in respect of the provider of unjustified benefits.

Under the Criminal Code, confession to the commission a crime, sincere repentance and active assistance in investigation of a crime are considered defences.

Overview of cross-border issues

Article 7 of the Criminal Code provides that citizens of Ukraine, who have committed crimes abroad, shall be held criminally liable under the Criminal Code, unless otherwise provided by the international treaties of Ukraine ratified by the Ukrainian parliament. If such individuals were brought to liability abroad for committing crimes envisaged by the Criminal Code, they may not be brought to criminal liability in Ukraine for these crimes.

Under the general rule stipulated by Article 8 of the Criminal Code, foreigners who do not permanently reside in Ukraine and committed crimes abroad, can be held liable in Ukraine under the Criminal Code in cases provided by the ratified international treaties of Ukraine, or if they committed grave or especially grave crimes against human rights and liberties or interests of Ukraine.

Part 2 of this Article 8 provides that foreigners, who do not permanently reside in Ukraine, can be prosecuted in Ukraine under the Criminal Code if they committed abroad, in complicity with Officials who are nationals of Ukraine, any of the following corruption crimes:

- accepting an offer or promise, or receiving unjustified benefits by an Official;
- corrupt payment to a Private Company Officer;
- corrupt payment to a Public Services Official;
- offering, promising or providing unjustified benefits to an Official; or
- improper influence.

In addition, such foreigners can be prosecuted in Ukraine under the Criminal Code if they offered, promised or provided unjustified benefits to such Officials, or accepted from them an offer or promise of unjustified benefits, or received such benefits.

FCPA/UKBA enforcement in Ukraine

To our knowledge, as of today there have been no precedents of the FCPA/UKBA enforcement in Ukraine. Ukrainian authorities cannot initiate any action in Ukraine under foreign law.

However, Ukraine is required to provide legal assistance for foreign law enforcement authorities on their request in accordance with a respective international treaty on legal assistance in civil or crime cases ratified by Ukraine. For instance, the Treaty between the US and Ukraine on Mutual Legal Assistance in Criminal Matters effective as of 27 February 2001 requires Ukrainian government bodies to cooperate with the US authorised agencies by providing legal assistance to the US authorities during the ongoing investigations, prosecution or for crime prevention purposes (e.g. to provide copies of the publicly accessible documents, to pass requests from the competent US agencies for a potential witness (including an Official) to testify before a US court, etc.).

We are also not aware of any FCPA- or UKBA-related investigations or prosecutions initiated by the US or UK authorities against a US or UK corporation or affiliated entity doing business in Ukraine, which would involve enforcement of FCPA or UKBA in Ukraine.

Article 72 of the Anti-Corruption Law provides that the competent Ukrainian agencies can give to/receive from the relevant foreign agencies information, including restricted data, related to preventing and fighting corruption.

Even though the number of publications on the FCPA and the UKBA and their extraterritorial application has increased recently in Ukraine, and more Ukrainian companies and enforcement agencies (especially those dealing with US or UK companies) are aware of the existence of the FCPA and the UKBA and their effect on US and UK companies (their subsidiaries, officers and employees, and agents), based on our observation it rarely influences their business and other decisions.

Corporate liability for bribery and corruption offences

The Anti-Corruption Law and the Criminal Code provide, among others, that a company may be brought to criminal liability for committing corruption crimes listed in Article 96[3] of the Criminal Code by the company's authorised representative (independently or in complicity with this legal entity) on behalf and in the interests of this company. In such case, according to the Anti-Corruption Law, to identify the reasons for and conditions of committing the crime by this company employee, the company's CEO orders (based on the action of the Anti-Corruption Bureau or the order of the Anti-Corruption Agency) to conduct an internal compliance investigation.

Criminal liability is introduced only for private companies (i.e. any companies that are not in state or municipal ownership).

A company may be brought to criminal liability for committing the following corruption crimes by the company's authorised representative on behalf and in the interests of this company:
• corrupt payment to a Private Company Officer;
• corrupt payment to a Public Services Official;
• offering, promising or providing unjustified benefits to an Official; or
• improper influence.

Under the Criminal Code, in case the company's authorised representative is found guilty in committing a corruption crime the company may be ordered to pay a fine in amount from 5,000 to 75,000 tax exempted incomes (currently being approximately €3,550 to €53,125), depending on the degree of a particular crime committed by the company's authorised representative.

Unlike the old anti-corruption legislation, the Anti-Corruption Law gives special attention to preventing corruption in activities of legal entities by dedicating its entire Section X to this issue. In particular, it requires Ukrainian companies to ensure developing and implementing adequate measures for preventing corruption in their activities. It also mandates companies' CEOs and founders (participants) to ensure regular assessment of the corruption risks their companies may face and implementation of relevant anti-corruption measures. A company may engage independent experts to facilitate detecting and elimination of corruption risks in the company's activities, including during anti-corruption due diligences.

The Anti-Corruption Law directly imposes the following obligations in the anti-corruption compliance area on all employees of any Ukrainian companies violation of which (if made part of the employment duties) may result in taking a disciplinary action against guilty employees, up to their dismissal:
• not to commit and not to participate in committing corrupt offences related to the company's activities;
• to refrain from behaving in a manner that might be interpreted as readiness to commit a corruption offence related to the company's activities;
• immediately inform the company's anti-corruption compliance officer, its CEO or founders (shareholders) on instances of incitement to commit a corruption offence related to the company's activities, as well as about actual commitment of corruption or corruption-related offences by other company employees or by other persons; and
• immediately inform the company's anti-corruption compliance officer, its CEO or founders (shareholders) of any actual or potential conflicts of interests.

For the first time in Ukraine, the Anti-Corruption Law introduces the notions of the anti-corruption compliance programme of a legal entity and an anti-corruption compliance officer of a company.

Based on the above, introduction and effective implementation by the Ukrainian companies of sound corporate anti-corruption programmes (including adoption by them of sophisticated anti-corruption policies/regulations) may mitigate the risk of potential criminal liability of these companies for corruption offences committed by their officers and other authorised representatives.

Proposed reforms / The year ahead

The Anti-Corruption Law is more consistent and clear in comparison to the earlier legislation, and generally seems to conform to the world's best practices. However, the Ukrainian anti-corruption legislative, regulatory and law enforcement environment still needs significant improvement to fully meet the world standard.

In general, the majority of the anti-corruption legislative initiatives introduced by the Cabinet of Ministers of Ukraine in the second part or 2014 were implemented in 2015.

It is expected that the year ahead will be marked with the following:
• The Anti-Corruption Agency will be fully created and staffed. This will enable the launching of the electronic system for financial declarations of Officials.
• By October 2015, the staffing of the Anti-Corruption Bureau with detectives is expected to be completed and the Bureau will commence its work.
• The Anti-corruption prosecutor's office should be formed in October 2015 to enable the Anti-Corruption Bureau to become fully operational.
• Several important legislative acts may be enacted (e.g. aimed at preventing political corruption, fighting corruption in the public procurement area, etc.).
• Significant cases can be prosecuted/initiated.
• Serious compliance initiatives (launching/amending compliance programmes, conducting internal compliance investigations, etc.) of Ukrainian companies can take place.

* * *

Endnote

1. Corrupt payment ('*підкуп*', in Ukrainian) is formally called in English 'commercial bribery'. For the purposes of this chapter, it was decided to replace it with the term 'corrupt payment' to avoid confusion with the term 'bribery', which was eliminated from the Ukrainian law in 2013.

Svitlana Kheda
Tel: +380 50 410 0259 / Email: skheda@sk.ua
Svitlana Kheda (LL.M., Ph.D.) is a counsel heading the firm's labour and compliance practice, in particular leading its anti-corruption/anti-bribery practice group.

Svitlana has over 18 years of professional experience in Ukraine and the US, advising clients on a wide range of sophisticated issues in the area of anti-corruption/anti-bribery legislation. She is known for her state-of-the-art, business-oriented and user-friendly work in the anti-corruption area.

Svitlana is an internationally recognised expert in the anti-corruption/anti-bribery area. She speaks and publishes extensively (in Ukraine and abroad) on the specifics of the Ukrainian anti-corruption legislative and regulatory environment. Svitlana is a member of the Society of Corporate Compliance and Ethics (USA) and regularly attends FCPA/UKBA trainings in the US and Europe.

Svitlana is recommended as one of the best lawyers in Ukraine, according to Ukrainian Law Firms 2015, Chambers Europe 2015, Best Lawyers International 2016, the all-Ukrainian survey Client's Choice: TOP-100 Lawyers in Ukraine 2014/2015.

Sayenko Kharenko

10 Muzeyny Provulok, Kyiv 01001, Ukraine
Tel: +380 44 499 6000 / Fax: +380 44 499 6250 / URL: http://www.sk.ua

United Arab Emirates

Khalid AlHamrani, Ibtissem Lassoued & Andrew Hudson
Al Tamimi & Company

Brief overview of the law and enforcement regime

<u>Legal system</u>

The UAE is a civil law jurisdiction, comprising seven Emirates (Abu Dhabi, Ajman, Dubai, Fujairah, Ras Al-Khaimah, Sharjah and Umm Al-Quwain). Each Emirate has its own court system, which applies local and federal laws at Court of First Instance and Court of Appeal levels. Beyond that, Dubai and Ras Al-Khaimah have their own Courts of Cassation, whereas appeals from the Courts of Appeal of the other five Emirates are heard by the Federal Supreme Court in Abu Dhabi.

Dubai also has a common law court in the Dubai International Financial Centre ("**DIFC**"), a financial free zone in Dubai. The DIFC Courts are considered part of the Dubai Courts in the sense that judgments of the DIFC Courts do not need to be ratified before they can be enforced in the Dubai Courts, but they operate under a separate, common law, English-language legal system and do not have jurisdiction over criminal matters.

<u>Legislation and offences</u>

The main legislation in the UAE governing bribery and corruption is Federal Law No. 3 of 1987, as amended ("**Federal Penal Code**"). Provisions combatting corruption in the public sector are also found in the following laws:

- Federal Law No. 11 of 2008 ("**Federal Government HR Law**").
- Dubai Law No. 27 of 2006 ("**Dubai Government HR Law**").
- Federal Law No. 3 of 1971 ("**Armed Forces Law**").
- Various Laws relating to governmental contracts and procurement.

The Federal Penal Code expressly criminalises active and passive bribery in the public sector, and passive bribery in the private sector.

In the public sector, bribery in all its forms includes soliciting or accepting, directly or indirectly, a donation or advantage of any kind, or a promise of anything of the like. These acts may be done either before or after the commission or omission of an act in violation of the public officer's duty. A bribe for the commission or omission of an act that is a legitimate duty of the public officer's function (facilitation payment) is also criminalised.

The provision relating to the private sector prohibits the direct or indirect demand or acceptance of a donation, or a promise thereof, in order to commit or omit any of the duties of one's job or to breach such duties. Although active bribery in the private sector is not specifically criminalised by the law, prosecution is possible by using the 'accomplice' provisions of the Federal Penal Code.

In all cases, it is the bribe that is criminalised, rather than the subsequent commission or omission of an act. As such, the offence shall be considered complete even if the recipient intends not to commit or omit such an act or if the offer of a bribe is declined.

A mediator to a bribe will be liable to the same penalty as the paying/promising and receiving/demanding parties. The bribe payer or mediator may be exempted from prosecution if he informs the authorities of the crime before it is discovered.

There is no separate offence under UAE law relating to bribery of foreign public officials.

Investigating and prosecuting authorities

The relevant Emirate's Public Prosecution oversees and directs the Police in the conduct of investigations into bribery and corruption. There is currently no special agency dedicated to anti-bribery and corruption investigations, although the establishment of an Anti-Corruption Unit has been announced.

Penalties

The maximum penalties for bribery offences are as follows:

- 15 years' imprisonment for passive bribery committed by a public officer in order to act in violation of his duties (10 years for facilitation payments).
- 10 years' imprisonment for passive bribery committed by a public officer after an act in violation of his duties (three years for facilitation payments).
- Five years' imprisonment for passive bribery committed by a public officer in order to commit an improper act which is not related to his function.
- Five years' imprisonment for bribery committed by a person in the private sector, whether before or after the improper act or omission.
- Five years' imprisonment for active bribery of a public officer. The same penalty applies to a mediator in the bribery.
- Three years' imprisonment for a person who requests payment to intervene or exert influence to get a public officer to act improperly.

In all cases, the offender shall also be punished with a fine equivalent to the amount of the bribe, provided that it is a minimum of Arab Emirates Dirhams (AED) 1,000. Further, any bribe accepted by the public officer shall be confiscated.

Other legal consequences

Bribery by a contractor or supplier in a government contract may lead to the revocation of the contract by the contracting government entity, seizure of the performance bond and the execution of the contract at the cost of the contractor or supplier.

Overview of enforcement activity and policy during the past two years

In 2012, the Federal Supreme Court convicted an individual of offering a bribe to a public official. The bribe was offered to a Customs Officer in Ajman Port and Customs, with the intention that he would allow the entry of certain goods without inspection. Offering a bribe to a public official for the exclusion of duties assigned to him is a violation of the Federal Penal Code. The Court of First Instance imposed a sentence of six months in prison and a fine of AED3,000 and confiscated the amount of the bribe. The sentence was reduced to three months on appeal.

Law and policy relating to issues such as facilitation payments and hospitality

Facilitation payments

Facilitation payments are not permitted under UAE law. The bribery articles of the Federal Penal Code prohibit bribery in return for the commission or omission of an act that is a legitimate duty of a public officer's function.

In addition, Article 70 of the Federal Government HR Law specifically prohibits any government employee from accepting, taking or offering any amount of money, service or anything of material or moral value to spoil the course of action by taking any act that would:

- Accelerate any work that the employee is required – by his job – to do.
- Lead to the employee's failure to do an assigned task.
- Lead one employee to influence another to finish an application or take any procedure in violation of the existing laws.

Hospitality

Hospitality of government officials is governed by the Federal Government HR Law, with mirror provisions in the Dubai Government HR Law.

Article 70 of the Federal Government HR Law prohibits the acceptance of gifts by government employees, unless the gift is a promotional product and bears the name and emblem of the presenting entity. Gifts may not be distributed unless in the name of the Ministry, so a personal gift may not be given by a government employee.

Key issues relating to investigation, decision-making and enforcement procedures

Self-reporting

Article 239 of the Federal Penal Code provides that the bribe payer or middle-man will be exempt from prosecution for the offence if the crime is self-reported to the authorities before it is discovered.

Reconciliation

Article 20*bis* of Federal Law No. 35 of 1992 as amended ("**Penal Procedures Law**") provides that the victim of certain offences, including Breach of Trust (embezzlement is one method of committing this offence), is entitled to request the Public Prosecution to confirm reconciliation between the offender and the victim, which may result in the termination of the criminal proceedings.

Overview of cross-border issues

The UAE is signatory to several regional and international bilateral and multilateral treaties, such as the Riyadh Arab Convention on Judicial Co-operation (ratified by Federal Decree No. 53 of 1999), the United Nations Convention Against Transnational Organised Crime ("**UNCTOC**") (ratified by Federal Decree No. 35 of 2007) and the United Nations Convention against Corruption ("**UNCAC**") (ratified by Federal Decree No. 8 of 2006). The UAE is also a member of the Middle East & North Africa Financial Action Task Force ("**MENA-FATF**") and the Egmont Group of Financial Intelligence Units. The UAE is ranked by Transparency International as 25th out of 175 in the Corruption Perceptions Index, making it the highest-ranking country in the Middle East.

Mutual legal assistance

The underlying law that governs matters of mutual legal assistance is Federal Law No. 39 of 2006 concerning International Judicial Assistance in Criminal Matters ("**International Assistance Law**"). This law contains comprehensive provisions on incoming and outgoing requests for judicial assistance in criminal matters and extradition.

In the absence of a treaty, the UAE authorities may extend co-operation on the basis of reciprocal treatment, as prescribed by Article 2 of the International Assistance Law. In practice, diplomatic channels are used to request judicial assistance. The request and all supporting documents must be translated into Arabic and submitted to the relevant authority via diplomatic channels. Article 45 provides that the competent judicial authority may act provisionally in urgent situations, upon requests that have not yet satisfied the procedural requirements of the law, for instance to secure evidence that may otherwise be dispersed or damaged.

Article 43 of the International Assistance Law lists the type of judicial assistance available under the law, such as providing assistance to Foreign Judicial Authorities in identifying or locating a suspect, conducting search operations, seizing property and obtaining information and evidence.

In line with international principles of law, and similarly to most other jurisdictions, the UAE includes the concepts of 'dual criminality' and 'specialty' in the International Assistance Law. Grounds for refusal of mutual legal assistance or extradition include the presence of substantial grounds for believing that the request is based on discrimination in terms of race, religion, nationality or political opinion. The UAE does not extradite its nationals.

Corporate liability for bribery and corruption offences

Article 65 of the Federal Penal Code imposes corporate liability on legal persons (with the exception of governmental agencies and public organisations) for criminal acts committed in the name, or for the benefit, of the entity. This is a general provision of the Federal Penal Code and is not limited to bribery and corruption offences. The maximum fine that can be imposed on a corporation is currently AED50,000. In addition to corporate liability, the individual(s) who committed the crime may also be prosecuted.

Proposed reforms / The year ahead

In May 2015, the Abu Dhabi Executive Council (the local Executive Authority for the Emirate of Abu Dhabi) issued a directive to the Abu Dhabi Accountability Authority instructing the establishment of an Anti-Corruption Unit. The date for establishment of the unit has not been announced at the time of writing. The unit's responsibilities will be twofold: (i) investigation into corruption and financial violations; and (ii) addressing deficiencies within the legislative framework so as to strengthen the defence mechanism and eventually lead to a reduction in the number of corruption-related crimes.

Khalid AlHamrani
Tel: +971 4 364 1641 / Email: k.hamrani@tamimi.com

Khalid AlHamrani is an Emirati lawyer and the Regional Head of Al Tamimi & Company's Financial Crime Practice. He has extensive experience representing government-owned corporations, financial institutions and high-profile clients in corporate commercial fraud, bribery and money laundering cases including multiple jurisdictions. Khalid has also dealt with compliance and regulatory matters involving government authorities in the UAE along with forgery and embezzlement-related matters.

Ibtissem Lassoued
Tel: +971 4 364 1641 / Email: i.lassoued@tamimi.com

Ibtissem Lassoued is a Partner in the Regional Financial Crime Practice at Al Tamimi & Company. She has extensive experience advising a variety of clientele on a spectrum of white-collar crime matters which have spanned the globe. These include complex corporate fraud, tracing, freezing and recovery of assets, anti-money laundering, anti-terrorism, extradition (acting both for States submitting extradition requests and individuals who are subject to a request) and mutual judicial cooperation, including issues relating to foreign judgments and Interpol notices.

Furthermore, she advises clients on international economic sanctions, boycott regulations, embezzlement, fraud and corruption, including advising multinational companies, global banks and international firms, and assisting with multijurisdictional investigations where the applicability of foreign regulations needs to be considered (e.g. the anti-corruption laws such as the US FCPA and the UK Bribery Act).

Andrew Hudson
Tel: +971 4 364 1641 / Email: a.hudson@tamimi.com

Andrew Hudson is an English-qualified Barrister and a Senior Associate in Al Tamimi & Company's Financial Crime Practice. He was previously a Prosecutor for the Crown Prosecution Service in England.

Andrew acts for individual and corporate clients in issues relating to white-collar crime including fraud and embezzlement, bribery and corruption. He also advises clients in respect of economic sanctions and other boycott regulations and has experience of dealing with cases involving mutual legal assistance and extradition.

Al Tamimi & Company

Floor 6, Building 4 East, Dubai International Financial Centre, PO Box 9275, Dubai, UAE
Tel: +971 4 364 1641 / Fax: +971 4 364 1777 / URL: http://www.tamimi.com

United Kingdom

Jonathan Pickworth & Jo Dimmock
White & Case LLP

Brief overview of the law and enforcement regime

The main legislation in the UK governing bribery and corruption is the Bribery Act 2010 (the "**Act**"), which came into force on 1 July 2011.

The Act defines the criminal offences of bribery very widely and includes the principal offences of bribing another person, being bribed and bribing a foreign public official. Significantly, the Act also introduced a new strict liability corporate offence of failure to prevent bribery, where the only defence available to commercial organisations is for them to show that they have "adequate procedures" in place to prevent bribery.

There have been very few cases prosecuted under the Act and those which have occurred we address below. The powers contained within the Act to prosecute corporate entities have not yet been used and, accordingly, the pre-existing authorities continue to be a determining factor for any intended prosecution in the pipeline. However, the Government has taken steps to raise the profile of the UK response to tackling corruption; in December 2014, the Government published the first *UK Anti-Corruption Plan,* in which it stated that its priorities were to raise international standards and lead the global fight against corruption in all its forms,[1] and in May 2015, a new government anti-corruption coordinator was appointed in the Cabinet Office. Accordingly, we expect to see a growing number of cases prosecuted under the 2010 Act.

The principal bribery offences

The offence of bribing another person includes offering, promising or giving a financial or other advantage intending to induce or reward improper conduct, or knowing or believing its acceptance to amount to improper conduct.[2] "Improper" means breaching an expectation of good faith, impartiality or trust. The bribe does not actually have to be given; just offering it, even if not accepted, could be sufficient to constitute bribery. In addition, the offer does not have to be explicit, and any offer made through a third party will fall within the Act.

An individual being bribed also commits an offence under the Act.[3] This includes requesting, agreeing to receive or accepting a financial or other advantage where that constitutes improper conduct, or intending improper conduct to follow, or as a reward for acting improperly.

There is a separate offence under the Act of bribing a foreign public official to gain or retain a business advantage.[4] In contrast to the offences above, this does not require evidence of an intention on the part of the person bribing to induce improper conduct, or knowledge or belief that its acceptance will amount to improper conduct; only that the person bribing intends to influence the official acting in his or her official capacity. Unlike the US Foreign Corrupt Practices Act 1977 ("**FCPA**"), as amended, facilitation payments (also known as "grease" payments) are not permitted under the Act.

The corporate offence of failure to prevent bribery

It is possible for a corporate body and its senior officers to be found guilty of any of the general offences of bribing, being bribed and bribing a foreign public official. For a corporate body to be found guilty of the general offences, the prosecution must show that the necessary mental element can be attributed to the directing mind of the corporate body. For senior officers, it is necessary to show that the offence has been committed with the consent or connivance of such a senior officer.[5]

The significance of the new and separate corporate offence of failing to prevent bribery is that it is not necessary to show that any senior officer had any particular mental element, removing a critical obstacle for the prosecution in taking action against corporate entities.

The corporate offence is committed by a relevant commercial organisation where a person "associated" with it bribes a person with the intention of obtaining business or a business advantage for that organisation.[6] For the purposes of the Act, an "associated" person is widely defined as a person who performs services for, or on behalf of, the relevant commercial organisation. This could include not only employees or agents but also, depending on the circumstances, subsidiaries, consultants, representatives or others who perform services on the relevant commercial organisation's behalf.

The only defence available to the commercial organisation is that it had "adequate procedures" in place to prevent bribery. Section 9 of the Act requires the Secretary of State to publish guidance about such procedures; this guidance was issued on 30 March 2011[7] and set out the following key principles:

- **Proportionate procedures** – the procedures to prevent bribery should be proportionate to the bribery risks faced by the organisation and the nature, scale and complexity of the organisation's activities.
- **Top-level commitment** – senior management should be committed to preventing bribery and a senior person should have overall responsibility for the programme.
- **Risk assessment** – the organisation should carry out periodic, informed and documented assessments of its internal and external exposure to bribery, and act on them.
- **Due diligence** – appropriate checks should be carried out on persons performing services for the organisation, and those persons should in turn be required to carry out similar checks on the persons they deal with.
- **Communication (including training)** – bribery prevention policies should be clearly communicated internally and externally, and there should be continuous training.
- **Monitoring and review** – the risks and procedures should be regularly monitored and reviewed to ensure that they are being followed in practice.

Extra-territorial reach

Importantly, under the Act, the act of bribery itself does not necessarily need to have occurred in the UK for the offence to have been committed.

In relation to the general offences of bribing, being bribed or bribing a foreign public official, provided the person committing the offence has a close connection with the UK (for example, they are, among others: a British citizen; a British overseas territories citizen; ordinarily resident in the UK; or a body incorporated in the UK), the physical act of bribery can occur inside or outside of the UK.[8] This means that an individual who is a citizen of, for example, the British Virgin Islands or Bermuda, will be subject to these laws even if the act occurs entirely outside of the UK mainland itself and the individual is not, and never has been, a British citizen.

The corporate offence of failure to prevent bribery is not just confined to acts of bribery carried out in the UK. Provided the organisation is incorporated or formed in the UK, or the organisation carries on a business or part of a business in the UK (wherever in the world it is incorporated), then the organisation is within the ambit of the offence, wherever the act of bribery takes place. The guidance issued by the Secretary of State asserts that the question of whether or not an organisation carries out a business or part of its business in any part of the UK will be answered by applying a common sense approach, and the final arbiter in any particular case will be the courts (who have not yet had the opportunity to do so at the date of writing). The guidance states that the Government would not expect, for example, the mere fact that a company's securities have been admitted to the UKLA's official list and are trading on the London Stock Exchange to, in itself, qualify that company as such for the purposes of the corporate offence. Likewise, in relation to a UK subsidiary of a foreign parent company, since a subsidiary may act independently of its parent company, its parent company may not necessarily be caught by the offence, but the point is yet to be tested.

Investigating and prosecuting authorities

According to the Joint Prosecution Guidance on the Bribery Act 2010 issued on 30 March 2011, the Serious Fraud Office ("**SFO**") is the primary agency in England and Wales for investigating and prosecuting cases of overseas corruption; the Crown Prosecution Service ("**CPS**") also prosecutes bribery offences investigated by the police, committed either overseas or in England and Wales.[9]

Accordingly, in England and Wales, consent needs to be sought from the Director of Public Prosecutions ("**DPP**") or the Director of the SFO for proceedings to be initiated for offences under the Act. They will make this decision in accordance with the Code for Crown Prosecutors (applying the two-stage test of whether there is sufficient evidence to provide a realistic prospect of conviction, and whether a prosecution is in the public interest), and also by taking into account the Joint Prosecution Guidance on the Bribery Act 2010, together with the Joint Guidance on Corporate Prosecutions, where relevant.

The prosecutor with responsibility for offences under the Act in Scotland is the Lord Advocate; in Northern Ireland, the Director of Public Prosecutions for Northern Ireland and the Director of the SFO are responsible.

Penalties

The penalty for an individual convicted of any of the general offences under the Act is a maximum of 10 years' imprisonment and/or an unlimited fine. A commercial organisation convicted under the Act can face an unlimited fine. In addition to any fine and/or imprisonment, a person can face forfeiture of the proceeds of crime (under the Proceeds of Crime Act 2002). Forfeiture can be by way of a criminal process known as confiscation, or by way of a civil process known as a civil recovery order ("**CRO**").

The Sentencing Council Definitive Guidelines on Fraud, Bribery and Money Laundering Offences, effective from 1 October 2014, provides Criminal Courts with guidance on how to approach sentence against individuals and commercial organisations in cases of bribery and corruption.

The high-level fines specified for the sentencing of corporate offenders suggest that heavy reliance has been placed upon deterrent sentencing as a means of enforcing the Bribery Act. The Guidelines indicate that the Criminal Courts must first consider making a compensation order, requiring an offender to pay compensation for any personal injury, loss or damage resulting from the offence. Confiscation must then be considered if either the Crown asks for it or if the court thinks that it may be appropriate. Confiscation must be dealt with before, and taken into account when assessing, any other fine or financial order (except compensation).[10] The Guidelines state that the level of fine will be determined by reference to the culpability and harm caused by the offending corporation. Examples of high culpability are:

- corporation plays a leading role in organised, planned unlawful activity (whether acting alone or with others);
- corruption of local or national government officials or ministers; and
- corruption of officials performing a law enforcement role.

An example of lesser culpability will be where some effort has been made to put bribery prevention measures in place but insufficient to amount to a defence (s.7 Bribery Act only).

Harm should be represented by a financial sum calculated as the gross profit from the contract obtained, retained or sought as a result of the offending. An alternative measure for offences under s.7 may be the likely cost avoided by failing to put in place appropriate measures to prevent bribery. The fine is calculated by the level of culpability multiplied by the harm figure. For instance, a case in which the court determines the corporation's role to have been of high culpability would multiply the harm figure by around 300%. In circumstances where the gross profit from a contract obtained was £1,000,000 the level of fine would, therefore, constitute *circa* £3,000,000 (300% x £1,000,000). A case determined by the court to involve low culpability would multiply the harm figure by around 100%.

Other consequences that may flow from a conviction under the Act include directors' disqualification and trade sanctions, such as disbarment from EU contract tenders.

Civil bribery

In addition to the criminal offences under the Act, there is long-established case law in the UK relating to the civil tort of bribery. This concerns the payment of secret commissions to agents without the principal's knowledge or consent. Where the payer is aware of the agency relationship and the payment is kept secret from the principal, there is an irrebuttable presumption of corruption. If a claim for bribery is made, the principal may be entitled to recovery of an amount equal to the bribe paid. Indeed, in a recent case (*FHR European Ventures LLP & Ors v Cedar Capital Partners LLC),* the Supreme Court decided that bribes and secret commissions are held on trust by an agent for his principal.

Overview of enforcement activity and policy during the past two years

Prosecutions of individuals

There have already been three individual prosecutions under the Act. The first case (*R v Patel (Munir)*) involved a clerk in the magistrates' court who had agreed to accept a £500 bribe in return for altering court records to help an individual avoid being charged for a road traffic violation. Even though the defendant in that case pled guilty to the bribery allegation, he was nonetheless sentenced on conviction to six years' imprisonment – three years for the Act offence and six years for misfeasance in public office (later reduced to four years on appeal) to run concurrently. The second case (*R v Mushtaq*) involved a person taking a test for a private hire taxi licence. When he failed, he offered £200 or £300 to the licensing officer to change the result. Mr Mushtaq was convicted of bribery and sentenced to two months' imprisonment, suspended for 12 months. In terms of penalties, these cases can be distinguished on their facts; the former related to an individual who held a public office, and the acts of receiving a bribe represented a severe breach of trust.

The third case (*R v Li*) involved a Chinese student attempting to bribe his professor at the University of Bath by placing £5,000 on the table and stating the professor could keep the money if his dissertation mark was raised to a pass. The professor refused and, when the student replaced the money in his pocket, he dropped an imitation firearm on the floor. Mr Li was convicted of bribery and possession of an imitation firearm and sentenced to 12 months' imprisonment and six months' imprisonment for the offences respectively, to run concurrently.

The fourth, and most recent, case resulted in the first convictions for the SFO under the Bribery Act 2010 on 5 December 2014. They secured sentences of 28 years in total for three men. The prosecution focused on the selling and promotion of Sustainable Agro Energy investment products based on "green biofuel" Jatropha tree plantations in Cambodia. The green biofuel products were sold to UK investors who invested primarily via self-invested pension plans (SIPPS). These investors were deliberately misled into believing that SAE owned land in Cambodia; that the land was planted with Jatropha trees and that there was an insurance policy in place to protect investors if the crops failed. When handing down sentence HHJ Beddoe described the fraud as a "*thickening quagmire of dishonesty... there were more than 250 victims of relatively modest means some of whom had lost all of their life savings and their homes*". The judge added that the bribery was an aggravating feature.[11]

In addition to these three prosecutions under the Bribery Act, the SFO has continued to take enforcement action under the pre-existing legislation. Four individuals were convicted in June 2014 of conspiracy to commit corruption and were sentenced in August 2014 to periods of imprisonment ranging from 16 months' suspended sentence to four years for their respective roles in the Innospec corruption case. Innospec itself was fined $12.7m in March 2010. In his sentencing remarks, the judge commented that "corruption in this company was endemic, institutionalised and ingrained... but despite being a separate legal entity it is not an automated machine; decisions are made by human minds". The one individual who received a suspended sentence avoided jail only because of the level of cooperation he provided to the investigating and prosecuting authority. Separately, the former CEO of Aluminium Bahrain B.S.C ("Alba") was sentenced to 16 months in prison in July 2014 for conspiracy to corrupt in relation to contracts for the supply of goods and services to Alba. In addition to his prison sentence (which was reduced because of his cooperation) he was required to pay a confiscation order of over £3m, compensation to Alba, and prosecution costs totalling in excess of £600,000. These cases demonstrate that the SFO has the ability and intent to prosecute under pre-existing bribery legislation, and the SFO has recently reiterated its "appetite to take on new cases... if the evidence leads that way".

Prosecutions of commercial organisations

At the time of writing, the UK is yet to see any corporate prosecutions under the Act, either for a principal offence or for the new corporate offence. Nonetheless, the SFO – which is the main investigating and prosecuting agency for cases of overseas corruption and serious and complex fraud – has stated publicly that it has a number of cases under investigation.

The new strict liability offence of failing to prevent bribery is perceived to be much easier to prosecute than the principal bribery offences under sections 1, 2 or 6 of the Act, referred to above. The main reason for this is that the section 7 offence is committed on a strict liability basis, where a bribe has been paid by someone who performs services for, or on behalf of, the relevant commercial organisation. Unlike the principal bribery offences, it does not require the prosecutor to establish intent on the part of a directing mind of the company.

The only defence for the corporate offence is for the company to show that it had in place "adequate procedures" to prevent the bribery from taking place. As a result, it is expected that any decision as to whether or not to prosecute will involve detailed consideration of the procedures that the suspect company has had in place and how they have been implemented. It is important to emphasise here that the focus will not just be on what the written procedures look like, but how they have operated in practice. The prosecutor will be looking at questions such as:

- What is the tone from the top, and does this company really subscribe to anti-corruption compliance in its truest sense?
- Has this company undertaken a properly documented risk assessment? Without this, it will be difficult for a company to show that it has put in place appropriate and proportionate procedures to plug the risk gaps.
- What do its written procedures look like, and are they adequate?
- How does the company go about the process of due diligence on third parties who perform certain services on its behalf?
- Is the training adequate?
- To what extent has the company monitored compliance, evaluated the adequacies of its procedures and assessed the true understanding of its employees and agents?

It remains to be seen how each of these aspects will be dealt with in practice as part of a prosecution, but to a large extent, the way that the section 7 offence is worded means that the onus of establishing "adequate procedures" will actually be on the company as defendant to the proceedings. All that the prosecutor will have to establish is that a bribe has been offered, promised or paid, even if the individual who committed the bribery offence has not himself been prosecuted.

The SFO has announced a number of investigations during 2014 including one into the commercial practices of GlaxoSmithKline plc and its subsidiary following the widely reported corruption allegations in China. In July 2014 the SFO announced criminal charges against Alstom in the UK in respect of three corruption offences under the Prevention of Corruption Act 1906 and three offences of conspiracy to corrupt contrary to the Criminal Law Act 1977 relating to matters which allegedly took place between June 2000 and November 2006 in India, Poland and Tunisia. The historic nature of the alleged offences and, in particular, the fact that they pre-date the coming into force of the Bribery Act, means that this matter will be dealt with under the old legislation rather than under the new Bribery Act.

Previous corporate prosecutions and civil settlements

Although the Act came into force on 1 July 2011, the UK had secured a number of corporate convictions prior to that date. Indeed, matters may still fall to be prosecuted under the pre-existing law for offences committed prior to 1 July 2011. In 2009, Mabey & Johnson, a bridge-building company, was the first corporate prosecution, convicted for paying bribes in Iraq, Jamaica and Ghana (three of its directors and officers were later prosecuted in February 2011). This prosecution was closely followed by Innospec (a fuel additives company which paid bribes in Indonesia and Iraq) and BAE Systems in 2010. It should be noted that BAE Systems was only convicted of keeping inadequate accounting records in the UK as part of a plea settlement reached, giving rise to some criticism of the SFO (there was also a conviction in the US).

There have also been a number of civil settlements, including those with Balfour Beatty, AMEC, Oxford University Press and M W Kellogg, where CROs of £2.25m, just under £5m, £1.9m and £7m respectively were agreed with the companies concerned. The approach of the SFO in resolving a number of potential corporate prosecutions by way of civil settlement has been criticised in some quarters. The OECD Bribery Working Group in its 2012 report criticised the UK Government not for the fact of its use of civil settlements *per se*, but rather because of the lack of transparency surrounding its decisions to adopt the civil settlement route rather than prosecution. As a result, we can expect to see much greater scrutiny of civil settlements in the future. Regardless of whether the trend for civil settlements with companies continues, it is anticipated that the individuals involved in bribery cases will still be prosecuted.

The recent position, however, of the current SFO leadership is that it is less inclined to use the civil settlement process than was the case under the previous regime. This is consistent with the approach taken in recent years by other UK prosecutorial agencies, with dual civil and criminal powers, such as the Financial Conduct Authority.

Interaction with other regulatory agencies

The interaction with the UK's money laundering regime, which requires reporting to the Serious Organised Crime Agency ("**SOCA**") and applies very strictly to the regulated sector (but also in a number of circumstances to other business sectors), further complicates the position. Any suspicion that a bribery offence has been committed (together with any past or future revenues that flow from contracts related to such bribes) may need to be reported to SOCA.

Any regulated firms in the financial services sector are also subject to the enforcement powers of the financial regulator in the UK: the Financial Conduct Authority ("**FCA**") or Prudential Regulatory Authority ("**PRA**"), as the case may be (previously the Financial Services Authority ("**FSA**")). The significance of this is that any conduct relating to bribery or corruption risks may also constitute a breach of the rules and/or principles of the FCA Handbook, but, unlike the SFO, there is no need for the FCA to necessarily prove the act of bribery itself. For example, the FSA took enforcement action against the companies Aon Limited, Willis Limited, JLT Speciality Limited and most recently, Besso Limited for failing to take reasonable care in establishing effective systems and controls for countering the risk of bribery and corruption, in relation to payments made to third party overseas representatives. The FSA fined Aon £5.25m in 2009; Willis was fined just under £7m in 2011, JLT Speciality Limited paid over £1.8m to the FCA in December 2013, and Besso Limited was fined £315,000 in March 2014.

The FCA (and before it, the FSA) has undertaken a number of thematic reviews into different sectors of the financial services industry. It started with insurance brokers, then the investment banks and at the end of 2013 published the findings of its thematic review into the activities of asset managers. The FCA has expressed great disappointment that the financial services industry as a whole has failed to learn the lessons of others, as it had identified similar themes throughout each of these thematic reviews. The most significant failings relate to the due diligence of agents (both from an anti-money laundering and anti-bribery perspective), as described in further detail below.

In May 2014, the British Bankers Association (BBA) published new guidance to assist the banking sector comply with the Bribery Act, again demonstrating that the Act is being viewed seriously by the financial sector.

There are also indications that Her Majesty's Revenue and Customs ("**HMRC**") is using the Act during its enquiries and investigations into taxpayers. Although the extent of this is not clear, UK taxpayers should be wary that there are permitted information gateways between HMRC (and other regulators) and the SFO in relation to the sharing of information regarding illegal activities. The relevance of the Act to HMRC is that some companies may be claiming tax deductions for overseas bribes (which is no longer permitted) and are therefore under-declaring tax.

Cooperation with other global enforcement agencies

The development of an increasing level of cooperation between the UK authorities and other global regulators in the fight against corruption is also apparent. For example, in the case of Depuy International Limited, a company designing orthopaedic and neurosurgery devices, the SFO obtained a CRO for £4.829m in April 2011, in recognition of the company's unlawful conduct in relation to the sale of orthopaedic products in Greece between 1998 and 2006. This case demonstrated cooperation between international enforcement agencies, as the SFO launched its investigation following a referral from the US Department of Justice (as the case involved payments from Depuy International Limited (a UK entity) to intermediaries for the purpose of making corrupt payments to Greek medical professionals) and worked closely with both the Department of Justice and the US Securities and Exchange Commission (SEC). More recently, the investigation into the corruption allegations against GlaxoSmithKline by Chinese authorities has been bolstered by investigations by the SFO and the US Department of Justice.

In the UK, the Crime (International Cooperation) Act 2003 empowers judges and prosecutors to issue requests to obtain evidence from another country for use in domestic proceedings or investigations. Additionally, the Proceeds of Crime Act 2002 enables prosecutors to send requests for restraint and confiscation to the Secretary of State for onward transmission to the relevant authority abroad. The UK is also party to numerous mutual legal assistance treaties, such as those with the US, Hong Kong and other EU Member States. The proposed treaty between the UK and China on Mutual Assistance in Criminal Matters was presented to the UK Parliament in July 2014, but at the time of writing, has not yet entered into force.

Hot topics

Three areas in particular have led to much debate in the UK: facilitation payments; gifts and entertainment; and due diligence of agents and third parties.

Facilitation payments

Facilitation payments are illegal under the Act. This is not a new offence, as facilitation payments (or so-called "grease" payments, whereby a modest sum of money or relatively small gifts are paid or given to government employees in order to encourage the recipient to exercise a function which he should be doing anyway) have always been contrary to UK law. Typical examples are: payments to customs officials to prevent or mitigate delay in passing goods through customs; or payments to secure licences, permits, etc. In outlawing facilitation payments, the UK takes a different approach from the USA (see the USA chapter in this book), with the UK's position in fact being in alignment with the law of most other countries around the world.

One common misconception is that facilitation payments must be modest in amount, and there is a significant risk that larger individual payments might not easily be characterised as "facilitation payments". It does not matter that there is no intent to corrupt the government official in question, provided that the payment is made in order to "influence" the official, or is made with the intention of obtaining or retaining business or an advantage in the conduct of business. If so, an offence is committed under the Act. The SFO guidance on facilitation payments was withdrawn in October 2012 and replaced with a new statement of policy, which removed any reference there had been in the previous guidance to acknowledging that it would take time to eradicate facilitation payments in certain countries.

In essence, the new SFO policy statement represents a hardening of the SFO's stance in relation to facilitation payments.

In May 2013, however, press reports in the UK indicated that there was a move to encourage the UK Government to soften the law in relation to facilitation payments, as it was causing an unnecessary burden on small and medium-sized enterprises. The Confederation of British Industries indicated that it supports this approach, but it remains to be seen whether there will indeed be any relaxation of the law in this regard. It is the authors' current view that any relaxation of the law, particularly in relation to businesses of a certain size, is unlikely in the near future.

Gifts and hospitality

Another issue which has caused much consternation since the coming into force of the Act relates to gifts and hospitality. In many respects there has been a disproportionate emphasis by companies on their gifts and entertainment policy. Cash gifts and other gifts, entertainments, or other advantage of a lavish and substantial nature, could potentially lead to allegations of bribery. The SFO is, however, keen to ensure that the emphasis of the requirements around gifts and entertainment is not overstated. David Green QC, the current Director of the SFO, said in October 2012 that the SFO was interested in the cases that were of the most serious nature, where it was in the public interest for the SFO to prosecute. "We are not the Serious Champagne Office," he said, thereby giving a stark indication of the likely level of interest the SFO would pay to corporate hospitality. This is consistent with the approach taken by the Ministry of Justice in its guidance that was issued prior to the implementation of the Act, whereby it was made clear that it was not the Government's intention to stamp out all forms of entertainment and hospitality.

It is clear that companies should have in place appropriate policies and procedures for gifts, entertainment and hospitality, but that this should not be to the detriment of any focus on other forms of potential bribery and corruption. There are much more significant risk areas for most companies.

Due diligence of agents and other third parties

It is submitted that the greatest area of risk for many companies operating across borders lies in the use of agents or other third parties to win business abroad. This is particularly so in the context of dealings with foreign governments (and where the threshold test, as discussed above, is much lower). The level and extent of appropriate due diligence is often difficult to determine, and represents a necessary but sometimes intrusive exercise. It is important to ensure that such due diligence is undertaken at a sufficiently early stage in the process, and that the results of the process are properly scrutinised. Most of the UK and US FCPA enforcement actions to date have related to bribery where an agent or other third party was involved.

Whistleblowing

The UK Government took action through the Enterprise and Regulatory Reform Act 2013 ('ERRA') to strengthen whistleblowing protections. The ERRA received Royal Assent on 25 April 2013 and makes an explicit requirement that all disclosures must be in the public interest, in order to be protected by the Public Interest Disclosure Act 1998. Given this new public interest test, the previous legal requirement that a disclosure had to be made in 'good faith' was removed. These two provisions were effective from 25 June 2013.

Under the ERRA, co-workers and other agents of an employer are to be made personally liable if they subject a worker to bad treatment or victimisation because they have made a protected disclosure. In addition, employers will be vicariously liable (partly responsible) for these actions, unless they can demonstrate that they have taken 'all reasonable steps' to prevent their workers from acting in this way. Given that fear of reprisals is a major barrier to people who wish to raise concerns, this will be a significant improvement.

In July 2013 the UK Government published a *Call for Evidence* to assess the existing protections and consider if further changes are required to the Whistleblowing Framework.[12] In December 2014, HM Government issued a *UK Anti-Corruption Plan* in which it stated that there was a need to support those who help to identify and disrupt corruption, and that the recent *Call for Evidence* consultation had highlighted support to introduce financial incentives for whistleblowers in cases of bribery and corruption. The results of a Home Office and BIS consultation on what more can be done to incentivise and support whistleblowers in such cases is due to be published in October 2015.

Key issues relating to investigation, decision making and enforcement

Self-reporting

Until October 2012, the SFO had indicated the potential for matters that had been self-reported to the SFO to be dealt with through a civil process. However, since 2012, the SFO has been very keen to emphasise its role as prosecutor, and has stated that "self-reporting is no guarantee that a prosecution will not follow". At most, it will be a public interest factor tending against prosecution, as explained in the Joint Guidance on Corporate Prosecutions. However, the SFO has also recently stated that the self-report can also be the single most important factor in a decision not to prosecute.

In recent speeches, the SFO has reiterated its stance on self-reporting; that is that it cannot accept such reports at face value, and that it will need to conduct its own independent investigation, especially in cases where the company in question denies any wrongdoing. It is for this reason that the SFO encourages companies to report early and to agree with the SFO whether, and if so, on what terms they might commission an investigation.

Despite the SFO's comments, however, the current regime for corporate self-reporting comes with a lot more uncertainty than was previously the case. The success of a self-reporting regime will depend on whether there is sufficient incentivisation to do so or, indeed, enough potential downside from not doing so. The considerations to take into account in such circumstances are numerous and complex and it is rare for a company to self-report to the SFO without taking legal advice. Companies considering a self-report should take specialist advice on the potential consequences, as well as the process.

Commercial pressure

The Act has received such publicity in the UK that most commercial organisations have been quick to put in place procedures to combat the risk of bribery and corruption. Anti-bribery compliance is now much more readily seen as an item on the board agenda than it has been at any point in the past. The extent to which compliance failings will in fact lead to prosecution or other action by the law enforcement authorities remains to be seen. The SFO has access to additional funding from the government where necessary, but nonetheless it is expected that funding will always present something of an issue, as will the SFO's own resources. That is not to say that it would be safe to rely on the assumption that the SFO would not have the funds and resources to investigate or prosecute a particular case. It does, however, mean that there will have to be some reliance on the corporate world policing itself and, in particular, making self-reporting work. The SFO cannot be expected to investigate every allegation, and the senior management of companies which uncover acts of suspected corruption need to be able to consider sensibly whether it is in the company's interests to report their suspicions to the SFO.

Witness accounts and legal privilege

The SFO has recently stated that its interest is focused on facts, as inherent in accurate and complete first accounts of witnesses spoken to as part of corporate investigations, and encourages companies to consult SFO investigators before questioning important witnesses.

The SFO has made it clear companies should be prepared to waive legal privilege in appropriate cases, stating that an assertion of legal privilege over witness accounts is unhelpful and impossible to reconcile with an assertion of a company's willingness to cooperate. A company's decision to waive legal privilege will be seen as an obvious sign of cooperation but if a company has a well-founded claim to privilege and opts to uphold privilege, then this will not be held against it. However, the SFO has indicated that it is prepared to litigate in cases where it finds claims of privilege to be false or exaggerated, but such litigation is to be a last resort. Lastly, if despite the existence of a well-made-out claim, a company still proceeds to disclose the witness accounts sought after, the SFO will view this as a significant mark of cooperation.

Plea agreements

English law does permit plea agreements in relation to criminal proceedings in certain restricted circumstances. In relation to offences under the Act, the rules are those as set out in the Consolidated Criminal Practice Direction: Pleas of Guilty in the Crown Court, and the Attorney-General's Guidelines on Plea Discussions in Cases of Serious or Complex Fraud. Significantly, the judge will always have complete discretion regarding what sentence is eventually given, which raises the question of how useful the settlement can actually be between the SFO and the defendant. The first case where the SFO used a plea agreement was in Mabey & Johnson, followed by Innospec and BAE Systems, however, the judiciary has been critical of such agreements, particularly in the latter two cases. In BAE Systems, given that the deal was structured so unusually (for BAE to pay the people of Tanzania £30m minus any fine imposed by the court), undue pressure was probably placed on the court to minimise any fine it imposed.

Deferred prosecution agreements

The Crime and Courts Act 2013, the relevant provisions of which came into force on 24 February 2014, introduced a new enforcement tool into the UK – deferred prosecution agreements ("**DPAs**") from 24 February 2014. DPAs can be used in cases involving financial crime, including bribery and corruption. Given that there have been very few prosecutions so far under the Act; it could be the case that we shall see some of the first DPAs used for bribery offences.

DPAs are voluntary agreements entered into between prosecutors and corporate and unincorporated entities (but not individuals) under which a prosecutor agrees not to commence criminal proceedings, provided there is compliance by the entity with a range of conditions. Such conditions, for example, may include the payment of penalties, and the implementation of training and compliance programmes. A pre-requisite appears to be a self-report from the company under investigation, which meets the standards expected by the SFO. In particular, the SFO has been keen to emphasise that it will not be prepared to engage in discussions about resolution by way of a DPA in circumstances where the company has declined to waive legal professional privilege over witness statements obtained by the company or its lawyers in the course of its own internal investigation, i.e. cooperation means full cooperation. It has also been very critical of self-reports prepared by law firms that do not have the right level of expertise or independence.

Once negotiations have begun in relation to a DPA, the Director of the SFO or the DPP (as the case may be) must apply to the Crown Court. The court will need to agree that the DPA is likely to be in the interests of justice and the proposed terms of the DPA are fair, reasonable and proportionate. This first hearing may be in private, with a further hearing in open court if the judge determines that the DPA is appropriate. If, once the DPA is agreed, the prosecutor believes that there has been a breach of the terms of the agreement, it can apply to the court, who can determine if there has been a breach and ask the parties to remedy the breach or terminate the DPA. Similarly, any variation will need to be approved by the court.

A joint code ("**the DPA Code**") published by the Director of the SFO and the DPP sets out the prosecutors' approach to the use of DPAs.

It is intended that any financial penalty under a DPA shall be broadly comparable to a fine that the court would have imposed upon the organisation following a guilty plea. This is intended to enable the parties and the courts to have regard to sentencing guidelines in order to determine the penalty. Under the new Sentencing Council Guidelines for corporate offenders introduced in January 2014, organisations can expect to receive a fine of 20 to 400 times the "harm" caused by the misconduct concerned. "Harm" is to be defined as the gross amount obtained or loss avoided as a result of the offence. The guidelines state that for bribery this will be the "gross profit from the contract obtained, retained or sought", or the cost of avoiding putting in place adequate procedures.

Organisations that enter into DPAs can expect a reduction of one-third of any fine (the same as entering an early guilty plea), or potentially a further reduction in certain cases, for example where an organisation assists the authorities. Any reduction in the financial penalty will very much depend upon the discretion of the judiciary: one indication from recent case law (*R v Dougall*) suggests that the judiciary will not welcome leniency that goes beyond what is offered for an early guilty plea. A further related consideration is how, in practice, the judiciary will react to agreements which have essentially been negotiated outside of the court system by the SFO or CPS rather than through the usual sentencing process. In *R v Innospec (2010)*, Lord Justice Thomas was reluctant in his approval of the global settlement reached by US and UK authorities in connection with bribing government officials in Indonesia, stating that the imposition of a sentence except for minor offences is a matter for the judiciary.

The DPA Code and sentencing guidelines bring greater clarity to the DPA process itself and the guiding factors for and against prosecution, particularly in relation to self-reporting. The factors set out in the DPA Code make it clear that DPAs are available only to pro-active, genuine and complete reports and the SFO has recently re-emphasised its position that a company which reports a problem to the SFO early and genuinely cooperates in resolving the issue is unlikely to be prosecuted. Recent guidance by the SFO has also given increased clarity as to what constitutes genuine cooperation, which refers to: (i) bringing new information to the regulator within a reasonable period of the incident being uncovered; (ii) allowing access to first-hand witness accounts by limiting legal privilege; and (iii) proper cooperation with the SFO case controller. Such cooperation will be judged by actions, not words. The Sentencing Guidelines Council issued a statement in January 2014 in which they noted that *while a DPA is not a criminal conviction and so the Sentencing Council cannot produce a guideline for them, the guidance can be used to inform the level of financial penalty that forms part of a DPA, which should be broadly comparable to the likely fine that would be imposed following a conviction after a guilty plea.*[13] The Definitive Guidelines on Fraud, Bribery and Money Laundering Offences are, therefore, to be referred to by judges operating the DPA scheme but will not yet be used in courts to sentence organisations that have been successfully prosecuted.

Accordingly, it appears that the onerous and deterrent sentencing regime that applies to corporate offenders under the bribery sentencing guidelines will also apply to DPAs.

In May 2015, the SFO confirmed that it had issued the first invitation letters to companies that had pled guilty to corporate wrongdoing, inviting them to enter into DPA negotiations.[14] It is yet to be seen whether these negotiations have proved successful.

It is not yet known how DPAs will interact with ongoing investigations by overseas regulators, and it remains to be seen how this discretionary tool will be used by prosecutors in practice.

Proposed reforms

There has been considerable development since 2010 in relation to the UK enforcement of bribery and corruption, both domestically and overseas. Now we expect to see a period of consolidation and testing of these new laws, policies and procedures. As this book reaches its third edition, we expect to be able to report on a number of corporate prosecutions under the Bribery Act and on several DPAs.

The UK Government and the SFO's current Director are enthused by the strict liability corporate offence of failing to prevent bribery. So much so that serious consideration is being given to expanding that offence to one of "failing to prevent financial crime". At a stroke, this would expand the current offence to one which counters not only bribery and corruption, but also fraud, money laundering, insider trading and economic sanctions, amongst others. It is not, however, expected that any such proposal will be put before UK Parliament prior to the next General Election in 2020.

* * *

Endnotes

1. https://www.gov.uk/government/uploads/system/uploads/attachment_data/file/388894/UKantiCorruptionPlan.pdf, p.6.
2. s. 1, Bribery Act 2010.
3. s. 2, Bribery Act 2010.
4. s. 6, Bribery Act 2010.
5. s. 14, Bribery Act 2010.
6. s. 7, Bribery Act 2010.
7. The Bribery Act 2010: Guidance about procedures that relevant commercial organisations can put in place to prevent persons associated with them from bribing another person (s. 9 of the Bribery Act 2010).
8. s. 12, Bribery Act 2010.
9. Proceedings for an offence under the Bribery Act 2010 may also be instituted with the consent of the Director of Revenue and Customs Prosecutions.
10. Sentencing Council Definitive Guideline, Fraud, Bribery and Money Laundering Offences, 1 October 2014, p.49.
11. http://www.sfo.gov.uk/press-room/latest-press-releases/press-releases-2014/city-directors-sentenced-to-28-years-in-total-for-23m-green-biofuel-fraud.aspx.
12. https://www.gov.uk/government/uploads/system/uploads/attachment_data/file/212076/bis-13-953-whistleblowing-framework-call-for-evidence.pdf.
13. https://www.sentencingcouncil.org.uk/news/item/new-sentencing-guideline-for-corporate-fraud/.
14. http://sfo.gov.uk/about-us/our-views/other-speeches/speeches-2015/ben-morgan-compliance-and-cooperation.aspx.

Jonathan Pickworth
Tel: +44 207 532 1663 / Email: jonathan.pickworth@whitecase.com
Jonathan Pickworth advises clients on regulatory and internal investigations, compliance and risk, with particular reference to corruption, market misconduct, fraud, tax fraud and money laundering. He has considerable expertise in relation to the handling of investigations by Government agencies such as the Serious Fraud Office, the Financial Conduct Authority and HM Revenue & Customs. He also advises and is a regular speaker on the Bribery Act, enforcement issues and managing investigations.

Mr. Pickworth's work has a strong international focus. He has advised on a significant number of government, regulatory and internal investigations particularly in relation to bribery and corruption, market misconduct, fraud and money laundering. He has been involved in a number of investigations and self-reports to the SFO, HMRC and investigations by the Financial Conduct Authority into allegations of market misconduct such as LIBOR and FX benchmark manipulation, insider trading and similar matters.

Mr. Pickworth is recognised as a leading lawyer on corporate crime in the legal directories Legal 500 and Chambers. Chambers UK ranked Mr. Pickworth as a key individual with "a noted presence in the world of corporate crime" and praised him for his "extremely strong grasp of detail".

Jo Dimmock
Tel: +44 207 532 1647 / Email: joanna.dimmock@whitecase.com
Jo has broad experience across a wide range of business crime-related areas and many of her cases have an international dimension. She has particular expertise in multi-jurisdictional investigations including complex extradition, Interpol red notices and mutual legal assistance matters as well as bribery and corruption and cartel investigations undertaken by various authorities in the UK, the US, Canada and the Middle East. Jo also has considerable experience in the field of international sanctions where she has represented individuals facing restrictive measures as well as corporations requiring compliance and litigious advice arising from the enforcement of sanctions by the European Council, OFAC and the Swiss Federal Council.

White & Case LLP

5 Old Broad St, London EC2N 1DW, United Kingdom
Tel: +44 20 7532 1000 / Fax: +44 20 7532 1001 / URL: http://www.whitecase.com

USA

Jeremy B. Zucker & Darshak Dholakia
Dechert LLP

Overview

The Foreign Corrupt Practices Act ("FCPA"),[1] was passed in 1977 but has been enforced aggressively only in the past decade or so. It is the US Government's primary tool in combatting overseas bribery and corruption. The Department of Justice ("DOJ") has jurisdiction over criminal prosecutions, while the Securities and Exchange Commission ("SEC") is empowered to bring civil enforcement actions. The FCPA has a broad geographical reach and creates significant exposure for both companies and individuals.

Notably, many of the most high-profile FCPA prosecutions have been against non-US companies. For instance, the record-breaking Siemens (Germany) case in 2008 led to $800m in fines in the United States alone. The government has also shown sustained interest in taking action against individuals and has increasingly touted its cooperation with non-US authorities in investigating and prosecuting cases.

While both prosecutions and civil enforcement actions have been on the rise, many aspects of the FCPA are still relatively untested in court because defendants tend to enter pleas and/or to settle civilly with the government, often entering into a Deferred Prosecution Agreement ("DPA") or Non-Prosecution Agreement ("NPA") rather than risking a larger fine or criminal conviction. Due to the increasingly real prospect of imprisonment for bribery offences, individuals are often more willing than corporations to test government theories in court; as a result, the current government focus on prosecuting individuals may yield more litigation and therefore more case law from judges interpreting the FCPA's provisions. Thus far, however, the evolution of the FCPA has emerged largely from the government's views, reflected in the cases it chooses to bring, in advisory opinions it occasionally issues, and in the 120-page Guidance jointly issued by the DOJ and SEC in late 2012.[2] One aspect of the FCPA's contours, however – the question of who qualifies as a foreign government official – received its first treatment from a federal court of appeals in 2014, signalling the possibility of greater clarity in that area.

While the FCPA does not provide an absolute defence based on adequate anti-bribery procedures and due diligence, robust procedures are essential to mitigating FCPA exposure. If the US Government becomes aware of potential red flags or suspicious payments by a corporation, it will look for real, substantial and sustained compliance efforts, including a strong anti-corruption message from the top. Companies subject to the FCPA also should carefully consider whether to self-report violations in order to maximise the chance of a favourable resolution with the government. Even self-reporting and swift action against individuals involved in any bribery, however, cannot necessarily shield a company from liability.[3]

Basic elements of the FCPA

Bribery provision

No "issuer" (an entity whose shares are publicly traded on a US exchange, including American Depository Receipts ("ADRs"), or any officer, director, employee or agent of such an entity) or "domestic concern" (US person, or officer, director, employee or agent of a US person) may *corruptly* pay, offer, authorise, or promise to pay money or *anything of value* to a *foreign government official*, candidate for office, or political party, in order to secure an *improper advantage* and to assist in *obtaining or retaining business*.

Additionally, no person, regardless of geography, may pay or offer a bribe if any act in furtherance of the bribe occurs within the territory of the United States. The US Government takes the position that if funds pass through a US bank or an email passes through US servers, that US connection would be sufficient to expose the participants in that activity to FCPA liability. In 2013, a federal judge in New York agreed with the government that sending an email that passes through US servers could be enough of a connection to the United States to enable the government to bring an FCPA suit against a participant in a bribery scheme concerning an issuer of ADRs that otherwise occurred entirely outside of the United States.[4]

As a result, both individuals and corporations have FCPA exposure. The FCPA covers, for instance, all US citizens regardless of location, foreign subsidiaries of US entities, US parents (which may be liable for the actions of their foreign subsidiaries), foreign entities traded on US exchanges, and indeed any non-US company or national that causes an act to be done within the United States by any person acting as an agent of the non-US person. Importantly, a principal can be liable for the actions of an agent even if the principal merely turns a blind eye to the high risk of a bribe.

Books and records provision

An "issuer" must also maintain its books and records in "reasonable detail" to "accurately and fairly reflect the transactions and dispositions of [the company's] assets", and maintain adequate internal controls. Thus, if a corporation paid a bribe but did not record the expenditure *as a bribe* in its books and records, it would be subject to additional, indeed in many cases higher, penalties. The issuer's responsibility to ensure accurate books and records extends to the books and records of subsidiaries and affiliates that the issuer controls. If the issuer owns less than 50% of a subsidiary or affiliate, however, the issuer must only use its "best efforts" to cause the subsidiary or affiliate to maintain adequate accounting controls.[5] In practice, the "books and records" provision has led to many of the largest FCPA fines. Individuals can also be held civilly or criminally liable for participating in such violations. Companies may also fall foul of this provision even if not all of the elements of a bribery offence, as described above, have been met. For instance, if a corporation allowed a third-party agent to make corrupt payments to another person, but it was doubtful whether that person was a "foreign government official", the corporation could still face FCPA prosecution under the books and records provision of the FCPA if the company's books and records characterised such payments in a misleading way, for instance, recording them as consulting fees.

Scope of prohibitions and risk

In assessing the FCPA's reach, corporations and individuals must focus on the wide range of activities that could fall under the law. For instance, providing a "thing of value" is not confined to paying a monetary bribe. Rather, the FCPA prohibits corruptly providing any benefit, such as:
- travel and lodging not directly related to business activities (e.g., providing for a detour to a tourist destination or paying expenses for a government official's family members);

- providing excessive gifts and entertainment;
- hiring a government official's relative; or
- making a charitable contribution, even to a *bona fide* charity, if that contribution benefits a foreign official or is part of a *quid pro quo*.

Similarly, one of the areas of greatest risk to corporations, especially those that operate in countries known for widespread corruption, is the activity of agents. A corporation can be liable for actions taken by their agents (including consultants, joint venture partners, distributors, "finders" and vendors) if the corporation authorises, has knowledge of, or turns a blind eye to corrupt payments by such agents. To combat exposure for such "deliberate ignorance" of bribery, a company must be alert to potential red flags in establishing a relationship with a third-party agent, for instance:

- a government official recommends the third party;
- the third party has previously engaged in illegal or suspicious activities;
- the third party has little relevant experience, or is not listed or known to people within the industry;
- the third party seeks unusual payment arrangements, unusually high commissions, or success fees dependent on favourable government action; or
- the third party is a charity (even *bona fide*) affiliated with foreign government or official(s).

Comparison with the UK Bribery Act

The FCPA and UK Bribery Act are similar in many respects, but in certain key areas the UK Bribery Act is wider in its reach. Nevertheless, the FCPA remains highly relevant to UK companies because the scope of the UK Bribery Act remains largely untested, whereas the US Government has an aggressive and much longer history of enforcement. Additionally, authorities may attempt to use whistleblower provisions under US law and information sharing between US and UK officials in order to bring cases against corporations and individuals based in the UK and elsewhere.

The key points of contrast between the FCPA and the UK Bribery Act are as follows:

FCPA	UK Bribery Act
Basics	
Prohibits paying bribes	Prohibits receiving bribes as well as paying bribes
Prohibits bribery only of foreign officials, though the US does prosecute commercial bribery through other laws, for instance the Travel Act	Includes specific offence of bribing a foreign public official, but prohibits commercial bribery as well as bribery of foreign officials
Exceptions for promotional expenses and routine facilitation payments (though facilitation payment exception may be narrowing in effect)	No exception for promotional expenses or facilitation payments, but as to corporate hospitality, officials are unlikely to pursue modest low-level gifts and entertainment
Intent	
Evidence of corrupt intent required (evidence of conscious disregard is sufficient)	No need to show corrupt intent; only need to show intent to "influence" (as regards foreign public officials)
No strict liability for corporations, except for books and records violations	Strict liability corporate offence for failing to prevent bribery

FCPA	UK Bribery Act
Compliance programmes not a defence but are a factor the DOJ and SEC will consider in determining whether to prosecute, and the terms of a settlement	Only one possible defence to strict liability: to show that the company had in place "adequate procedures" to prevent bribery
Jurisdiction	
"Issuers," and their officers, directors, employees, and agents	
"Domestic concerns" and their officers, directors, employees, and agents; this includes any individual who is a citizen, national or resident of the US and any corporation or other entity that has its principal place of business in the US or is organised under US law	Any commercial organisation that carries on business or part of a business in the UK (including any company that has any UK affiliate), regardless of where the act or omission took place or whether the person(s) paying the bribe has any connection to the UK
Any person or entity, including foreign individuals or entities, if they commit "any act in furtherance" of an FCPA violation "while in the territory of the United States"	
Sanctions	
Criminal: • Individuals: up to five years' imprisonment (20 years for books and records); fines of up to $250,000 or twice the benefit sought or received, whichever is greater ($5m for books and records) • Corporations: fines of up to $2m or twice the benefit sought or received, whichever is greater ($25m for books and records)	
Civil: • Disgorgement • Anti-bribery provision: fines up to $16,000 • Books & records provision: fine equal to the greater of gross pecuniary advantage, or up to $160,000 for individuals or $775,000 for corporations	• Unlimited fine for both individuals and corporations • Confiscation • Imprisonment (up to 10 years) • Debarment • Independent monitor • Civil recovery of sums wrongfully obtained
Companies frequently agree to an independent monitor or other reporting requirements as part of terms of a settlement (e.g., NPA or DPA), which imposes ongoing remediation costs	
Debarment may also be imposed	

Areas of focus or controversy

While it would be impossible to cover all current trends in FCPA enforcement in this space, we would highlight a few areas as attracting particular attention and presenting the potential for further development in the near future.

Definition of foreign instrumentality and foreign government official

The DOJ and SEC have taken a broad view of who qualifies as a "foreign government official", and that view was recently largely endorsed by a court of appeals. For instance, the US Government views all employees, no matter how senior or junior, of state-owned entities ("instrumentalities" of a foreign government) as foreign government officials. This category includes all doctors employed by non-US health ministries (such as the UK's National Health Service), individuals representing foreign sovereign wealth funds, and professors at public universities.

In May 2014, a US court of appeals weighed in for the first time concerning what constitutes a "foreign instrumentality", such that the employees of the "instrumentality" are "foreign officials" under the FCPA. The US Court of Appeals for the Eleventh Circuit — which has jurisdiction over federal cases in Florida, Georgia, and Alabama — essentially sided with the government, affirming the criminal convictions of two owners of a Florida-based company who had been found to have bribed employees of the Haitian telecommunications company, Teleco.

The Eleventh Circuit's decision clarifies that a separate inquiry into an entity's function — as well as the level of governmental control — is required by the FCPA, holding that "[a]n 'instrumentality' under . . . the FCPA is [1] an entity controlled by the government of a foreign country that [2] performs a function the controlling government treats as its own".[6] Each of these two separate requirements must be satisfied: "[P]rovision of a service by a government-owned or controlled entity is *not* by itself sufficient" for that entity to qualify as an "instrumentality" under the FCPA. Furthermore, the decision's "definition of 'instrumentality' *requires* that the entity perform a function the government treats as its own".[7]

As to the *first* requirement, the Court put forth several non-exhaustive factors to guide the determination of whether a foreign government controls an entity:
- the foreign government's designation of the entity;
- whether the government has a majority interest in the entity;
- the government's ability to hire and fire the entity's principals;
- the extent to which the entity's profits, if any, go directly into government coffers and, conversely, whether the government funds the entity if it fails to break even; and
- the length of time these indicia have existed.[8]

As to the *second* requirement, the Court found that the following non-exhaustive list of factors should be considered in determining whether the entity "performs a function the government treats as its own":
- whether the entity has a monopoly;
- whether the government subsidises the entity's costs;
- whether the entity provides services to the public at large; and
- whether the public and the government of the foreign country generally perceive the entity to be performing a governmental function.[9]

The US Supreme Court denied a petition from the defendants to review this decision. The influential case therefore stands as the first appellate decision to address the crucial definition of a "foreign official". Notably, the court set no bright-line rules, nor did it opine on which factor or factors may be most significant, but instead established a fact-based framework to be applied in each case's particular circumstances. This decision underlines the need for a case-by-case analysis, and for companies to implement policies and procedures that ensure genuine engagement with compliance or legal personnel on these sensitive issues.

Whistleblowers

The Dodd-Frank Wall Street Reform and Consumer Protection Act of 2010 established, among other things, a whistleblower programme intended to create incentives for whistleblowers to inform the government of potential violations of US securities laws including the FCPA. The whistleblower need not report his or her concern internally before contacting the government. In response, the Securities and Exchange Commission established an Office of the Whistleblower to process tips, including those relating to the FCPA.[10] In 2014, the SEC announced its largest ever whistleblower award – to a non-US resident – for more than $30m, more than twice the previous record.[11]

In April 2015, the SEC brought its first enforcement action against a company for using restrictive language in confidentiality agreements that could illegally stifle whistleblowing. KBR Inc. agreed to pay a penalty of $130,000 to settle charges that it impeded potential whistleblowers from reporting possible securities violations to the SEC by requiring witnesses in certain internal investigations to sign agreements stating that they could face discipline (up to termination) for discussing matters with anyone outside of the company without prior approval from the company's legal department.[12] In addition, among the protections the Act offers to prospective whistleblowers is a provision that a company may not retaliate against a whistleblower.[13] Notably, in 2014, the SEC entered into a settlement agreement with Paradigm Capital under which the company agreed to pay a total of $2.2 million in connection with charges that it engaged in prohibited financial transactions and then retaliated against a former employer who reported the potential misconduct to the SEC.[14] In 2015, the SEC awarded $600,000 to the whistleblower involved the Paradigm Capital case, representing the maximum possible award that could be awarded to the whistleblower under those circumstances.[15]

However, in a 2014 decision, the US Court of Appeals for the Second Circuit, which covers New York, Connecticut, and Vermont, ruled that the anti-retaliation provision of the Dodd-Frank Act did not apply extraterritorially – in other words, Congress had not manifested a clear intent to apply that provision to activities that occurred outside "the territorial jurisdiction of the United States".[16] As a result, the Act did not prohibit an employer from retaliating against an FCPA whistleblower where "[t]he facts alleged in the complaint reveal essentially no contact with the United States regarding either the wrongdoing or the protected activity [the reporting of alleged violations]": all of the relevant activity was outside the United States, the whistleblower was not a US citizen, and the company was not a US company. The only connection to the United States was that the German parent company of the Chinese subsidiary where the plaintiff had been employed was publicly listed on the New York Stock Exchange.[17] In contrast, the SEC, in announcing the $30m whistleblower award less than six weeks later, found that it was empowered to make a monetary award to a foreign whistleblower whose tip led to a successful enforcement action, explaining:

> *In our view, there is a sufficient US territorial nexus whenever a claimant's information leads to the successful enforcement of a covered action brought in the United States, concerning violations of the US securities laws, by the [SEC], the US regulatory agency with enforcement authority for such violations. When these key territorial connections exist, it makes no difference whether, for example, the claimant was a foreign national, the claimant resides overseas, the information was submitted from overseas, or the misconduct comprising the US securities law violation occurred entirely overseas.*[18]

The SEC explicitly acknowledged the Second Circuit's recent decision, but found that that decision was not controlling because the anti-retaliation provisions of the law have a focus and purpose different from the whistleblower award provisions.[19] This award sends a significant message that the SEC intends to encourage tips regarding corporations with operations outside of the United States and that such corporations must remain vigilant in their compliance with US securities laws and should establish robust procedures to encourage internal reporting of potential wrongdoing. While the ultimate effect of this ruling remains to be seen, FCPA enforcement will continue to be affected by a tightening securities enforcement environment in the US generally. Foreign whistleblowers are now on notice: while Dodd-Frank's rewards are fully available, its protections are not.

Compliance programmes, voluntary disclosures and cooperation with the US Government

Several commentators, including the US Chamber of Commerce, have urged the US Government to adopt a formal affirmative defence based on compliance efforts and due diligence, allowing a corporation to avoid criminal liability if it has a vigorous anti-bribery programme in place. Similarly, commentators have taken the government to task for giving inadequate comfort to companies deciding whether or not to self-report.

Recent cases illustrate the wide range of government discretion in this area. In mid-2015, the government declined to prosecute PetroTiger Ltd., a British Virgin Islands oil and gas company, for the actions of three former executives who individually pleaded guilty to violating the FCPA. The government noted PetroTiger's extensive cooperation and remediation efforts in a public statement announcing that no charges would be brought against the company.[20] On the other hand, also in 2015, the government entered into a settlement with Mead Johnson Nutrition Co. to resolve allegations of FCPA violations (via a cease-and-desist order with the SEC), despite Mead Johnson's comprehensive compliance programme, "extensive and thorough" cooperation with the SEC and implementation of significant remediation measures.[21]

SEC and DOJ enforcement guidance explicitly provide companies with significant mitigation opportunities for cooperation in investigations related to potential FCPA violations. The DOJ's *Principles of Federal Prosecution of Business Organizations* states that "[i]n determining whether to charge a corporation and how to resolve corporate criminal cases, the corporation's timely and voluntary disclosure of wrongdoing and its cooperation with the government's investigation may be relevant factors". Factors to be considered in this regard include a corporation's willingness to provide relevant information and identify relevant actors within and outside the corporation.[22] Similarly, the SEC's so-called "Seaboard report" identifies self-reporting and cooperation as factors to be considered when assessing appropriate charges and remedies.[23] In 2010, the SEC launched a formal cooperation programme and issued a related policy statement setting forth a framework for evaluating cooperation in an SEC investigation, which includes factors such as the value and nature of the cooperation provided, the danger posed by the misconduct, and the cooperator's efforts to remediate the harm caused by violations.[24]

In a recent speech, the Director of the SEC's Division of Enforcement stated that "when a company commits to cooperation and expects credit for that assistance, the Enforcement staff expects them to provide us with all relevant facts, including facts implicating senior officials and other individuals".[25] Echoing these statements, the Assistant Attorney General for the DOJ's Criminal Division recently stated that "put simply, if a company wants cooperation credit, we expect that company to conduct a thorough internal investigation and to turn over evidence of wrongdoing to our prosecutors in a timely and complete way. Perhaps most critically, we expect cooperating companies to identify culpable individuals – including senior executives if they were involved – and provide the facts about their wrongdoing".[26]

Companies involved in FCPA investigations often are concerned regarding the scope and nature of information to be provided to the government in order to receive full credit for cooperation. Companies have been concerned that providing detailed information regarding the results of an internal investigation, even if the report is considered to be protected by attorney-client privilege, could form the basis for potential claims brought by employees or shareholders. A recent decision by the Texas Supreme Court provided some comfort to companies that such reports are considered to be "absolutely privileged," and therefore cannot be used as evidence in claims filed by employees against their employers, when submitted to the government as part of an ongoing investigation into potential criminal behaviour.[27] As background, the DOJ had been conducting an investigation of potential FCPA violations by a freight forwarder (Panalpina) used by Shell Oil Co. and other companies. In connection with this investigation, the DOJ requested Shell to conduct its own internal review and submit its confidential findings to the DOJ. The resulting report by Shell included allegations of misconduct by a Shell employee who was subsequently terminated by the company. The employee then sued Shell for wrongful termination and defamation, claiming that the report contained false accusations regarding his participation in the alleged bribery. After various appeals, the Texas Supreme Court ultimately ruled that the provision of a report regarding potential criminal activity to a government agency was "absolutely privileged" and could not be used as part of the employee's claims against the company.

Other laws and other consequences of FCPA violations

As noted above, US authorities employ a number of tools other than the FCPA to combat bribery. For instance, the Travel Act prohibits commercial bribery (bribery of a non-government official), even though the FCPA does not. Additionally, corporations may face considerable exposure as a result of civil lawsuits by customers, competitors, and even their own shareholders. The US authorities have also begun to go after bribery from the "demand" side, by prosecuting allegedly corrupt foreign officials for offences such as money-laundering and wire fraud, and attempting to seize any US assets of such foreign officials. Corporations can also be debarred from federal contracts, and institutional investors may be barred from doing business with a firm that is subject to FCPA action. Other institutions, such as the World Bank, may also debar a firm for bribery violations.

The monitorships to which many corporations consent in order to resolve FCPA violations are also costly and may increase government scrutiny of other areas of the corporation's activities. The DOJ has continued to impose hybrid monitorships as a requirement of some – but not all – enforcement actions, meaning that an independent monitor was required for part, but not all, of the term of the DPA. The decision whether to impose a monitorship appears to be based on the company's ability to remediate past wrongdoing and on the severity of the company's unlawful conduct. Hybrid monitorships are more likely to be imposed where a company has substantially cooperated with an investigation and has undertaken remediation efforts, but the original conduct or the remediation efforts leave the Department of Justice with concerns. In contrast, where the original offence is considered serious and the extent of remediation is unclear or lacking, the government may insist on a monitorship throughout the term of the settlement.[28]

Additionally, US Government officials have increasingly worked closely with other governments, including the UK government, in investigating potential cross-border corruption. In a recent speech, the Assistant Attorney General for the DOJ's Criminal Division stated that "fighting corruption is not some service [the DOJ] provide[s] to the global community; this is a fight in which we have critical international allies. Far from acting as the world's corruption police, the United States is part of a formidable and growing coalition of international enforcement partners who together combat corruption around the world – at home as well as abroad – that threatens each of our nations".[29] While not involving FCPA charges specifically, the DOJ's ongoing prosecution of multiple FIFA officials for alleged conspiracy to engage in racketeering (among other charges) reportedly has involved close coordination between the DOJ's Office of International Affairs and multiple governments to obtain evidence from around the globe. US authorities continue to signal that anti-corruption is a law enforcement priority, and we expect US enforcement of the FCPA to remain a prime driver of international anti-corruption efforts for years to come.

* * *

Endnotes

1. 15 U.S.C. § 78dd-1, *et seq.*
2. The Criminal Division of the US Dep't of Justice & the Enforcement Division of the US Securities and Exchange Commission, *FCPA: A Resource Guide to the US Foreign Corrupt Practices Act* (November 2012) (hereinafter, *FCPA Resource Guide*), *available at* http://www.justice.gov/criminal/fraud/fcpa/guide.pdf.
3. *See,* for example, the April 2013 Non-Prosecution Agreements that Ralph Lauren signed with both the DOJ and the SEC. *See* US Department of Justice, *Press Release: Ralph Lauren Corporation Resolves Foreign Corrupt Practices Act Investigation and Agrees to Pay $882,000 Monetary Policy* (22 April 2013), *available at* http://www.justice.gov/opa/pr/2013/April/13-crm-456.html; US Securities & Exchange Commission, *Press Release: SEC Announces Non-Prosecution Agreement With Ralph Lauren Corporation Involving FCPA Misconduct* (22 April 2013), *available at* http://www.sec.gov/news/press/2013/2013-65.htm. Though Ralph Lauren self-reported the alleged violations, which involved customs activities in Argentina, within two weeks of discovering them, and though there was no allegation of knowledge or involvement by the US parent company, Ralph Lauren paid $1.6m to resolve the claims. *See, e.g., Former DOJ FCPA Enforcement Attorney Blasts Ralph Lauren Enforcement Action* (9 May 2013), http://www.fcpaprofessor.com/former-doj-fcpa-enforcement-attorney-blasts-ralph-lauren-enforcement-action; *Ralph Lauren Enforcement Action Commentary – Hits And Misses* (29 April 2013), http://www.fcpaprofessor.com/ralph-lauren-enforcement-action-commentary-hits-and-misses. Government officials later stated publicly that greater indications of US involvement existed than had been spelled out in court documents.
4. *See Securities & Exchange Commission v. Straub,* 921 F. Supp. 2d 244 (S.D.N.Y. 2013). Less than two weeks later, a different federal judge in New York dismissed claims against a foreign FCPA defendant, finding that any connection to false US filings was "far too attenuated" to establish jurisdiction over the defendant. *US Securities & Exchange Commission v. Sharef,* 924 F. Supp. 2d 539, 546 (S.D.N.Y. 2013). The second court, however, did not have occasion to address the question of whether emails sent through US servers form a sufficient basis for jurisdiction.
5. *FCPA Resource Guide* at 43.
6. *United States v. Esquenazi,* 752 F.3d 912, 925 (11th Cir. 2014).
7. *Id.* at 927, 929.
8. *Id.* at 925.
9. *Id.* at 926.
10. *See* http://www.sec.gov/whistleblower.
11. *See* US Securities & Exchange Commission, Press Release: SEC Announces Largest-Ever Whistleblower Award (Sept. 22, 2014), available at http://www.sec.gov/News/PressRelease/Detail/PressRelease/1370543011290; Securities & Exchange Commission, Release No. 73174, Whistleblower Award Proceeding, File No. 2014-10, Order Determining Whistleblower Award Claim (Sept. 22, 2014), available at http://www.sec.gov/rules/other/2014/34-73174.pdf (hereinafter, Whistleblower Order).

12. *See* US Securities & Exchange Commission, *In the Matter of KBR, Inc.,* Administrative Proceeding File No. 3-16466 (1 April 2015), *available at* http://www.sec.gov/litigation/admin/2015/34-74619.pdf.

13. 15 U.S.C. § 78u–6(h)(1)(A).

14. *See* US Securities & Exchange Commission, *Press Release: SEC Charges Hedge Fund Adviser With Conducting Conflicted Transactions and Retaliating Against Whistleblower* (16 June 2014), *available at* http://www.sec.gov/News/PressRelease/Detail/PressRelease/1370542096307.

15. *See* US Securities & Exchange Commission, *Press Release: SEC Announces Award to Whistleblower in First Retaliation Case* (28 April 2015), *available at* http://www.sec.gov/news/pressrelease/2015-75.html.

16. *Liu Meng-Lin v. Siemens AG,* --- F.3d ----, 2014 WL 3953672, at *2, *4-*7 (2d Cir. Aug. 14, 2014).

17. *Id.* at *3-*4.

18. Whistleblower Order at 2 n.2.

19. See *id.*

20. See US Department of Justice, *Press Release: Former Chief Executive of Oil Services Company Pleads Guilty to Foreign Bribery Charge* (15 June 2015), *available at* http://www.justice.gov/opa/pr/former-chief-executive-officer-oil-services-company-pleads-guilty-foreign-bribery-charge.

21. *See* US Securities & Exchange Commission, *In the Matter of Mead John Nutrition Company*, Administrative Proceeding File No. 3-16704 (28 July 2015), *available at* http://www.sec.gov/litigation/admin/2015/34-75532.pdf.

22. *See* US Department of Justice, *Principles of Federal Prosecution of Business Organizations*, US Attorney's manual Section 9-28.000, *available at* http://www.justice.gov/usam/usam-9-28000-principles-federal-prosecution-business-organizations.

23. *See* US Securities & Exchange Commission, *Report of Investigation Pursuant to Section 21(a) of the Securities Exchange Act of 1934 and Commission Statement on the Relationship of Cooperation to Agency Enforcement Decisions, Release No. 34-44969* (Oct. 23, 2001), *available at* http://www.sec.gov/litigation/investreport/34-44969.htm.

24. *See* US Securities & Exchange Commission, *Policy Statement of the Securities and Exchange Commission Concerning Cooperation by Individuals in its Investigations and Related Enforcement Actions*, SEC Rel. No. 34-61340 (Jan. 13, 2010), available at https://www.sec.gov/rules/policy/2010/34-61340.pdf.

25. Andrew Ceresney, Director, SEC Division of Enforcement, "The SEC's Cooperation Program: Reflections on Five Years of Experience," Remarks at University of Texas School of Law's Government Enforcement Institute in Dallas, Texas (13 May 2015), *available at* http://www.sec.gov/news/speech/sec-cooperation-program.html.

26. Leslie R. Caldwell, Assistant Attorney General of DOJ's Criminal Division, Remarks at New York University Law School's Program on Corporate Compliance and Enforcement (17 April 2015), *available at* http://www.justice.gov/opa/speech/assistant-attorney-general-leslie-r-caldwell-delivers-remarks-new-york-university-law.

27. *See* Shell Oil Company and Shell International, E&P, Inc. v. Robert Writt, No. 13-0552 (Tex. 2015).

28. *See, e.g.,* Deferred Prosecution Agreement, *United States v. Total, S.A.*, No. 13-CR-239, at 8-10 (E.D. Va. May 29, 2013), *available at* http://www.justice.gov/iso/opa/resources/9392013529103746998524.pdf.

29. Leslie R. Caldwell, Assistant Attorney General of DOJ's Criminal Division, Remarks at the 26th Annual Association of Certified Fraud Examiners Global Fraud Conference (15 June 2015), *available at* http://www.justice.gov/opa/speech/assistant-attorney-general-leslie-r-caldwell-delivers-remarks-26th-annual-association.

Jeremy B. Zucker
Tel: +1 202 261 3322 / Email: jeremy.zucker@dechert.com
Jeremy Zucker advises clients on international trade regulatory compliance matters, including in relation to the U.S. Foreign Corrupt Practices Act, the Export Administration Regulations, the International Traffic in Arms Regulations, economic sanctions programmes administered by the Office of Foreign Assets Control, the anti-money laundering provisions of the USA Patriot Act and national security reviews under Exon-Florio by the Committee on Foreign Investment in the United States. He has represented clients before the U.S. Departments of Commerce, Defense, Homeland Security, Justice, State and Treasury, as well as at the White House. Mr. Zucker assists clients in all phases of their compliance and risk mitigation programmes, including evaluating existing programmes, developing and drafting new policies and procedures and providing training, as well as conducting risk assessments, compliance audits and complex internal investigations. He also performs due diligence for planned mergers and acquisitions, and helps prepare and submit applications and disclosures to government authorities. Mr. Zucker has been recognised as a leading lawyer in the area of International Trade by the Legal 500, and was also named one of the Top 10 Rising Stars Under 40 in International Trade by Law360.

Darshak Dholakia
Tel: +1 202 261 3467 / Email: darshak.dholakia@dechert.com
Darshak Dholakia's practice focuses primarily on international trade and national security regulatory compliance matters, including with respect to the U.S. Foreign Corrupt Practices Act and other anti-corruption measures, U.S. export control laws, U.S. economic sanctions and national security reviews by the Committee on Foreign Investment in the United States. In these areas, Mr. Dholakia assists clients by conducting risk assessments, internal investigations and due diligence on behalf of multinationals related to potential violations of anti-corruption, export control and economic sanctions laws. Mr. Dholakia also assists clients in developing, implementing and improving effective trade compliance programmes and conducting training in this regard.

Dechert LLP

1900 K Street NW, Washington, DC 20006, USA
Tel: +1 202 261 3300 / Fax: +1 202 261 3333 / URL: dechert.com